THE WRITER'S
CHAPBOOK

THE WRITER'S
CHAPBOOK

A Compendium of Fact, Opinion, Wit, and Advice from the Twentieth Century's Preeminent Writers

EDITED FROM *THE PARIS REVIEW* INTERVIEWS
AND WITH AN
INTRODUCTION BY GEORGE PLIMPTON

THE MODERN LIBRARY

NEW YORK

1999 Modern Library Edition

Copyright © 1989, 1999 by The Paris Review, Inc.

All rights reserved under International and Pan-American Copyright Conventions.
Published in the United States by Random House, Inc., New York, and
simultaneously in Canada by Random House of Canada Limited, Toronto.

Modern Library and colophon are registered trademarks of Random House, Inc.

This is a revised edition of *The Writer's Chapbook,*
published in 1989 by Viking Penguin.

This collection is derived from interviews first published in *The Paris Review.*

LIBRARY OF CONGRESS CATALOGING-IN-PUBLICATION DATA
The Writer's chapbook: a compendium of fact, opinion, wit, and advice from
the twentieth century's preeminent writers/edited from The Paris Review
interviews and with an introduction by George Plimpton.
p. cm.
Collected from Writers at work.
Includes index.
ISBN 0-679-60315-8
1. Authors—Interviews. 2. Authorship. I. Plimpton, George.
II. Paris review. III. Writers at work.
PN453.W75 1998
809—dc21 98-34158

Modern Library website address: www.modernlibrary.com

Printed in the United States of America on acid-free paper

2 4 6 8 9 7 5 3 1

GEORGE PLIMPTON

George Plimpton, the editor, essayist, sportswriter, humorist, and adventurer whose highly original brand of participatory journalism has earned him a singular place in American letters, was born in New York City on March 18, 1927. His father, Francis T. P. Plimpton, was a Wall Street lawyer who served as United States deputy representative to the United Nations. Plimpton attended St. Bernard's School in New York City and Phillips Exeter Academy, where he wrote for the student paper, *The Exonian*. He entered Harvard University in 1944, leaving soon thereafter for military service in the United States Army. He returned to Harvard in 1948 and became editor of *The Lampoon* before his graduation in 1950. Later he earned two additional degrees, a B.A. and an M.A., from King's College, Cambridge.

In 1953 Plimpton co-founded *The Paris Review,* a distinguished literary quarterly, with a group of young Americans, including Peter Matthiessen, Harold L. Humes, Thomas Guinzburg, and Donald Hall. Beginning in 1958, he has brought out numerous volumes of the *Writers at Work* series, acclaimed compilations of discussions with contemporary authors regularly featured in the magazine. According to *The New York Times,* Plimpton "developed a new kind of extended and articulate interview that combined the Boswellian aim with an exploration of the ideas of major contemporary writers on the art of fiction and poetry." Among the books Plimpton has compiled from the pages of *The Paris Review* include *Poets at*

Work (1989), *Women Writers at Work* (1989; revised edition 1998), *The Paris Review Anthology* (1990), *The Writer's Chapbook* (1990; revised edition 1999), a compendium of fact, opinion, wit, and advice from the twentieth century's preeminent writers, and *Beat Writers at Work* (1998). In addition he co-edited the first three volumes of *The American Literary Anthology* (1968–1970).

Plimpton's remarkable career as a sportswriter, distinguished by his competing in professional athletics he is describing, dates from 1961, the year he published *Out of My League*. It is a chronicle of every baseball fan's fantasy that recounts Plimpton's experience pitching to an all-star lineup of National League and American League players in a post-season exhibition game in Yankee Stadium. "Beautifully observed and incredibly conceived [George Plimpton's writing] is the dark side of the moon of Walter Mitty," said Ernest Hemingway. Plimpton first hit national bestseller lists with *Paper Lion* (1966), an engaging account of his seasoning as a third-string rookie quarterback at the summer training camp of the Detroit Lions. "*Paper Lion* is the best book written about pro football—maybe about any sport—because Plimpton captures with absolute fidelity how the average fan might feel given the opportunity to try out for a professional football team," explained *The Saturday Review*.

Several of Plimpton's other books similarly explore his exploits in various sports. Following the success of *Paper Lion,* he related his foray into the world of professional golf in *The Bogey Man* (1968). In his review of the book, critic Eliot Fremont-Smith, in effect, summarized all of Plimpton's chronicles when he wrote, "[Plimpton] conveys a tremendous sense of empathy which comes from his putting himself through the paces of a pro, so that he feels and gets to know intimately the emotions of the sport—despair, self-consciousness, suspense, boredom, yearning, panic and, every once in a while, exultation." And Gerald Clarke noted: "It is Plimpton's triumph that he has restored the word *amateur*—which today is so often a synonym for bungler—to its original and true connotation: someone who takes up an art or craft not for gain but for love."

Plimpton returned to the subject of football in *Mad Ducks and Bears* (1973) and *One More July* (1977), and in *One for the Record* (1974) he told the inside story of Hank Aaron's chase for the home-run record. *Shadow Box* (1977), arguably Plimpton's most humorous book, is an amalgam of boxing lore that includes a vintage rendition of his own exhibition bout with heavyweight champ Archie Moore. *Open Net* (1985) is the story of his experience on the ice as a goalie for the Boston Bruins. "Plimpton, the professional amateur, the dashing public hero, is first and best a writer," observed *The New Yorker*. "Plimpton's writing is so fascinating, not only for sports fans but for students of human behavior as well," said *People* magazine. "[He is] sincerely inquisitive, a receptive listener, and a fluid funny writer."

Plimpton's other books, which cover a wide range of intriguing subjects, make it clear why *The New York Times* praised his "endless curiosity, unshakable enthusiasm and nerve, and deep respect for the world he enters." He collaborated with interviewer Jean Stein on *American Journey* (1970), a narrative of the life and times of Robert F. Kennedy, and *Edie* (1982), an oral biography of Edie Sedgwick, the quintessential Andy Warhol superstar whose brief life mirrored the explosive 1960s. Plimpton also edited *Pierre's Book* (1971), a look at *jeu de paume*, the game of court tennis that was played by French royalty. In addition he wrote the text for *Sports!* (1978), a lavish album of photographs by Neil Leifer, and *Sports Bestiary* (1982), an amusing lexicon of sports terminology illustrated by Arnold Roth. In 1984 he brought out *D. V.*, the recollections of fashion editor Diana Vreeland, and *Fireworks*, a spectacular history and celebration of pyrotechnic displays from around the world.

Plimpton's belated first novel, *The Curious Case of Sidd Finch*, came out in 1987. At once a hilarious and suspenseful tale, it chronicles the adventures of an oddball mystic whose phenomenal pitching skills threaten to destroy the game of baseball. "Plimpton has written a funny, knowing, and poignant first novel," said *The New York Times Book Review*. "[The baseball] culture is splendidly rendered with an experienced insider's knowledge, and the whole saga of Finch's brief, astonishing passage through big-league baseball is at once a parody of every player's as-told-to biography, a satire on professional sports, and an extended (and intriguing) meditation on our national pastime."

Plimpton's recent collections include *The Best of Plimpton* (1990) and *The Norton Book of Sports* (1992), an anthology of sports literature. He worked with Jean Kennedy Smith on *Chronicles of Courage* (1993), a series of candid and revealing interviews with disabled artists, and in *The X Factor* (1995) he attempted to identify the qualities that enable a champion to consistently overcome his competitors. Plimpton's latest book, *Truman Capote*, a compelling oral biography in which the author's many friends and enemies recall his turbulent career, was published in 1998. George Plimpton lives in New York City, where he continues to edit *The Paris Review*. He is a frequent contributor to *Harper's* and *Sports Illustrated*, and his humorous articles on birdwatching have appeared in *Audubon* and other magazines.

In gratitude to
E. M. Forster
and to both interviewers
and interviewed

I don't know exactly how it's done. I let it alone a
good deal. —SAUL BELLOW

A writer is somebody for whom writing is more
difficult than it is for other people.
—THOMAS MANN

There are three rules for writing the novel.
Unfortunately, no one knows what they are.
—SOMERSET MAUGHAM

READER: Miss Moore, your poetry is very
                 difficult to read.
MARIANNE MOORE: It is very difficult to write.

NOTE

Following, in alphabetical order, are the names of the authors interviewed with the names of the interviewers in parentheses. In many cases, the authors were interviewed by more than one person.

Chinua Achebe (Jerome Brooks), **Conrad Aiken** (Robert Hunter Wilbur), **Edward Albee** (William Flannagan), **Nelson Algren** (Alston Anderson, Terry Southern), **Woody Allen** (Michiko Kakutani), **Yehuda Amichai** (Lawrence Joseph), **Kingsley Amis** (Michael Barber), **A. R. Ammons** (David Lehman), **Maya Angelou** (George Plimpton), **John Ashbery** (Peter Stitt), **Margaret Atwood** (Mary Morris), **Louis Auchincloss** (George Plimpton), **W. H. Auden** (Michael Newman).

James Baldwin (Jordan Elgrably), **J. G. Ballard** (Thomas Frick), **Donald Barthelme** (J. D. O'Hara), **Simone de Beauvoir** (B. Frechtman, translator; Madelein Gobeil), **Saul Bellow** (Gordon Lloyd Harper), **John Berryman** (Peter Stitt), **Elizabeth Bishop** (Elizabeth Spires), **Harold Bloom** (Antonio Weiss), **Heinrich Böll** (A. Leslie Wilson), **Jorge Luis Borges** (Ronald Christ), **Paul Bowles** (Jeffrey Bailey), **Joseph Brodsky** (Sven Birkerts), **William F. Buckley, Jr.** (Sam Vaughan), **Anthony Burgess** (John Cullinan), **William Burroughs** (Conrad Knickerbocker).

Erskine Caldwell (Elizabeth Pell Broadwell, Ronald Wesley Hoag), **Hortense Calisher** (Allan Gurganus, Pamela McCordick, Mona Simpson), **Italo Calvino** (Damien Pettigrew, William Weaver), **Truman Capote** (Pati Hill), **Raymond Carver** (Mona Simpson), **Joyce Cary** (John Burrows, Alex Hamilton), **Camilo José Cela** (Valerie Miles), **Louis-Ferdinand Céline** (J. Darribehaude; J. Guenot; James Sherwood, translator), **Blaise Cendrars** (William Brandon, translator; Michael Manoll), **John Cheever** (Annette Grant), **Amy Clampitt** (Robert E. Hosmer, Jr.), **Jean Cocteau** (William Fifield), **Julio Cortázar** (Jason Weiss), **Malcolm Cowley** (John McCall, George Plimpton), **Robert Creeley** (Lewis MacAdam, Jr., Linda Wagner).

Robertson Davies (Elisabeth Sifton), **Don DeLillo** (Adam Begley),

James Dickey (Franklin Ashley), **Joan Didion** (Linda Kuehl), **Isak Dinesen** (Eugene Walter), **E. L. Doctorow** (George Plimpton), **J. P. Donleavy** (Molly McKaughan), **John Dos Passos** (David Sanders), **Margaret Drabble** (Barbara Milton), **John Gregory Dunne** (George Plimpton), **Lawrence Durrell** (Gene Andrewski, Julian Mitchell).

Leon Edel (Jeanne McCulloch), **T. S. Eliot** (Donald Hall), **Stanley Elkin** (Thomas LeClair), **Ralph Ellison** (Alfred Chester, Vilma Howard).

William Faulkner (Jean Stein), **Robert Fitzgerald** (Edwin Frank, Andrew McCord), **Richard Ford** (Bonnie Lyons), **E. M. Forster** (P. N. Furbank, F. J. H. Haskell), **John Fowles** (James Baker), **Robert Frost** (Richard Poirier), **Carlos Fuentes** (Alfred MacAdam, Charles Ruas), **Athol Fugard** (Lloyd Richards).

William Gaddis (Zoltan Abadi-Nagy), **John Gardner** (Paul Ferguson, John R. Maier, Sara Matthiessen, Frank McConnell), **William Gass** (Thomas LeClair), **Allen Ginsberg** (Gerald Clarke), **Nadine Gordimer** (Jannika Hurwitt), **Robert Gottlieb** (Larissa MacFarquhar), **William Goyen** (Robert Phillips), **Robert Graves** (Peter Buckman, William Fifield), **Francine du Plessix Gray** (Regina Weinreich), Henry Green (Terry Southern), **Graham Greene** (Simon Raven), **John Guare** (Anne Cattaneo), **Thom Gunn** (Clive Wilmer).

Donald Hall (Peter Stitt), **Elizabeth Hardwick** (Darryl Pinckney), **Jim Harrison** (Jim Fergus), **Seamus Heaney** (Henri Cole), **Joseph Heller** (George Plimpton), **Lillian Hellman** (Anne Hollander, John Phillips), **Mark Helprin** (James Linville), **Ernest Hemingway** (George Plimpton), **John Hersey** (Jonathan Dee), **John Hollander** (J. D. Clatchy), **Ted Hughes** (Drue Heinz), **Aldous Huxley** (Ray Frazer, George Wickes).

David Ignatow (Gerard Malanga), **Gillermo Cabrera Infante** (Alfred MacAdam), **Eugène Ionesco** (Shusha Guppy), **John Irving** (Ron Hansen), **Christopher Isherwood** (W. I. Scobie).

P. D. James (Shusha Guppy), **James Jones** (Nelson W. Aldrich, Jr.).

Garrison Keillor (George Plimpton), **William Kennedy** (George Plimpton), **Jack Kerouac** (Ted Berrigan), **Ken Kesey** (Robert Faggen), **Arthur Koestler** (Duncan Fallowell), **Jerzy Kosinski** (Rocco Landesman, George Plimpton), **Milan Kundera** (Christian Salmon), **Stanley Kunitz** (Chris Busa).

Philip Larkin (Robert Phillips), **James Laughlin** (Richard Ziegfield), **John le Carré** (George Plimpton), **Rosamund Lehmann** (Shusha Guppy), **Doris Lessing** (Thomas Frick), **Peter Levi** (Jannika Hurwitt),

Primo Levi (Gabriel Motola), **Philip Levine** (Mona Simpson), **Mario Vargas Llosa** (Ricardo A. Settee), **Christopher Logue** (Shusha Guppy), **Robert Lowell** (Frederick Seidel).

Archibald MacLeish (Benjamin DeMott), **Naguib Mahfouz** (Charlotte El Shabrawy), **Norman Mailer** (Steven Marcus), **Bernard Malamud** (Daniel Stern), **David Mamet** (John Lahr), **Gabriel García Márquez** (Peter H. Stone), **François Mauriac** (John leMarchand, translator; John Train), **William Maxwell** (George Plimpton, John Seabrook), **Mary McCarthy** (Elisabeth Niebuhr), **Thomas McGuane** (Sinda Gregory, Larry McCaffery), **William Meredith** (Edward Hirsch), **James Merrill** (J. D. Clatchy), **W. S. Merwin** (Edward Hirsch), **Arthur Miller** (Olga Carlisle, Rose Styron), **Henry Miller** (George Wickes), **Czeslaw Milosz** (Robert Faggen), **Marianne Moore** (Donald Hall), **Toni Morrison** (Claudia Brodsky Lacour, Elissa Schappell), **John Mortimer** (Rosemary Herbert), **Iris Murdoch** (James Atlas, Jeffrey Meyers).

Vladimir Nabokov (Herbert Gold), **Pablo Neruda** (Rita Guibert, Ronald Christ).

Joyce Carol Oates (Robert Phillips), **Patrick O'Brian** (Stephen Becker), **Edna O'Brien** (Shusha Guppy), **Frank O'Connor** (Anthony Whittier), **Amos Oz** (Shusha Guppy), **Cynthia Ozick** (Tom Teicholz).

Grace Paley (Jonathan Dee, Barbara Jones, Larissa MacFarquhar), **Dorothy Parker** (Marion Capron, George Plimpton), **Octavio Paz** (Alfred MacAdam), **Walker Percy** (Zoltan Abadi-Nagy), **S. J. Perelman** (William Cole, George Plimpton), **Robert Pinsky** (Ben Downing, Daniel Kunitz), **Katherine Anne Porter** (Barbara Thompson), **Ezra Pound** (Donald Hall), **Anthony Powell** (Michael Barber), **Reynolds Price** (Frederick Busch), **Richard Price** (James Linville), **V. S. Pritchett** (Allan Gurganus, Anthony Weller).

Jean Rhys (Elizabeth Vreeland), **Alain Robbe-Grillet** (Shusha Guppy), **Barney Rosset** (Ken Jordan), **Philip Roth** (Hermione Lee).

Françoise Sagan (Blair Fuller, Robert B. Silvers), **James Salter** (Edward Hirsch), **Nathalie Sarraute** (Shusha Guppy, Jason Weiss), **May Sarton** (Karen Saum), **George Seferis** (Edmund Keeley), **Anne Sexton** (Barbara Kevles), **Karl Shapiro** (Robert Phillips), **Irwin Shaw** (Lucas Matthiessen, Willie Morris), **Sam Shepard** (Benjamin Howe, Jeanne McCulloch, Mona Simpson), **Georges Simenon** (Carvel Collins), **Claude Simon** (Alexandra Eyle; Magali Saporito, translator), **John Simon** (Davi Napoleon), Neil Simon (James Lipton), **Isaac Bashevis**

Singer (Harold Fender), **W. D. Snodgrass** (Alexandra Eyle), **Gary Snyder** (Eliot Weinberger), **Stephen Sondheim** (James Lipton), **Susan Sontag** (Edward Hirsch), **Stephen Spender** (Peter Stitt), **William Stafford** (William Young), **Wallace Stegner** (James R. Hepworth), **Gertrude Stein** (William Lundell), **John Steinbeck** (from his letters), **George Steiner** (Ronald A. Sharp), **Robert Stone** (William Crawford Woods), **Tom Stoppard** (Shusha Guppy), **William Styron** (Peter Matthiessen, George Plimpton).

Peter Taylor (Barbara Thompson), **James Thurber** (George Plimpton, Max Steele), **P. L. Travers** (Edwina Burress, Jerry Griswold), **William Trevor** (Mira Stout), **Calvin Trillin** (George Plimpton).

John Updike (Charles Thomas Samuels).

Helen Vendler (Henri Cole), **Gore Vidal** (Gerald Clarke), **Kurt Vonnegut** (David Michaelis, George Plimpton, Richard Rhodes), **Andrei Voznesensky** (Quentin Vest, William Crawford Woods).

Robert Penn Warren (Ralph Ellison, Eugene Walter), **Wendy Wasserstein** (Laurie Winer), **Evelyn Waugh** (Julian Jebb), **Eudora Welty** (Linda Kuehl), **Jessamyn West** (Carolyn Doty), **Rebecca West** (Marina Warner), **John Hall Wheelock** (William Cahill, Molly McKaughan), **E. B. White** (Frank Crowther, George Plimpton), **Edmund White** (Jordan Elgrably), **Elie Wiesel** (John S. Friedman), **Richard Wilbur** (McCloy Ellison), **Billy Wilder** (James Linville), **Thornton Wilder** (Richard H. Goldstone), **Tennessee Williams** (Dotson Raider), **William Carlos Williams** (Stanley Koehler), **Angus Wilson** (Michael Millgate), **Jeanette Winterson** (Audrey Bilger), **P. G. Wodehouse** (Gerald Clarke), **Tom Wolfe** (George Plimpton), **James Wright** (Peter Stitt).

Marguerite Yourcenar (Shusha Guppy).

CONTENTS

PART III

DIFFERENT FORMS

PART IV

THE WRITER'S LIFE

INTRODUCTION

In 1953 *The Paris Review,* a fledgling literary quarterly, initiated a series of interviews with famous writers on their craft. For over forty years it has continued to do so—with frequently a pair of interviews in each issue. Nearly two hundred and fifty novelists, poets, biographers, and essayists have talked about their work and how they go about it. Viking Penguin has collected many of these interviews in a series of volumes entitled *Writers at Work.*

The purpose of this present volume is to cull what the various authors have said about specific topics and present these under a series of headings—the focus on subject matter rather than author. Thus, if a reader is curious about the importance of "plot" to the novelist, under that heading in the *Chapbook* are to be found any number of comments and views on that particular subject. It saves browsing through all the issues of the *Review,* which in sum would stretch the length of a twenty-five-foot library shelf.

In a sense that is behind the choice of "Chapbook" for the book's title—that a volume is provided in which it is less time-consuming (and expensive) to find what one is looking for. There the comparison ends! The original chapbooks were sold in medieval times by a "chapman" (hence the common family name), an itinerant peddler who in the village square sold little rag-paper booklets about Tom Thumb, Reynard the Fox, and other such folk heroes.

This is the third revised and expanded edition of the *Chapbook*. The first was published in 1989, the second in 1992. Material from over forty interviews conducted for *The Paris Review* since 1992 has been added to the present volume.

A word about the arrangement of this book. It has been divided into four major sections. The first is a kind of general profile of the writer in which the major steps in a literary career are arranged chronologically— starting from earliest influences (childhood reading, early mentors) through the initial impulse for becoming a writer, then to the actual process of creation (the inspiration for a work, first drafts, work habits [the quintessential *Paris Review* question: Do you use a pen or a pencil?], and so forth), and finally on to publication and the effects of success or failure along with observations, quite pithy, on critics.

Next is a section in which the writers talk about the actual mechanics of writing: plot, characters, symbols, experimental work, writer's block, the use of artificial stimulants, among them. Here we discover that when W. H. Auden took LSD experimentally, "nothing much happened, but I did get the distinct impression that some birds were trying to communicate with me."

In the third section the writers are concerned with different fields of writing—journalism, the theater, children's books, the short story, writing for the film, free-lancing. Of this last, John Cheever describes an assignment from the *Saturday Evening Post* to do an interview with Sophia Loren. He accepted the offer. "I got to kiss her. I've had other offers but nothing as good."

The final section focuses on the social life of the writer (writers' colonies, readings, teaching jobs, grants, and the like). In the interviews authors tended to talk most engagingly about their contemporaries; this section contains a number of these "portraits"—Malcolm Cowley on Ford Madox Ford, Aldous Huxley on James Joyce, Robert Frost on Ezra Pound, James Laughlin on Gertrude Stein, among them. The section concludes with some views on the future of the written word.

Since the various headings are fairly arbitrary and the authors' statements so often discursive, a cross-checking index has been provided so that under the heading "plot," for instance, the reader will find additional references in other parts of the book. The reader will also note that to provide even further insight into the various topics, each subject is prefaced by a collection of epigrams and quotations from authors as far back as Aristophanes (c. 450 B.C.–c. 388 B.C.).

A word about *The Paris Review*. The magazine, planned as a literary quarterly, was first published in the spring of 1953. Its policy from the start was to concentrate on publishing fiction and poetry rather than the critical essays which were the mainstay in almost all the literary magazines of the time. Its one concession to critical evaluation was that rather than getting a third party to provide an essay on a contemporary author, it would go to the authors themselves and, using the interview form, ask them firsthand about their work and their working methods. The first author *The Paris Review* went to see was E. M. Forster, then a senior fellow at King's College, Cambridge. He was an admirable choice. Perhaps the greatest living author at the time *(A Passage to India, Howards End)*, in fact he had not published a novel since 1924. The interview, which was conducted by P. N. Furbank and F. J. H. Haskel, one scribbling down the answers while the other concentrated on the questions (tape recorders were still a few years away), was a feature in the first issue of the *Review* and raised an immediate stir. For in it Forster talked about the problems that made it so difficult for him to write fiction, namely what he called "fiction technicalities." The result furnished the best of patterns for the interviews that followed.

In the introduction to the first volume of *Writers at Work*, Malcolm Cowley suggested why such famous authors as Forster devoted so much of their time to a project from which they had very little to gain. "Some of them disliked the idea of being interviewed," he wrote, "but consented anyway, either out of friendship for someone on the *Review* or because they wanted to help a struggling magazine of the arts, perhaps in memory of their own early struggles to get published. . . . Authors are sometimes like tomcats: they distrust all the other toms, but they are kind to kittens."

Of particular importance to the series was that so many of the writers turned out to be absorbed by the writing process and glad to talk about it—almost as if they had never been asked, and perhaps thought it too self-indulgent to write about. In many cases they added additional material on their own; they were free to make what changes they wished since the intention of the editors was never to think of the interviews as inquisitions but rather as documentations of the authors-at-work.

The series gathered momentum. Because a number of distinguished writers agreed to be interviewed in its earliest numbers—E. M. Forster,

François Mauriac, Graham Greene, Irwin Shaw, William Styron, Alberto Moravia, Joyce Cary, Ralph Ellison, Georges Simenon, James Thurber, Nelson Algren, William Faulkner were all in the first four years—the series began to assume the aura of a Pantheon. Writers were pleased to be asked to contribute. There were exceptions, of course—writers who made a point of their reclusivity: Samuel Beckett, J. D. Salinger, Alexander Solzhenitsyn, Thomas Pynchon—but many others agreed who rarely granted interviews: Faulkner, Hemingway, Henry Green. The length of the interviews increased. E. M. Forster's required only fourteen pages of the first issue. Many since have run to forty or fifty pages. The record is the interview of James Laughlin, the poet/publisher, whose reminiscences about his immersion in the literary world ran through two numbers of the magazine.

There is such diversity of opinion in the *Chapbook* that it may be hard to construct a composite writer out of the material at hand. The working habits are different: Hemingway rises at dawn to work; James Baldwin works late at night after the hour is quiet. Truman Capote, Paul Bowles, and Evelyn Waugh often work in bed. Robert Frost takes off a shoe and uses the sole for a desk. John Dos Passos rewrites a chapter seven or eight times. William Kennedy's rewrites of *Legs* stacked up to match the height of his six-year-old son. Yet Eudora Welty only corrects or changes an occasional word; to do more would make her feel that "someone would start looking over my shoulder." Writers have divergent views about the importance of plot. Norman Mailer doesn't work from plots. Neither does Elizabeth Hardwick. She says that if she wants a plot she'll watch the TV series *Dallas*. John Irving disagrees. So does Kurt Vonnegut, who doesn't believe a reader can be satisfied unless the rudiments of an old-fashioned plot are smuggled into the book someplace. Joseph Heller sees his novels in an astounding blast of insight provoked by a first line which evolves into a whole series of scenes, characters, resolutions. For a time James Merrill used a Ouija board for his creative impulses. E. M. Forster loses control of his characters. They wander away like disembodied puppets. John Cheever is contemptuous of this. So is Nabokov. He refers to his characters as galley slaves.

All this may be confusing to readers who hope to find direction for their own work in fiction or poetry. But then the vast complexity of material suggests that it is possible to come across ideas and comments with which associations can be made: "Ah, that seems to fit," and a key will be provided.

For the general reader, another matter. A reviewer once said of the *Writers at Work* series that a reader could dip into a volume and not reemerge for days. I have had very much that feeling compiling the material for the book. Reading through this series was a time of reacquaintance. The interview is obviously the most direct of relationships; the authors' voices are preeminent. One listens on a summer porch or in a library. It seemed almost an indignity to clip words out of their commentary. But the piles under various headings grew. Sometimes I even hoped the interview would be bland so that nothing had to be clipped. Never the case. The stacks increased. I tried grading the excerpts, thinking to cut down on them. A–, B+, A–, A, A, A–. A star class.

Interviews tend to be derided as a form. Too easy. Tape recorders do not necessarily catch true meanings. The interviewers set their machines down nervously on the coffee table. "Do you mind?" No matter. At the conclusion of his introduction to one of the *Writers at Work* volumes, Wilfrid Sheed wrote that he would trade half of *Childe Harold* for an interview with Lord Byron and all of *Adam Bede* for one with George Eliot. He said he was speaking for his "frivolous self," but I suspect he meant it. He would certainly have my support if he did.

—G.A.P.

PART I

THE WRITER: A PROFILE

ON READING

Poetry is the only art people haven't yet learned to consume
like soup.   —W. H. AUDEN

I never desire to converse with a man who has written more
than he has read.   —SAMUEL JOHNSON

Reading is to the mind what exercise is to the body.
                                              —RICHARD STEELE

KINGSLEY AMIS: Well, there's the early Joyce, P. G. Wodehouse, Evelyn Waugh, Anthony Powell, Elizabeth Taylor, and early Angus Wilson among novelists. And poets . . . oh, Hardy I admire, but don't feel very warm to—A. E. Housman, Philip Larkin, John Betjeman, the early R. S. Thomas, parts of Robert Frost, parts of Robert Graves, some poems by Yeats. It's not a complete list—in fact I was once worried by this, that I couldn't name more than a dozen admired contemporaries. But I mentioned it to Robert Graves, and he said, "Nonsense. You ought to be concerned if you admire *more* than that number. It shows you have no discrimination." Which is a good point!

MAYA ANGELOU: My mother knew Shakespeare, but my grandmother was raising us. When I told her I wanted to recite—it was actually Portia's speech—Mama said to me, "Now, sistah, what are you goin' to render?" The phrase was so fetching. The phrase was: "Now, little mistress Marguerite will render her rendition." Mama said, "Now, sistah, what are you goin' to render?" I said, "Mama, I'm going to render a piece written by William Shakespeare." My grandmother asked me, "Now, sistah, who is this very William Shakespeare?" I had to tell her that he was white, it was going to come out. Somebody would let it out. So I told Mama, "Mama, he's white, but he's dead." Then I said, "He's been dead for centuries," thinking she'd forgive him because of this little idiosyncrasy. She said, "No Ma'am, little mistress you will not. No Ma'am, little mistress you will not." So I rendered James Weldon Johnson, Paul Laurence Dunbar, Countee Cullen, Langston Hughes.

W. H. AUDEN: The only poetry I had read, as a child, were certain books of sick jokes—Belloc's *Cautionary Tales, Strubel Peter* by Hoffman, and Harry Graham's *Ruthless Rhymes for Heartless Homes.* I had a favorite, which went like this:

> Into the drinking well
> The plumber built her
> Aunt Maria fell;
> We must buy a filter.

Of course I read a good deal about geology and lead mining. Sopwith's *A Visit to Alston Moore* was one, *Underground Life* was another. I can't remember who wrote it. I read all the books of Beatrix Potter, and also Lewis Carroll. Andersen's *The Snow Queen* I loved, and also Haggard's *King Solomon's Mines.* And I got my start reading detective stories with Sherlock Holmes.

JOHN BARTH: The great guides were the books I discovered in the Johns Hopkins Library, where my student job was to file books away. One was more or less encouraged to take a cart of books and go back into the stacks and not come out for seven or eight hours. So I read what I was filing. My great teachers (the best thing that can happen to a writer) were Scheherazade, Homer, Virgil, and Boccaccio; also the great Sanskrit taletellers. I was impressed forever with the width as well as the depth of literature—just what a kid from the sticks, from the swamp, in my case, needed.

JORGE LUIS BORGES: I remember a time when I used to come here [Borges's office in the Biblioteca Nacional] to read. I was a very young man, and I was far too timid to ask for a book. Then, I was rather, I won't say poor, but I wasn't too wealthy in those days—so I used to come every night here and pick out a volume of the *Encyclopaedia Britannica,* the old edition. The eleventh or twelfth because those editions are far above the new ones. They were meant to be *read.* Now they are merely reference books. While in the eleventh or twelfth edition of the *Encyclopaedia Britannica,* you had long articles by Macaulay, by Coleridge, De Quincey, and so on. So that I used to take any volume from the shelves—there was no need to ask for them: they were reference books—and then I opened the book till I found an article that interested me, for example about the Mormons or about any particular writer. I sat down and read it because those articles were really monographs, really books or short books. The same goes for the German encyclopedias—Brockhaus or Meyers. When we got the new copy, I thought that was what they call the *Shorter Brockhaus,* but it wasn't. It was explained to me that because people live in small flats, there is no longer room for books in thirty volumes. Encyclopedias have suffered greatly; they have been packed in.

ERSKINE CALDWELL: Oh, I used to read the Sears and Roebuck Catalogue, every year when it came out. But I learned early in life that you can be a reader or a writer. I decided to be a writer.

TRUMAN CAPOTE: Anything, including labels and recipes and advertisements. I have a passion for newspapers ... read all the New York dailies every day, and the Sunday editions of several foreign magazines too. The ones I don't buy I read standing at newsstands. I average about five books a week . . . the normal length novel takes me about two hours. I enjoy thrillers and would like someday to write one. Though I prefer first-rate fiction, for the last few years my reading seems to have been concentrated on letters and journals and biographies. It doesn't bother me to read while I am writing . . . I mean, I don't suddenly find another writer's style seeping out of my pen. Though once, during a lengthy spell of James, my own sentences *did* get awfully long.

BLAISE CENDRARS: Captain Lacroix ... is an old sailor and his books are a feast. I've never had the luck to meet him. I looked for him in Nantes, at Saint-Nazaire. I was told that he is in his eighties and that he doesn't want to give up. When he was no longer able to navigate, he became a marine insurer, and it appears that he doesn't hesitate to put on a deep-sea diving rig in order to see for himself the state of his hulls. At his age, admirable. I imagine that the winter nights seemed long to him by the fireplace, when the wind from the sea poured down on his village of the Loire-Inférieure and blew around in his chimney, and I suppose it was to kill time that this man, who has knocked about on all the Seven Seas and aboard all sorts of ships possible and imaginable, began to write books. These are thick books, strongly built, full of solid documentation, sometimes a little too heavy but nearly always fresh, thus never tedious, all the less so in that the old seaman even searches out reproductions of illustrated post cards and photos of joyous ports of call of his youth, and he recounts things as they happened, his experience and all that he has learned and all that he has seen from Cape Horn to the China Sea, from Tasmania to Ushant, speaking of everything, of lighthouses, currents, wind, reefs, tempests, crews, traffic, shipwrecks, fish and birds, celestial phenomena and maritime catastrophes, history, customs, nations, people of the sea, relating thousands of anecdotes intimate or dramatic, all his life of an honest seaman carried along by the very movement of the sea and dominated by his exclusive love of ships. Ah, it is, certainly, not the work of a littérateur. His pen is a marlinspike, and each page brings you something, and there are ten big volumes! It's as moving as it can be and as simple as good morning. In a word, miraculous. One touches the globe with a finger.

JOHN CHEEVER: The books that you really love give the sense, when you first open them, of having been there. It is a creation, almost like a chamber in the memory. Places that one has never been to, things that one has never seen or heard, but their fitness is so sound that you've been there somehow.

AMY CLAMPITT: Naming names, or giving homage to the predecessors I'd declared indispensable, I was bound to mention Hopkins, whom I'm conscious of revering more than any other. After him I'd name Virginia Woolf, John Keats, Shakespeare, Milton, maybe Proust. After that, the list could vary from day to day, even hour to hour. Hopkins comes first because I simply can't imagine having become a poet without having read his work—the delight in all things physical, the wallowing in sheer sound, in the extravagance of the possibilities of language. For me there is still nobody like him, though Keats comes close, for similar reasons. Reading Virginia Woolf for the first time I thought, "She's writing for me." The book was *The Waves.* I don't feel quite so strongly about it on rereading; but the diaries are something else, as are the letters and the essays. I began reading Proust while I was still in college, before I got around to either George Eliot or Henry James—both of whom have tended to mean more to me since—and the sense of discovery I felt, all that lingering over the hawthorns, Marcel having to inform the person he'd been, over and over, that Albertine is gone—the sense of discovery at the time was simply enormous. Now that I think of it, another, totally different writer who gave me that feeling of momentousness was Thoreau. As for Shakespeare, it was the sonnets I can't imagine having been without. As for Milton, what I really mean is "Lycidas."

JULIO CORTÁZAR: I read Edgar Allan Poe for the first time when I was only nine. I stole the book to read because my mother didn't want me to read it; she thought I was too young and she was right. The book scared me and I was ill for three months, because I believed in it . . . *dur comme fer* as the French say. For me, the fantastic was perfectly natural; I had no doubts at all. That's the way things were. When I gave those kinds of books to my friends, they'd say, "But no, we prefer to read cowboy stories." Cowboys were especially popular at the time. I didn't understand that. I preferred the world of the supernatural, of the fantastic.

ROBERTSON DAVIES: I admire writers who are sometimes enviably self-indulgent, like Victor Hugo. Last summer, I was rereading *Les Misérables,* and really that book has sometimes as much as ninety pages about something which just happens to interest him, something political or religious or something of the sort. And you think, When is he ever going to get on with the story? But the story is so good that you put up with his digressions, and also he writes so fascinatingly about his odds and ends that you can't stop.

I'm very fond of Victor Hugo, and a book which I read when I was eleven years old which I've reread many times through my life and admired enormously is *Notre Dame de Paris.* I wish that people who see those many movies called *The Hunchback of Notre Dame* would read the novel. It's worth any of those movies twenty times over. A great nineteenth-century novelist like Balzac—infinitely enchanting. You cannot put him down. Even when he is telling you the details of rural newspaper publishing. Well, of course that is very interesting. It absolutely grips you. You cannot stop reading Balzac. You cannot stop reading any of the great Russians. The great English writers: Dickens more than Thackeray, but Thackeray is much finer than some people are prepared to admit. Trollope is endlessly gripping, though it's rather crunchy granola: you chomp your way resolutely through it, and it's worth it because the story is so good. It's the storytellers' quality that they have. Nabokov said that he thought that the most important element in a novelist's armory was what he called by a Russian word, *shamanstvo.* It means the enchanter-quality. The word *shamanen* is familiar to everyone. The enchanter-quality, the ability to keep people wanting more, it's not something which can be taught, and often it is associated with what critics call a "bad literary style," but it is irresistible. Dickens had it. Nobody praises Dickens's style, but who can resist his enchantment? Only professors, and only some of those.

DON DELILLO: When I was eighteen, I got a summer job as a playground attendant—a parkie. And I was told to wear a white T-shirt and brown pants and brown shoes and a whistle around my neck—which they provided, the whistle. But I never acquired the rest of the outfit. I wore blue jeans and checkered shirts and kept the whistle in my pocket and just sat on a park bench disguised as an ordinary citizen. And this is where I read Faulkner, *As I Lay Dying* and *Light in August.* And got paid for it. And then James Joyce, and it was through Joyce that I learned to see something in language that carried a radiance, something that made me feel the beauty and fervor of words, the sense that a word has a life and a history. And I'd look at a sentence in *Ulysses* or in *Moby-Dick* or in Hemingway— maybe I hadn't gotten to *Ulysses* at that point, it was *Portrait of the Artist*— but certainly Hemingway and the water that was clear and swiftly moving and the way the troops went marching down the road and raised dust that powdered the leaves of the trees. All this in a playground in the Bronx.

JOAN DIDION: I always say Hemingway, because he taught me how sentences worked. When I was fifteen or sixteen I would type out his stories to learn how the sentences worked. I taught myself to type at the same time. A few years ago when I was teaching a course at Berkeley I reread *A Farewell to Arms* and fell right back into those sentences. I mean they're perfect sentences. Very direct sentences, smooth rivers, clear water over granite, no sinkholes.

Henry James wrote perfect sentences too, but very indirect, very complicated. Sentences *with* sinkholes. You could drown in them. I wouldn't dare to write one. I'm not even sure I'd dare to read James again. I loved those novels so much that I was paralyzed by them for a long time. All those possibilities. All that perfectly reconciled style. It made me afraid to put words down.

JOHN DOS PASSOS: [Hemingway] and I used to read the Bible to each other. He began it. We read separate little scenes. From *Kings, Chronicles.* We didn't make anything out of it—the reading—but Ernest at that time talked a lot about style. He was crazy about Stephen Crane's *The Blue*

Hotel. It affected him very much. I was very much taken with him. He took me around to Gertrude Stein's. I wasn't quite at home there. A Buddha sitting up there, surveying us. Ernest was much less noisy then than he was in later life. He felt such people were instructive.

LEON EDEL: In 1926, I heard stories about Joyce's banned book *Ulysses* and what an oppressed author he was; nobody wanted to publish him. I sympathized; I explored. I finally got a smuggled copy. For a youth of eighteen the prose was dazzling. I thought of Joyce as a kind of Paganini of prose: a trickster who carried all English literature in his head. I was fascinated by the way Joyce tried to put the reader into the minds of his characters—that long soliloquy of Molly Bloom's, the way Joyce flitted from Bloom's thoughts into street smells and street incidents and then back into the stream of consciousness. Great stuff! Did I fall in love with Joyce? No, he wasn't lovable. But he was a great performer and youth likes performance. So I went to my favorite professor and announced I would write a dissertation on the "stream of consciousness" in Joyce. "Impossible," said the professor. Joyce was forty. His book wasn't available. There were only some poems, *Dubliners,* and *Portrait of the Artist as a Young Man.* And anyhow, he was alive; at that time you wrote dissertations only on the dead, whose work was complete and who could be fully appraised.

GABRIEL GARCÍA MÁRQUEZ: One night [at college] a friend lent me a book of short stories by Franz Kafka. I went back to the pension where I was staying and began to read *The Metamorphosis.* The first line almost knocked me off the bed, I was so surprised. The first line reads, "As Gregor Samsa awoke that morning from uneasy dreams, he found himself transformed in his bed into a gigantic insect. . . ." When I read the line I thought to myself that I didn't know anyone was allowed to write things like that. If I had known, I would have started writing a long time ago. So I immediately started writing short stories.

NADINE GORDIMER: You know what made me want to become a journalist? Reading Evelyn Waugh's *Scoop* when I was about eleven. Enough to make anybody want to be a journalist!

WILLIAM GOYEN: I still read, I still study, the *Cantos* of Pound. I found Pound in Texas when I was eighteen or nineteen through a young friend named William Hart. Hart was one of those prodigies, *enfants terribles,* that materialize in small towns, young men bearing a sense of art and poetry and life as naturally as others bore the instinct to compete and to copulate. He had a great deal to do with my early enlightenment and spiritual salvation in a lower middle class environment in an isolated (then) Texas town, where a boy's father considered him a sissy if he played the piano, as I've said, and questioned the sexual orientation of any youth who read poetry.

William Hart was a true pioneer; he brought me Pound, Eliot, and Auden. He was self-taught, finding things for himself out of hunger. He had a high-school education, barely, but afterwards he came and sat in my classes at Rice and listened. He knew more than the professors did sometimes—he really did ... about Elizabethan drama, and medieval romances. He knew these things. He was a delicate boy, obviously, but not effete. He was French Cajun, from a poor family, and he was on the streets, and could have been in trouble a lot. But he ended up in the library. They felt they had a revolutionary in there. In the Houston Public Library at nineteen he would get up and speak about literature, and Archibald MacLeish, of all people. And oh, how this man Hart spoke. The whole library would turn and listen. He became that kind of town creature, one of those who go down in cities, unheralded ... they go down into beds of ashes. Well, he brought me Pound.

Pound's *Cantos* hold for me madness and beauty, darkness and mystery, pain, heartbreak, nostalgia. Some of the most beautiful and most haunting were written as a prisoner. He made, above all, *songs,* and he told his stories lyrically, as I have felt driven to tell mine. By ordinary speech, ordinary people. I mean that it seems to me that Pound sometimes speaks from a sort of sub-tone in his poems like a con-man, a back-street hustler, using pieces of several languages, bits of myth, literary quotations and mixed dialects and plain beguiling nonsense. There is a stream, flowing and broken, of *voices* in Pound, echoes, town speech, songs, that deeply brought to me my own predicament, in the home of my parents and in the town where I lived. He helped show me a way to sing about it—it was, as most influences have been for me, as much a *tone,* a sound, a quality, as anything else.

The same for T. S. Eliot. He seemed then so much more American than Pound—but then Pound has the Chinese calligraphy and the heavy Greek and Latin. Eliot's wan songs broken suddenly by a crude word or a street phrase directly influenced me as a way to tell *The House of Breath;* and doom cut through by caprice shocked me and helped me survive in my own place until I could escape; showed me a way of managing the powerful life that I felt tearing through me, and trying to kill me. I saw a way: "Cry, what shall I cry?"—the dark Biblical overtone of the great poem; "the voice of one calling Stetson!" Oh, Eliot got hold of me at that early age and helped me speak for my own place.

The storytelling method of Eliot and Pound—darting, elliptical, circular, repetitive, lyric, self-revealing, simple speech within grand cadence and hyperbole—educated me and showed me a way to be taken out of my place, away from my obsessing relations: saved me from locality, from "regionalism." I knew then that it was "style" that would save me. I saw Pound as the most elegant of poets and the most elemental. Both. His madness partakes of both (elegance and elementalness) and is a quality of his poetry: "hast 'ou seen the rose in the steel dust / (or swansdown ever?) / so light is the urging, so ordered the dark / petals of iron / we who have passed over Lethe." That's Canto 74, from the *Pisan Cantos.*

HENRY GREEN: As far as I'm consciously aware, I forget everything I read at once, including my own stuff.

ELIZABETH HARDWICK: As I have grown older I see myself as fortunate in many ways. It is fortunate to have had all my life this passion for studying and enjoying literature and for trying to add a bit to it as interestingly as I can. This passion has given me much joy, it has given me friends who care for the same things, it has given me employment, escape from boredom, everything. The greatest gift is the passion for reading. It is cheap, it consoles, it distracts, it excites, it gives you knowledge of the world and experience of a wide kind. It is a moral illumination.

ERNEST HEMINGWAY: Mark Twain, Flaubert, Stendhal, Bach, Turgenev, Tolstoy, Dostoevsky, Chekhov, Andrew Marvell, John Donne, Maupassant, the good Kipling, Thoreau, Captain Marryat, Shakespeare, Mozart, Quevedo, Dante, Vergil, Tintoretto, Hieronymus Bosch, Brueghel, Patinir, Goya, Giotto, Cézanne, Van Gogh, Gauguin, San Juan de la Cruz, Góngora—it would take a day to remember everyone. Then it would sound as though I were claiming an erudition I did not possess instead of trying to remember all the people who have been an influence on my life and work. This isn't an old dull question. It is a very good but a solemn question and requires an examination of conscience. I put in painters, or started to, because I learn as much from painters about how to write as from writers. You ask how this is done? It would take another day of explaining. I should think what one learns from composers and from the study of harmony and counterpoint would be obvious.

ALDOUS HUXLEY: I never got very much out of *Ulysses*. I think it's an extraordinary book, but so much of it consists of rather lengthy demonstrations of how a novel ought *not* to be written, doesn't it? He does show nearly every conceivable way it should not be written, and then goes on to show how it might be written.

P. D. JAMES: I read widely—from adventure stories to Jane Austen. I came under her spell early on, though she usually appeals to older people. One of my first loves was the Book of Common Prayer—I loved its beautiful language and the sense of history, of timelessness it gave me. What in particular attracted me to Jane Austen was her irony and control of structure. One's response to literature is like one's response to human beings—if you asked me what appeals to me in a certain person, I might say his courage, or humor, or intelligence. In Jane Austen it was her style and her irony, the way she creates so distinctive a world in which I feel at home. I called my second daughter after her. She was born during some of the worst bombing in London. I went from Queen Charlotte's Maternity Hospital to a basement flat in Hampstead because I thought it was safer being underground, and we could hear the flying bombs overhead and the guns trying to shoot them down, and I just read Jane Austen for the hundredth time! I read Dickens and recognized his genius, but he is not my favorite. I find many of his female characters unsuccessful—wonderful caricatures, wicked, odd, grotesque, evil, but not true. There isn't the subtlety of characterization you get, say, in Trollope, whose understanding and description of women is astonishing. Jane Austen never described two men talking together if a woman was not present—she would have thought that was outside her experience. In Trollope, by contrast, you get continual conversations between women—for example Alice Vavasor and Lady Glencora Palliser in *Can You Forgive Her*—without a man there, and he gets it absolutely right. This plain, grumpy looking man had obviously an astonishing knowledge of women's psychology.

NORMAN MAILER: *The Amateur Gentleman* and *The Broad Highway* were glorious works. So was *Captain Blood*. I think I read every one of Farnol's books and there must be twenty of them. And every one of Sabatini's.

Now I have no real idea of their merit. But I never enjoyed a novel more than *Captain Blood.* Nor a movie. Do you remember Errol Flynn as Captain Blood? Some years ago I was asked by a magazine what were the ten most important books in my development. The book I listed first was *Captain Blood.* Then came *Das Kapital.* Then *The Amateur Gentleman.*

I have learned a lot from E. M. Forster. You remember in *The Longest Journey* somewhere about the fourth chapter, you turn the page and read, "Gerald was killed that day. He was beaten to death in a football game."* It was quite extraordinary. Gerald had been very important through the beginning of the book. But now that he was suddenly and abruptly dead, everyone else's character began to shift. It taught me that personality was more fluid, more dramatic and startling, more inexact than I had thought. I was brought up on the idea that when you wrote a novel you tried to build a character who could be handled and walked around like a piece of sculpture. Suddenly character seemed related more closely to the paintings of the new realists. For instance I saw one recently which had a painted girl reclining on a painted bed, and there was a television set next to her in the canvas, a real one which you could turn on. Turning on the literal factual set changes the girl and the painting both. Well, Forster gives you something of that sensation in his novels.

BERNARD MALAMUD: At eight or nine I was writing little stories in school and feeling the glow. To anyone of my friends who'd listen I'd recapitulate at tedious length the story of the last movie I'd seen. The movies tickled my imagination. As a writer I learned from Charlie Chaplin. Let's say the rhythm, the snap of comedy; the reserved comic presence—that beautiful distancing; the funny with sad; the surprise of surprise.

JAMES MERRILL: In Europe the *Paris Herald*—I get very American over there, and it's so concise. Here, I never learned how to read a newspaper. My first year away at school, I watched my classmates, some of them littler than I was, frowning over the war news or the financial page. They already knew how! I realized then and there I couldn't hope to catch up. I told this to Marianne Moore before introducing her at her Amherst reading in 1956. She looked rather taken aback, as I did myself, a half hour later, when in the middle of a poem she was reading—a poem I thought I

---

*Actually kicked in the head by a horse.—Ed.

knew—I heard my name. "Now Mr. Merrill," she was saying, "tells me he doesn't read a newspaper. That's hard for me to understand. The things one would miss! Why, only last week I read that our U.S. Customs Bureau was collecting all the egret and bird-of-paradise feathers we'd confiscated during the twenties and thirties—collecting them and sending them off to Nepal, where they're *needed.* . . ." And then she went right on with her poem.

ARTHUR MILLER: When I was about twelve, I think it was, my mother took me to a theater one afternoon. We lived in Harlem and in Harlem there were two or three theaters that ran all the time and many women would drop in for all or part of the afternoon performances. All I remember was that there were people in the hold of a ship, the stage was rocking—they actually rocked the stage—and some cannibal on the ship had a time bomb. And they were all looking for the cannibal: it was thrilling. The other one was a morality play about taking dope. Evidently there was much excitement in New York then about the Chinese and dope. The Chinese were kidnapping beautiful, blond, blue-eyed girls who, people thought, had lost their bearings morally; they were flappers who drank gin and ran around with boys. And they inevitably ended up in some basement in Chinatown where they were irretrievably lost by virtue of eating opium or smoking some pot. Those were the two masterpieces I had seen.

HENRY MILLER: That's hard to say, the writers I love are so diverse. They are the writers who are more than writers. They have this mysterious X quality which is metaphysical, occult, or whatnot—I don't know what term to use—this little extra something beyond the confines of literature. You see, people read to be amused, to pass the time, or to be instructed. Now I never read to pass the time, I never read to be instructed; I read to be taken out of myself, to become ecstatic. I'm always looking for the author who can lift me out of myself.

AMOS OZ: When I was nine or ten I read Zionist books about the glories of the ancient kingdoms of Israel. I decided to become a terrorist against the British Mandate, I built an intercontinental rocket with the wreck of a refrigerator and the relic of a motorcycle. My plan was to aim this rocket at Buckingham Palace, then send a letter to the King of England saying, "Either you get out of my country or off you go!" I was an Intifada child against the British—I threw stones at British soldiers and shouted "go home." So my early reading was nationalistic, in the spirit of third world freedom-fighting: books about the Italian risorgimento, like De Amicis's *Heart*, about little children who save their country by some heroic deed or self-sacrifice. Later I discovered the Russians, in particular Dostoevsky, Tolstoy and above all Chekhov. I felt Chekhov must have come from our neighborhood in Jerusalem, no one had ever captured those little paralyzed work reformers who use big words as he did.

My father was asked by the Jewish underground to hide a couple of Molotov cocktails in our home; it was risky, as there was a death penalty for terrorist activities. Our apartment was tiny and choking with thousands of books, and my father hid the explosives behind some books on a shelf, and told us about it so that we didn't set them off by mistake. The British arrived—I still have a vivid memory of the incident—they wore khaki shorts down to their knees and khaki socks up to their knees and in between their knees were exposed, white as snow on the Alps. The officer was extremely polite and, apologizing profusely for the inconvenience, began the search with a couple of soldiers. We were terrified. They evidently thought my father was too bookish to be a terrorist and searched perfunctorily. As they turned to go, the officer made some polite remark about the books and asked if there were any interesting English ones. That set my father off: "How do you mean, Sir? Of course we have English books!" he said, and began to pull out one English classic after another. My mother and I were petrified, lest having forgotten about the explosives, he might suddenly expose them or cause an explosion, while he was showing off. The reason we survived was that he had hidden the explosives behind Russian books—with the anarchists and terrorists of nineteenth-century Russia—Bakunin, Nechaev, Kropotkin, Dostoevsky.

DOROTHY PARKER: I went to a convent in New York—The Blessed Sacrament. Convents do the same things progressive schools do, only they don't know it. They don't teach you how to read; you have to find out for yourself. At my convent we *did* have a textbook, one that devoted a page and a half to Adelaide Ann Proctor; but we couldn't read Dickens; he was vulgar, you know. But *I* read him and Thackeray, and I'm the one woman you'll ever know who's read every word of Charles Reade, the author of *The Cloister and the Hearth*. But as for helping me in the outside world, the convent taught me only that if you spit on a pencil eraser it will erase ink. And I remember the smell of oilcloth, the smell of nuns' garb. I was fired from there, finally, for a lot of things, among them my insistence that the Immaculate Conception was spontaneous combustion.

BORIS PASTERNAK: The greatness of a writer has nothing to do with subject matter itself, only with how much the subject matter touches the author. It is the density of style which counts. Through Hemingway's style you feel matter, iron, wood. I admire Hemingway but I prefer what I know of Faulkner. *Light in August* is a marvelous book. The character of the little pregnant woman is unforgettable. As she walks from Alabama to Tennessee something of the immensity of the South of the United States, of its essence, is captured for us who have never been there.

KATHERINE ANNE PORTER: All the old houses that I knew when I was a child were full of books, bought generation after generation by members of the family. Everyone was literate as a matter of course. Nobody told you to read this or not to read that. It was there to read, and we read. I grew up in a sort of mélange. I was reading Shakespeare's sonnets when I was thirteen years old, and I'm perfectly certain that they made the most profound impression upon me of anything I ever read. For a time I knew the whole sequence by heart; now I can only remember two or three of them. That was the turning point of my life, when I read the Shakespeare sonnets, and then all at one blow, all of Dante—in that great big book illustrated by Gustave Doré. The plays I saw on the stage, but I don't remember reading them with any interest at all. Oh, and I read all kinds of poetry—Homer, Ronsard, all the old French poets in translation. We also had a very good library of—well, you might say secular philosophers. I was incredibly influenced by Montaigne when I was very young. And one day when I was about fourteen, my father led me up to a great big line of books and said, "Why don't you read this? It'll knock some of the nonsense out of you!" It happened to be the entire set of Voltaire's philosophical dictionary with notes by Smollett. And I plowed through it; it took me about five years.

And of course we read all the eighteenth-century novelists, though Jane Austen, like Turgenev, didn't really engage me until I was quite mature. I read them both when I was very young, but I was grown up before I really took them in. And I discovered for myself *Wuthering Heights;* I think I read that book every year of my life for fifteen years. I simply adored it. Henry James and Thomas Hardy were really my introduction to modern literature; Grandmother didn't much approve of it. She thought Dickens might do, but she was a little against Mr. Thackeray; she thought he was too trivial. So that was as far as I got into the modern world until I left home!

RICHARD PRICE: At Cornell the class of 1958 or 1959 was amazing—with Richard Farina, Ronald Sukenick, Thomas Pynchon, Joanna Russ, Steve Katz, all of whom are working writers now in various degrees of acclaim or obscurity. When I was at Cornell from 1967 to 1971 two or three of them came back to teach. It was the first time I sat in a room with a teacher who wasn't as old as my father. Here was a guy wearing a vest over a T-shirt. He had boots on, and his hair was longer than mine. A novelist! I couldn't take my eyes off him. I felt, "Ah, to be a writer! I could be like this teacher and have that long, gray hair . . . boots up on the table and cursing in class!" It made me dizzy just to look at the guy. I don't remember a thing he said to me, except that he usually made encouraging noises: "You're good. You're okay, keep writing, blah, blah . . ." He gave us this reading list that ranged from Céline to Walter Abish to Mallarmé and Rimbaud, names I'd never even heard of. The books looked so groovy, so cool and so hip. I bought every one of them. I walked around with Alfred Jarry and Henri Michaux under my arm, but I didn't understand what they were trying to do, to *say*. I had no context for any of them. The only one I could get through on the list was Henry Miller. One writing teacher gave us his own novel, and frankly, I couldn't understand that either.

SUSAN SONTAG: Well, literature does educate us about life. I wouldn't be the person I am, I wouldn't understand what I understand, were it not for certain books. I'm thinking of the great question of nineteenth-century Russian literature: how should one live? A novel worth reading is an education of the heart. It enlarges your sense of human possibility, of what human nature is, of what happens in the world. It's a creator of inwardness.

HELEN VENDLER: I don't think the mind is gendered. I know that's not a popular position these days, but I never felt the mind to be gendered and perhaps that may be because I always read poetry. When I was a young girl reading and the page said, "My heart aches, and a drowsy numbness pains my sense," or "So are you to my thoughts as food to life," it never occurred to me that these thoughts were not available to me because they had been uttered by an author who was male. I didn't care who had uttered them. They seemed good things to say at a given moment.

KURT VONNEGUT: My education was as a chemist at Cornell and then an anthropologist at the University of Chicago. Christ—I was thirty-five before I went crazy about Blake, forty before I read *Madame Bovary,* forty-five before I'd even heard of Céline. Through dumb luck, I read *Look Homeward, Angel* exactly when I was supposed to—at the age of eighteen.

I grew up in a house crammed with books. But I never had to read a book for academic credit, never had to write a paper about it, never had to prove I'd understood it in a seminar. I am a hopelessly clumsy discusser of books. My experience is nil.

ROBERT PENN WARREN: *How They Brought the Good News from Aix to Ghent* (at about age nine). I thought it was pretty nearly the height of human achievement. I didn't know whether I was impressed by riding a horse that fast or writing the poem. I couldn't distinguish between the two, but I knew there was something pretty fine going on. . . . Then *Lycidas.* . . .

By thirteen, something like that, I knew it wasn't what was happening in the poem that was important—it was the poem. I had crossed the line.

EVELYN WAUGH: I enjoyed him [Ronald Firbank] very much when I was young. I can't read him now. I think there would be something wrong with an elderly man who could enjoy Firbank.

E. B. WHITE: I was never a voracious reader and, in fact, have done little reading in my life. There are too many other things I would rather do than read. In my youth I read animal stories—William J. Long and Ernest Seton Thompson. I have read a great many books about small boat voyages—they fascinate me even though they usually have no merit. In the twenties, I read the newspaper columns: F.P.A., Christopher Morley, Don Marquis. I tried contributing and had a few things published. (As a child, I was a member of the St. Nicholas League and from that eminence was hurled into the literary life, wearing my silver badge and my gold badge.) My reading habits have not changed over the years, only my eyesight has changed. I don't like being indoors and get out every chance I get. In order to read, one must sit down, usually indoors. I am restless and would rather sail a boat than crack a book. I've never had a very lively literary curiosity, and it has sometimes seemed to me that I am not really a literary fellow at all. Except that I write for a living.

I admire anybody who has the guts to write anything at all. As for what comes out on paper, I'm not well equipped to speak about it. When I should be reading, I am almost always doing something else. It is a matter of some embarrassment to me that I have never read Joyce and a dozen other writers who have changed the face of literature. But there you are. I picked up *Ulysses* the other evening, when my eye lit on it, and gave it a go. I stayed with it only for about twenty minutes, then was off and away. It takes more than a genius to keep me reading a book. But when I latch onto a book like *They Live by the Wind*, by Wendell P. Bradley, I am glued tight to the chair. It is because Bradley wrote about something that has always fascinated (and uplifted) me—sailing. He wrote about it very well, too.

I was deeply impressed by Rachel Carson's *Silent Spring*. It may well be the book by which the human race will stand or fall.

TENNESSEE WILLIAMS: What writers influenced me as a young man? *Chekhov!*

As a dramatist? Chekhov! As a story writer? Chekhov! D. H. Lawrence, too, for his spirit, of course, for his understanding of sexuality, of life in general.

ON FIRST EFFORTS

Most of the basic material a writer works with is acquired
before the age of fifteen.   —WILLA CATHER

The beginnings of all things are small.   —CICERO

The first step is the hardest.
                    —A COMMENT MADE BY MME DU DUFFAND,
    a celebrated eighteenth-century *salon* personage, on the legend of Saint
    Denis, who after his execution picked up his head and walked with it from
    Montmartre to the town which now bears his name a few miles north of
    Paris.

The difficult thing is to get your foot in the stirrup.
                                                   —OLD SAYING

CHINUA ACHEBE: The English department [of the University of
Ibadan] was a very good example of what I mean. The people there would
have laughed at the idea that any of us would become a writer. That didn't
really cross their minds. I remember on one occasion a departmental
prize was offered. They put up a notice: Write a short story over the long
vacation for the departmental prize. I'd never written a short story before,
but when I got home, I thought, Well, why not. So I wrote one and submitted it. Months passed; then finally one day there was a notice on the
board announcing the result. It said that no prize was awarded because no
entry was up to the standard. They named me, said that my story deserved
mention. Ibadan in those days was not a dance you danced with snuff in
one palm. It was a dance you danced with all your body. So when Ibadan
said you deserved mention, that was very high praise.

I went to the lecturer who had organized the prize and said, "You said
my story wasn't really good enough, but it was interesting. Now what was
wrong with it?" She said, "Well, it's the form. It's the wrong form." So I said,
"Ah. Can you tell me about this?" She said, "Yes, but not now. I'm going to
play tennis; we'll talk about it. Remind me later, and I'll tell you." This went

on for a whole term. Every day when I saw her, I'd say, "Can we talk about form?" She'd say, "No, not now. We'll talk about it later." Then at the very end she saw me and said, "You know, I looked at your story again, and actually there's nothing wrong with it." So that was it! That was all I learned from the English department about writing short stories. You really have to go out on your own and do it.

TRUMAN CAPOTE: When I was a child of about ten or eleven and lived near Mobile, I had to go into town on Saturdays to the dentist and I joined the Sunshine Club that was organized by the Mobile *Press Register.* There was a children's page with contests for writing and for coloring pictures and then every Saturday afternoon they had a party with free Nehi and Coca-Cola. The prize for the short story writing contest was either a pony or a dog, I've forgotten which, but I wanted it badly. I had been noticing the activities of some neighbors who were up to no good, so I wrote a kind of *roman à clef* called *Old Mr. Busybody* and entered it in the contest. The first installment appeared one Sunday, under my real name of Truman Streckfus Persons. Only somebody suddenly realized that I was serving up a local scandal as fiction, and the second installment never appeared. Naturally, I didn't win a thing.

ISAK DINESEN: I painted a little in Africa, but every time I'd get to work someone would come and say an ox has died or something and I'd have to go out in the fields. I did write there to entertain myself and I told stories constantly to the natives, all kinds of nonsense: they loved it. I'd say, "Once there was a man who had an elephant with two heads," and right away the natives would say, "Oh? Yes, well, Mem-Sahib, how did he find it, and how did he manage to feed it," or whatever. They loved such invention. I delighted my people there by speaking in rime for them; they have no rime, you know, had never discovered it. I'd say things like "Wakamba na kula mamba"—"The such-and-such tribe eats snakes": which in prose would have infuriated them, but amused them mightily in rime. Afterwards they'd say, "Please, Mem-Sahib, talk like rain," so then I knew they liked it, for rain was very precious to us there.

JOHN DOS PASSOS: I never felt I wanted to be a writer. . . . I didn't much like the literary world as I knew it. I studied architecture. I've always been a frustrated architect. But there are certain periods of life when you take in an awful lot of impressions. I kept a good diary—very usual sort of thing—and I was consistent about putting down my impressions. But I had no intention, really, of being a writer then. It may have been Barbusse that got me going. Or more likely something to keep the dry rot from settling in the brain. Robert Hillyer and I began what we called the Great Novel, or more simply the GN. Our schedule then at the front was twenty-four hours on, twenty hours off, and I remember we worked on the novel in a cement tank that protected us from the shelling. We wrote alternate chapters. I sent the manuscript up to the University of Virginia the other day. I didn't dare look at it.

FRANCINE DU PLESSIX GRAY: One childhood episode stands out as particularly vivid, in Paris, in the 1930s. My father was an eccentric, extremely conservative Frenchman who deplored most aspects of the twentieth century, particularly the laxness of its education. And according to his wishes, I spent my first nine years confined to my room, tutored at home by a governess quite as tyrannical as my father. She was a rabid hypochondriac, convinced that the mere *sight* of another child might lead me to catch some deadly germ. . . . I lived in extreme isolation. Once a week we commuted to a correspondence school where I'd receive the assignments for the following week—typically French, didactic, desiccating assignments, memorizing Latin verbs and the dates of battles won by Napoleon. But when I was eight years old an unprecedented event took place—a new teacher came in and gave us the following assignment: "Write a Story About Anything You Wish." I was filled with excitement and anguish by this novel freedom. I began as a severe minimalist. Here's the cautionary tale I wrote: "The little girl was forbidden by her parents to walk alone to the lake at the other end of the green lawn. But she wished to visit a green-eyed frog who could offer her the key to freedom. One day she disobeyed her parents and walked to the lake, and was immediately drowned. The End." The following day, during his daily visit to the study room my father perused the composition and raised a storm. "Pathetic dribble! You dare call that a story? What will become of you if you don't ever finish anything!" And he grabbed the paper from my little desk and tore it to shreds. It was a May evening in 1939, fourteen months before he died in the Resistance. My father had been the love of my life, and he'd warned me that I should never write again. I didn't attempt fiction again for over thirty years.

GRAHAM GREENE: I wanted to be a businessman and all sorts of other things; I wanted to prove to myself that I could do something else [than write]. The business career lasted for a fortnight. They were a firm, I remember, of tobacco merchants. I was to go up to Leeds to learn the business and then go abroad. I couldn't stand my companion. He was an insufferable bore. We would play double noughts and crosses and he always won. What finally got me was when he said: "We'll be able to play this on the way out, won't we?" I resigned immediately.

JOHN GUARE: If you can't be arrogant in drama school, where can you be? You learn to approach, say, Chekhov as a peer. How does he deal with entrances and exits? You study how Chekhov gets somebody offstage: you see how he takes a simple exit in *Uncle Vanya,* in which Sonya leaves to ask permission to play the piano and builds to Sonya's sudden return—"He says no."—a heart-stopping moment that sums up a life.

· · ·

In college I was editor of the literary magazine and wrote sensitive short stories overly inspired by Flaubert. Our English teacher actually knew Katherine Anne Porter; he showed her a short story I had written. She told him she would pay $1500 for the first sentence: "After Pinky vomited, Ingrid Aldamine sat up in bed." She liked the rhythm. She didn't mention anything about the rest.

EUGÈNE IONESCO: When I was nine, the teacher asked us to write a piece about our village *fête.* He read mine in class. I was encouraged and continued. I even wanted to write my memoirs at the age of ten. At twelve I wrote poetry, mostly about friendship—"Ode to Friendship." Then my class wanted to make a film and one little boy suggested that I write the script. It was a story about some children who invite some other children to a party, and they end up throwing all the furniture and the parents out of the window. Then I wrote a patriotic play, *Pro Patria.* You see how I went for the grand titles!

P. D. JAMES: I don't make a distinction between the so-called "serious" or "literary" novel and the crime novel. I suppose one could say mainstream novel. But I didn't hesitate long before I decided to try to write a detective story, because I so much enjoyed reading them myself. And I thought I could probably do it successfully, and the detective story being a popular genre, it would have a better chance of being accepted for publication. I didn't want to use the traumatic experiences of my own life in an autobiographical book, which would have been another option for a first attempt. But there were two other reasons. First, I like structured fiction, with a beginning, a middle and an end. I like a novel to have narrative drive, pace, resolution, which a detective novel has. Second, I was setting out at last on the path of becoming a writer, which I had longed for all my life, and I thought writing a detective story would be a wonderful apprenticeship for a "serious" novelist, because a detective story is very easy to write badly but difficult to write well. There is so much you have to fit into eighty or ninety thousand words—not just creating a puzzle, but an atmosphere, a setting, characters . . . Then, when the first one worked, I continued, and I came to believe that it is perfectly possible to remain within the constraints and conventions of the genre *and* be a serious writer, saying something true about men and women and their relationships and the society in which they live.

NORMAN MAILER: It was a science fiction novel about people on Earth taking a rocket ship to Mars. The hero had a name which sounded like Buck Rogers. His assistant was called Dr. Hoor. That's the way we used to pronounce whore in Brooklyn. He was patterned directly after Dr. Huer in Buck Rogers, who was then appearing on radio. This novel filled two and a half paper notebooks. You know the type, about 7 × 10. They had soft shiny blue covers and they were, oh, only ten cents in those days, or a nickel. They ran to perhaps 100 pages each, and I used to write on both sides. My writing was remarkable for the way I hyphenated words. I loved hyphenating, so I would hyphenate "the" and make it th-e if it came at the end of the line. Or "they" would become the-y. Then I didn't write again for a long time. I didn't even try out for the high school literary magazine. I had friends who wrote short stories, and their short stories were far better than the ones I would write for assignments in high school English and I felt no desire to write. When I got to college I started again. The jump from Boys' High School in Brooklyn to Harvard came as a shock. I started reading some decent novels for the first time.

When I first began to write again at Harvard, I wasn't very good. I was doing short stories at the time. If there were fifty people in the class, let's say I was somewhere in the top ten. My teachers thought I was fair, but I don't believe they ever thought for a moment that I was really talented. Then in the middle of my sophomore year I started getting better. I got on the *Harvard Advocate,* and that gave me confidence, and about this time I did a couple of fairly good short stories for English A-1, one of which won *Story* magazine's college contest for that year. I must say that Robert Gorham Davis, who was my instructor then, picked the story to submit for the contest and was confident it would win.

And when I found out it had won—which was at the beginning of the summer after my sophomore year (1941)—well, that fortified me, and I sat down and wrote a novel. It was a very bad novel. I wrote it in two months. It was called *No Percentage*. It was just terrible. But I never questioned any longer whether I was *started* as a writer.

MARY MCCARTHY: I didn't have any other ambitions at all. Then I married Edmund Wilson, and after we'd been married about a week, he said, "I think you have a talent for writing fiction." And he put me in a little room. He didn't literally lock the door, but he said, "Stay in there!" And I did. I just sat down, and it just came. It was the first story I had ever written, really: the first story in *The Company She Keeps*. Robert Penn Warren published it in *The Southern Review*. And I found myself writing fiction to my great surprise.

ARTHUR MILLER: The first play I wrote was in Michigan in 1935. It was written on a spring vacation in six days. I was so young that I dared do such things, begin it and finish it in a week. I'd seen about two plays in my life, so I didn't know how long an act was supposed to be, but across the hall there was a fellow who did the costumes for the University theater and he said, "Well, it's roughly forty minutes." I had written an enormous amount of material and I got an alarm clock. It was all a lark to me, and not to be taken too seriously . . . that's what I told myself. As it turned out, the acts were longer than that, but the sense of the timing was in me even from the beginning, and the play had a form right from the start.

Being a playwright was always the maximum idea. I'd always felt that the theater was the most exciting and the most demanding form one could try to master. When I began to write, one assumed inevitably that one was in the mainstream that began with Aeschylus, and went through about 2500 years of playwrighting. There are so few masterpieces in the theater, as opposed to the other arts, that one can pretty well encompass all of them by the age of nineteen.

MARIANNE MOORE: I had written something first about "the adder and the child with a bowl of porridge," and she [my mother] said, "Well, it won't do."

"All right," I said, "but I have to produce something." Cyril Connolly had asked me for something for *Horizon*. So I wrote "A Face." That is one of the few things I ever set down and it didn't give me any trouble. And she said, "I like it." I remember that.

Then, much before that, I wrote "The Buffalo." I thought it would probably outrage a number of persons because it had to me a kind of pleasing jerky progress. I thought, "Well, if it seems bad my brother will tell me, and if it has any point he'll detect it."

And he said, with a considerable gusto, "It takes my fancy." I was happy as could be.

FRANK O'CONNOR: From the time I was nine or ten, it was a toss-up whether I was going to be a writer or a painter, and I discovered by the time I was sixteen or seventeen that paints cost too much money, so I became a writer because you could be a writer with a pencil and a penny notebook.

ROBERT PINSKY: I think my first experience of art, or the joy in making art, was playing the horn at some high-school dance or bar mitzvah or wedding, looking at a roomful of people moving their bodies around in time to what I was doing. There was a piano player, a bass player, a drummer, and my breath making the melody. The audience may not have been thinking, My God, that kid is the best saxophone player I've ever heard; I'm *positive* they weren't. But we were making music, and the fact that it was my breath making a party out of things was miraculous to me, a physical pleasure. So maybe the horn, this fumbling after a kind of melodic grace and ease I know I'll never have, stands for a rededication to art itself—with that eager, amateur's love.

KATHERINE ANNE PORTER: I started out with nothing in the world but a kind of passion, a driving desire. I don't know where it came from, and I do not know why—or why I have been so stubborn about it that nothing could deflect me. But this thing between me and my writing is the strongest bond I have ever had—stronger than any bond or any engagement with any human being or with any other work I've ever done.

ANNE SEXTON: One night I saw I. A. Richards on educational television reading a sonnet and explaining its form. I thought to myself, "I could do that, maybe; I could try." So I sat down and wrote a sonnet. The next day I wrote another one, and so forth. My doctor encouraged me to write more. "Don't kill yourself," he said. "Your poems might mean something to someone else someday." That gave me a feeling of purpose, a little cause, something to *do* with my life, no matter how rotten I was.

ROBERT STONE: My early life was very strange. I was a solitary; radio fashioned my imagination. Radio narrative always has to embody a full account of both action and scene. I began to do that myself. When I was seven or eight, I'd walk through Central Park like Sam Spade, describing aloud what I was doing, becoming both the actor and the writer setting him into the scene. That was where I developed an inner ear.

EUDORA WELTY: I remember a sentence I opened one story with, to show you how bad I was: "Monsieur Boule inserted a delicate dagger in Mademoiselle's left side and departed with a poised immediacy." I like to think I didn't take myself seriously then, but I did.

JOHN HALL WHEELOCK: When I was at Harvard in 1906, I was so influenced by Swinburne that I kept after my father, saying that I wanted to go over to England to see him. My father wasn't very well-off that year—it was a recession year—but he said, "Well, since you're so persistent you can go, but you'll have to go steerage; I can't afford to send you even cabin class." I said, "Well, that's fine with me," and I went over in the steerage and it wasn't bad at all. But I made the pilgrimage stupidly; I didn't get a letter of introduction. All I knew was that Swinburne was living with Theodore Watts-Dunton—a much lesser poet but quite well known as a critic—in "The Pines" in London, in a part of the city called Putney.

So I just went over and hung around "The Pines" for several days. I waited for I forget how many days, and then one August afternoon Swinburne appeared—this very short man wearing a turban—an odd idea, it was very hot—and I was disappointed because he was so short, almost giving the effect of being a dwarf—and he was talking to himself. At that time he must have been about seventy, and, of course, to me, as a youth, he seemed very old. As he came near me I thought I was going to faint, because my heart began palpitating so rapidly that I didn't know whether I'd be able to make it, I mean walk the rest of the distance without fainting. But I did, and as he passed me I touched his coat with my hand, and I hardly dared look at him. You must remember that I'd been reading Swinburne devoutly and knew many of his poems by heart. He had a very powerful influence on any poet, particularly a young poet, because he has such a marked style; I think after Pope probably the most marked style of any English poet. So, seeing the source of all this verbal magic and music, the poetry that so intoxicated me, was almost like, well, seeing God. I survived it, however, and passed him, and I went back to my room in a small, inexpensive hotel and lay down on the bed and just thought about it all the rest of the day. I went back for several days in the hope of seeing Swinburne again, thinking that I might even have the courage to say a word to him. I'd written him many letters, and also I'd written poems and an essay about him, which came out in *The Harvard Advocate*, and I had sent these to him. But, of course, I added in all my letters, "I would never forgive you if you answered this. Do not answer it, please." The *thought* of his being bothered to answer it—it was real hero-worship.

E. B. WHITE: I never knew for sure that I would follow a literary profession. I was twenty-seven or twenty-eight before anything happened that gave me any assurance that I could make a go of writing. I had *done* a great deal of writing, but I lacked confidence in my ability to put it to good use. I went abroad one summer and on my return to New York found an accumulation of mail at my apartment. I took the letters, unopened, and went to a Child's restaurant on 14th Street, where I ordered dinner and began opening my mail. From one envelope, two or three checks dropped out, from *The New Yorker*. I suppose they totaled a little under a hundred dollars, but it looked like a fortune to me. I can still remember the feeling that "this was it"—I was a pro at last. It was a good feeling and I enjoyed the meal.

On Motivation: Why I Write

I write to ease the passing of time.   —JORGE LUIS BORGES

I know that poetry is indispensable, but to what I could not say.
—JEAN COCTEAU

I felt like poisoning a monk.
—UMBERTO ECO on why he wrote
The Name of the Rose

I was too slow a mover. It was much easier to be a poet.
—T. S. ELIOT on giving up
boxing in college

Poetry is a way of taking life by the throat.   —ROBERT FROST

I write because I hate. A lot. Hard.   —WILLIAM GASS

I don't want to be a doctor, and live by men's diseases; nor a
minister to live by their sins; nor a lawyer to live by their
quarrels. So I don't see there's anything left for me but to be an
author.   —NATHANIEL HAWTHORNE

Sir, no man but a blockhead ever wrote except for money.
—SAMUEL JOHNSON

The only end of writing is to enable readers better to enjoy life
or better to endure it.   —SAMUEL JOHNSON

A work of art has no importance whatever to society. It is only
important to the individual.   —VLADIMIR NABOKOV

The role of the writer is not to say what we can all say, but
what we are unable to say.   —ANAÏS NIN

My main reason for adopting literature as a profession was
that, as the author is never seen by his clients, he need not
dress respectably.   —GEORGE BERNARD SHAW

I write for myself and strangers. The strangers, dear Readers,
are an afterthought.   —GERTRUDE STEIN

WOODY ALLEN: A woman I went to school with said, "Oh yes, I married this guy. He's a plumber but he's very creative." It's very important for people to have that credential. Like if he wasn't creative, he was less.

I hate when art becomes a religion. I feel the opposite. When you start putting a higher value on works of art than people, you're forfeiting your humanity. There's a tendency to feel the artist has special privileges, and that anything's okay if it's in the service of art. I tried to get into that in *Interiors*. I always feel the artist is much too revered: it's not fair and it's cruel. It's a nice but fortuitous gift—like a nice voice or being left-handed. That you can create is a kind of nice accident. It happens to have high value in society, but it's not as noble an attribute as courage. I find funny and silly the pompous kind of self-important talk about the artist who takes risks. Artistic risks are like show-business risks—laughable. Like casting against type, wow, what danger! Risks are where your life is on the line. The people who took risks against the Nazis or some of the Russian poets who stood up against the state—those people are courageous and brave, and that's really an achievement. To be an artist is also an achievement, but you have to keep it in perspective. I'm not trying to undersell art. I think it's valuable, but I think it's overly revered. It is a valuable thing, but no more valuable than being a good schoolteacher, or being a good doctor. The problem is that being creative has glamour. People in the business end of film always say, "I want to be a producer, but a creative producer."

KINGSLEY AMIS: When starting to think about any novel, part of the motive is: I'm going to show them, this time. Without that, a lot of what passes under the name of creative energy would be lost. It's an egotistical self-assertion, if you like—the mere act of writing a book is that.

· · ·

There's always vanity. You remember that Orwell said, when he was answering his own question, why I write, that his leading motive was the desire to be thought clever, to be talked about by people he had never met. I don't think he was being arrogant, I think he was being very honest.

JAMES BALDWIN: Something that irritates you and won't let you go. That's the anguish of it. Do this book, or die. You have to go through that. Talent is insignificant. I know a lot of talented ruins. Beyond talent lie all the usual words: discipline, love, luck, but, most of all, endurance.

. . .

When you're writing, you're trying to find out something which you don't know. The whole language of writing for me is finding out what you don't want to know, what you don't want to find out. But something forces you to anyway.

JOHN BARTH: It's a combination of an almost obscene self-confidence and an ongoing terror. You remember the old story of how Hemingway would always record the number of words he wrote each day. When I learned that detail about Hemingway I understood why the poor chap went bonkers and did himself in at the end. The average professional, whether he's good or mediocre, learns enough confidence in himself so that he no longer fears the blank page. About my own fiction: my friend John Hawkes once said of it that it seems spun out against nothingness, simply so that there should not be silence. I understand that. It's Scheherazade's terror: the terror that comes from the literal or metaphorical equating of telling stories with living, with life itself. I understand that metaphor to the marrow of my bones. For me there is always a sense that when this story ends maybe the whole world will end; I wonder whether the world's really there when I'm not narrating it. Well, at this stage of my life I have enough confidence in myself to know that the page will fill up. Indeed, because I'm not a very consistent fiction writer (my books don't resemble one another very much), I have an ongoing curiosity about what will happen next. Stendhal said that once when he wanted to commit suicide, he couldn't abide to do it because he wanted to find out what would happen next in French politics. I have a similar curiosity . . . when this long project is over, what will fill the page next? I've never been able to think that far ahead; I can't do it until the project in hand is out of the shop and going through the publisher's presses. Then I begin to think about what will be next. I'm just as curious as the next chap. Maybe more so.

JORGE LUIS BORGES: I was very timid, because when I was young I thought of myself as a poet. So I thought: "If I write a story everybody will know I'm an outsider, that I am intruding in forbidden ground." Then I had an accident. You can feel the scar. If you touch my head here, you will see. Feel all those mountains, bumps? Then I spent a fortnight in a hospital. I had nightmares and sleeplessness—insomnia. After that they told me that I had been in danger, well, of dying, that it was really a wonderful thing that the operation had been successful. I began to fear for my mental integrity—I said, "Maybe I can't write anymore." Then my life would have been practically over, because literature is very important to me. Not because I think my own stuff particularly good, but because I know that I can't get along without writing. If I don't write, I feel, well, a kind of remorse, no? Then I thought I would try my hand at writing an article or a poem. But I thought: "I have written hundreds of articles and poems. If I can't do it, then I'll know at once that I am done for, that everything is over with me." So I thought I'd try my hand at something I hadn't done: if I couldn't do it, there would be nothing strange about it, because why should I write short stories?—It would prepare me for the final overwhelming blow: knowing that I was at the end of my tether. I wrote a story called, let me see, I think, "*Hombre de la esquina rosada*" [This is, perhaps, a slip of memory: the story was "*Pierre Menard, autor del Quijote*," published in *Sur* number 56 (May 1959).], and everyone enjoyed it very much. It was a great relief to me. If it hadn't been for that particular knock on the head I got, perhaps I would never have written short stories.

ANTHONY BURGESS: My eight-year-old son said the other day: "Dad, why don't you write for *fun*?" Even he divined that the process as I practice it is prone to irritability and despair. I suppose, apart from my marriage, I was happiest when I was doing a teaching job and had nothing much to think about in the vacations. The anxiety involved is intolerable. And—I differ here from Simenon—the financial rewards just don't make up for the expenditure of energy, the damage to health caused by stimulants and narcotics, the fear that one's work isn't good enough. I think if I had enough money, I'd give up writing tomorrow.

LOUIS-FERDINAND CÉLINE: Emotion. Savy, the biologist, said something appropriate: In the beginning there was emotion, and the verb wasn't there at all. When you tickle an amoeba she withdraws, she has emotion, she doesn't speak but she does have emotion. A baby cries, a horse gallops. Only us, they've given us the verb. That gives you the politician, the writer, the prophet. The verb's horrible. You can't smell it. But to get to the point where you can translate this emotion, that's a difficulty no one imagines.... It's ugly.... It's superhuman.... It's a trick that'll kill a guy.

AMY CLAMPITT: Women who are inclined to write poetry at all are inspired by being mad at something. It doesn't affect them in an obvious way but I suspect it's there. You can't help but be affected more than men. Women have been given reason to recognize a lot of things that have been covered up for a long time. What preceded the rage was a lot of anxiety. When you get over the anxiety you discover you should have been mad a long time ago. Women are full of steam, and mostly they're making a lot of noise. I don't necessarily like it, but some very plausible stuff is being written by women in a way that most men are not doing.

ROBERT CREELEY: One time, again some years ago, Franz Kline was being questioned—not with hostility but with intensity, by another friend—and finally he said, "Well, look, if I paint what *you* know, then that will simply bore you, the repetition from me to you. If I paint what *I* know, it will be boring to myself. Therefore I paint what I don't know." Well, I believe that. I write what I don't know. Communication is a word one would have to spend much time defining. For example, can you make a blind man see? That has always been a question in my own mind. And if it is true that you cannot tell someone something he has no experience of, then the act of reading is that one is reading *with* someone. I feel when people read my poems most sympathetically, they are reading *with* me. So communication is mutual feeling with someone, not a didactic process of information.

DON DELILLO: Writing is a concentrated form of thinking. I don't know what I think about certain subjects, even today, until I sit down and try to write about them. Maybe I wanted to find more rigorous ways of thinking. We're talking now about the earliest writing I did and about the power of language to counteract the wallow of late adolescence, to define things, define muddled experience in economical ways. Let's not forget that writing is convenient. It requires the simplest tools. A young writer sees that with words and sentences on a piece of paper that costs less than a penny he can place himself more clearly in the world. Words on a page, that's all it takes to help him separate himself from the forces around him, streets and people and pressures and feelings. He learns to think about these things, to ride his own sentences into new perceptions.

JOAN DIDION: I wrote stories from the time I was a little girl, but I didn't want to be a writer. I wanted to be an actress. I didn't realize then that it's the same impulse. It's make-believe. It's performance. The only difference being that a writer can do it all alone. I was struck a few years ago when a friend of ours—an actress—was having dinner here with us and a couple of other writers. It suddenly occurred to me that she was the only person in the room who couldn't plan what she was going to do. She had to wait for someone to ask her, which is a strange way to live.

E. L. DOCTOROW: I subscribe to what Henry James tries to indicate when he gives that wonderful example of a young woman who has led a sheltered life walking along beside an army barracks and hearing a snatch of soldier's conversation coming through the window. On the basis of that, said James, if she's a novelist she's capable of going home and writing a perfectly accurate novel about army life. I've always subscribed to that idea. We're supposed to be able to get into other skins. We're supposed to be able to render experiences not our own and warrant times and places we haven't seen. That's one justification for art, isn't it—to distribute the suffering? Writing teachers invariably tell students, Write about what you know. That's, of course, what you have to do, but on the other hand, how do you know what you know until you've written it? Writing is knowing. What did Kafka know? The insurance business? So that kind of advice is foolish, because it presumes that you have to go out to a war to be able to do war. Well, some do and some don't. I've had very little experience in my life. In fact, I try to avoid experience if I can. Most experience is bad.

LAWRENCE DURRELL: It doesn't really matter whether you're first rate, second rate, or third rate, but it's of vital importance that the water finds its own level and that you do the very best you can with the powers that are given you. It's idle to strive for things out of your reach, just as it's utterly immoral to be slothful about the qualities you have. You see, I'm not fundamentally interested in the artist. I use him to try to become a happy man, which is a good deal harder for me. I find art easy. I find life difficult.

WILLIAM FAULKNER: He must never be satisfied with what he does. It never is as good as it can be done. Always dream and shoot higher than you know you can do. Don't bother just to be better than your contemporaries or predecessors. Try to be better than yourself. An artist is a creature driven by demons. He doesn't know why they choose him and he's usually too busy to wonder why. He is completely amoral in that he will rob, borrow, beg, or steal from anybody and everybody to get the work done.

The writer's only responsibility is to his art. He will be completely ruthless if he is a good one. He has a dream. It anguishes him so much he must get rid of it. He has no peace until then. Everything goes by the board: honor, pride, decency, security, happiness, all, to get the book written. If a writer has to rob his mother, he will not hesitate; the "Ode on a Grecian Urn" is worth any number of old ladies.

RICHARD FORD: I want to write, partly at least, for the kind of reader I was when I was nineteen years old. I want to address that person because he or she is young enough that life is just beginning to seem a mystery which literature can address in surprising and pleasurable ways. When I was nineteen I began to read *Absalom, Absalom!* slowly, slowly, page by patient page, since I was slightly dyslexic. I was working on the railroad, the Missouri-Pacific in Little Rock. I hadn't been doing well in school, but I started reading. I don't mean to say that reading altogether changed my life, but it certainly brought something into my life—possibility—that had not been there before. With *Absalom, Absalom!* it was the language—a huge suffusing sea of wonderful words, made into beautiful, long paragraphs and put to the service of some great human conundrum it meant to console me about if not completely resolve. When I was old enough to think about myself as trying to be a writer, I always thought I would like to write a book and have it do that for someone else.

WILLIAM GADDIS: If the work weren't difficult I'd die of boredom. After *The Recognitions,* where there is a great deal of authorial intrusion and little essays along the way, on alchemy or what have you, I found it was too easy and I didn't want to do it again. I wanted to write something different. I wanted to do something which was challenging, to create other problems, to force this discipline on myself.

JOHN GARDNER: As I tried to make plain in *On Moral Fiction,* I think that the difference right now between good art and bad art is that the good artists are the people who are, in one way or another, creating, out of deep and honest concern, a vision of life-in-the-twentieth-century that is worth pursuing. And the bad artists, of whom there are many, are whining or moaning or staring, because it's fashionable, into the dark abyss. If you believe that life is fundamentally a volcano full of baby skulls, you've got two main choices as an artist: you can either stare into the volcano and count the skulls for the thousandth time and tell everybody, "There are the skulls; that's your baby, Mrs. Miller." Or you can try to build walls so that fewer baby skulls go in. It seems to me that the artist ought to hunt for positive ways of surviving, of living. You shouldn't lie. If there aren't any, so far as you can see, you should say so, like the *Merdistes.* But I don't think the *Merdistes* are right—except for Céline himself, by accident, because Céline (as character, not as author) is comic; a villain so outrageous—miserable, and inept—that we laugh at him and at all he so earnestly stands for. I think the world is not all merde. I think it's possible to make walls around at least some of the smoking holes.

· · ·

The ones that last are the ones that are true. You look at Faulkner and John O'Hara. John O'Hara outsold Faulkner, he circled Faulkner at the time they were writing. Ten years after his death, O'Hara's books are out of print. We all read Faulkner, nobody reads O'Hara. Dreiser in some ways, some of the time, is one of the worst writers who ever lived. *An American Tragedy,* for instance, is an endless book with terrible sentences like "He found her extremely intellectually interesting." But by the time you finish the book, you've sopped your vest. He's a great writer, though he wrote badly. But what he does morally, that is to say what he does in terms of analysis of character and honest statement about the way the world is, is very good. Of course, some writers last a long time because of their brilliance, their style; Fitzgerald is a good example—a fine stylist. But he never quite got to the heart of things. *That's* what should concern the critics. If a critic is concerned with only how well the sentences go, or how neat the symbolic structure is, or how new the devices are, he's going to exaggerate the importance of mediocre books. Samuel Beckett—surely one of the great writers of our time despite my objections—is loved by critics, but except for John Fowles, I hear no one pointing out that the tendency of all he says is wrong. He says it powerfully, with comi-tragic brilliance, and he believes it, but what he says is not quite sound. Every night Samuel Beckett goes home to his wife, whom he's lived with all these years; he lies down in bed with her, puts his arms around her, and says, "No meaning again today . . ." Critics can say, and do say, well, it doesn't matter what he says, it's how well he says it. But I think in the long run Beckett is in for it. Because great writers tell the truth exactly—and get it right.

WILLIAM GOYEN: I can't imagine *not* writing. Writing simply is a way of life for me. The older I get, the more a way of life it is. At the beginning, it was totally a way of life excluding everything else. Now it's gathered to it marriage and children and other responsibilities. But still, it is simply a way of life before all other ways, a way to observe the world and to move through life, among human beings, and to record it all above all and to shape it, to give it sense, and to express something of myself in it. Writing is something I cannot imagine living without, nor scarcely would want to. Not to live daily as a writing person is inconceivable to me.

FRANCINE DU PLESSIX GRAY: Over the years I've come to realize that my greatest fear in life is a dread of a certain kind of solitude, of abandonment. And I've come to know that by writing I'm creating a presence which fills that solitude, which takes the place of some ideal Other. Mind you, I'm not afraid of any *chosen* solitude—I'm fiercely independent, I love traveling alone, going to restaurants and theater alone—I'm only terrified of abandonment. This is rooted certainly in the evenings of my childhood. Night was a very threatening time. I don't remember having one single dinner with my parents during all of my childhood in Paris. They were each off in a different direction every night, and there I was in the dark apartment alone with this terrifying predatory governess who I felt was always ready to ravage, destroy me. So the act of writing—I'm dealing with the most primitive, elemental fears here—the act of writing, this creation of a *controllable* presence, seems to be a mature way of exorcising the fear of abandonment, the dread of annihilation which filled my early years. The text in progress is like a fire in the room, an animal, it speaks, hollers, barks, growls back at me, like a magical dog guarding my body from evils, guarding me against the threat of void, of extinction.

· · ·

Rousseau made the point that writing becomes necessary when speech fails to protect our identity. The written word may be a weak second best to lived experience, but it's still pretty powerful—our only path to meaning and inner order. I keep being haunted by this phrase of Valéry's: "I thought to erect a minor monument of language on the menacing shore of the ocean of gibberish."

HENRY GREEN: The purpose of art is to produce something alive, in my case, in print, but with a separate, and of course one hopes, with an everlasting life of its own. The miracle is that it should live in the person who reads it. And if it is real and true it does, for five hundred years, for generation after generation. It's like having a baby, but in print. If it's really good, you can't stop its living. Indeed once the thing is printed, you simply cannot strangle it, as you could a child, by putting your hands around its little wet neck.

GRAHAM GREENE: Talent, even of a very high order, cannot sustain an achievement, whereas a ruling passion gives to a shelf of novels the unity of a system.

MARK HELPRIN: The motto of my first book, intended to apply to everything that followed, is, "*amor mi mosse, che mi fa parlare*," from the second canto of *Inferno* in Dante's *Commedia*. I translate it, "Love moved me, and makes me speak." Beatrice is explaining to Virgil why she is asking him to help Dante after he has fallen. I have always taken this as Dante's answer to the *Paris Review* question, "Why do you write?" And it is certainly mine.

ERNEST HEMINGWAY: A writer without a sense of justice and of injustice would be better off editing the Year Book of a school for exceptional children than writing novels. Another generalization. You see; they are not so difficult when they are sufficiently obvious. The most essential gift for a good writer is a built-in, shock-proof shit detector. This is the writer's radar and all great writers have had it.

TED HUGHES: There is ever a desire to do something else. I've sometimes wondered if it wouldn't be a good idea to write under a few pseudonyms. Keep several quite different lines of writing going. Like Fernando Pessoa, the Portuguese poet who tried four different poetic personalities. They all worked simultaneously. He simply lived with the four. What does Eliot say? "Dance, dance, / Like a dancing bear, / Cry like a parrot, chatter like an ape, / To find expression." It's certainly limiting to confine your writing to one public persona, because the moment you publish your own name you lose freedom. It's like being in a close-knit family. The moment you do anything new, the whole family jumps on it, comments, teases, advises against, does everything to make you self-conscious. There's a unanimous reaction to keep you as you were. You'd suppose any writer worth his salt could be bold and fearless and not give a damn. But in fact very few can. We're at the mercy of the groups that shaped our early days. We're so helplessly social—like cells in an organ. Maybe that's why madness sometimes works—it knocks out the oversensitive connection. And maybe that's why exile is good. I wonder if the subjective impression of most writers is that whenever they take a new step, some big, unconscious reaction among readers tries to stop them . . . often a big conscious reaction among colleagues. Hardy stopped writing novels by just that. In his late years, while he was up in an apple tree, pruning it, he had a vision of the most magnificent novel—all the characters, many episodes, even some dialogue . . . the one ultimate novel that he absolutely had to write. What happened? By the time he came down out of the tree the whole vision had fled. And it never reappeared. Even Goethe, back then, made some remark about the impossibility of producing a natural oeuvre of fully ripened works when everything was instantly before the public and its hectic, printed reactions.

ALDOUS HUXLEY: There are lots of excellent story tellers who are simply story tellers, and I think it's a wonderful gift, after all. I suppose the extreme example is Dumas: that extraordinary old gentleman, who sat down and thought nothing of writing six volumes of *The Count of Monte Cristo* in a few months. And my God, *Monte Cristo* is damned good! But it isn't the last word. When you can find story-telling which carries at the same time a kind of parable-like meaning (such as you get, say, in Dostoevsky or in the best of Tolstoy), this is something extraordinary, I feel. I'm always flabbergasted when I re-read some of the short things of Tolstoy, like *The Death of Ivan Ilych*. What an astounding work that is! Or some of the short things of Dostoevsky, like *Notes from Underground*.

• • •

Fiction, history, and biography are *immensely* important, not only for their own sake, because they provide a picture of life now and of life in the past, but also as vehicles for the expression of general philosophic ideas, religious ideas, social ideas. My goodness, Dostoevsky is six times as profound as Kierkegaard, because he writes *fiction*. In Kierkegaard you have this Abstract Man going on and on—like Coleridge—why, it's *nothing* compared with the really profound Fictional Man, who has always to keep these tremendous ideas *alive* in a concrete form. In fiction you have the reconciliation of the absolute and the relative, so to speak, the expression of the general in the particular. And this, it seems to me, is the exciting thing—both in life and in art.

GUILLERMO CABRERA INFANTE: Any literary work that aspires to the condition of art must forget politics, religion, and, ultimately, morals.

Otherwise it will be a pamphlet, a sermon, or a morality play. Even the greatest moralist of our century, Joseph Conrad, was first and foremost an entertainer. Solzhenitsyn is a failed artist but a very successful moralist. His novels are pretentious junk, but his political writing, *The Gulag Archipelago* books, for example, are precious masterpieces of indictment. George Orwell is a failure as an artist, but a superb pamphleteer. His political essays, together with Camus's, are the best written in Europe since World War II. These men are heroes because they fight swords with words—but that doesn't make them artists.

EUGÈNE IONESCO: I can't do anything else. I have always regretted having gotten involved with literature up to my neck. I would have preferred to have been a monk; but, as I said, I was torn between wanting fame and wishing to renounce the world. The basic problem is that if God exists, what is the point of literature? And if He *doesn't* exist, what is the point of literature? Either way, my writing, the only thing I have ever succeeded in doing, is invalidated.

JOHN IRVING: I'm old-fashioned. I believe in plot, of all things; in narrative, all the time; in storytelling; in character. Very traditional forms interest me. This nonsense about the novel being about "the word" . . . what can that mean? Are we novelists going to become like so many modern poets, writing only for and to each other, not comprehensible to anyone who isn't another writer? I have only a prep school education in the poems of John Milton. Yet I can read Milton; I really understand him. All that time has passed, and yet he's still clear. But when I read the poems of someone my own age and can't understand a single thing, is that supposed to be a failure of my education, or of the poetry?

· · ·

A writer is a vehicle. I feel the story I am writing existed before I existed; I'm just the slob who finds it, and rather clumsily tries to do it, and the characters, justice. I think of writing fiction as doing justice to the people in the story, and doing justice to *their* story—it's not *my* story. It's entirely ghostly work; I'm just the medium. As a writer, I do more listening than talking. W. H. Auden called the first act of writing "noticing." He meant the vision—not so much what we make up but what we *witness*. Oh, sure: writers "make up" the language, the voice, the transitions, all the clunking bridges that span the story's parts—that stuff, it's true, is invented. I am still old-fashioned enough to maintain that what *happens* in a novel is what distinguishes it, and what happens is what we *see*. In that sense, we're all just reporters. Didn't Faulkner say something like it was necessary only to write about "the human heart in conflict with itself" in order to write well? Well, I think that's all we do: we find more than we create, we simply see and expose more than we fabulate and invent. At least I do. Of course, it's necessary to make the atmosphere of a novel more real than real, as we say. Whatever its *place* is, it's got to feel, concretely, like a place with richer detail than any place we can actually remember. I think what a reader likes best is memories, the more vivid the better. That's the role of atmosphere in fiction: it provides details that feel as good, or as terrifying, as memories. Vienna, in my books, is more Vienna than Vienna; St. Cloud's is more Maine than Maine.

CHRISTOPHER ISHERWOOD: I think I'm a very unobservant person, one who goes straight to concepts about people and ignores evidence to the contrary and the bric-a-brac surrounding that person. Stephen Spender said an amusing thing about Yeats—that he went for days on end without noticing anything, but then, about once a month, he would look out of a window and suddenly be aware of a swan or something, and it gave him such a stunning shock that he'd write a marvelous poem about it. That's more the kind of way I operate: suddenly something pierces the reverie and self-absorption that fill my days, and I see with a tremendous flash the extraordinariness of that person or object or situation.

WILLIAM KENNEDY: I used to say on Thursday afternoons when I was on my day off from the Albany *Times Union* and I was waiting for the muse to descend and I discovered that it was the muse's day off too, you have to beat the bastards. I didn't even know who the bastards were, but you have to beat somebody. You have to beat your own problematic imagination, to discover what it is you're saying and how to say it and move forward into the unknown. I always knew that (a) I wanted to be a writer and (b) if you persist in doing something, sooner or later you will achieve it. It's just a matter of persistence—and a certain amount of talent. You can't do anything without talent, but you can't do anything without persistence, either. Bellow and I once talked about that. We were talking just in general about writing and publishing and so on, and he said there's a certain amount of talent that's necessary. After that, it's character. I said, "What do you mean by character?" He smiled at me and never said anything. So I was left to define what he meant that night. What I concluded was that character is equivalent to persistence. That you just refuse to give up. Then, the game's not over. You know, I had an enormous success in everything I'd done in life . . . up until the time I decided to be a writer. I was a good student; I was a good soldier; I was good at this and that. I got a hole-in-one one day on the golf course. I bowled 299, just like Billy Phelan. I was a very good newspaperman. I became a managing editor. Anything I wanted to do in journalism, it seemed to work; it just fell into place. So I didn't understand why I was so successful as a journalist and yet zilch as a novelist and a short-story writer. It was just that time was working against me. You just have to learn. It's such a complicated craft . . . such a complicated thing to understand what you're trying to bring out of your own imagination, your own life.

KEN KESEY: It was my last day of class, and I was trying to give some kind of closing lecture to tie it up in a little package they could take home with them. I told them they had all read and studied, that they could all write. They knew fiction far better than I did. If there had been a test, they'd have just walked all over me because they knew the history of literature and the history of style better than I did. But I told them, "So you guys can write, and well enough that one of these days you're going to have a visitation. You're going to be walking down the street and across the street you're going to look and see God standing over there on the street corner motioning to you, saying, 'Come to me, come to me.' And you will know it's God, there will be no doubt in your mind—he has slitty little eyes like Buddha, and he's got a long nice beard and blood on his hands. He's got a big Charlton Heston jaw like Moses, he's stacked like Venus, and he has a great jeweled scimitar like Mohammed. And God will tell you to come to him and sing his praises. And he will promise that if you do, all of the muses that ever visited Shakespeare will fly in your ear and out of your mouth like golden pennies. It's the job of the writer in America to say, 'Fuck you God, fuck you and the Old Testament that you rode in on, fuck you.' The job of the writer is to kiss no ass, no matter how big and holy and white and tempting and powerful. Anytime anybody says come to me and says, 'Write my advertisement, be my ad manager,' tell him, 'Fuck you.' " The job is always to be exposing God as the crook, as the sleaze ball. Nelson Algren says the job of the writer in America is to pull the judge down into the docket, get the person who is high down where he's low, make him feel what it's like where it's low.

MILAN KUNDERA: The great European novel started out as entertainment, and every true novelist is nostalgic for it. In fact, the themes of those great entertainments are terribly serious—think of Cervantes! In *The Farewell Party*, the question is, does man deserve to live on this earth? Shouldn't one "free the planet from man's clutches"? My lifetime ambition has been to unite the utmost seriousness of question with the utmost lightness of form. Nor is this purely an artistic ambition. The combination of a frivolous form and a serious subject immediately unmasks the truth about our dramas (those that occur in our beds as well as those that we play out on the great stage of History) and their awful insignificance. We experience the unbearable lightness of being.

Every one of my novels could be entitled *The Unbearable Lightness of Being* or *The Joke* or *Laughable Loves;* the titles are interchangeable, they reflect the small number of themes that obsess me, define me, and, unfortunately, restrict me. Beyond these themes, I have nothing else to say or to write.

PHILIP LARKIN: You've been reading Auden: "To ask the hard question is simple." The short answer is that you write because you have to. If you rationalize it, it seems as if you've seen this sight, felt this feeling, had this vision, and have got to find a combination of words that will preserve it by setting it off in other people. The duty is to the original experience. It doesn't feel like self-expression, though it may look like it. As for *whom* you write, well, you write for everybody. Or anybody who will listen.

· · ·

I think a young poet, or an old poet, for that matter, should try to produce something that pleases himself personally, not only when he's written it but a couple of weeks later. Then he should see if it pleases anyone else, by sending it to the kind of magazine he likes reading. But if it doesn't, he shouldn't be discouraged. I mean, in the seventeenth century every educated man could turn a verse and play the lute. Supposing no one played tennis because they wouldn't make Wimbledon? First and foremost, writing poems should be pleasure. So should reading them, by God.

· · ·

You must realize I've never had "ideas" about poetry. To me it's always been a personal, almost physical release or solution to a complex pressure of needs—wanting to create, to justify, to praise, to explain, to externalize, depending on the circumstances. And I've never been much interested in other people's poetry—one reason for writing, of course, is that no one's written what you want to read.

Probably my notion of poetry is very simple. Some time ago I agreed to help judge a poetry competition—you know, the kind where they get about 35,000 entries, and you look at the best few thousand. After a bit I said, Where are all the love poems? And nature poems? And they said, Oh, we threw all those away. I expect they were the ones I should have liked.

· · ·

I think a poet should be judged by what he does with his subjects, not by what his subjects are. Otherwise you're getting near the totalitarian attitude of wanting poems about steel production figures rather than "*Mais où sont les neiges d'antan?*" Poetry isn't a kind of paint-spray you use to cover selected objects with. A good poem about failure is a success.

NORMAN MAILER: Jean Malaquais always has a terrible time writing. He once complained with great anguish about the unspeakable difficulties he was having with a novel. And I asked him, "Why do you do it? You can do many other things well. Why do you bother with it?" I really meant this. Because he suffered when writing like no one I know. He looked up in surprise and said, "Oh, but this is the only way one can ever find the truth. The only time I know that something is true is at the moment I discover it in the act of writing." I think it's that. I think it's this moment when one knows it's true. One may not have written it well enough for others to know, but you're in love with the truth when you discover it at the point of a pencil. That in and by itself is one of the few rare pleasures in life.

FRANÇOIS MAURIAC: I have never begun a novel without hoping that it would be the one that would make it unnecessary for me to write another. I have had to start again from scratch with each one. What had gone before didn't count. . . . I was not adding to a fresco. Like a man who has decided to start his life over again, I have told myself that I had so far accomplished nothing: for I have always believed that my *chef d'oeuvre* would be the novel I was working on at the time.

WILLIAM MEREDITH: It's the nature of the work that a poem is getting at something mysterious, which no amount of staring at straight-on has ever solved, something like death or love or treachery or beauty. And we keep doing this corner-of-the-eye thing. I remember when we were in training to be night fliers in the Navy, I learned, very strangely, that the rods of the eye perceive things at night in the corner of the eye that we can't see straight ahead. That's not a bad metaphor for the vision of art. You don't stare at the mystery, but you *can* see things out of the corner of your eye that you weren't supposed to see.

TONI MORRISON: What makes me feel as though I belong here, out in this world, is not the teacher, not the mother, not the lover but what goes on in my mind when I am writing. Then I belong here, and then all of the things that are disparate and irreconcilable can be useful. I can do the traditional things that writers always say they do, which is to make order out of chaos. Even if you are reproducing the disorder, you are sovereign at that point. Struggling through the work is extremely important—more important to me than publishing it.

If I didn't do this, then I would be part of the chaos.

JOHN MORTIMER: I knew early on that I was going to be a writer. I think it's something rather like a curse that you're born with. I knew I wanted to be a writer and my father was far too intelligent to tell me not to be one. Instead of that, he said, "Of course you'll be a writer. Of course you'll be a very successful writer but just till you make a fortune by writing, just divorce a few people. You know, just a few. There's nothing in it." He thought that writers' wives led such terrible lives because the writer was always at home brewing tea and stumped for words. And he said, "Your marriage will be much happier if you go down to Temple tube station and go to the law courts and divorce people." And he told me there was really nothing to being a lawyer except a certain amount of common sense, and relatively clean fingernails. You see, I was practically born into the divorce courts. My father was the *doyen* of the divorce barristers. He was an extremely erudite and very famous divorce barrister. So that when I was a little boy in the nursery, instead of a story like "Snow White and the Seven Dwarfs," I used to get "The Duchess and the Seven Co-Respondents." My father used to return to me glowing with his triumphs in the divorce courts and give me wonderful lines which I was afterwards able to use in a play I wrote about him. He did really come home to me one night in the nursery and say, "I had a wonderful day in court, John. Terrific trial," he said. "Managed to prove adultery by evidence of inclination and opportunity," he said. "The only piece of evidence we had was a pair of footprints upside down on the dashboard of an Austin 711 parked in a Hampstead garden suburb."

FRANK O'CONNOR: I really got into this row, big, at the novel conference at Harvard when I had a couple of people talking about the various types of novel—and analyzing them, and then we had a novelist get up and speak about the responsibilities of the novelist. I was with Anthony West on the stage and I was gradually getting into hysterics. It's never happened to me before in public; I was giggling, I couldn't stop myself. And, "all right," I said at the end of it, "if there are any of my students here I'd like them to remember that writing is fun." That's the reason you do it, because you enjoy it, and you read it because you enjoy it. You don't read it because of the serious moral responsibility to read, and you don't write it because it's a serious moral responsibility. You do it for exactly the same reason that you paint pictures or play with the kids. It's a creative activity.

JEAN RHYS: It seems as if I was fated to write.... Which is horrible. But I can only do one thing. I'm rather useless, but perhaps not as useless as everyone thinks. I tried to be an actress—a chorus girl—and the whole thing ended when I was handed a line to say: "Oh Lottie, don't be epigrammatic." But, when the cue came, the words just disappeared. That was that. I was interested in beauty—cosmetics—but when I tried to make a face cream, it blew up.

PHILIP ROTH: Writing novels is not the road to power. I don't believe that, in my society, novels effect serious changes in anyone other than the handful of people who are writers, whose own novels are of course seriously affected by other novelists' novels. I can't see anything like that happening to the ordinary reader, nor would I expect it to. Novels provide readers with something to read. At their best writers change the *way* readers read. That seems to me the only realistic expectation. It also seems to me quite enough. Reading novels is a deep and singular pleasure, a gripping and mysterious human activity that does not require any more moral or political justification than sex.

· · ·

A writer needs his poisons. The antidote to his poisons is often a book.

JAMES SALTER: What is the ultimate impulse to write? Because all this is going to vanish. The only thing left will be the prose and poems, the books, what is written down. Man was very fortunate to have invented the book. Without it the past would completely vanish, and we would be left with nothing, we would be naked on earth.

MARY LEE SETTLE: Anyone who has a choice and doesn't choose *not* to write is a fool. Don't people know that it's the hardest work in the world? Joseph Conrad said that he had loaded hundredweights of coal all day long on a ship in Amsterdam in the wintertime, and that it was nothing to the energy demanded for a day's work writing. The work is hard, the perks are few, the pay is terrible, and the product, when it's finally finished, is pure joy. If you set out to write for money and fame, as Freud said writers did, then you should sell junk bonds or shoot somebody instead. It's easier.

IRWIN SHAW: Writing is like a contact sport, like football. Why do kids play football? They can get hurt on any play, can't they? Yet they can't wait until Saturday comes around so they can play on the high-school team, or the college team, and get smashed around. Writing is like that. You can get hurt, but you enjoy it.

JOHN SIMON: A German writer whom I love and whom I've translated, Erich Kästner, gives advice, in one of his poems, to a would-be suicide. He tries to give this man various reasons for not blowing his brains out. The man remains unconvinced, so Kästner says, in essence, "All right, the world is full of idiots and they're in control of everything. You fool, stay alive to annoy them!" And that, in a sense, is my function in life, and my consolation. If I can't convince these imbeciles of anything, I can at least annoy them, and I think I do a reasonably good job of that.

ISAAC BASHEVIS SINGER: In the later years before I began to publish, my brother gave me a number of rules about writing which seem to me sacred. Not that these rules cannot be broken once in a while, but it's good to remember them. One of his rules was that while facts never become obsolete or stale, commentaries *always* do. When a writer tries to explain too much, to psychologize, he's already out of time when he begins. Imagine Homer explaining the deeds of his heroes according to the old Greek philosophy, or the psychology of his time. Why, nobody would read Homer! Fortunately, Homer just gave us the images and the facts, and because of this the *Illiad* and the *Odyssey* are fresh in our time. And I think this is true about all writing. Once a writer tries to explain what the hero's motives are from a psychological point of view, he has already lost. This doesn't mean that I am against the psychological novel. There are some masters who have done it well. But I don't think it is a good thing for a writer, especially a young writer, to imitate them.

SUSAN SONTAG: I read the biography of Madame Curie by her daughter Eve Curie when I was about six, so at first I thought I was going to be a chemist. Then for a long time, most of my childhood, I wanted to be a physician. But literature swamped me. What I really wanted was every kind of life, and the writer's life seemed the most inclusive.

GEORGE STEINER: The Everyman's Library is for the first time issuing an Old Testament, and I've been asked to do the long preface. It took all summer. Now I'm not a Hebraist or a biblical scholar; the sensible thing would be now to send out ten copies to specialists and ask them what errors I have committed. Maybe this time I am going to do that, but I've never done it before—at my cost. This goes very much against the present collaborative trend. I think a page that sings, that lives in us, is a wildly autistic act; it's mad to do it at all. It's mad to think you might have something new to say, for God's sake, about the Old Testament. How many books are there on it already? Hundreds of thousands? I can't even guess: libraries full. So how can you be so crazy? How can you, after Proust and Joyce and Kafka and Faulkner, sit down and write a novel? I've never quite understood. Answer: you have to. And the *you have to* is a private cancer, a private tumor of the soul.

ROBERT STONE: "Fiction must justify itself in every line." Yes. I'm beginning to frame one—and along rather Conradian lines. Prose fiction must first of all perform the traditional functions of storytelling. We *need* stories. We can't identify ourselves without them. We're always telling ourselves stories about who we are: that's what history is, what the idea of a nation or an individual is. The purpose of fiction is to help us answer the question we must constantly be asking ourselves: who do we think we are and what do we think we're doing?

JOHN UPDIKE: I think of my books not as sermons or directives in a war of ideas but as objects, with different shapes and textures and the mysteriousness of anything that exists. My first thought about art, as a child, was that the artist brings something into the world that didn't exist before, and that he does it without destroying something else. A kind of refutation of the conservation of matter. That still seems to me its central magic, its core of joy.

ROBERT PENN WARREN: Once you start illustrating virtue as such you had better stop writing fiction. Do something else, like Y-work. Or join a committee. Your business as a writer is not to illustrate virtue but to show how a fellow may move toward it—or away from it.

EVELYN WAUGH: An artist must be a reactionary. He has to stand out against the tenor of the age and not go flopping along; he must offer some little opposition. Even the great Victorian artists were all anti-Victorian, despite the pressures to conform.

E. B. WHITE: A writer should concern himself with whatever absorbs his fancy, stirs his heart, and unlimbers his typewriter. I feel no obligation to deal with politics. I do feel a responsibility to society because of going into print: a writer has the duty to be good, not lousy; true, not false; lively, not dull; accurate, not full of error. He should tend to lift people up, not lower them down. Writers do not merely reflect and interpret life, they inform and shape life.

. . .

The writer's role is what it has always been: he is a custodian, a secretary. Science and technology have perhaps deepened his responsibility but not changed it. In "The Ring of Time," I wrote: "As a writing man, or secretary, I have always felt charged with the safekeeping of all unexpected items of worldly or unworldly enchantment, as though I might be held personally responsible if even a small one were to be lost. But it is not easy to communicate anything of this nature."

A writer must reflect and interpret his society, his world; he must also provide inspiration and guidance and challenge. Much writing today strikes me as deprecating, destructive, and angry. There are good reasons for anger, and I have nothing against anger. But I think some writers have lost their sense of proportion, their sense of humor, and their sense of appreciation. I am often mad, but I would hate to be nothing but mad: and I think I would lose what little value I may have as a writer if I were to refuse, as a matter of principle, to accept the warming rays of the sun, and to report them, whenever, and if ever, they happen to strike me. One role of the writer today is to sound the alarm. The environment is disintegrating, the hour is late, and not much is being done. Instead of carting rocks from the moon, we should be carting the feces out of Lake Erie.

RICHARD WILBUR: It seems to me that there has to be a sudden, confident sense that there is an exploitable and interesting relationship between something perceived out there and something in the way of incipient meaning within you. And what you see out there has to be seen freshly, or the process is not going to be provoked. Noting a likeness or resemblance between two things in nature can provide this freshness, but I think there must be more. For example, to perceive that the behavior of certain tree leaves is like the behavior of birds' wings is not, so far as I am concerned, enough to justify the sharpening of the pencil. There has to be a feeling that some kind of idea is implicit within that resemblance. It is strange how confident one can be about this. I always detest it when artists and writers marvel at their own creativity, but I think this is a very strange thing which most practiced artists would have in common, the certainty which accompanies these initial, provocative impressions. I am almost always right in feeling that there is a poem in something if it hits me hard enough. You can spoil your material, of course, but that doesn't mean the original feeling was false.

THORNTON WILDER: I suspect that all writers have some didactic intention. That starts the motor. Or let us say: many of the things we eat are cooked over a gas stove, but there is no taste of gas in the food.

- · ·

I think I write in order to discover on my shelf a new book which I would enjoy reading, or to see a new play that would engross me. That is why the first months of work on a new project are so delightful: you see the book already bound, or the play already produced, and you have the illusion that you will read or see it as though it were a work by another that will give you pleasure.

On Work Habits

I like writing with a Peacock's Quill; because its Feathers are
all Eyes.   —THOMAS FULLER, *Gnomologia*

I have a great deal of company in my house; especially in the
morning when nobody calls.   —HENRY DAVID THOREAU

I put a piece of paper under my pillow, and when I could not
sleep I wrote in the dark.   —HENRY DAVID THOREAU

I never travel without my diary. One should always have
something sensational to read in the train.   —OSCAR WILDE

CONRAD AIKEN: I never used a carbon because that made me self-
conscious. I can remember discussing the effect of the typewriter on our
work with Tom Eliot, because he was moving to the typewriter about the
same time I was. And I remember our agreeing that it made for a slight
change of style in the prose—that you tended to use more periodic sentences, a little shorter, and a rather choppier style—and that one must be
careful about that. Because, you see, you couldn't look ahead quite far
enough, for you were always thinking about putting your fingers on the
bloody keys. But that was a passing phase only. We both soon discovered
that we were just as free to let the style throw itself into the air as we had
been writing manually.
                            · · ·
I compelled myself all through to write an exercise in verse, in a different
form, every day of the year. I turned out my page every day, of some
sort—I mean I didn't give a damn about the meaning, I just wanted to
master the form—all the way from free verse, Walt Whitman, to the most
elaborate of villanelles and ballad forms. Very good training. I've always
told everybody who has ever come to me that I thought that was the first
thing to do. And to study all the vowel effects and all the consonant effects
and the variation in vowel sounds. For example, I gave Malcolm Lowry an

exercise to do at Cuernavaca: writing ten lines of blank verse with the caesura changing one step in each line. Going forward, you see, and then reversing on itself. I still have a group of them sent to me at his rented house in Cuernavaca, sent to me by hand from the bar with a request for money, and in the form of a letter—and unfortunately not used in his collected letters; very fine, and very funny. As an example of his attention to vowel sounds, one line still haunts me, "Airplane or aeroplane, or just plain plane." Couldn't be better.

EDWARD ALBEE: There's a time to go to the typewriter. It's like a dog—the way a dog before it craps wanders around in circles—a piece of earth, an area of grass, circles it for a long time before it squats. It's like that—figuratively circling the typewriter getting ready to write, and then finally one sits down. I think I sit down to the typewriter when it's time to sit down to the typewriter. That isn't to suggest that when I do finally sit down at the typewriter, and write out my plays with a speed that seems to horrify all my detractors and half of my well-wishers, that there's no work involved. It *is* hard work, and one *is* doing all the work oneself. Still, I know playwrights who like to kid themselves into saying that their characters are so well formed that *they* just take over. *They* determine the structure of the play. By which is meant, I suspect, only that the unconscious mind has done its work so thoroughly that the play just has to be filtered through the conscious mind. But there's work to be done—and discovery to be made. Which is part of the pleasure of it. It's a form of pregnancy I suppose, and to carry that idea further, there are very few people who are pregnant who can recall specifically the moment of conception of the child—but they discover that they are pregnant, and it's rather that way with discovering that one is thinking about a play.

MAYA ANGELOU: I have kept a hotel room in every town I've ever lived in. I rent a hotel room for a few months, leave my home at six, and try to be at work by 6:30. To write, I lie across the bed, so that this elbow is absolutely encrusted at the end, just so rough with callouses. I never allow the hotel people to change the bed, because I never sleep there. I stay until 12:30 or 1:30 in the afternoon, and then I go home and try to breathe; I look at the work around five; I have an orderly dinner: proper, quiet, lovely dinner; and then I go back to work the next morning. Sometimes in hotels I'll go into the room, and there'll be a note on the floor which says, "Dear Miss Angelou, let us change the sheets. We think they are moldy." But I only allow them to come in and empty wastebaskets. I insist that all things are taken off the walls. I don't want anything in there. I go into the room, and I feel as if all my beliefs are suspended. Nothing holds me to anything. No milkmaids, no flowers, nothing. I just want to *feel* and then when I start to work I'll remember. I'll read something, maybe the Psalms, maybe, again, something from Mr. Dunbar, James Weldon Johnson. And I'll remember how beautiful, how pliable the language is, how it will lend itself. If you pull it, it says, "Okay." I remember that, and I start to write.

W. H. AUDEN: I don't like the phone very much, and never stay on long if I can help it. You get some people who simply will not get off the line! I remember the story of the man who answered the phone and was kept prisoner for what seemed an age. The lady talked and talked. Finally, in desperation, he told her, "Really, I must go. I hear the phone ringing!"

JAMES BALDWIN: I start working when everyone has gone to bed. I've had to do that ever since I was young—I had to wait until the kids were asleep. And then I was working at various jobs during the day. I've always had to write at night. But now that I'm established I do it because I'm alone at night.

JOHN BARTH: I write in longhand. My Baltimore neighbor Anne Tyler and I are maybe the only two writers left who actually write with a fountain pen. She made the remark that there's something about the muscular movement of putting down script on the paper that gets her imagination back in the track where it was. I feel that too, very much so. My sentences in print, as in conversation, tend to go on a while before they stop: I trace that to the cursiveness of the pen. The idea of typing out first drafts, where each letter is physically separated by a little space from the next letter, I find a paralyzing notion. Good old script, which connects this letter to that, and this line to that—well, that's how good plots work, right? When this loops around and connects to that...

PAUL BOWLES: I don't use a typewriter. It's too heavy, too much trouble. I use a notebook, and I write in bed. Ninety-five percent of everything I've written has been done in bed.

ERSKINE CALDWELL: I have a red rug in my room. Wherever I've lived in life, I've carried my red rug with me. I keep it in excellent shape.

I have it vacuumed; I have it dry-cleaned. We are sitting on it now, in fact. Why is it here? We have a very good carpet underneath. But I've got a reason for wanting it here. It's part of my life. Back in the early days I had to live on cold and splintery floors. There was a hardwood floor in Maine that was especially cold because the room I worked in was unheated. Now, an unheated room in a New England winter is sort of a difficult dungeon. Then, in South Carolina, I was confined to write for a while in a rented room with a linoleum floor. The linoleum was cracked and it bristled with splinters. Anytime I didn't have my shoes on, I'd get a splinter in my foot. Well, as soon as I could afford to get a good rug, I bought my red one. And I decided then that I'd carry my red rug with me wherever I went.

· · ·

I used to have all kinds of schedules. Years ago, in the state of Maine, I chose to write my book on even days and work outside on odd days. When winter came, I shoveled snow and slept a little during the day, then stayed up all night to write. Another early method I used was to take a trip to write a short story. I'd ride a bus, from Boston to Cleveland maybe, and get off at night once in a while to write. I'd do a story that way in about a week's time. Then, for a while, I took the night boats between Boston and New York. The Fall River Line, the New Bedford Line, the Cape Cod Line, all going to New York at night. The rhythm of the water might have helped my sentence structure a little; at least I thought it did.

ITALO CALVINO: I have two different handwritings. One is large, with fairly big letters: The Os and As have a big hole in the center. This is the hand I use when I'm copying or when I'm rather sure of what I'm writing. My other hand corresponds to a less confident mental state and is very small: the Os are like dots. This is very hard to decipher, even for me. I use a magnifying glass to figure out what I've written.

TRUMAN CAPOTE: I suppose my superstitiousness could be termed a quirk. I have to add up all numbers: there are some people I never telephone because their number adds up to an unlucky figure. Or I won't accept a hotel room for the same reason. I will not tolerate the presence of yellow roses . . . which is sad because they're my favorite flower. I can't allow three cigarette butts in the same ashtray. Won't travel on a plane with two nuns. Won't begin or end anything on a Friday. It's endless, the things I can't and won't. But I derive some curious comfort from obeying these primitive concepts.

. . .

I am a completely horizontal author . . . I can't think unless I'm lying down, either in bed or stretched on a couch and with a cigarette and coffee handy. I've got to be puffing and sipping. As the afternoon wears on, I shift from coffee to mint tea to sherry to martinis. I write my first version in longhand (pencil). Then I do a complete revision, also longhand. Essentially I think of myself as a stylist and stylists can become notoriously obsessed with the placing of a comma, the weight of a semicolon. Obsessions of this sort, and the time I take over them, irritate me beyond endurance.

Then I type a third draft on yellow paper, a very special certain kind of yellow paper. I don't get out of bed to do this. . . . I balance the machine on my knees. I can manage a hundred words a minute. Well, when the yellow draft is finished, I put the manuscript away for a while, a week, a month, sometimes longer. When I take it out again, I read it as coldly as possible, then read it aloud to a friend or two, and decide what changes I want to make and whether or not I want to publish it. I've thrown away rather a few short stories, an entire novel, and half of another. But if all goes well, I type the final version on white paper and that's that.

CAMILO JOSÉ CELA: I always write longhand. The truth is I don't know how to type and I don't have a computer. There is a computer in the house, but my wife uses it, not me, because I'm afraid it will give me cramps. It's true! Confronted with such machines—computers, even automobiles—I'm like a person from a very remote and distant area. I look at them distrustfully and don't touch them for fear that they may give off sparks. It seems very convenient for my wife, and I'm happy for her, but I prefer to write longhand. Whether I use a fountain pen, a ballpoint pen, a pencil, or a marker is all the same to me. I'm not superstitious or maniacal about such things. One young journalist asked me once, "Do you plan on writing until you don't have anything more to say?" and I responded by saying, "No, until I no longer have anything to write!"

BLAISE CENDRARS: A writer should never install himself before a panorama, however grandiose it may be. . . . Like Saint Jerome, a writer should work in his cell. Turn the back. Writing is a view of the spirit. . . . "The world is my representation." Humanity lives in its fiction. This is why a conqueror always wants to transform the face of the world into his image. Today, I even veil the mirrors.

The workroom of Rémy de Gourmon was on a court, 71 rue des Saints-Pères, in Paris. At 202 Boulevard Saint-Germain, Guillaume Apollinaire, who had a vast apartment with large rooms and with a belvedere and terrace on the roof, wrote by preference in his kitchen, at a little card table where he was very uncomfortable, having had to shrink this little table even smaller in order to succeed in sliding it under a bull's-eye window in the mansard, which was also on a court. Edouard Peisson, who has a nice little house in the hills near Aix-en-Provence, does not work in one of the front rooms where he could enjoy a beautiful view of the valley and the play of light in the distance, but has had a little library corner constructed in back, the window of which gives on an embankment bordered with lilacs. And myself, in the country, in my house at Tremblay-sur-Mauldre, I've never worked on the upper floor, which looks out on the orchards, but in the lower room, which looks in one direction on an impasse behind a stable and in another on a wall which encloses my garden.

Among the very few writers I've had occasion to see much of, only one man of letters, celebrated for his frenetic cult of Napoleon, installed himself before a panorama to work—a historical one—the window of his study had a full view of the Arc de Triomphe. But this window was most often closed because the living spectacle of the glory of his great man, far from inspiring him, clipped his wings. He could be heard through the door coming and going in his study, beating his sides, roaring his phrases, trying out phrases and cadences, groaning, weeping, laboring himself sick like Flaubert in his "*gueuloir.*" His wife then said to the servants, "Pay no attention. It is Monsieur castigating his style."

· · ·

I like long sea voyages, and the unique life at sea, too much to ever dream of working. It's the apotheosis of idleness; a triumph—to do nothing while the deck rocks, the boat moves, the engines knock, the ocean rolls, the wind blows, the earth revolves with the heavens and the stars, and the entire universe rushes to open for you to pass. I'm never in a hurry to arrive, and I've tried dozens of times to seduce the captain into taking his boat elsewhere than the designated port. "There's no way, alas!" an old Dutchman told me. "For thirty years I've been making the trip between Rotterdam and Buenos Aires, as if I was the engineer of a train. Impossible to change anything, the route is set in advance, the timetable fixed, I must get there on such a day at such a time, it's outlined in advance by the company, who are masters after God. But the most annoying thing is that it's always the same people who get on, always the same heads I'm obliged to have at my table—the same chargés d'affaires, the same diplomats, the same nabobs, the same big bankers. After thirty years, I know them too well! If only I had the courage to follow your infernal ideas, swing the helm and point elsewhere, to the east or the west, no matter . . . pass the Cape, dive into the southern seas."

All that to tell you that on board, I don't write.

AMY CLAMPITT: My own original handwritten drafts are usually on the backs of those silly announcements law firms send out, that so-and-so has just been appointed a partner, which would otherwise go into the wastebasket, and which my best friend Hal, a law professor, saves for me. They're printed on fine creamy vellum, and they're very small—four-by-six inches or so, though maddeningly there isn't even a standard size. I've put away stacks of these things for a single poem.

· · ·

My favorite place for writing, the place where I'm most likely to get something written, is the coast of Maine, where I've spent some time—never more than six weeks at a stretch, usually less—nearly every summer since 1974. I find a place to put my typewriter where I can look at the water. I tend to work best in the morning—I'm not a night person, although I have occasionally woken up with a phrase in my head and not been able to sleep. I used to keep something to write with under the pillow just in case something like that came to me—sometimes it was very hard to decipher because I don't like to turn the light on.

MALCOLM COWLEY: Almost all of them are certainly procrastinators, but a few people really like to write. Kay Boyle used to say that she loved the smell of paper. Anthony Trollope trained himself to turn out forty-nine pages of manuscript a week, seven pages a day, and he was so rigorous about keeping to that exact number of pages that if he finished a novel halfway through the last day, he'd write the title of a new book and "Chapter One" on the next page and go right on until he'd done his proper quota of seven pages.

ROBERT CREELEY: Allen Ginsberg, for example, can write poems anywhere—trains, planes, in any public place. He isn't the least self-conscious. In fact, he seems to be stimulated by people around him. For myself, I need a very kind of secure quiet. I usually have some music playing, just because it gives me something, a kind of drone that I like, as relaxation. I remember reading that Hart Crane wrote at times to the sound of records because he liked the stimulus and this pushed him to a kind of openness that he could use. In any case, the necessary environment is that which secures the artist in the way that lets him be *in* the world in a most fruitful manner.

DON DELILLO: A writer takes earnest measures to secure his solitude and then finds endless ways to squander it. Looking out the window, reading random entries in the dictionary. To break the spell I look at a photograph of Borges, a great picture sent to me by the Irish writer Colm Tóibín. The face of Borges against a dark background—Borges fierce, blind, his nostrils gaping, his skin stretched taut, his mouth amazingly vivid; his mouth looks painted; he's like a shaman painted for visions, and the whole face has a kind of steely rapture. I've read Borges of course, although not nearly all of it, and I don't know anything about the way he worked—but the photograph shows us a writer who did not waste time at the window or anywhere else. So I've tried to make him my guide out of lethargy and drift, into the otherworld of magic, art and divination.

JOAN DIDION: Another thing I need to do, when I'm near the end of the book, is sleep in the same room with it. That's one reason I go home to Sacramento to finish things. Somehow the book doesn't leave you when you're asleep right next to it. In Sacramento nobody cares if I appear or not. I can just get up and start typing.

ISAK DINESEN: During the German occupation of Denmark I thought I should go mad with boredom and dullness. I wanted so to be amused, to amuse myself, and besides I was short of money, so I went to my publisher in Copenhagen and said, look here, will you give me an advance on a novel, and send me a stenographer to dictate it to? They said they would, and she appeared and I started dictating. I had no idea at all of what the story would be about when I began. I added a little every day, improvising. It was very confusing to the poor stenographer.

I'd start one day by saying, "Then Mr. So-and-So entered the room," and the stenographer would cry out, "Oh dear, but he can't. He died yesterday in Chapter Seventeen."

WILLIAM FAULKNER: The best job that was ever offered to me was to become a landlord in a brothel. In my opinion it's the perfect milieu for an artist to work in. It gives him perfect economic freedom; he's free of fear and hunger; he has a roof over his head and nothing whatever to do except keep a few simple accounts and to go once every month and pay off the local police. The place is quiet during the morning hours, which is the best time of the day to work. There's enough social life in the evening, if he wishes to participate, to keep him from being bored; it gives him a certain standing in his society; he has nothing to do because the madam keeps the books; all the inmates of the house are females and would defer to him and call him "sir." All the bootleggers in the neighborhood would call him "sir." And he could call the police by their first names.

So the only environment the artist needs is whatever peace, whatever solitude, and whatever pleasure he can get at not too high a cost. All the wrong environment will do is run his blood pressure up; he will spend more time being frustrated or outraged. My own experience has been that the tools I need for my trade are paper, tobacco, food, and a little whiskey.

RICHARD FORD: I've written everywhere. I wrote a novella *The Womanizer* on a plane coming back from Paris. I've written in hotel rooms in Milan and Great Falls. I wrote a screenplay in the Chateau Marmont. I've worked in fifty rented houses, in friends' apartments. I like that, actually. It's a challenge to go into someplace that's not yours, and let the fact that you're doing important work there be the accommodating force. I don't think I could stay in one house continuously. I'm not contemplative enough, not interior enough, and that's another way of saying I'm probably not smart enough. I need a lot of external stimulation bulleting into my life. I'm not talking about exhilaration or thrill, I just want new sounds coming into my ears.

JOHN FOWLES: I am a great believer in diaries, if only in the sense that bar exercises are good for ballet dancers: it's often through personal diaries (however embarrassing they are to read now) that the novelist discovers his true bent—that he can narrate real events and distort them to please himself, describe character, observe other beings, hypothesize, invent, all the rest. I think that is how I became a novelist, eventually.

ROBERT FROST: I never write except with a writing board. I've never had a table in my life. And I use all sorts of things. Write on the sole of my shoe.

GABRIEL GARCÍA MÁRQUEZ: When I was working for *El Espectador* in Bogotá, I used to do at least three stories a week, two or three editorial notes every day, and I did movie reviews. Then at night, after everyone had gone home, I would stay behind writing my novels. I liked the noise of the Linotype machines, which sounded like rain. If they stopped, and I was left in silence, I wouldn't be able to work. Now, the output is comparatively small. On a good working day, working from nine o'clock in the morning to two or three in the afternoon, the most I can write is a short paragraph of four or five lines, which I usually tear up the next day.

WILLIAM GASS: I get very tense working, so I often have to get up and wander around the house. It is very bad on my stomach. I have to be mad to be working well anyway, and then I am mad about the way things are going on the page in addition. My ulcer flourishes and I have to chew lots of pills. When my work is going well, I am usually sort of sick.

NADINE GORDIMER: I can't understand writers who feel they shouldn't have to do any of the ordinary things of life, because I think that this is necessary; one has got to keep in touch with that. The solitude of writing is also quite frightening. It's quite close sometimes to madness, one just disappears for a day and loses touch. The ordinary action of taking a dress down to the dry cleaner's or spraying some plants infected with greenfly is a very sane and good thing to do. It brings one back, so to speak. It also brings the world back. I have formed the habit, over the last two books I've written, of spending half an hour or so reading over what I'd written during the day just before I go to bed at night. Then, of course, you get tempted to fix it up, fuss with it, at night. But I find that's good. But if I've been with friends or gone out somewhere, then I won't do that. The fact is that I lead a rather solitary life when I'm writing.

ROBERT GRAVES: Everything is made by hand—with one exception: this nasty plastic triple file which was given me as a present. I've put it here out of politeness for two or three weeks, then it will disappear. Almost everything else is made by hand. Oh yes, the books have been printed, but many have been printed by hand—in fact some I printed myself. Apart from the electric light fixtures, everything else is handmade; nowadays very few people live in houses where anything at all is made by hand. One secret of being able to think is to have as little as possible around you that is not made by hand.

JOSEPH HELLER: I keep a small sheath of 3 × 5 cards in my billfold. If I think of a good sentence, I'll write it down. It won't be an idea ("have him visit a brothel in New Orleans"). What I put down is an actual line of intended text ("In the brothel in New Orleans was like the time in San Francisco"). Of course, when I come back to it, the line may change considerably. Occasionally, there's one that sings so perfectly the first time that it stays, like "My boy has stopped speaking to me and I don't think I can bear it." I wrote that down on a 3 × 5 card, perhaps on a bus, or after walking the dog. I store them in filing cabinets. The file on *Something Happened* is about four inches deep, the one on *Catch-22* about the length of a shoe-box.

. . .

I have to be alone. A bus is good. Or walking the dog. Brushing my teeth is marvelous—it was especially so for *Catch-22*. Often when I am very tired, just before going to bed, while washing my face and brushing my teeth, my mind gets very clear . . . and produces a line for the next day's work, or some idea way ahead. I don't get my best ideas while actually writing . . . which is the agony of putting down what I think are good ideas and finding the words for them and the paragraph forms for them . . . a laborious process. I don't think of myself as a naturally gifted writer when it comes to using language. I distrust myself. Consequently I try every which way with a sentence, then a paragraph, and finally a page, choosing words, selecting pace (I'm obsessed with that, even the pace of a sentence). I say to myself what I hope to put down on paper, but I hope not aloud. I think sometimes I move my lips, not only when I'm writing, but when I'm thinking of what I'm going to be having for dinner.

ERNEST HEMINGWAY: When I am working on a book or a story I write every morning as soon after first light as possible. There is no one to disturb you and it is cool or cold and you come to your work and warm as you write. You read what you have written and, as you always stop when you know what is going to happen next, you go on from there. You write until you come to a place where you still have your juice and know what will happen next and you stop and try to live through until the next day when you hit it again. You have started at six in the morning, say, and may go on until noon or be through before that. When you stop you are as empty, and at the same time never empty but filling, as when you have made love to someone you love. Nothing can hurt you, nothing can happen, nothing means anything until the next day when you do it again. It is the wait until the next day that is hard to get through.

TED HUGHES: Hotel rooms are good. Railway compartments are good. I've had several huts of one sort or another. Ever since I began to write with a purpose I've been looking for the ideal place. I think most writers go through it. I've known several who liked to treat it as a job—writing in some office well away from home, going there regular hours. Sylvia had a friend, a novelist, who used to leave her grand house and go into downtown Boston to a tiny room with a table and chair where she wrote facing a blank wall. Didn't Somerset Maugham also write facing a blank wall? Subtle distraction is the enemy—a big beautiful view, the tide going in and out. Of course, you think it oughtn't to matter, and sometimes it doesn't. Several of my favorite pieces in my book *Crow* I wrote traveling up and down Germany with a woman and small child—I just went on writing wherever we were. Enoch Powell claims that noise and bustle help him to concentrate. Then again, Goethe couldn't write a line if there was another person anywhere in the same house, or so he said at some point. I've tried to test it on myself, and my feeling is that your sense of being concentrated can deceive you. Writing in what seems to be a happy concentrated way, in a room in your own house with books and everything necessary to your life around you, produces something noticeably different, I think, from writing in some empty silent place far away from all that. Because however we concentrate, we remain aware at some level of everything around us. Fast asleep, we keep track of the time to the second. The person conversing at one end of a long table quite unconsciously uses the same unusual words, within a second or two, as the person conversing with somebody else at the other end—though they're amazed to learn they've done it. Also, different kinds of writing need different kinds of concentration. Goethe, picking up a transmission from the other side of his mind, from *beyond* his usual mind, needs different tuning than Enoch Powell when he writes a speech. Brain rhythms would show us what's going on, I expect. But for me, successful writing has usually been a case of having found good conditions for real, effortless concentration. When I was living in Boston, in my late twenties, I was so conscious of this that at one point I covered the windows with brown paper to blank out any view and wore earplugs—simply to isolate myself from distraction. That's how I worked for a year. When I came back to

England, I think the best place I found in that first year or two was a tiny cubicle at the top of the stairs that was no bigger than a table really. But it was a wonderful place to write. I mean, I can see now, by what I wrote there, that it was a good place. At the time it just seemed like a convenient place.

· · ·

I made an interesting discovery about myself when I first worked for a film company. I had to write brief summaries of novels and plays to give the directors some idea of their film potential—a page or so of prose about each book or play, and then my comment. That was where I began to write for the first time directly onto a typewriter. I was then about twenty-five. I realized instantly that when I composed directly onto the typewriter my sentences became three times as long, much longer. My subordinate clauses flowered and multiplied and ramified away down the length of the page, all much more eloquently than anything I would have written by hand. Recently I made another similar discovery. For about thirty years I've been on the judging panel of the W. H. Smith children's writing competition. Annually there are about sixty thousand entries. These are cut down to about eight hundred. Among these our panel finds seventy prizewinners. Usually the entries are a page, two pages, three pages. That's been the norm. Just a poem or a bit of prose, a little longer. But in the early 1980s we suddenly began to get seventy- and eighty-page works. These were usually space fiction, always very inventive and always extraordinarily fluent—a definite impression of a command of words and prose, but without exception strangely boring. It was almost impossible to read them through. After two or three years, as these became more numerous, we realized that this was a new thing. So we inquired. It turned out that these were pieces that children had composed on word processors. What's happening is that as the actual tools for getting words onto the page become more flexible and externalized, the writer can get down almost every thought or every extension of thought. That ought to be an advantage. But in fact, in all these cases, it just extends everything slightly too much. Every sentence is too long. Everything is taken a bit too far, too attenuated. There's always a bit too much there, and it's too thin. Whereas when writing by hand you meet the terrible resistance of what happened your first year at it when you couldn't write at all ... when you were making attempts, pretending to form letters. These ancient feelings are there, wanting to be expressed. When you sit with your pen, every year of your life is right there, wired into the communication between your brain and your writing hand. There is a natural characteristic resistance that produces a certain kind of result analogous to your actual handwriting. As you force your expression against that built-in resistance, things become automatically more compressed, more summary and, perhaps, psychologically denser. I suppose if you use a word processor and deliberately prune everything back, alert to the tendencies, it should be possible to get the best of both worlds.

Maybe what I'm saying applies only to those who have gone through the long conditioning of writing only with a pen or pencil up through their mid-twenties. For those who start early on a typewriter or, these days, on a computer screen, things must be different. The wiring must be different. In handwriting the brain is mediated by the drawing hand, in typewriting by the fingers hitting the keyboard, in dictation by the idea of a vocal style, in word processing by touching the keyboard and by the screen's feedback. The fact seems to be that each of these methods produces a different syntactic result from the same brain. Maybe the crucial element in handwriting is that the hand is simultaneously drawing. I know I'm very conscious of hidden imagery in handwriting—a subtext of a rudimentary picture language. Perhaps that tends to enforce more cooperation from the other side of the brain. And perhaps that extra load of right brain suggestions prompts a different succession of words and ideas. Perhaps that's what I am talking about.

Word processing is a new discipline that these particular children haven't learned. And which I think some novelists haven't learned. "Brevity is the soul of wit." It makes the imagination jump. I think I recognize among some modern novels the supersonic hand of the word processor uncurbed. When Henry James started dictating, his sentences became interminable, didn't they? And the physical world, as his brother William complained, suddenly disappeared from them. Henry hadn't realized. He was astonished.

EUGÈNE IONESCO: I work in the morning. I sit comfortably in an armchair, opposite my secretary. Luckily, although she's intelligent, she knows nothing about literature and can't judge whether what I write is good or worthless. I speak slowly, as I'm talking to you, and she takes it down. I let characters and symbols emerge from me, as if I were dreaming. I always use what remains of my dreams of the night before. Dreams are reality at its most profound, and what you invent is truth because invention, by its nature, can't be a lie. Writers who try to prove something are unattractive to me, because there is nothing to prove and everything to imagine. So I let words and images emerge from within. If you do that, you might prove something in the process. As for dictating the text to my secretary, for twenty-five years I wrote by hand. But now it is impossible for me; my hands shake and I am too nervous. Indeed, I am so nervous that I kill my characters immediately. By dictating, I give them the chance to live and grow.

JOHN IRVING: I am compulsive about writing, I need to do it the way I need sleep and exercise and food and sex; I can go without it for a while, but then I need it. A novel is such a long involvement; when I'm beginning a book, I can't work more than two or three hours a day. I don't know more than two or three hours a day about a new novel. Then there's the middle of a book. I can work eight, nine, twelve hours then, seven days a week— if my children let me; they usually don't. One luxury of making enough money to support myself as a writer is that I can afford to have those eight-, nine-, and twelve-hour days. I resented having to teach and coach, not because I disliked teaching or coaching or wrestling but because I had no time to write. Ask a doctor to be a doctor two hours a day. An eight-hour day at the typewriter is easy; and two hours of reading over material in the evening, too. That's routine. Then when the time to finish the book comes, it's back to those two- and three-hour days. Finishing, like beginning, is more careful work. I write very quickly; I rewrite very slowly. It takes me nearly as long to rewrite a book as it does to get the first draft. I can write more quickly than I can read.

JAMES JONES: I get up earlier than most guys—between seven and eight—but only because I like to go out in the afternoons while there's still sun. After I get up it takes me an hour and a half of fiddling around before I can get up the courage and nerve to go to work. I smoke half a pack of cigarettes, drink six or seven cups of coffee, read over what I wrote the day before. Finally there's no further excuse. I go to the typewriter. Four to six hours of it. Then I quit and we go out. Or stay home and read.

JACK KEROUAC: I had a ritual once of lighting a candle and writing by its light and blowing it out when I was done for the night . . . also kneeling and praying before starting (I got that from a French movie about George Frederick Handel)...but now I simply hate to write. My superstition? I'm beginning to suspect that full moon. Also I'm hung up on the number 9 though I'm told a Piscean like myself should stick to number 7; but I try to do 9 touchdowns a day, that is, I stand on my head in the bathroom, on a slipper, and touch the floor 9 times with my toe tips, while balanced. This is incidentally more than Yoga, it's an athletic feat, I mean imagine calling me "unbalanced" after that. Frankly I do feel that my mind is going. So another "ritual," as you call it, is to pray to Jesus to preserve my sanity and my energy so I can help my family: that being my paralyzed mother, and my wife, and the ever-present kitties. Okay?

PHILIP LARKIN: My life is as simple as I can make it. Work all day, cook, eat, wash up, telephone, hack writing, drink, television in the evenings. I almost never go out. I suppose everyone tries to ignore the passing of time: some people by doing a lot, being in California one year and Japan the next; or there's my way—making every day and every year exactly the same. Probably neither works.

JAMES LAUGHLIN: There was a period when Delmore Schwartz wrote a sonnet every day. He didn't really like sonnets, but he wrote them for discipline. It certainly helped him. If you look at his best short poems, they're not sonnets, but they're very well structured. So too with Pound. There was a time early on when Ezra used to chant his lines to a metronome, though he gave it up after a while—another way to learn verbal discipline and control.

NORMAN MAILER: I like a room with a view, preferably a long view. I dislike looking out on gardens. I prefer looking at the sea, or ships, or anything which has a vista to it. Oddly enough, I've never worked in the mountains.

· · ·

If you tell yourself you're going to work the next day, you go to work. Even if you don't feel like it, even if you were enough of a fool to go out and get dead drunk the night before and you've forgotten what you were going to writer—you sit down at your desk, because I believe that there is a relation that goes on between the writer and his or her unconscious. It's a little bit like the relation of a general to troops. If you call the troops out, you can't leave them standing in the rain. You have to do something with them. You don't have to do much, you just have to show up and be the medium for that unconscious to deliver what it's prepared.

WILLIAM MAXWELL: I prefer small messy rooms that don't look out on anything interesting. I wrote the last two sections of *They Came Like Swallows* beside a window looking out on a tin roof. It was perfect. The roof was so boring it instantly drove me back to my typewriter.

HENRY MILLER: I generally go to work right after breakfast. I sit right down to the machine. If I find I'm not able to write, I quit.

PATRICK O'BRIAN: Pen, ink and paper (generally the back of proof sheets, for the surface) are my tools. I have occasionally beaten out an unimportant letter on a typewriter; and some people with quicker minds than I can use a word processor with great speed; but upon the whole there is much to be said for the reflective pen. Many capital books have been written with it, and then it is comparatively economical—Dr. Lodge is said to have completed his famous translation of Josephus (812 folio pages) with one single goose quill.

DOROTHY PARKER: I tried to keep one [a notebook] but I never could remember where I put the damn thing. I always say I'm going to keep one tomorrow.

S. J. PERELMAN: Raymond Chandler and I discussed this once, and he admitted to the most bitter reluctance to commit anything to paper. He evolved the following scheme: he had a tape recorder into which he spoke the utmost nonsense—a stream of consciousness which was then transcribed by a secretary and which he then used as a basis for his first rough draft. Very laborious. He strongly advised me to do the same . . . in fact became so excited that he kept plying me with information for months about the machine that helped him.

PHILIP ROTH: I don't ask writers about their work habits. I really don't care. Joyce Carol Oates says somewhere that when writers ask each other what time they start working and when they finish and how much time they take for lunch, they're actually trying to find out "Is he as crazy as I am?" I don't need that question answered.

NATHALIE SARRAUTE: I don't work at home because at first the house was full of children; my husband was a lawyer and received his clients here, so I couldn't work. Going to a café is like traveling—you get out of your own environment and its distractions. Writing is difficult; it is like jumping into the void. One tries to avoid it by any means—looking for a lost piece of paper, making a cup of tea, anything. In a café you jump in. Nobody disturbs me there and I don't hear the conversations. I had the same setup in the country, until one day they installed a jukebox in the café where I worked, and that *does* stop you from thinking. So I arranged a cowshed across the courtyard, and every morning I go there and work.

MAY SARTON: I sometimes start the day with the letters. Just to get the oil into the machine.

Music. I play records, mostly eighteenth-century music. I find that the Romantics—Beethoven—don't work for me. I love them to listen to, but not to work with, alongside of, whereas Mozart, Bach, Albinoni . . . Haydn, I love. I feel the tremendous masculine joy of Haydn. That gets me going.

ANNE SEXTON: I might, if I felt the poem come on, put on a certain record, sometimes the "Bachianas Brasileiras" by Villa-Lobos. I wrote to that for about three or four years. It's my magic tune.

GEORGES SIMENON: The beginning will be always the same; it is almost a geometrical question: I have such a man, such a woman, in such surroundings. What can happen to them to oblige them to go to their limit? That's the question. It will be sometimes a very simple incident, anything which will change their lives. Then I write my novel chapter by chapter. When I am doing a novel now I don't see anybody, I don't speak to anybody, I don't take a phone call—I live just like a monk. All the day I am one of my characters. I feel like him. And it's almost unbearable after five or six days. That is one of the reasons my novels are so short; after eleven days I can't—It's impossible. I have to—It's physical. I am too tired. And it's awful. That is why, before I start a novel—this may sound foolish here, but it is the truth—generally a few days before the start of a novel I look to see that I don't have any appointments for eleven days. Then, I call the doctor. He takes my blood pressure, he checks everything. And he says, "Okay." Because I have to be sure that I am good for the eleven days. He thinks it is all right but unhealthy to do it too often. Sometimes he will say, "Look, after this novel take two months off." For example, yesterday he said, "Okay, but how many novels do you want to do before you go away for the summer?" I said, "Two." "Okay," he said.

NEIL SIMON: I have this office. There are four or five rooms in it, and no one is here but me. No secretary, no one, and I've never once in the many years that I've come here ever felt lonely, or even alone. I come in and the room is filled with—as corny as it might sound—these characters I'm writing, who are waiting each day for me to arrive and give them life. I've also written on airplanes, in dentist's offices, on subways. I think it's true for many writers. You blank out whatever is in front of your eyes. That's why you see writers staring off into space. They're not looking at "nothing," they're visualizing what they're thinking. I never visualize what a play will look like on stage, I visualize what it looks like in *life*. I visualize being in that room where the mother is confronting the father.

W. D. SNODGRASS: Stay up all night, sleep all day. One way and another burn your time away. I became an absolute master of filing my nails. The best looking nails in the country.

STEPHEN SPENDER: The poet Walter de la Mare said that if there is a leak of attention when you are trying to concentrate, the leak can be stifled by smoking a cigarette, or in Schiller's case, by inhaling the rotten apples which he kept in a drawer.

JOHN STEINBECK: On the third finger of my right hand I have a great callus just from using a pencil for so many hours every day. It has become a big lump by now and it doesn't ever go away. Sometimes it is very rough and other times, as today, it is as shiny as glass. It is peculiar how touchy one can become about little things. Pencils must be round. A hexagonal pencil cuts my fingers after a long day. You see I hold a pencil for about six hours every day. This may seem strange but it is true. I am really a conditioned animal with a conditioned hand.

GEORGE STEINER: From western Portugal to St. Petersburg, you have cafés, places where you can come in the morning, order a cup of coffee or a glass of wine, spend the day reading the world's newspapers, playing chess and writing. The bibliography of magnificent books written in cafés is enormous. There are people who have always worked that way and preferred to. You don't have them in Moscow, which is an Asian frontier city. The line can be sharply drawn: Odessa is about the limit of the café. I'm a café creature, not a pub creature. The English pub is a very different animal, and the American bar is a profoundly different animal again. I'm at home everywhere in Europe because I go to a café the moment I arrive, either have a chess game, challenge somebody, or have them bring the papers for me on those wooden sticks, the old-fashioned ones where you roll them up, and it's the most egalitarian society in the world because the price of one cup of coffee or glass of wine buys you the day at the table, and you can write, you can do anything. After my lectures in Geneva, my students always knew at which café I would have my second coffee of the morning, or a glass of white wine, and they could come and chat. That's where the intellectual life really blazes.

. . .

These are very difficult issues; there's no use negotiating one's passions or negotiating with one's major errors. My children would say that America is the future and perhaps already the present. They've chosen, and I'm proud of them and delighted to visit them often. But the memories are too powerful, the French schooling was too strong. Why am I not going to heaven? Certainly for very good moral reasons, but for much more practical reasons too: *I've already been there.* What is heaven? It is the Galleria in Milan. I'm sitting with a real cappuccino, in front of me is *La Stampa,* the Frankfurter *Allgemeine, Le Monde* and the *Times.* I've got a ticket to La Scala in my pocket, and coming at me are the ten or twelve complex smells in that Galleria—of the chocolate, the bakery, the twenty bookstores (which are among the world's best bookstores); the sound of the steps of people moving towards the opera or the theaters that night; the way Milan vibrates around you. I've been to heaven, so I'm not getting a second one.

JAMES THURBER: I don't have to do the sort of thing Fitzgerald did with *The Last Tycoon*—the voluminous, the tiny and meticulous notes, the long descriptions of character. I can keep all these things in my mind. I wouldn't have to write down "three roses in a vase," or something, or a man's middle name. Henry James dictated notes just the way that I write. His note-writing was part of the creative act, which is why his prefaces are so good. He dictated notes to see what it is that they might come to.

GORE VIDAL: I often read for an hour or two. Clearing the mind. I'm always reluctant to start work, and reluctant to stop. The most interesting thing about writing is the way that it obliterates time. Three hours seem like three minutes. Then there is the business of surprise. I never know what is coming next. The phrase that sounds in the head changes when it appears on the page. Then I start probing it with a pen, finding new meanings. Sometimes I burst out laughing at what is happening as I twist and turn sentences. Strange business, all in all. One never gets to the end of it. That's why I go on, I suppose. To see what the next sentences I write will be.

ANDREI VOZNESENSKY: I don't schedule. Nobody does. In Russia, everything is improvisation. Nobody can tell where he'll be on Friday night. Let me give you an example. When I came to America, I wanted very much to visit my dear friend Robert Lowell's grave. We drove out from Boston in the late afternoon—a dinner had been arranged for that evening. It was dark by the time we found the grave in the forest. I was with a young poet from Boston, and I said to him, "Please, I'm sorry, excuse me, it is impolite, but leave me alone, go to your car, I want half-an-hour alone." Then I began to write poetry. Later I asked him to find a phone and call the people and tell them we wouldn't come to dinner. They were all friends of Lowell's and they were very upset with me. But how could I have gone to a dinner party and broken the mood of that encounter?

REBECCA WEST: My memory is certainly in my hands. I can remember things only if I have a pencil and I can write with it and I can play with it. I think your hand concentrates for you. I don't know why it should be so.

E. B. WHITE: Delay is natural to a writer. He is like a surfer—he bides his time, waits for the perfect wave on which to ride in. Delay is instinctive with him. He waits for the surge (of emotion? of strength? of courage?) that will carry him along. I have no warm-up exercises, other than to take an occasional drink. I am apt to let something simmer for a while in my mind before trying to put it into words. I walk around, straightening pictures on the wall, rugs on the floor—as though not until everything in the world was lined up and perfectly true could anybody reasonably expect me to set a word down on paper.

There are two faces to discipline. If a man (who writes) feels like going to a zoo, he should by all means go to a zoo. He might even be lucky, as I once was when I paid a call at the Bronx Zoo and found myself attending the birth of twin fawns. It was a fine sight, and I lost no time writing a piece about it. The other face of discipline is that, zoo or no zoo, diversion or no diversion, in the end a man must sit down and get the words on paper, and against great odds. This takes stamina and resolution. Having got them on paper, he must still have the discipline to discard them if they fail to measure up; he must view them with a jaundiced eye and do the whole thing over as many times as is necessary to achieve excellence, or as close to excellence as he can get.

EDMUND WHITE: Writers say two things that strike me as nonsense. One is that you must follow an absolute schedule every day. If you're not writing well, why continue it? I just don't think this grinding away is useful. The other thing they say: I write because I must. Well, I have never felt that, and I doubt most of them do either. I think they are mouthing a cliché. I don't think most people write because they must; perhaps economically they must, but spiritually? I wonder. I think many writers would be perfectly happy to lay down their pens and never write again if they could maintain their prestige, professorship, and PEN membership.

RICHARD WILBUR: I proceed as Dylan Thomas once told me he proceeded—it is a matter of going to one's study, or to the chair in the sun, and starting a new sheet of paper. On it you put what you've already got of a poem you are trying to write. Then you sit and stare at it, hoping that the impetus of writing out the lines that you already have will get you a few lines farther before the day is done. I often don't write more than a couple of lines in a day of, let's say, six hours of staring at the sheet of paper. Composition for me is, externally at least, scarcely distinguishable from catatonia.

. . .

There are some circumstances under which it is easier to translate than to try to go ahead with a poem of your own. I think that in order to work on your own poem you need to baby yourself sort of totally, not to have the telephone ring, not otherwise to be vulnerable. I somehow can't work on poetry, which is the most important thing in my life, until I've taken care of all the unimportant things: written that silly letter, marked the class papers, *mowed the lawn!* At any rate, I've gotten into that fussy frame of mind now, whereas I can translate Molière riding on a plane, sitting in a motel. I have with me on this trip a translation of *The Learned Ladies*, which has almost reached the end of the second act, and in a frustrating recent day full of flights, limousines, and buses I got four lines done to my satisfaction. And that's a fair average even if one were sitting in a living room. Some days you get sixteen lines done, some days none.

THORNTON WILDER: Many writers have told me that they have built up mnemonic devices to start them off on each day's writing task. Hemingway once told me he sharpened twenty pencils; Willa Cather that she read a passage from the Bible (not from piety, she was quick to add, but to get in touch with fine prose; she also regretted that she had formed this habit, for the prose rhythms of 1611 were not those she was in search of). My springboard has always been long walks. I drink a great deal, but I do not associate it with writing.

TENNESSEE WILLIAMS: In Key West I get up just before daybreak, as a rule. I like being completely alone in the house in the kitchen when I have my coffee and ruminate on what I'm going to work on. I usually have two or three pieces of work going at the same time, and then I decide which to work on that day.

I go to my studio. I usually have some wine there. And then I carefully go over what I wrote the day before. You see, baby, after a glass or two of wine I'm inclined to extravagance. I'm inclined to excesses because I drink while I'm writing, so I'll blue pencil a lot the next day. Then I sit down, and I begin to write.

My work is *emotionally* autobiographical. It has no relationship to the actual events of my life, but it reflects the emotional currents of my life. I try to work every day because you have no refuge but writing. When you're going through a period of unhappiness, a broken love affair, the death of someone you love, or some other disorder in your life, then you have no refuge but writing.

TOM WOLFE: I use a typewriter. My wife gave me a word processor two Christmases ago which still stares at me accusingly from a desk in my office. One day I am going to be compelled to learn how to use it. But for the time being, I use a typewriter. I set myself a quota—ten pages a day, triple-spaced, which means about eighteen hundred words. If I can finish that in three hours, then I'm through for the day. I just close up the lunch box and go home—that's the way I think of it anyway. If it takes me twelve hours, that's too bad, I've got to do it. To me, the idea "I'm going to work for six hours" is of no use. I can waste time as handily at the desk as I can window-shopping, which is one of my favorite diversions. So I try to be very methodical and force myself to stick to that schedule. I always have a clock in front of me. Sometimes, if things are going badly, I will force myself to write a page in a half an hour. I find that can be done. I find that what I write when I force myself is generally just as good as what I write when I'm feeling inspired. It's mainly a matter of forcing yourself to write. There's a marvelous essay that Sinclair Lewis wrote on how to write. He said most writers don't understand that the process begins by actually sitting down.

ON INSPIRATION: THE STARTING POINT

It is not *in*spiration; it is expiration. [the gaunt, fine hands on the thorax; evacuation of the chest; a great breathing out from himself] —JEAN COCTEAU

There is no subject so old that something new cannot be said about it. —FYODOR DOSTOEVSKY

Mostly, we authors must repeat ourselves—that's the truth. We have two or three great moving experiences in our lives — experiences so great and moving that it doesn't seem at the time that anyone else has been caught up and pounded and dazzled and astonished and beaten and broken and rescued and illuminated and rewarded and humbled in just that way ever before. —F. SCOTT FITZGERALD

A poem is never a put-up job so to speak. It begins as a lump in the throat, a sense of wrong, a homesickness, a lovesickness. It is never a thought to begin with. —ROBERT FROST

Thoughts fly and words go on foot. —JULIEN GREEN

There are no dull subjects. There are only dull writers. —H. L. MENCKEN

Listening to the rhythm of his water drinking [her dog, Basset's] made me recognize the difference between sentences and paragraphs, that paragraphs are emotional and sentences are not. —GERTRUDE STEIN

We are stricken by memory sometimes, and old affections rush back on us as vivid as in the time when they were our daily talk. —WILLIAM MAKEPEACE THACKERAY

JOHN BARTH: Different books start in different ways. I sometimes wish that I were the kind of writer who begins with a passionate interest in a character and then, as I've heard other writers say, just gives that character elbow room and sees what he or she wants to do. I'm not that kind of writer. Much more often I start with a shape or form, maybe an image. The floating showboat, for example, which became the central image in *The Floating Opera,* was a photograph of an actual showboat I remember seeing as a child. It happened to be named *Captain Adams' Original Unparalleled Floating Opera,* and when nature, in her heavy-handed way, gives you an image like that, the only honorable thing to do is to make a novel out of it. This may not be the most elevated of approaches. Aleksandr Solzhenitsyn, for example, comes to the medium of fiction with a high moral purpose; he wants, literally, to try to change the world through the medium of the novel. I honor and admire that intention, but just as often a great writer will come to his novel with a much less elevated purpose than wanting to undermine the Soviet Government. Henry James wanted to write a book in the shape of an hourglass. Flaubert wanted to write a novel about *nothing.* What I've learned is that the muses' decision to sing or not to sing is not based on the elevation of your moral purpose—they will sing or not regardless.

HEINRICH BÖLL: It begins with one person (at the most two) in a specific situation that produces conflict and tension. How much "breathing space" or length is determined by the number of persons who necessarily become involved.

ITALO CALVINO: I'm very slow getting started. If I have an idea for a novel, I find every conceivable pretext to not work on it. If I'm doing a book of stories, short texts, each one has its own starting time. Even with articles, I'm a slow starter. Even with articles for newspapers, every time I have the same trouble getting under way. Once I have started, then I can be quite fast. In other words, I write fast, but I have huge blank periods. It's a bit like the story of the great Chinese artist: the Emperor asked him to draw a crab, and the artist answered, "I need ten years, a great house, and twenty servants." The ten years went by, and the Emperor asked him for the drawing of the crab. "I need another two years," he said. Then he asked for a further week. And finally he picked up his pen and drew the crab in a moment, with a single, rapid gesture.

JOYCE CAREY: Often I don't know the real origin. I had an odd experience lately which gave me a glimpse of the process, something I hadn't suspected. I was going round Manhattan on a steamer with an American friend, Elizabeth Lawrence, of *Harper's*. And I noticed a girl sitting all by herself on the other side of the deck—a girl of about thirty, wearing a shabby skirt. She was enjoying herself. A nice expression, with a wrinkled forehead, a good many wrinkles. I said to my friend, "I could write about that girl—what do you think she is?" Elizabeth said that she might be a schoolteacher taking a holiday, and asked me why I wanted to write about her. I said I didn't really know—I imagined her as sensitive and intelligent, and up against it. Having a hard life but making something of it, too. In such a case I often make a note. But I didn't—and I forgot the whole episode. Then, about three weeks later, in San Francisco, I woke up one night at four—I am not so much a bad sleeper as a short sleeper—I woke up, I say, with a story in my head. I sketched the story at once—it was about an English girl in England—a purely English tale. Next day an appointment fell through and I had a whole day on my hands. I found my notes and wrote the story—that is, the chief scenes and some connecting tissue. Some days later, in a plane—ideal for writing—I began to work it over, clean it up, and I thought, why all these wrinkles, that's the third time they come in. And I suddenly realized that my English heroine was the girl on the Manhattan boat. Somehow she had gone down into my subconscious, and came up again with a full-sized story. And I imagine that has happened before. I notice some person because he or she exemplifies some part of my feeling about things. The Manhattan girl was a motive. And she brought up a little piece of counterpoint. But the wrinkles were the first crude impression—a note, but one that counted too much in the final writing.

CAMILO JOSÉ CELA: Ideas? My head is full of them, one after the other, but they serve no purpose there. They must be put down on paper, one after the other.

DON DELILLO: I don't always know when or where an idea first hits the nervous system, but I remember *Americana*. I was sailing in Maine with two friends, and we put into a small harbor on Mt. Desert Island. And I was sitting on a railroad tie waiting to take a shower, and I had a glimpse of a street maybe fifty yards away and a sense of beautiful old houses and rows of elms and maples and a stillness and wistfulness—the street seemed to carry its own built-in longing. And I felt something, a pause, something opening up before me. It would be a month or two before I started writing the book and two or three years before I came up with the title *Americana,* but in fact it was all implicit in that moment—a moment in which nothing happened, nothing ostensibly changed, a moment in which I didn't see anything I hadn't seen before. But there was a pause in time, and I knew I had to write about a man who comes to a street like this or lives on a street like this. And whatever roads the novel eventually followed, I believe I maintained the idea of that quiet street if only as counterpoint, as lost innocence.

JAMES DICKEY: I remember when I was in Okinawa and the war was over and we went out to one of the invasion beaches near Buckner Bay, me and my co-flyers, and we went swimming and there was an old amtrac there in ten feet of water that the Japanese had stove in—big holes in the sides of it—and I swam down and sat in the driver's seat. That image stayed with me and years later, twenty or twenty-five years later, I wrote "The Driver."

JOAN DIDION: What's so hard about that first sentence is that you're stuck with it. Everything else is going to flow out of that sentence. And by the time you've laid down the first *two* sentences, your options are all gone.

Yes, and the last sentence in a piece is another adventure. It should open the piece up. It should make you go back and start reading from page one. That's how it *should* be, but it doesn't always work. I think of writing anything at all as a kind of highwire act. The minute you start putting words on paper you're eliminating possibilities. Unless you're Henry James.

I suppose that's part of the dynamic. I start a book and I want to make it perfect, want it to turn every color, want it to *be the world.* Ten pages in, I've already blown it, limited it, made it less, marred it. That's very discouraging. I hate the book at that point. After a while I arrive at an accommodation: well, it's not the ideal, it's not the perfect object I wanted to make, but maybe—if I go ahead and finish it anyway—I can get it right next time. Maybe I can have another chance.

E. L. DOCTOROW: Well, it can be anything. It can be a voice, an image; it can be a deep moment of personal desperation. For instance, with *Ragtime* I was so desperate to write something, I was facing the wall of my study in my house in New Rochelle and so I started to write about the wall. That's the kind of day we sometimes have, as writers. Then I wrote about the house that was attached to the wall. It was built in 1906, you see, so I thought about the era and what Broadview Avenue looked like then:

trolley cars ran along the avenue down at the bottom of the hill; people wore white clothes in the summer to stay cool. Teddy Roosevelt was President. One thing led to another and that's the way that book began, through desperation to those few images. With *Loon Lake*, in contrast, it was just a very strong sense of place, a heightened emotion when I found myself in the Adirondacks after many, many years of being away ... and all this came to a point when I saw a sign, a road sign: Loon Lake. So it can be anything.... I liked the sound of the two words together—loon lake. I had these opening images of a private railroad train on a single track at night going up through the Adirondacks with a bunch of gangsters on board, and a beautiful girl standing, naked, holding a white dress up in front of a mirror to see if she should put it on. I didn't know where these gangsters came from. I knew where they were going—to this rich man's camp. Many years ago the very wealthy discovered the wilderness in the American eastern mountains. They built these extraordinary camps— C. W. Post, Harriman, Morgan—they made the wilderness their personal luxury. So I imagined a camp like this, with these gangsters, these low-down people going up there on a private railroad train. That's what got me started. I published this material in the *Kenyon Review,* but I wasn't through. I kept thinking about the images and wondering where they'd come from. The time was in the 1930s, really the last era a man would have had his own railroad car, as some people today have their own jetliners. There was a depression then, so the person to see this amazing train was obviously a hobo, a tramp. So then I had my character, Joe, out there in this chill, this darkness, seeing the headlamp of the engine coming around the bend and blinding him, and then as the train goes by seeing these people at green baize tables being served drinks and this girl standing in a bedroom compartment holding the dress. And at dawn he follows the track in the direction the train has gone. And he's off and running, and so am I.

J. P. DONLEAVY: I remember the day when I started *A Singular Man.* I was sitting in the sunroom of a house out in the west of Ireland, near Clifden in County Galway, and out my window I could see the Atlantic. I was in the middle of my litigations with the Olympia Press over *The Ginger Man* then and I could see the mailman on his bicycle on the winding mountain road coming to me four hours before he arrived, and I'd sit and wonder what bad news he had for me.

I think it must have been the glamour of America, the glamour of New

York, as opposed to the isolation and poverty of Ireland that started me on the book. There was a cemetery just over a couple of fields where there were no gravestones. When anyone was buried they'd just pile some boulders on the grave. There were no markings, nothing. One was so isolated out there that I remember that day when the local farmer came rushing across the lawn, pointing up to the sky, and yelling, "There's a dog up there." My two children, Philip and Karen, were playing in front of the house. I remember warning my wife that the children should be pulled inside because there was a maniac wandering around. I was struck with terror. I had no contact with the outside world and no way of knowing that the Russians had sent a dog up in a spaceship. In Ireland when you buy a newspaper, as often as not they put a recent cover on it, but inside will be an old, old newspaper. They think news is news and vintage news is better than anything. Indeed, in Ireland, to read a local paper that's fifty years old is not much different than reading today's. In that kind of isolation *A Singular Man* came into being.

LAWRENCE DURRELL: It's simply a sort of premonitory sense that one day one was going to put one's whole shoulder behind a particular punch. But one had to be patient and wait and let it [*The Quartets*] form up, and not catch it in the early jelly stage before it had set properly, and ruin it by a premature thing. That explains why I have hung around in the Foreign Service for so long—keeping the machine running by writing other sorts of things, but waiting patiently, and now I suddenly felt this was it, and this was the moment, and bang—at least I hope, bang.

LEON EDEL: You begin, I suppose, the way all storytellers begin. Remember, a biography is a narrative, and the biographer has a story to tell. Inside the mind there is the classical beginning: "Once upon a time . . ." In my Thoreau, I found my first sentence an expression of my thematic sense of Thoreau's narcissism. I began something like this: "Of the creative spirits that flourished in Concord, Massachusetts, it might be said that Hawthorne loved men but felt estranged from them, Emerson loved ideas even more than men, and Thoreau loved himself." A cruel beginning, but I think the reader wants to go right on.

WILLIAM FAULKNER: *The Sound and the Fury* began with a mental picture. I didn't realize at the time it was symbolical. The picture was of the muddy seat of a little girl's drawers in a pear tree, where she could see through a window where her grandmother's funeral was taking place and report what was happening to her brothers on the ground below. By the time I explained who they were and what they were doing and how her pants got muddy, I realized it would be impossible to get all of it into a short story and that it would have to be a book. And then I realized the symbolism of the soiled pants, and that image was replaced by the one of the fatherless and motherless girl climbing down the rainpipe to escape from the only home she had, where she had never been offered love or affection or understanding.

I had already begun to tell the story through the eyes of the idiot child, since I felt that it would be more effective as told by someone capable only of knowing what happened, but not why. I saw that I had not told the story that time. I tried to tell it again, the same story through the eyes of another brother. That was still not it. I told it for the third time through the eyes of the third brother. That was still not it. I tried to gather the pieces together and fill in the gaps by making myself the spokesman. It was still not complete, not until fifteen years after the book was published, when I wrote as an appendix to another book the final effort to get the story told and off my mind, so that I myself could have some peace from it. It's the book I feel tenderest towards. I couldn't leave it alone, and I never could tell it right, though I tried hard and would like to try again, though I'd probably fail again.

· · ·

I don't know anything about inspiration, because I don't know what inspiration is—I've heard about it, but I never saw it.

WILLIAM GADDIS: I think first it was that towering kind of confidence of being quite young, that one can do anything—"All's brave that youth mounts and folly guides," as we're told in *As You Like It. The Recognitions* started as a short piece of work, quite undirected, but based on the Faust story. Then as I got into the idea of forgery, the entire concept of forgery became—I wouldn't say an obsession—but a central part of everything I thought and saw; so the book expanded from simply the central character of the forger to the forgery, falsification, and cheapening of values and what have you, everywhere. Looking at it now with its various faults, I suppose excess would be the main charge. I remember Clive Bell looking back on his small fine book, *Art,* thirty-five years after it was published in 1913, and listing *its* faults, finding it too confident and aggressive, even too optimistic—I was never accused of that!—but still feeling, as he said, "a little envious of the adventurous young man who wrote it."

GABRIEL GARCÍA MÁRQUEZ: One of the most difficult things is the first paragraph. I have spent many months on a first paragraph and once I get it, the rest just comes out very easily. In the first paragraph you solve most of the problems with your book. The theme is defined, the style, the tone. At least in my case, the first paragraph is a kind of sample of what the rest of the book is going to be. That's why writing a book of short stories is much more difficult than writing a novel. Every time you write a short story, you have to begin all over again.

WILLIAM GOYEN: I thought I was going to die in the war. I was on a terrible ship. It was the *Casablanca,* the first baby flattop. There were always holes in it, and people dying and it was just the worst place for me to be. I really was desperate. I just wanted to jump off. I thought I was going to die anyway, be killed, and I wanted to die because I couldn't endure what looked like an endless way of life with which I had nothing to do—the war, the ship, and the water . . . I have been terrified of water all my life. I would have fits when I got close to it.

Suddenly—it was out on a deck in the cold—I saw the breath that came from me. And I thought that the simplest thing that I know is what I belong to and where I came from and I just called out to my family as I stood there that night, and it just . . . I saw this breath come from me and I thought—in that breath, in that call is *their* existence, is their reality . . . and I must shape that and I must write about them—*The House of Breath.*

I saw this whole thing. I saw what was going to be four or five years' work. Isn't that amazing? But I knew it was there. Many of my stories happen that way. It's dangerous to tell my students this because then these young people say, "Gee, all I've got to do, if I really want to write, is wait around for some ship in the cold night, and I'll blow out my breath, and I've got my thing."

ROBERT GRAVES: Some people have gifts, like a friend of mine who can balance a glass on his finger and make it turn round by just looking at it. I have the gift of being occasionally able to put myself back in the past and see what's happening. That's how historical novels should be written.

I also have a very good memory for anything I want to remember, and none at all for what I don't want to remember. *Wife to Mr. Milton*—my best novel—started when my wife and I were making a bed in 1943 and I suddenly said: "You know, Milton must have been a trichomaniac"—meaning a hair-fetishist. The remark suddenly sprang out of my mouth. I realized how often his imagery had been trichomanic. So I read all I could find about him, and went into the history of his marriages. I'd always hated Milton, from earliest childhood; and I wanted to find out the reason. I found it. His jealousy. It's present in all his poems . . . Marie Powell had long hair with which he could not compete.

HENRY GREEN: I got the idea of *Loving* from a manservant in the Fire Service during the war. He was serving with me in the ranks, and he told me he had once asked the elderly butler who was over him what the old boy most liked in the world. The reply was: "Lying in bed on a summer morning, with the window open, listening to the church bells, eating buttered toast with cunty fingers." I saw the book in a flash.

JOSEPH HELLER: I was lying in bed in my four-room apartment on the West Side when suddenly this line [the first line of *Catch-22*] came to me: "It was love at first sight. The first time he saw the chaplain, Someone fell madly in love with him." I didn't have the name Yossarian. The chaplain wasn't necessarily an army chaplain—he could have been a *prison* chaplain. But as soon as the opening sentence was available, the book began to evolve clearly in my mind—even most of the particulars . . . the tone, the form, many of the characters, including some I eventually couldn't use. All of this took place within an hour and a half. It got me so excited that I did what the cliché says you're supposed to do: I jumped out of bed and paced the floor. That morning I went to my job at the advertising agency and wrote out the first chapter in longhand. Before the end of the week I had typed it out and sent it to Candida Donadio, my agent. One year later, after much planning, I began chapter two. I don't understand the process of imagination—though I know that I am very much at its mercy. I feel that these ideas are floating around in the air and they pick me to settle upon. The ideas come to me; I don't produce them at will. They come to me in the course of a sort of controlled daydream, a directed reverie. It may have something to do with the disciplines of writing advertising copy (which I did for a number of years) where the limitations involved provide a considerable spur to the imagination. There's an essay of T. S. Eliot's in which he praises the disciplines of writing, claiming that if one is forced to write within a certain framework the imagination is taxed to its utmost and will produce its richest ideas. Given total freedom, however, the chances are good that the work will sprawl.

. . .

As for *Something Happened,* in 1962 I was sitting on the deck of a house on Fire Island. I was frightened. I was worried because I had lost interest in my job then—which was writing advertising and promotion copy. *Catch-22* was not making much money. It was selling steadily (eight hundred to two thousand copies a week)—mostly by word-of-mouth—but it had never come close to the *The New York Times* best-seller list. I had a wife and two children. I had no idea for another book. I was waiting for something to happen(!), wishing I had a book to start. My novels begin in a strange way. I don't begin with a theme, or even a character. I begin with a first sentence that is independent of any conscious preparation. Most often nothing comes out of it: a sentence will come to mind that doesn't lead to a second sentence. Sometimes it will lead to thirty sentences which then come to a dead end. I was alone on the deck. As I sat there worrying and wondering what to do, one of those first lines suddenly came to mind: "In the office in which I work, there are four people of whom I am afraid. Each of these four people is afraid of five people." Immediately, the lines presented a whole explosion of possibilities and choices—characters (working in a corporation), a tone, a mood of anxiety or insecurity. In that first hour (before someone came along and asked me to go to the beach) I knew the beginning, the ending, most of the middle, the whole scene of that particular "something" that was going to happen; I knew about the brain-damaged child, and especially, of course, about Bob Slocum, my protagonist, and what frightened him, that he wanted to be liked, that his immediate hope was to be allowed to make a three-minute speech at the company convention. Many of the actual lines throughout the book came to me—the entire "something happened" scene with those solar plexus lines (beginning with the doctor's statement and ending with "Don't tell my wife" and the rest of them) all coming to me in that first hour on that Fire Island deck. Eventually I found a different opening chapter with a different first line ("I get the willies when I see closed doors") but I kept the original, which had spurred everything, to start off the second section.

JOHN HERSEY: I think the first impulse comes from some deep emotion. It may be anger, it may be some sort of excitement. I recognize in the real world around me something that triggers such an emotion, and then the emotion seems to cast up pictures in my mind that lead me towards a story. To give you an example, the impulse to write *The Wall* came from seeing some camps in Eastern Europe when I was working as a correspondent in Moscow for *Time*. We were taken first to Estonia, and there we saw a camp where the Germans had had orders to kill everybody before they left; they had done it in a crude and awful way, making the prisoners build their own pyres before shooting them. We went later to Poland, and though the Warsaw ghetto itself was completely razed, we saw a couple of camps where the same thing had happened, the Germans had been ordered to kill everybody. In each case, there had been a few survivors to talk to. This came at a time when the West had not yet known very much about the Holocaust; there had been some vague rumors of the camps, but we had no real pictures of them. To see these bodies, to hear from the people who survived, created a sense of horror and anger in me that made me want to write. I thought at first to write about one of the camps like Auschwitz, and I did a lot of research on that; then it appeared to me, later on, that the life in the ghettos was at least something like real life for a long time, and so would, I thought, lend itself better to a novel. But it was the sense of distress, fear, anger that I felt seeing those camps that got me launched on that work.

ALDOUS HUXLEY: I don't believe for a moment that creativity is a neurotic symptom. On the contrary, the neurotic who succeeds as an artist has had to overcome a tremendous handicap. He creates in spite of his neurosis, not because of it.

JOHN IRVING: I begin by telling the truth, by remembering real people, relatives and friends. The landscape detail is pretty good, but the people aren't quite interesting enough—they don't have quite enough to do with one another; of course, what unsettles me and bores me is the absence of plot. . . . And so I find a little something that I exaggerate, a little; gradually, I have an autobiography on its way to becoming a lie. The lie, of course, is more interesting. I become much more interested in the part of the story I'm making up, in the "relative" I never had. And then I begin to think of a novel; that's the end of the diary. I promise I'll start another one as soon as I finish the novel. Then the same thing happens; the lies become much more interesting—always.

· · ·

Henry Robbins, my late editor at E. P. Dutton, called this my enema theory: keep from writing the book as long as you can, make yourself *not begin*, store it up. This is an advantage in historical novels. *Setting Free the Bears* and *The Cider House Rules,* for example. I had to learn so much before I could begin those books; I had to gather so much information, take so many notes, see, witness, observe, study—whatever—that when I finally was able to begin writing, I knew everything that was going to happen, in advance. That never hurts. I want to know how a book feels after the main events are over. The authority of the storyteller's voice—of mine, anyway—comes from knowing how it all comes out before you begin. It's very plodding work, really.

JACK KEROUAC: Burroughs and I were sitting in a bar one night and we heard a newscaster saying . . . "and so the Egyptians attacked blah blah . . . and meanwhile there was a great fire in the zoo in London and the fire raced across the fields and the hippos were boiled in their tanks! Goodnight, everyone!" That's Bill, he noticed that. Because he notices them kind of things.

STANLEY KUNITZ: What triggered "King of the River," I recall, was a brief report in *Time* of some new research on the aging process of the Pacific salmon. I wrote the poem in Provincetown one fall—my favorite writing season. The very first lines came to me with their conditional syntax and suspended clauses, a winding and falling movement. The rest seemed to flow, maybe because I'm never very far from the creature world. Some of my deepest feelings have to do with plants and animals. In my bad times they've sustained me. It may be pertinent that I experienced a curious elation while confronting the unpleasant reality of being mortal, the inexorable process of my own decay. Perhaps I had managed to "distance" my fate—the salmon was doing my dying for me.

A poem has secrets that the poet knows nothing of. It takes on a life and a will of its own. It might have proceeded differently—towards catastrophe, resignation, terror, despair—and I still would have no claim to it. Valéry said that poetry is a language within a language. It is also a language beyond language, a meta-medium—that is, metabolic, metaphoric, metamorphic. A poet's collected work is his book of changes. The great meditations on death have a curious exaltation. I suppose it comes from the realization, even on the threshold, that one isn't done with one's changes.

· · ·

The poem in the head is always perfect. Resistance starts when you try to convert it into language. Language itself is a kind of resistance to the pure flow of self. The solution is to become one's language. You cannot write a poem until you hit upon its rhythm. That rhythm not only belongs to the subject matter, it belongs to your interior world, and the moment they hook up there's a quantum leap of energy. You can ride on that rhythm, it will carry you somewhere strange. The next morning you look at the page and wonder how it all happened. You have to triumph over all your diurnal glibness and cheapness and defensiveness.

PHILIP LEVINE: I remember what "On the Edge" came out of very clearly . . . a lecture on Edgar Allan Poe, delivered in French, a language I don't understand. I sat right in the front; I didn't know it was going to be in French. The speaker was a very nice young man, an Argentine I'd met; there was almost no one there—maybe ten people—so once he began in French I couldn't leave, it would have been too rude; so I sat through fifty minutes, an academic hour. I focused on small things, like the delightful way he said Poe's name in this French way, ED-ga-PO . . . so much more delicious than Edgar Allan Poe in a heavy Midwestern voice, the way my high-school lit teacher had said it. So musical, ED-ga-PO. The French take Poe much more seriously than we do. I've always thought of Poe as the last poet in the world I would want to be, so I just imagined myself as Poe. The poem also came out of not writing. I was going through one of my extensive three-month dry spells or maybe I was simply dissatisfied with what I was writing. So I became Poe. The poem is really, I guess, about not writing, about the power one gains by not committing oneself; one becomes almost God-like. That was the vision of the poem, for God won't commit himself. We don't see Him, we have these rumors of His existence, hints of His immense power, we're told of His enormous concern for us, and we don't see it. So I said, Well, maybe I'll be God-like, I will remain silent, I will give away nothing. I'm sure the idea came from my encounters with certain people who never seem to commit themselves and gain a temporary power, especially over a loudmouth like me.

ROBERT LOWELL: Some bit of scenery or something you've felt. Almost the whole problem of writing poetry is to bring it back to what you really feel, and that takes an awful lot of maneuvering. You may feel the doorknob more strongly than some big personal event, and the doorknob will open into something that you can use as your own. A lot of poetry seems to me very good in the tradition but just doesn't move me very much because it doesn't have personal vibrance to it. I probably exaggerate the value of it, but it's precious to me. Some little image, some detail you've noticed—you're writing about a little country shop, just describing it, and your poem ends up with an existentialist account of your experience. But it's the shop that started it off. You didn't know why it meant a lot to you. Often images and often the sense of the beginning and end of a poem are all you have—some journey to be gone through between those things: you know that, but you don't know the details. And that's marvelous; then you feel the poem will come out. It's a terrible struggle, because what you really feel hasn't got the form, it's not what you can put down in a poem. And the poem you're equipped to write concerns nothing that you care very much about or have much to say on. Then the great moment comes when there's enough resolution of your technical equipment, your way of constructing things, and what you can make a poem out of, to hit something you really want to say. You may not know you have it to say.

NORMAN MAILER: An appropriate image for me might be that I start with the idea of constructing a treehouse and end with a skyscraper made of wood. With *The Naked and the Dead*, I wanted to write a short novel about a long patrol. All during the war I kept thinking about this patrol. I even had the idea before I went overseas. Probably it was stimulated by a few war books I had read: John Hersey's *Into the Valley*, Harry Brown's *A Walk in the Sun*, and a couple of others I no longer remember. Out of these books came the idea to do a novel about a long patrol. And I began to create my characters. All the while I was overseas a part of me was working on this long patrol. I even ended up in a reconnaissance outfit which I had asked to get into. A reconnaissance outfit, after all, tends to take long patrols. Art kept traducing life. At any rate, when I started writing *The Naked and the Dead* I thought it might be a good idea to have a preliminary chapter or two in which to give the reader a chance to meet my characters before they went on patrol. But the next six months and the first five hundred pages went into that, and I remember in the early days I was annoyed at how long it was taking me to get to the patrol.

BERNARD MALAMUD: When I start I have a pretty well-developed idea what the book is about and how it ought to go, because generally I've been thinking about it and making notes for months if not years. Generally I have the ending in mind, usually the last paragraph almost verbatim. I begin at the beginning and stay close to the track, if it is a track and not a whalepath. If it turns out I'm in the open sea, my compass is my narrative instinct, with assistance from that astrolabe, theme. The destination, wherever it is, is, as I said, already defined. If I go astray it's not a long excursus, good for getting to know the ocean if not the world. The original idea, altered but recognizable, on the whole remains.

WILLIAM MAXWELL: When I was at Harvard I got to know Robert Fitzgerald, and I used to show my poems to him. In spite of the fact that I was older than he was—I was a graduate student and he was a sophomore—I had enormous respect for him. He was better educated than I was, and intransigent, and he despised anything that wasn't first rate. One day he looked at my poem and then he looked at me, rather in the way you look at children who present a problem, and he said, "Why don't you write prose?" I was so happy that he thought I could write *anything* that I just turned to and wrote prose—as if he'd given me permission to try. The prose took the form of fiction because I do like stories and don't have a very firm grasp on ideas.

THOMAS MCGUANE: When I start something it's like being a bird dog getting a smell; it's a matter of running it down in prose and then trying to figure out what the thing is that's out there. Sometimes it might be a picture. This morning when I was writing I was chasing down one of those images. It was just a minute thing that happened to me while I was recently down in Alabama. We had rented a little cottage on the edge of Mobile Bay and at one point there was stormy weather out on the bay; I wandered out to see what kind of weather it was and the door blew closed and locked me out of the cottage. I thought about getting back inside and

I sat down and there was one of those semi-tropical warm summer rains starting to come down like buckshot. Somehow the image of stepping outside to see what's going on and having the wind blow the door shut has stuck in my head. I don't know what that image *is* exactly, or what it means, but I know that ever since I came home I've been trying to pursue that image in language, find out what it is. That image begins to ionize the prose and narrative particles around it so that words are drawn in, people and language begin to appear. That's when things are going well. When that's happening, any reader will recognize that flame-edge of discovery, that excitement of proceeding on the page that is shared between the reader, the writer, and the page.

JAMES MERRILL: Whether you're at your desk or not when a poem's under way, isn't there that constant eddy in your mind? If it's strong enough all sorts of random flotsam gets drawn into it, how selectively it's hopeless to decide at the time. I try to break off, get away from the page, into the kitchen for a spell of mixing and marinating which gives the words a chance to sort themselves out behind my back. But there's really no escape, except perhaps the third drink. On "ordinary" days, days when you've nothing on the burner, it might be safe to say that you're not a poet at all: more like a doctor at a dinner party, just another guest until his hostess slumps to the floor or his little beeper goes off. Most of those signals are false alarms—only they're not. Language *is* your medium. You can be talking or writing a letter, and out comes an observation, a "sentence-sound" you rather like. It needn't be your own. And it's not going to make a poem, or even fit into one. But the *twinge* it gives you—and it's this, I daresay, that distinguishes you from the "citizen"—reminds you you've got to be careful, that you've a condition that needs watching.

HENRY MILLER: Each man has his own way. After all, most writing is done away from the typewriter, away from the desk. I'd say it occurs in the quiet, silent moments, while you're walking or shaving or playing a game or whatever, or even talking to someone you're not vitally interested in. You're working, your mind is working, on this problem in the back of your head. So, when you get to the machine it's a mere matter of transfer.

What is an artist? He's a man who has antennae, who knows how to hook up to the currents which are in the atmosphere, in the cosmos; he merely has the facility for hooking on, as it were. Who is original? Everything that we are doing, everything that we think, exists already, and we are only intermediaries, that's all, who make use of what is in the air. Why do ideas, why do great scientific discoveries often occur in different parts of the world at the same time? The same is true of the elements that go to make up a poem or a great novel or any work of art. They are already in the air, they have not been given voice, that's all. They need *the* man, *the* interpreter, to bring them forth.

FRANK O'CONNOR: "Get black on white," used to be Maupassant's advice—that's what I always do. I don't give a hoot what the writing's like; I write any sort of rubbish which will cover the main outlines of the story, then I can begin to see it. When I write, when I draft a story, I never think of writing nice sentences about, "It was a nice August evening when Elizabeth Jane Moriarty was coming down the road." I just write roughly what happened, and then I'm able to see what the construction looks like. It's the design of the story which to me is most important, the thing that tells you there's a bad gap in the narrative here and you really ought to fill that up in some way or another. I'm always looking at the design of a story, not the treatment. Yesterday I was finishing off a piece about my friend A. E. Coppard, the greatest of all the English storytellers, who died about a fortnight ago. I was describing the way Coppard must have written these stories, going around with a notebook, recording what the lighting looked like, what that house looked like, and all the time using metaphor to suggest it to himself: "The road looked like a mad serpent going up the hill," or something of the kind, and, "she said so-and-so, and the man in the pub said something else." After he had written them all out, he must have got the outline of his story and he'd start working in all the details. Now, I could never do that at all. I've got to see what these people did, first of all, and then I start thinking of whether it was a nice August evening or a spring evening. I have to wait for the theme before I can do anything.

GRACE PALEY: A lot of them begin with a sentence—they all begin with language. It sounds dopey to say that, but it's true. Very often one sentence is absolutely resonant. A story can begin with someone speaking. "I was popular in certain circles," for example; an aunt of mine said that, and it hung around in my head for a long time. Eventually I wrote a story, "Goodbye and Good Luck," that began with that line, though it had nothing to do with my aunt. Another example: "There were two husbands disappointed by eggs," which is the first sentence of "The Used-Boy Raisers." I was at the house of a friend of mine, thirty-five years ago, and there were her two husbands complaining about the eggs. It was just *right*—so I went home and began the story, though I didn't finish it for months. I'm almost invariably stuck after one page or one paragraph—at which point I have to begin thinking about what the story could possibly be about. I begin by writing paragraphs that don't have an immediate relation to a plot. The sound of the story comes first.

OCTAVIO PAZ: Each poem is different. Often the first line is a gift, I don't know if from the gods or from that mysterious faculty called inspiration. Let me use *Sun Stone* as an example: I wrote the first thirty verses as if someone were silently dictating them to me. I was surprised at the fluidity with which those hendecasyllabic lines appeared one after another. They came from far off and from nearby, from within my own chest. Suddenly the current stopped flowing. I read what I'd written: I didn't have to change a thing. But it was only a beginning, and I had no idea where those lines were going. A few days later, I tried to get started again, not in a passive way but trying to orient and direct the flow of verses. I wrote another thirty or forty lines. I stopped. I went back to it a few days later and, little by little, I began to discover the theme of the poem and where it was all heading. It was a kind of a review of my life, a resurrection of my experiences, my concerns, my failures, my obsessions. I realized I was living the end of my youth and that the poem was simultaneously an end and a new beginning.

HAROLD PINTER: I can't remember exactly how a given play developed in my mind. I think what happens is that I write in a very high state of excitement and frustration. I follow what I see on the paper in front of me—one sentence after another. That doesn't mean I don't have a dim, possible overall idea—the image that starts off doesn't just engender what happens immediately, it engenders the possibility of an overall happening, which carries me through. I've got an idea of what *might* happen—sometimes I'm absolutely right, but on many occasions I've been proved wrong by what does actually happen. Sometimes I'm going along and I find myself writing "C. comes in" when I didn't know that he was going to come in; he *had* to come in at that point, that's all.

KATHERINE ANNE PORTER: The truth is, I have never written a story in my life that didn't have a very firm foundation in actual human experience—somebody else's experience quite often, but an experience that became my own by hearing the story, by witnessing the thing, by hearing just a word perhaps. It doesn't matter, it just takes a little—a tiny seed. Then it takes root, and it grows. It's an organic thing. That story ["Flowering Judas"] had been on my mind for years, growing out of this one little thing that happened in Mexico. It was forming and forming in my mind, until one night I was quite desperate—people are always so sociable, and I'm sociable too, and if I live around friends... Well, they were insisting that I come and play bridge. But I was very firm, because I knew the time had come to write that story, and I had to write it.

Something I saw as I passed a window one evening. A girl I knew had asked me to come and sit with her, because a man was coming to see her, and she was a little afraid of him. And as I went through the courtyard, past the flowering Judas tree, I glanced in the window and there she was sitting with an open book on her lap, and there was this great big fat man sitting beside her. Now Mary and I were friends, both American girls living in this revolutionary situation. She was teaching at an Indian school, and I was teaching dancing at a girls' technical school in Mexico City. And we were having a very strange time of it. I was more skeptical, and so I had already begun to look with a skeptical eye on a great many of the revolutionary leaders—oh, the idea was all right, but a lot of men were misapplying it.

And when I looked through that window that evening, I saw something in Mary's face, something in her pose, something in the whole situation, that set up a commotion in my mind. Because until that moment I hadn't really understood that she was not able to take care of herself, because she was not able to face her own nature and was afraid of everything.

I don't know why I saw it. I don't believe in intuition. When you get sudden flashes of perception, it is just the brain working faster than usual. But you've been getting ready to know it for a long time, and when it comes, you feel you've known it always.

RICHARD PRICE: My grandmother, who was a big influence on my life, would take me under her wing because there was something wrong with my hand. She was a very unhappy person herself, very heavy, about five feet tall. Really overweight. Like two hundred pounds or more. It was her against the world, and she saw me as her ally. I think she tended to see herself as a freak. There was something wrong with my hand, so we were fellow freaks... although she never said that to me. To go to her house on a Saturday was like getting parole for a day. I didn't understand how unhappy and isolated she was, but she'd be all filled with this melodrama about everything. We'd sit and look out her Bronx kitchen window and watch the East 172nd Street follies. She'd see a black man who lived across the street and she'd say, "Oh, this one is a gentleman, married to this white piece of trash. She goes with anything in pants. She has him wrapped around her little finger. Do you know how much of a gentleman this man is? If he goes into his building lobby to go into the elevator and he sees a white woman there who's gonna get spooked by him because he's a black man, do you know what he does? He steps *out* of the lobby so she can go up the elevator herself. Now, *this* is a gentleman. But that whore he's married to . . . ?"

Then there'd be some other guy. "Oh, this son-of-a-bitch, he's a junkie. Every time he sticks a needle in his arm it's like sticking a needle in his mother's heart. She comes to me, she says, 'Mrs. Rosenbaum, what can I do! What can I do!' Richard, what am I going to tell her?"

It was this constant rat-tat-tat. I'm six and I'm with the fattest, biggest ball of love to me. This is my grandmother. Then we'd go all day to monster movies in a neighborhood you wouldn't go into with a tank. She'd be talking back to the screen the whole time. We'd watch *The Attack of the Praying Mantis,* along with *The Crawling Eye* and *The Creature From Green Hell.* She'd be the only person over fourteen in the whole theater. Not only that, the only person over one hundred and fifty pounds. She'd pack up these big, big, vinyl, sort of, beach bags. She'd make sandwiches, thermoses of coffee and chocolate milk, and bring plums and nectarines. If there was a turkey carcass, she'd wrap it in silver foil so we could pick on the bones. We'd go into the movies with all this. We were ready for anything. And when we came out of the theater we'd have those little light dots in front of our eyes because we'd gone in at noon and we'd be coming out at five o'clock. Coming out, she'd walk all hunched over. She was only in her fifties, but she was so arthritic and rheumatic and heavy. We'd walk all the way back home, about one block every twenty minutes with that nonstop commentary about everybody who crossed our path. She lived on the third floor of a walk-up, so that took another hour, one step at a time. Then we get up there, and even after the triple horror feature we'd watch "Zacherly's Shock Theater," pro wrestling, Roller Derby—everything—drama, stories, tragedies, drama, drama.

One time she took me to a wrestling arena in the early fifties in the height of summer. She had me on her lap and when one of the villains walked by she jabbed him with a hatpin. She was what was known as a Hatpin Mary. So, for the next match, when Nature Boy Buddy Rogers, this peroxide pompadoured villain, who wore a leopard-skin Tarzan getup, came strutting down the aisle, people were looking at my grandmother, and they started chanting, "Stick him! Stick him!" He heard the chant and stood right over us, daring her. She was paralyzed, so he took her hand with the hatpin, a woman who probably felt very unloved by the world, bowed down and kissed it, said, "Madam." And then he continued walking toward the ring. At which point my grandmother dropped me, just dropped me on the floor. I remember ten, fifteen years later, when I would watch wrestling with my grandmother, every once in a while she'd say, "I wonder how Nature Boy Buddy Rogers is doing. He's such a nice guy."

My grandmother's house was heaven for me. When I started writing in earnest I just thought back to the time with her, all those Saturdays, all those movies, all that commentary on the world under her window, then I started thinking about my friends, about other aspects of my childhood; the out-of-whack passions, crushes, terrors, and I began writing this sort of magic realism bullshit, aka stories about the Bronx.

As I always told my students, "We all grow up with ten great stories about our families, our childhoods . . . they probably have nothing to do with the truth of things, but they're yours. You know them. And you love them. So use them." And that's what I did. That's what I reached for, to become a writer.

Now, at this point in my life I've paid all my bills, I've fulfilled all my screenwriting obligations. I'm financially flush, for the next year I have nothing to do but work on this novel without distraction. So, I'm looking at all my notes, at my nice clean desk, my stack of unwrapped ready-to-go legal pads, and all I can think of is that saying: "If God hates your guts he grants you your deepest wish."

ALAIN ROBBE-GRILLET: It is hard to describe. I have an idea of the beginning. I write the first line and continue to the last. I correct a great deal, work hard and write several drafts, but I never question the finished work. So I start with the first words which will be the first words of the book, but I never know how it will develop or end. The first idea is vague, but I know that it is the generating force—later everything can change. I can well imagine Proust writing: "For a long time I used to go to bed early . . ." and not knowing what story he was going to tell.

MAY SARTON: Many of my poems are love poems. I'm only able to write poetry, for the most part, when I have a Muse, a woman who focuses the world for me. She may be a lover, may not. In one case it was a person I saw only once, at lunch in a room with a lot of other people, and I wrote a whole book of poems. Many of these poems have not been published. But this is the mystery. Something happens which touches the source of poetry and ignites it. Sometimes it is the result of a long love affair, as with "The Divorce of Lovers" poems, the sonnet sequence. But not always. So who is the audience for my poetry? The audience is the loved one for me. But usually "the loved one" isn't really interested in the poems.

IRWIN SHAW: Watching, listening, remembering. A lot of them from my friends or people I meet. Sometimes from a general feeling or belief which is strong enough to make me invent characters and situations to state it. For example, my story "The Eighty-Yard Run," which was about an ex-football player, a minor hero, who turns into a complete failure by the age of thirty-five, came as a result of my seeing around me so many men, all of whose best moments had come in their youth. I wanted to express that and show the subtle disappointments and inadequacies which bring so many promising young men to failure so early. Americans are at their best in their youth, and for me, at least, nothing is more characteristic of that best side and best moment of Americans than the race down the football field under a kickoff, in which are mingled gaiety, grace, recklessness, good-humored ferocity, skill at high speed, all taking place in a particular atmosphere of health and holiday that is duplicated nowhere else in the world. It was a productive symbol both for me and for the reader, and I built my story around the feelings of past joy and present regret that remembering it gave me.

STEPHEN SPENDER: There are two theories of inspiration. One idea is that poetry can actually be dictated to you, like it was to William Blake. You are in a hallucinated state, and you hear a voice or you are in communication with something outside, like James Merrill's new poem, which he says is dictated through the Ouija board by Auden and other people.

The other idea is Paul Valéry's, what he calls *une ligne donnée*, that you are given one line and you try to follow up this clue, pulling the whole poem out of it. My own experience is that a rhythm or something comes into my head which I feel I must do, I must write it, create it.

For example, I recall looking out of a railway window and seeing an industrial landscape, factories, slag heaps, and the line coming into my head: "A language of flesh and roses." The thought at the back of this was that the industrial landscape was a language, what people have made out of nature, the contrast of nature and the industrial, "A language of flesh and roses." The problem of the poem was to work this connection out, trying to go back to remember what you really thought at that instant, and trying to re-create it. If I think of a poem, I may spend six months writing, but what I am really trying to do is remember what I thought of at that instant.

GERTRUDE STEIN: I was walking in the gardens of the Luxembourg in Paris it was the end of summer the grass was yellow I was sorry that it was the end of summer and I saw the big fat pigeons in the yellow grass and I said to myself, pigeons on the yellow grass, alas, and I kept on writing pigeons on the grass, alas, short longer grass short longer longer shorter yellow grass pigeons large pigeons on the shorter longer yellow grass, alas pigeons on the grass, and I kept on writing until I had emptied myself of the emotion. If a mother is full of her emotion toward a child in the bath the mother will talk and talk and talk until the emotion is over and that's the way a writer is about an emotion.

ROBERT PENN WARREN: Something I read or see stays in my head for five or six years. I always remember the date, the place, the room, the road, when I first was struck. For instance, *World Enough and Time*. Katherine Anne Porter and I were both at the Library of Congress as Fellows. We were in the same pew, had offices next to each other. She came in one day with an old pamphlet, the trial of Beauchamp for killing Colonel Sharp. She said, "Well, Red, you better read this." There it was. I read it in five minutes. But I was six years making the book. Any book I write starts with a flash but takes a long time to shape up. All of your first versions are in your head so by the time you sit down to write you have some line developed in your head.

TENNESSEE WILLIAMS: The process by which the idea for a play comes to me has always been something I really couldn't pinpoint. A play just seems to materialize, like an apparition it gets clearer and clearer and clearer. It's very vague at first, as in the case of *Streetcar,* which came after *Menagerie.* I simply had the vision of a woman in her late youth. She was sitting in a chair all alone by a window with the moonlight streaming in on her desolate face, and she'd been stood up by the man she planned to marry.

I believe I was thinking of my sister because she was madly in love with some young man at the International Shoe Company who paid her court. He was extremely handsome, and she was profoundly in love with him. Whenever the phone would ring, she'd nearly faint. She'd think it was he calling for a date, you know? They saw each other every other night, and then one time he just didn't call anymore. That was when Rose first began to go into a mental decline. From that vision *Streetcar* evolved. I called it, at the time, *Blanche's Chair in the Moon,* which is a very bad title. But it was from that image, you know, of a woman sitting by a window that *Streetcar* came to me.

On the Audience

Those who write clearly have readers; those who write
obscurely have commentators.　　　　　　—ALBERT CAMUS

I've written some poetry I don't understand myself.
　　　　　　—CARL SANDBURG

Those big-shot writers . . . could never dig the fact that there
are more salted peanuts consumed than caviar.
　　　　　　—MICKEY SPILLANE

To have great poets, there must be great audiences, too.
　　　　　　—WALT WHITMAN

MAYA ANGELOU: It's myself . . . and my reader. I would be a liar, a hypocrite, or a fool—and I'm not any of those—to say that I don't write for the reader. I do. But for the reader who hears, who really will work at it, going behind what I seem to say. So I write for myself and that reader who will pay the dues. There's a phrase in West Africa, in Ghana; it's called "deep talk." For instance, there's a saying: "The trouble for the thief is not how to steal the chief's bugle, but where to blow it." Now, on the face of it, one understands that. But when you really think about it, it takes you deeper. In West Africa they call that "deep talk." I'd like to think I write "deep talk." When you read me, you should be able to say "Gosh, that's pretty. That's lovely. That's nice. Maybe there's something else? Better read it again."

W. H. AUDEN: I just try to put the thing out and hope somebody will read it. Someone says: "Whom do you write for?" I reply: "Do you read me?" If they say "Yes," I say, "Do you like it?" If they say "No," then I say, "I don't write for you."

SAUL BELLOW: In bed last night I was reading a collection of articles by Stendhal. One of them amused me very much, touched me. Stendhal was saying how lucky writers were in the age of Louis XIV not to have anyone take them very seriously. Their obscurity was very valuable. Corneille had been dead for several days before anyone at court considered the fact important enough to mention. In the 19th century, says Stendhal, there would have been several public orations, Corneille's funeral covered by all the papers. There are great advantages in not being taken *too* seriously. Some writers are excessively serious about themselves. They accept the ideas of the "cultivated public." There is such a thing as overcapitalizing the A in Artist. Certain writers and musicians understand this. Stravinsky says the composer should practice his trade exactly as a shoemaker does. Mozart and Haydn accepted commissions—wrote to order. In the 19th century, the artist loftily waited for Inspiration. Once you elevate yourself to the rank of a cultural institution, you're in for a lot of trouble.

· · ·

I have in mind another human being who will understand me. I count on this. Not on perfect understanding, which is Cartesian, but on approximate understanding, which is Jewish. And on a meeting of sympathies, which is human. But I have no ideal reader in my head, no. Let me say just this, too. I seem to have the blind self-acceptance of the eccentric who can't conceive that his eccentricities are not clearly understood.

HEINRICH BÖLL: My "imaginary reader" can be "uneducated," but with a vacillating optimism that sometimes approaches pessimism. I still consider language to be a means of communication with this reader. Even complicated events—which form topics in essays or reviews—are communicable to the "uneducated" reader. The most difficult aspect of writing, considering my "imaginary reader," is being able to be understood without having to compromise by making something easy that isn't easy, or by making something unnecessarily difficult when it is easy in the first place.

JORGE LUIS BORGES: Perhaps a few personal friends of mine. Not myself because I never reread what I've written. I'm far too afraid to feel ashamed of what I've done.

JOSEPH BRODSKY: As I write I think about Auden, what he would say—would he find it rubbish, or kind of entertaining? Auden and Orwell.

ANTHONY BURGESS: The ideal reader of my novels is a lapsed Catholic and failed musician, short-sighted, color-blind, auditorially biased, who has read the books that I have read. He should also be about my age.

JOHN CHEEVER: All sorts of pleasant and intelligent people read the books and write thoughtful letters about them. I don't know who they are, but they are marvelous and seem to live quite independently of the prejudices of advertising, journalism, and the cranky academic world. Think of the books that have enjoyed independent lives. *Let Us Now Praise Famous Men. Under the Volcano. Henderson the Rain King.* A splendid book like *Humboldt's Gift* was received with confusion and dismay, but hundreds of thousands of people went out and bought hardcover copies. The room where I work has a window looking into a wood, and I like to think that these earnest, lovable, and mysterious readers are in there.

JEAN COCTEAU: You are always concentrated on the inner thing. The moment one becomes aware of the crowd—performs for the crowd—it is spectacle. It is *fichu.*

DON DELILLO: When my head is in the typewriter the last thing on my mind is some imaginary reader. I don't have an audience; I have a set of standards. But when I think of my work out in the world, written and published, I like to imagine it's being read by some stranger somewhere who doesn't have anyone around him to talk to about books and writing— maybe a would-be writer, maybe a little lonely, who depends on a certain kind of writing to make him feel more comfortable in the world.

J. P. DONLEAVY: I suppose very isolated, lonely folk. I remember one letter from a girl in a Midwestern town who read one of my books and thought she had discovered it—that no one had ever read it or knew about it. Then one day in her local library she found cards for one or two of my other books. They were full of names—the books were borrowed all the time. She resented this a bit and then walked around the town looking in everybody's face and wondering if they were the ones who were reading my books. That is someone I write for.

MARGARET DRABBLE: What really annoys me are the ones who write to say, I am doing your book for my final examinations and could you please tell me what the meaning of it is. I find it just so staggering—that you're supposed to explain the meaning of your book to some total stranger! If I knew what the meanings of my books were, I wouldn't have bothered to write them.

WILLIAM FAULKNER: I myself am too busy to care about the public. I have no time to wonder who is reading me. I don't care about John Doe's opinion on my or anyone else's work. Mine is the standard which has to be met, which is when the work makes me feel the way I do when I read *La Tentation de Saint-Antoine*, or the Old Testament. They make me feel good. So does watching a bird make me feel good. You know that if I were reincarnated, I'd want to come back a buzzard. Nothing hates him or envies him or wants him or needs him. He is never bothered or in danger, and he can eat anything.

WILLIAM GADDIS: When I write I *don't* think of the audience. After the fact I think, "Well there. I hope they like it."

GABRIEL GARCÍA MÁRQUEZ: In general I think you usually do write for someone. When I'm writing I'm always aware that this friend is going to like this, or that another friend is going to like that paragraph or chapter, always thinking of specific people. In the end all books are written for your friends. The problem after writing *One Hundred Years of Solitude* was that now I no longer know whom of the millions of readers I am writing for; this upsets and inhibits me. It's like a million eyes are looking at you and you don't really know what they think.

WILLIAM GASS: I don't think much about the reader. Ways of reading are adversaries—those theoretical ways. As far as writing something is concerned, the reader really doesn't exist. The writer's business is somehow to create in the work something which will stand on its own and make its own demands; and if the writer is good, he discovers what those demands are, and he meets them, and creates this thing which readers can then do what they like with. Gertrude Stein said, "I write for myself and strangers," and then eventually she said that she wrote only for herself. I think she should have taken one further step. You don't write *for* anybody. People who send you bills do that. People who want to sell you things so they can send you bills do that. People who want to tell you things so they can sell you things so they can send you bills do that. You are advancing an art—the art. That is what you are trying to do.

KEN KESEY: I was in a quandary about my audience when I was working on *Notion* until I realized that I'm not writing for the east coast literary establishment. I am writing for Mountain Girl and Jerry Garcia's oldest girl, Annabelle—she's a great Stephen King fan. She just reads and reads. She likes something that's got a little zip to it. At one point, I realized that's whom I'm writing for. If Annabelle Garcia reads this book, gets excited and grins about it, then I have hit my audience, and all the rest just ricochets.

NORMAN MAILER: I suppose it's that audience which has no tradition by which to measure their experience but the intensity and clarity of their inner lives. That's the audience I'd like to be good enough to write for.

ARTHUR MILLER: There are some biological laws in the theater which can't be violated. It should not be made into an activated chess game. You can't have a theater based upon anything other than a mass audience if it's going to succeed. The larger the better. It's the law of the theater. In the Greek audience fourteen thousand people sat down at the same time to see a play. Fourteen thousand people! And nobody can tell me that those people were all readers of *The New York Review of Books*! Even Shakespeare was smashed around in his time by university people. I think for much the same reasons—because he was reaching for those parts of man's makeup which respond to melodrama, broad comedy, violence, dirty words, and blood. Plenty of blood, murder, and not very well motivated at that.

· · ·

People are pretty primitive—they really want the thing to turn out all right. After all, for a century and half *King Lear* was played in England with a happy ending. I wrote a radio play about the boy who wrote that version—William Ireland—who forged Shakespeare's plays, and edited *King Lear* so that it conformed to a middle-class view of life. They thought, including all but Malone, who was the first good critic, that this was the real Shakespeare. He was an expert forger. He fixed up several of the other plays, but this one he really rewrote. He was seventeen years old. And they produced it—it was a big success—and Boswell thought it was the greatest thing he'd ever seen, and so did all the others. The only one was Malone, who on the basis of textual impossibilities—aside from the fact that he sensed it was a bowdlerization—proved that it couldn't have been Shakespeare. It's what I was talking about before: the litmus paper of the playwright: you see Ireland sensed quite correctly what those people really wanted from *King Lear,* and he gave it to them. He sentimentalized it; took out any noxious references. It ended with a kind of happy family reunion . . . like a Jewish melodrama. A family play.

. . .

There's a wonderful naivete that the Parisian theater public has; they're not bored to death. They're not coming in out of the rain, so to speak, with nothing better to do. When they go to the theater, it has great weight with them. They come to see something that'll change their lives. Ninety percent of the time, of course, there's nothing there, but they're open to a grand experience. This is not the way we go to the theater.

JOHN MORTIMER: I found writing novels rather a lonely business. You very rarely actually catch anyone reading them. I've heard of a novelist who got onto the tube at Piccadilly Circus for the purpose of getting out at Green Park, a distance of one stop. And as he got onto the tube he found himself sitting next to a girl who was in fact reading one of his novels. And he knew that two hundred pages further on there was a joke. So he sat on till Cockfosters, the end of the line, in the faint hope of hearing a laugh which never came.

PATRICK O'BRIAN: I have never written for an audience. On the other hand I do not write merely to please myself. When words are flowing faster than one's pen can catch them, writing is a strong though wearing delight; but these splendid bursts are rare and they are paid for by many, many days of only a thousand words or so, and long periods of silent reflection. And for me the process works best with no interruption, no breaks in the steady application, no letters to be answered, very little social life, no holidays; it is therefore a form of happy imprisonment to which no man would submit without at least the hope of publication and its rewards, often dimly seen, often illusory.

EDNA O'BRIEN: When you are writing you are not conscious of the reader, so that you don't feel embarrassed. I'm sure Joyce had a most heady and wonderful time writing the last fifty pages of *Ulysses*—glorious Molly Bloom. He must have written it in one bout, thinking: I'll show the women of the world that I am omniscient!

WALKER PERCY: I hold out for some sort of contractual relationship between novelist and reader, however flawed, misapprehended or fragmentary. Perhaps the contract is ultimately narratological, perhaps not.

But something keeps—or fails to keep—the reader reading the next sentence. Even the "antinovel" presupposes some sort of contractual venture at the very moment the "antinovelist" is attacking narrativity. Such a venture implies that the writer is up to something, going abroad like Don Quixote—if only to attack windmills—and that the reader is with him. Otherwise why would the latter bother? The antinovelist is like a Protestant. His protests might be valid, but where would he be without the Catholic Church? I have no objection to "antihistory" novels. What I object to is any excursion by the author which violates the novelistic contract between writer and reader which I take to be an intersubjective transaction entailing the transmission of a set of symbols, a text. The writer violates the contract when he trashes the reader by pornography or scatological political assaults, e.g., depicting President Nixon in a novel buggering Ethel Rosenberg in Times Square, or LBJ plotting the assassination of JFK. Take pornography, a difficult, slippery case. It is not necessary to get into a discussion of First Amendment rights—for all I know it has them. And for all I know, pornography has its uses. All I suggest is that pornography and literature stimulate different organs. If we can agree that a literary text is a set of signals transmitted from sender to receiver in a certain code, pornography is a different set of signals and a different code.

S. J. PERELMAN: I don't know if that grocer on my shoulder digs all the references, but other than him, I write pretty much for myself. If, at the close of business each evening, I myself can understand what I've written, I feel the day hasn't been totally wasted.

PHILIP ROTH: I occasionally have an anti-Roth reader in mind. I think, "How he is going to hate this!" That can be just the encouragement I need.

GEORGE SEFERIS: This situation of not having a very large audience has something good in it too. I mean that it educates you in a certain way: not to consider that great audiences are the most important reward on this earth. I consider that even if I have three people who read me, I mean really read me, it is enough. That reminds me of a conversation I had once upon a time during the only glimpse I ever had of Henri Michaux. It was when he had a stopover in Athens, coming from Egypt, I think. He came ashore while his ship was in Piraeus just in order to have a look at the Acropolis. And he told me on that occasion: "You know, my dear, a man who has only one reader is not a writer. A man who has two readers is not a writer either. But a man who has *three* readers (and he pronounced "three readers" as though they were three million), that man is *really* a writer."

. . .

I'm sorry to say that I never felt I was the spokesman for anything or anybody. There are no credentials which appoint anybody to be a spokesman for something. Now others consider that a sort of function which must be performed; but I think that is, after all, why I have written so little. I've never felt the obligation; I have to consider only that I am not dried up as a poet and to write. I mean that has been my feeling from the very beginning. I remember when I published my first book, there were lots of people who said: "Mr. Seferis, you must now try to show us that you can do more." I answered them: "Gentlemen, you must consider that every poem published by me is the last one. I never have any feeling about its continuation." My last poem. And if I write another one, it's a great blessing.

IRWIN SHAW: I wrote "The Girls in Their Summer Dresses" one morning while my wife, Marian, was lying in bed and reading. And I knew I had something good there, but I didn't want her to read it, knowing that the reaction would be violent, to say the least, because it's about a man who tells his wife that he's going to be unfaithful to her. So I turned it face-down, and I said, "Don't read this yet. It's not ready." It was the only copy I had. Then I went out and took a walk, had a drink, and came back. She was raging around the room. She said, "It's a lucky thing you came back just now, because I was going to open the window and throw it out." Since then she's become reconciled to it, and I think she reads it with pleasure, too.

. . .

I have a fine play in mind I'll write for them [theater audiences] someday. The curtain slides up on a stage bare except for a machine gun facing the audience. Then after a pause in which the audience is given time to rustle their paper bags and their programs, wheeze and cough and settle in their seats, the actor enters. He's a tall man dressed in evening clothes. He comes downstage to the footlights and after a little bow smiles charmingly at the audience, giving them more time to mumble and rustle and cough and whisper and settle in their seats. Then he walks upstage, adjusts the machine gun, and blasts them.

SUSAN SONTAG: I don't write because there's an audience. I write because there is literature.

WILLIAM STAFFORD: I think language does bring us together. Fragile and misleading as it is, it's the best communication we've got, and poetry is language at its most intense and potentially fulfilling. Poems do bring people together. And not just the people who come to a workshop. But everybody—they are addicts of poetry without knowing it. Walking down the street, someone comes out of church and says, "Oh, Bill, hello, been writing? How come people don't pay any attention to poetry these days?" When they've just been in church with hundreds of people reciting the Psalms in responsive readings, singing the songs, responding to the rhymes in the hymns. They are addicted to it. They're victims of it. And yet they come out and say, "How come people aren't interested in poetry?" It's because they've compartmentalized their minds. Maybe it's our fault that they feel that poems only appear in literary magazines. Poetry is everywhere. Here I am preaching about it. Oh yes, I think it brings people together. When they go to church and they hear, "Though I speak with the tongues of men and of angels, and have not love," and so on, they're into poetry.

JOHN STEINBECK: I've always tried out my material on my dogs first. You know, with Angel, he sits there and listens and I get the feeling he understands everything. But with Charley, I always felt he was just waiting to get a word in edgewise. Years ago, when my red setter chewed up the manuscript of *Of Mice and Men,* I said at the time that the dog must have been an excellent literary critic.

WILLIAM STYRON: Faulkner doesn't give enough help to the reader. I'm all for the complexity of Faulkner, but not for the confusion. That goes for Joyce, too. All that fabulously beautiful poetry in the last part of *Finnegans Wake* is pretty much lost to the world simply because not many people are ever going to put up with the chaos that precedes it. As for *The Sound and the Fury,* I think it succeeds in spite of itself. Faulkner often simply stays too damn intense for too long a time. It ends up being great stuff, somehow, though, and the marvel is how it could be so wonderful being pitched for so long in that one high, prolonged, delirious key.

JAMES THURBER: Someone once wrote a definition of the difference between English and American humor. I wish I could remember his name. I thought his definition very good. He said that the English treat the commonplace as if it were remarkable and the Americans treat the remarkable as if it were commonplace. I believe that's true of humorous writing. Years ago we did a parody of *Punch* in which Benchley did a short piece depicting a wife bursting into a room and shouting, "The primroses are in bloom"—treating the commonplace as remarkable, you see. In *The Secret Life of Walter Mitty* I tried to treat the remarkable as commonplace.

JOHN UPDIKE: When I write, I aim in my mind not toward New York but toward a vague spot a little to the east of Kansas. I think of the books on library shelves, without their jackets, years old, and a countryish teenaged boy finding them, and having them speak to him. The reviews, the stacks in Brentano's, are just hurdles to get over, to place the books on that shelf.

EUDORA WELTY: At the time of writing, I don't write for my friends or myself, either; I write for *it*, for the pleasure of *it*. I believe if I stopped to wonder what So-and-so would think, or what I'd feel like if this were read by a stranger, I would be paralyzed. I care what my friends think, very deeply—and it's only after they've read the finished thing that I really can rest, deep down. But in the writing, I have to just keep going straight through with only the *thing* in mind and what it dictates.

It's so much an inward thing that reading the proofs later can be a real shock. When I received them for my first book—no, I guess it was for *Delta Wedding*—I thought, *I* didn't write this. It was a page of dialogue—I might as well have never seen it before. I wrote to my editor, John Woodburn, and told him something had happened to that page in the typesetting. He was kind, not even surprised—maybe this happens to all writers. He called me up and read me from the manuscript—word for word what the proofs said. Proofs don't shock me any longer, yet there's still a strange moment with every book when I move from the position of writer to the position of reader, and I suddenly see my words with the eyes of the cold public. It gives me a terrible sense of exposure, as if I'd gotten sunburned.

JOHN HALL WHEELOCK: I think it was a Spanish poet—it may have been Calderón—who said that all his life he had been like a swimmer who could only use one arm, because with the other arm he had to hold his poems up over the waters. The things that he really cared about. It's strange, but we live in a world which is even more alienated from poetry than it used to be; most people don't care or know anything about poetry.

Most civilized, cultivated people know something about painting, they go to galleries; they know something about music, they go to concerts; but no one cares or knows anything about poetry except the poets themselves. Since the poets don't expect anyone else to read them, many of them have devised a way of communicating with one another through their poems, and readers often find such poetry difficult. Prose is, of course, easier.

On Performance

Write something, even if it's just a suicide note. —Anon.

If . . . it makes my whole body so cold no fire can warm me, I
know that is poetry. —Emily Dickinson

When my horse is running good, I don't stop to give him sugar.
—William Faulkner

I listen to the voices. —William Faulkner

Genius is the ability to put into effect what is in your mind.
—F. Scott Fitzgerald

When I described how Emma Bovary poisoned herself, I had
such a strong taste of arsenic in my mouth, I was so poisoned
myself, that I had two attacks of indigestion, one after the other,
very real attacks, for I vomited my entire dinner.
—Gustave Flaubert

How do I know what I think until I see what I say?
—E. M. Forster

They can't yank a novelist like they can a pitcher. A novelist
has to go the full nine, even if it kills him.
—Ernest Hemingway

We are all apprentices in a craft where no one ever becomes a
master. —Ernest Hemingway

I have seldom written poetry unless I was rather out of health,
and the experience, though pleasurable, was generally agitating
and exhausting. —A. E. Houseman

Who casts a living line, must sweat. —Ben Jonson

The idea is to get the pencil moving quickly.
—Bernard Malamud

There is no need for the writer to eat a whole sheep to be able
to tell what mutton tastes like. It is enough if he eats a cutlet.
—Somerset Maugham

Nothing, unless it is difficult, is worth while. —OVID

All bad poetry springs from genuine feeling. —OSCAR WILDE

EDWARD ALBEE: Naturally, no writer who's any good at all would sit down and put a sheet of paper in a typewriter and start typing a play unless he knew what he was writing about. But at the same time, writing has got to be an act of discovery. Finding out things about what one is writing about. To a certain extent I imagine a play is completely finished in my mind—in my case at any rate—without my knowing it, before I sit down to write. So in that sense, I suppose, writing a play is *finding out* what the play is. I always find that the better answer to give. It's a question I despise, and it always seems to me better to slough off the answer to a question which I consider to be a terrible invasion of privacy—the kind of privacy that a writer must keep for himself. If you intellectualize and examine the creative process too carefully, it can evaporate and vanish. It's not only terribly difficult to talk about, it's also dangerous. You know the old story about the—I think it's one of Aesop's Fables, or perhaps not, or a Chinese story—about the very clever animal that saw a centipede that he didn't like. He said, "My God, it's amazing and marvelous how you walk with all those hundreds and hundreds of legs. How do you do it? How do you get them all moving that way?" The centipede stopped and thought and said, "Well, I take the left front leg and then I—" and he thought about it for a while, and he couldn't walk.

KINGSLEY AMIS: Graham Greene said he would find an episode or a character turning up after the first ten thousand words which he had no idea how to use. But then thirty thousand words later it would come up. And experience had taught him never to destroy what he had written, because it would always be fitted into the design later.

MARTIN AMIS: I would say they are more *inspirers* than influences. When I am stuck with a sentence that isn't fully born, it isn't yet there, I sometimes think: How would Dickens go at this sentence, how would Bellow or Nabokov go at this sentence? What you hope to emerge with is how *you* would go at that sentence, but you get a little shove in the back by thinking about writers you admire. I was once winding up a telephone conversation with Saul Bellow and he said, "Well you go back to work now," and I said all right, and he said, "Give 'em hell." And it's Dickens saying, "Give 'em hell." Give the reader hell. Stretch the reader.

JOHN BARTH: It is simply this: a writer has to take all the risks of putting down what he sees. No one can tell him about that. No one can control that reality. It reminds me of something Pablo Picasso was supposed to have said to Gertrude Stein while he was painting her portrait. Gertrude said, "I don't look like that." And Picasso replied, "You will." And he was right.

· · ·

I have a pretty good sense of where the book is going to go. By temperament I am an incorrigible formalist, not inclined to embark on a project without knowing where I'm going. It takes me about four years to write a novel. To embark on such a project without some idea of what the landfall and the estimated time of arrival were would be rather alarming. But I have learned from experience that there are certain barriers that you cannot cross until you get to them; in a thing as long and complicated as a novel you may not even know the real shape of the obstacle until you heave in sight of it, much less how you're going to get around it. I can see in my plans that there will be this enormous pothole to cross somewhere around the third chapter from the end; I'll get out my little pocket calculator and estimate that the pothole will be reached about the second of July, 1986, let's say, and then just trust to God and the muses that by the time I get there I'll know how to get around it.

TRUMAN CAPOTE: Work is the only device I know of. Writing has laws of perspective, of light and shade, just as painting does, or music. If you are born knowing them, fine. If not, learn them. Then rearrange the rules to suit yourself. Even Joyce, our most extreme disregarder, was a superb craftsman; he could write *Ulysses because* he could write *Dubliners.* Too many writers seem to consider the writing of short stories as a kind of finger exercise. Well, in such cases, it is certainly only their fingers they are exercising.

· · ·

Since each story presents its own technical problems, obviously one can't generalize about them on a $2 \times 2 = 4$ basis. Finding the right form for your story is simply to realize the most *natural* way of telling the story. The test of whether or not a writer has divined the natural shape of his story is just this: after reading it, can you imagine it differently, or does it silence your imagination and seem to you absolute and final? As an orange is final. As an orange is something nature has made just right.

JEAN COCTEAU: I feel myself inhabited by a force or being—very little known to me. *It gives* the orders; I follow. The conception of my novel *Les Enfants Terribles* came to me from a friend, from what he told me of a circle: a family closed from societal life. I commenced to write: exactly seventeen pages per day. It went well. I was pleased with it. Very. There was in the original life story some connection with America, and I had something I wanted to say about America. Poof! The being in me did not want to write that! Dead halt. A month of stupid staring at paper unable to say anything. One day it commenced again in its own way.

· · ·

When it goes well—the euphoria of such moments has been much the most intense and joyous of my life experience.

JULIO CORTÁZAR: It's like improvising in jazz. You don't ask a jazz musician, "But what are you going to play?" He'll laugh at you. He has a theme, a series of chords he has to respect, and then he takes up his trumpet or his saxophone and he begins. It's not a question of *idea*. He performs through a series of different internal pulsations. Sometimes it comes out well, sometimes it doesn't. It's the same with me. I'm a bit embarrassed to sign my stories sometimes. The novels, no, because the novels I work on a lot; there's a whole architecture. But my stories, it's as if they were dictated to me by something that is in me, but it's not me who's responsible. Well, since it does appear they are mine even so, I guess I should accept them!

ROBERTSON DAVIES: I do know the story when I begin, but I don't know how it's going to end. I know about two-thirds of it, and then the end emerges as I go on. I shrink from saying this, but I've agreed to come here and talk about it, and it's true: I hear the story, I am told the story, I record the story. I don't pretend that some remarkable person somewhere else is whispering in my ear, or that a beautiful lady in a diaphanous garment is telling me what I should write. It is just part of my own creative process which I am not immediately in touch with and certainly not in full control of. And so the story emerges. There can be no two ways about how it's going to end. It just ends the way it's going to end. I don't think that that is very mysterious, for if the story is any good, it must have an inevitability, although some critics dispute that. They say they're full of coincidence and this, that or the other; but the fact is that my life seems to be much fuller of coincidence and curious happenings than the lives of critics. What I mean is, the kind of mind which makes a critic is an analytical, cool, infinitely, unenviably, cautious mind. A recent professorial criticism of *What's Bred in the Bone* was very severe with me for my attraction to arcane lore and weird belief—no use explaining that to me the arcane lore isn't arcane at all, and makes wonderful sense, and that almost all belief is strange, if you catch it with the light falling on it in a certain way. I wish professorial critics, who often write so dully, would give me the credit for a minimum of wits, and stop elevating themselves as the standard by which all belief and understanding should be measured! What sort of books would Balzac and Dickens have written if they had listened to such stuff?

· · ·

My family background was Welsh, and the Welsh are very, very fond of storytelling and tend to be rather good at it. They're also fond of children, but they are not in the modern way infinitely tolerant of children. They think children need to be *taught* and they *teach* them. They teach them very often through stories. I feel that this quality of storytelling is basic to the novelist's art. Sometimes I am asked to talk to groups of students about writing, and the poor souls are filled to the brim with all the complex business about theories and types of narrative and this, that and the other. What I say to them is, "If you're a writer, a real writer, you're a descendant of those medieval storytellers who used to go into the square of a town and spread a little mat on the ground and sit on it and beat on a bowl and say, 'If you give a copper coin I will tell you a golden tale.' If the storyteller had what it took, he collected a little group and told them a golden tale until it got to the most exciting point and then he passed the bowl again. That was the way he made his living, and if he failed to hold his audience, he was through and had to take up some other line of work. Now this is what a writer must do." I get so sick of writers who make tedious demands on their readers and expect them to bear with them through infinitely refined analyses of meaning and this, that and the other. You really must have a story and you must tell it, or people will just put the book down and they will find it to be one of those books (unlike the ones you sometimes read about in book reviews) that once put down is impossible to take up again.

DON DELILLO: I think the scene comes first, an idea of a character in a place. It's visual, it's Technicolor—something I see in a vague way. Then sentence by sentence into the breach. No outlines—maybe a short list of items, chronological, that may represent the next twenty pages. But the basic work is built around the sentence. This is what I mean when I call myself a writer. I construct sentences. There's a rhythm I hear that drives me through a sentence. And the words typed on the white page have a sculptural quality. They form odd correspondences. They match up not just through meaning but through sound and look. The rhythm of a sentence will accommodate a certain number of syllables. One syllable too many, I look for another word. There's always another word that means nearly the same thing, and if it doesn't then I'll consider altering the meaning of a sentence to keep the rhythm, the syllable beat. I'm completely willing to let language press meaning upon me. Watching the way in which words match up, keeping the balance in a sentence—these are sensuous pleasures. I might want *very* and *only* in the same sentence, spaced a particular way, exactly so far apart. I might want *rapture* matched with *danger*—I like to match word endings. I type rather than write longhand because I like the way the words and letters look when they come off the hammers onto the page—finished, printed, beautifully formed.

JAMES DICKEY: One of the difficulties in writing poetry is to maintain your sense of excitement and discovery about what you write. American literature is full of people who started off excited about poetry and their own contribution to it and their own relationship to poetry and have had, say, a modicum of success and have just gone on writing poetry as a kind of tic, a sort of reflex, when they've lost all their original excitement and enthusiasm for what they do. They do it because they have learned to do it, and that's what they *do*. You have to find private stratagems to keep up your original enthusiasm, no matter what it takes. As you get older, that's tougher and tougher to do. You want to try to avoid, if you possibly can, the feeling of doing it simply because you *can* do it.

E. L. DOCTOROW: As the book goes on it becomes inevitable. Your choices narrow, the thing picks up speed. And there's the exhilaration of a free ride—like a downhill ski run. You know before you get there what the last scene is. Sometimes what the last line is. But even if none of that happens, even if you find yourself at the end before you expected to, a kind of joy breaks over you, spills out of your eyes. And you realize you've finished. And then you want to be sure, you see. You need confirmation. You ask somebody you love to read it and see if it works. I remember when I finished *The Book of Daniel.* We were living in a house on the beach in Southern California. One of those houses with sliding glass doors for windows. I asked my wife if she would read the manuscript. She said she would be pleased to. And I left her sitting and reading with the sun coming through those big windows, and I went for a walk on the beach. It was a Sunday and the beach was crowded; they really use their beaches in California, every inch of them. Back toward the road were the volleyball players and the kite flyers. Boys throwing footballs or Frisbees. Then the sunbathers, the children with their sandpails, the families. Then the runners splashing along at the edge of the surf. Or the people looking for little shells in the tide pools in the rocks. Then the swimmers. Beyond them the surfers in their wet suits waiting on their boards. Further out snorkelers' flags bobbing in the water. Out past the buoys the water skiers tearing along. Or rising into the air in their parachutes. And beyond that sailboats, flotillas of them, to the horizon. And all in this light. It was like a Brueghel, a Southern Californian Brueghel. I walked for several hours and thought about my book, and worried in my mind, in that California light worrying about this dark book, very much a New York City book. Was it done? Was it any good? And I came back to the house in the late afternoon, the house in shadows now, and there was Helen sitting in the same chair and the manuscript was all piled upside down on the table and she couldn't speak; she was crying, there were these enormous tears running down her cheeks, and it was the most incredible moment—never before had I known such happiness.

JOHN DOS PASSOS: You get a great deal off your chest—emotions, impressions, opinions. Curiosity urges you on—the driving force. What is collected must be got rid of. That's one thing to be said about writing. There is a great sense of relief in a fat volume.

MARGARET DRABBLE: I've often worried about this—if one got really very happy in life, one might not want to write at all. I think grief is creative. And, in some awful way, boredom is creative. When I'm really deeply bored (inevitably I'm rather miserable at the same time) I find this a creative phase because one's got to get something. One's got to rise out of it in some way. And the way that I'm most familiar with is by writing.

LAWRENCE DURRELL: Poetry is form, and the wooing and seduction of form is the whole game. You can have all the apparatus in the world, but what you finally need is something like a—I don't know what—a lasso . . . a very delicate thing, for catching wild deer. Oh, no, I'll give you an analogy for it. To write a poem is like trying to catch a lizard without its tail falling off. In India when I was a boy they had great big green lizards there, and if you shouted or shot them their tails would fall off. There was only one boy in the school who could catch lizards intact. No one knew quite how he did it. He had a special soft way of going up to them, and he'd bring them back with their tails on. That strikes me as the best analogy I can give you. To try and catch your poem without its tail falling off.

LEON EDEL: It's a little like falling in love; at any rate that's the way it usually begins. You never know how long the affair or the infatuation will last. Of course, it's a one-sided love affair since the love object is dead or, if alive, relatively unwooable. Most biographies are begun out of enchantment or affection; you read a poem and want to find the poet, you hear a statesman and are filled with admiration, or you are stirred by the triumphs of a general or an admiral. In the writing of the life changes occur, discoveries are made. Realities emerge. The love affair, however exhilarating, has to be terminated if a useful biography is to emerge. Sometimes there is disenchantment and even hate; the biographer feels deceived. Isn't that the way all love affairs run—from dream and cloud-journey to earth-firmness?

E. M. FORSTER: People will not realize how little conscious one is of these things; how one flounders about. They want us to be so much better informed than we are. If critics could only have a course on writers' *not* thinking things out—a course of lectures.

ROBERT FROST: Very first one I wrote I was walking home from school and I began to make it—a March day—and I was making it all afternoon and making it so I was late at my grandmother's for dinner. I finished it, but it burned right up, just burned right up, you know. And what started that? What burned it? So many talk, I wonder how falsely, about what it costs them, what agony it is to write. I've often been quoted: "No tears in the writer, no tears in the reader. No surprise for the writer, no surprise for the reader." But another distinction I made is: however sad, no grievance, grief without grievance. How could I, how could anyone have a good time with what cost me too much agony, how could they? What do I want to communicate but what a *hell* of a good time I had writing it? The whole thing is performance and prowess and feats of association. Why don't critics talk about those things?—what a feat it was to turn that that way, and what a feat it was to remember that, to be reminded of that by this? Why don't they talk about that?

Scoring. You've got to *score*. They say not, but you've got to score—in all the realms—theology, politics, astronomy, history, and the country life around you.

. . .

I look at a poem as a performance. I look on the poet as a man of prowess, just like an athlete. He's a performer. And the things you can do in a poem are very various. You speak of figures, tones of voice varying all the time. I'm always interested, you know, when I have three or four stanzas, in the way I *lay* the sentences in them. I'd hate to have the sentences all lie the same in the stanzas. Every poem is like that: some sort of achievement in performance. Somebody has said that poetry among other things is the marrow of wit. That's probably way back somewhere—marrow of wit. There's got to be wit. And that's very, very much left out of a lot of this labored stuff. It doesn't sparkle at all. Another thing to say is that every thought, poetical or otherwise, every thought is a feat of association. They tell of old Gibbon—as he was dying he was the same Gibbon as his historical parallels. All thought is a feat of association: having what's in front of you bring up something in your mind that you almost didn't know you knew. Putting this and that together. That click.

JOHN GARDNER: Bernard Malamud and I had a conversation one time in which he said that he doesn't know how he does those magnificent things he sometimes does. He just keeps writing until it comes out right. If that's the way a writer works, then that's the way he has to work and that's fine. But I like to be in control as much of the time as possible. One of the first things you have to understand when you are writing fiction— or teaching writing—is that there are different ways of doing things, and each one has a slightly different effect. A misunderstanding of this leads you to the Bill Gass position: that fiction can't tell the truth, because every way you say the thing changes it. I don't think that's to the point. I think that what fiction does is sneak up on the truth by telling it six different ways and finally releasing it. That's what Dante said, that you can't really get at the poetic, inexpressible truths, that the way things are leaps up like steam between them. So you have to determine very accurately the potential of a particular writer's style and help that potential develop at the same time, ignoring what you think of his moral stands.

· · ·

I get great pleasure out of stealing other people's writings. Actually, I do that at least partly because of a peculiar and unfortunate quality of my mind: I remember things. Word for word. I'm not always aware of it. Once in college, I wrote a paragraph of a novel which was word for word out of Joyce's "The Dead," and I wasn't aware of it at all. I absolutely wasn't. My teacher at the time said why did you do this? He wasn't accusing me of plagiarism, he was just saying it was a very odd thing to do. I realized then that I had a problem. Of course, it was a big help when I was a teacher, because I could quote long passages of Beowulf and things like that. Once I realized that I also accidentally quote, that I'm constantly alluding to things I'm not consciously aware of, I began to develop this allusive technique—at least when it's fiction—so that nobody could accuse me of plagiarism since it's so obvious that I'm alluding. In fact, sometimes I have great fun with it. Particularly in *Jason and Medeia,* where I took long sections of writing by Bill Gass, whom I'm enormously fond of, and with whom I completely disagree on almost everything unimportant, and altered a few words to mess up his arguments. And in *The Wreck of Agathon* I took long sections out of Jean-Paul Sartre, changed all the images, but kept the rest directly translated. So I use everything.

ROBERT GRAVES: The leading atomic scientist in Australia agreed with me the other day that time does not really exist. The finished poem is present before it is written and one corrects it. It is the final poem that dictates what is right, what is wrong.

THOM GUNN: T. S. Eliot gave us a pleasing example, didn't he, quoting from people without acknowledgment? I remember a line in *Ash Wednesday* which was an adaptation of "Desiring this man's art and that man's scope." When I was twenty, I thought that was the most terrific line I'd read in Eliot! I didn't know that it was a line from Shakespeare's sonnets. I don't resent that in Eliot and I hope people don't resent it in me. I don't make such extensive use of unacknowledged quotation as Eliot does, but every now and again I'll make a little reference. This is the kind of thing that poets have always done. On the first page of *The Prelude,* Wordsworth slightly rewrites a line from the end of *Paradise Lost:* "The earth is all before me" instead of "The world was all before them." He was aware that many an educated reader would recognize that as being both a theft and an adaptation. He was also aware, I'm sure, that a great many of his readers wouldn't know it was and would just think it was original. That's part of the process of reading: you read a poem for what you can get out of it.

ELIZABETH HARDWICK: I'm not sure I understand the process of writing. There is, I'm sure, something strange about imaginative concentration. The brain slowly begins to function in a different way, to make mysterious connections. Say, it is Monday, and you write a very bad draft, but if you keep on trying, on Friday, words, phrases, appear almost unexpectedly. I don't know why you can't do it on Monday, or why I can't. I'm the same person, no smarter, I have nothing more at hand. I think it's true of a lot of writers. It's one of the things writing students don't understand. They write a first draft and are quite disappointed, or often *should* be disappointed. They don't understand that they have merely begun, and that they may be merely beginning even in the second or third draft.

ERNEST HEMINGWAY: If a writer stops observing he is finished. But he does not have to observe consciously nor think how it will be useful. Perhaps that would be true at the beginning. But later everything he sees goes into the great reserve of things he knows or has seen. If it is any use to know it, I always try to write on the principle of the iceberg. There is seven-eighths of it underwater for every part that shows. Anything you know you can eliminate and it only strengthens your iceberg. It is the part that doesn't show. If a writer omits something because he does not know it then there is a hole in the story.

The Old Man and the Sea could have been over a thousand pages long and had every character in the village in it and all the processes of how they made their living, were born, educated, bore children, etc. That is done excellently and well by other writers. In writing you are limited by what has already been done satisfactorily. So I have tried to learn to do something else. First I have tried to eliminate everything unnecessary to conveying experience to the reader so that after he or she has read something it will become a part of his or her experience and seem actually to have happened. This is very hard to do and I've worked at it very hard.

• • •

The stories you mention I wrote in one day in Madrid on May sixteenth when it snowed out the San Isidro bullfights. First I wrote "The Killers," which I'd tried to write before and failed. Then after lunch I got in bed to keep warm and wrote "Today Is Friday." I had so much juice I thought maybe I was going crazy and I had about six other stories to write. So I got dressed and walked to Fornos, the old bullfighters' café, and drank coffee and then came back and wrote "Ten Indians." This made me very sad and I drank some brandy and went to sleep. I'd forgotten to eat and one of the waiters brought me up some *bacalao* and a small steak and fried potatoes and a bottle of Valdepeñas.

The woman who ran the Pension was always worried that I did not eat enough and she had sent the waiter. I remember sitting up in bed and eating, drinking the Valdepeñas. The waiter said he would bring up another bottle. He said the Señora wanted to know if I was going to write all night. I said no, I thought I would lay off for a while. Why don't you try to write just one more, the waiter asked. I'm only supposed to write one, I said. Nonsense, he said. You could write six. I'll try tomorrow, I said. Try it tonight, he said. What do you think the old woman sent the food up for?

I'm tired, I told him. Nonsense, he said (the word was not nonsense). You tired after three miserable little stories. Translate me one.

Leave me alone, I said. How am I going to write it if you don't leave me alone? So I sat up in bed and drank the Valdepeñas and thought what a hell of a writer I was if the first story was as good as I'd hoped.

JOHN HERSEY: When the writing is really working, I think there is something like dreaming going on. I don't know how to draw the line between the conscious management of what you're doing and this state. It usually takes place in the earlier stages, in the drafting process. I would say that it's related to day-dreaming. When I feel really engaged with a passage, I become so lost in it that I'm unaware of my real surroundings, totally involved in the pictures and sounds that that passage evokes. So I think it's a kind of dream state of some sort, though it has baffled most people who've tried to analyze just what takes place in the creative process. Even Freud, who gave up on almost nothing, seemed to have given up on that. It remains mysterious; and it's probably a good thing that it does. It may be that the mystery is among the things that attract those of us who write.

ARTHUR KOESTLER: If I stop working and just try to enjoy myself, I get very neurotic and guilt-ridden. Orwell was the same. Like the man who, if he stops running, becomes afraid. Or the shark which must move to breathe. But I love playing games like Scrabble. That's not wasting time because it's an effort. Like climbing mountains, which I used to do too. Everything which is an effort is virtuous, is work, and is worth doing.

JERZY KOSINSKI: I think the longest uninterrupted stretch I ever had was twenty-seven hours. I wrote nineteen pages of *The Painted Bird* which in the drafts that followed shrank to one page. On an average I probably "produce" about a page, maybe a page and a half, in a sitting. I write very much the way some of my poet friends do. I select from the novel's master plan, from its topography, a fragment of a scene I find most inspiring at the given time, and then write it moving either "above it" or "below it." Since I start with an image, let's say, of a man being driven in his car through the West Virginia countryside—I might first write about the rain, or his car, or what he felt at the end of the drive, and only then confront the scene's dramatic center. I usually start a novel by writing its opening and its end, which seem to survive relatively unchanged through all the following drafts and galley-proof changes.

PHILIP LEVINE: Over the course of my writing life the process has changed. When I was a kid speaking poetry I never wrote it down; those poems began with a phrase and then I would try to employ the vocabulary and the structure of the phrase to create a fabric of repetitions. When I started writing poetry at eighteen the poems seemed to spring outward from a visual image; it was that precise visual image I was out to capture; that's what excited me; the poem became the means for pushing forward the images I wanted the reader to devour. Then Yeats set me on fire. I mean the language is exalted, yet it sounds like somebody talking and singing at the same time. I thought, *this is it.* And I still kind of feel *this is it.* This is the perfection of form. It's got speech, song, it's high rhetoric and yet it doesn't sound remote or false. A poem like "Easter, 1916." I said, Jesus Christ, this is so much what I want. It doesn't matter about his stupid attitudes. He wrote one poem about his daughter, such a sexist poem.

But it's so beautifully done. I remember telling a woman friend of mine, isn't this an incredible poem? and she got very angry with me; she said it's so sexist, look at this! I said, sure, it's like Eliot's anti-Semitic stuff, "the Jew squats on the windowsill," fuck you Eliot, but the poem is exquisite.

Then somewhere in my forties I hit a kind of phase of automatic writing. I would really be taken, sort of seized, and just write the stuff! It would just come pouring out, hundreds of lines. Then the process of making a poem became quite different: it became seeing what was inside this great blast of language and imagery, and finding the core.

ARCHIBALD MACLEISH: You delight me by saying some of my poems sound as though they had come in a rush, but none of them have with the exception of "You, Andrew Marvell," which was there at the end of a morning and finished by night. I am sure—I mean I am not sure at all but I believe—the master poets must come at their poems as a hawk on a pigeon in one dive. I can't. I chip away like a stonemason who has got it into his head that there is a pigeon in that block of marble. But there's a delight in the chipping. At least there's a delight in it when your hunch that the pigeon in there is stronger than you are carries you along. There is no straining then nor *are* you strained—all assurance and confidence. Oh, you can be fooled, of course—there may be nothing there but a stone. But until you are . . .

. . .

The first discipline is the realization that there *is* a discipline—that all art begins and ends with discipline, that any art is first and foremost a craft. We have gone far enough on the road to self-indulgence now to know that. The man who announces to the world that he is going to "do his thing" is like the amateur on the high-diving platform who flings himself into the void shouting at the judges that he is going to do whatever comes naturally. He will land on his ass. Naturally. You'd think, to listen to the loudspeakers which surround us, that no man had ever tried to "do his thing" before. Every poet worth reading has, but those really worth reading have understood that to do your thing you have to learn first what your thing is and second how to go about doing it. The first is learned by the difficult labor of living, the second by the endless discipline of writing and rewriting and rerewriting. There are no shortcuts. Young writers a while back, misreading Bill Williams, decided to ignore the fact that poems are made of words as sounds as well as of words as signs—decided not to learn the art of words as sounds, not to be bothered with it. They were not interested in poems. They were interested in doing their thing. They did—and that was that.

· · ·

A book takes on its own life in the writing. It has its laws, it becomes a creature to you after a while. One feels a bit like a master who's got a fine animal. Very often I'll feel a certain shame for what I've done with a novel. I won't say it's the novel that's bad; I'll say it's I who was bad. Almost as if the novel did not really belong to me, as if it was something raised by me like a child. I know what's potentially beautiful in my novel, you see. Very often after I've done the novel I realize that that beauty which I recognize in it is not going to be recognized by the reader. I didn't succeed in bringing it out. It's very odd—it's as though I had let the novel down, owed it a duty which I didn't fulfill.

NORMAN MAILER: Occasionally I have to look something up. But I'm always unhappy about that and mistrust the writing which comes out of it. I feel in a way that one's ignorance is part of one's creation, too. I don't know quite how to put it, but for instance if I, as a Jew, am writing about other Jews, and if my knowledge of Jewish culture is exceptionally spotty, as indeed it is, I am not so sure that that isn't an advantage in creating a modern American Jew. Because *his* knowledge of Jewish culture is also extremely spotty, and the way in which his personality is composed may be more in accordance with my ignorance than with a cultivated Jew's immersion in the culture. So in certain limited ways one's ignorance can help to buttress the validity of a novel.

· · ·

A friend once said that a novelist is capable of creating any character in the world except one—he cannot create a novelist better than himself. It's absolutely true. I could give a prescription for how to have a fighting chance to become a good novelist. To begin with, you need the ability to contain great opposites in the self. You've got to be on the one hand capable of nobility; on the other hand it helps if you're a touch evil and aware of it. And you certainly have to be wicked, which I separate from evil. Wickedness is an essential ingredient for getting things done because, if we keep waiting to know if something is perfect before we do it, then almost always it's stillborn—or just not that good. You have to take chances. You need a mixture of arrogance and modesty. You have to be arrogant enough to do something large and important and worth doing, because writing itself is not the most exciting activity. You have to be modest enough to realize that you have limitations—there's a piece of white paper in front of you, so you can't be that good at it. You have to pay attention to those limitations. A good novelist has got to be a mad drunk on the one hand and absolutely sober on the other. These opposites are exactly the reasons so few people become novelists. You have to be both cultivated and ignorant. You have to know a lot and be astonishingly innocent about serious subjects as well. With it there has to be some kind of navigator at the core of yourself that deals with these opposites—knows when to satisfy one, when to satisfy the other.

BERNARD MALAMUD: Take chances. "Dare to do," Eudora Welty says. She's right. One drags around a bag of fears he has to throw to the winds every so often if he expects to take off in his writing. I'm glad Virginia Woolf did *Orlando*, though it isn't my favorite of her books, and in essence she was avoiding a subject. Still, you don't have to tell everything you know. I like Updike's *Centaur*, Bellow's *Henderson*. Genius, after it has got itself together, may give out with a *Ulysses* or *Remembrance of Things Past*. One doesn't have to imitate the devices of Joyce or Proust, but if you're not a genius imitate the daring. If you are a genius assert yourself, in art and humanity.

DAVID MAMET: I never try to make it hard for the audience. I may not succeed, but . . . Vakhtangov, who was a disciple of Stanislavsky, was asked at one point why his films were so successful, and he said, "Because I never for one moment forget about the audience." I try to adopt that as an absolute tenet. I mean, if I'm not writing for the audience, if I'm not writing to make it easier for *them*, then who the hell am I doing it for? And the way you make it easier is by following those tenets: cutting, building to a climax, leaving out exposition and always progressing toward the single goal of the protagonist. They're very stringent rules, but they are, in my estimation and experience, what makes it easier for the audience.

· · ·

Get into the scene late, get out of the scene early. That's how *Glengarry* got started. I was listening to conversations in the next booth and I thought, My God, there's nothing more fascinating than the people in the next booth. You start in the middle of the conversation and wonder, What the hell are they talking about? And you listen heavily.

JAMES MERRILL: Frederick Buechner gave me a Ouija board as a birthday present in 1953. As I recall, we sat down then and there to try it, and got a touching little story from a fairly simple soul—that engineer "dead of cholera in Cairo," who'd met Goethe. I used it in the first thing I ever wrote about the Ouija board (a poem called "Voices from the Other World"), although by that time the *experiences* behind this poem were mine and David's. We started in the summer of 1955. But the spirit *we* contacted—Ephraim—was anything but simple. So much so that for a long time I felt that the material he dictated really couldn't be used—then or perhaps ever. I felt it would be like cheating, or plagiarizing from some unidentifiable source. Oh, I put a few snippets of it into *The Seraglio,* but that was just a novel, and didn't count. Twenty years later, though, I was yet again trying to tell the whole story as fiction, through a set of characters bearing little resemblance to David or me. I'd got about fifty pages done, hating every bit of it. I'm not a novelist, and never was. No accident, then, that I simply "forgot" the manuscript in a taxi in Atlanta, and never recovered it—well, all that's described in "The Book of Ephraim." But I went on, I didn't take the hint. I put together all the drafts and notes for those lost pages, and proceeded to forget *these* in a hotel room in Frankfurt! By now I was down to just two pages of an opening draft. As I sat glaring at them, the prose began to dissolve into verse. I marked the line-breaks with a pencil, fiddled a bit, typed it up, and showed the two versions to a friend who said quite firmly: "You must never write prose again." At that point "The Book of Ephraim" crystallized, and got written without any particular trouble.

Most of the time, we never knew what to expect. Last summer, for instance, we were about to sit down at the board—no, I was already in my chair—when David called from the kitchen. He can never keep abreast of the rising postal rates, and wanted to know which stamp to put on his letter. I called back, "Put on an Edna St. Vincent Millay"—I'd bought a sheet of her commemoratives just that week. And when we started at the board, there she was. Very embarrassing on both sides, as it dawned on the poor creature that we hadn't meant to talk to *her* at all.

An overturned teacup is our pointer. The commercial boards come with a funny see-through planchette on legs. I find them too cramped. Besides, it's so easy to make your own—just write out the alphabet, and the numbers, and your YES and NO (punctuation marks too, if you're going all out) on a big sheet of cardboard. Or use brown paper—it travels better. On our Grand Tour, whenever we felt lonely in the hotel room, David and I could just unfold our instant company. He puts his right hand lightly on the cup, I put my left, leaving the right free to transcribe, and away we go. We get, oh, 500 to 600 words an hour. Better than gasoline.

HENRY MILLER: Dostoevsky was always in a miserable state, but you can't say he deliberately chose psychological discomforts. No, I doubt that strongly. I don't think anyone chooses these things, unless unconsciously. I do think many writers have what you might call a demonic nature. They are always in trouble, you know, and not only while they're writing or because they're writing, but in every aspect of their lives, with marriage, love, business, money, everything. It's all tied together, all part and parcel of the same thing. It's an aspect of the creative personality.

CZESLAW MILOSZ: I have a quarrel with the genre. It's an impure form. I taught Dostoevsky at Berkeley for twenty years. A born novelist, he would sacrifice everything; he knows no obligations of honor. He would put anything in a novel. Dostoevsky created a character in *The Idiot,* General Ivolgin, who is a liar and tells stories—how he lost his leg in a war, how he buried his leg, and then what he inscribed on the tombstone. The inscription is taken from the tomb of Dostoevsky's mother. There you have a true novelist. I couldn't do that.

MARIANNE MOORE: Oh, I never knew anyone who had a passion for words who had as much difficulty in saying things as I do. I very seldom say them in a manner I like. If I do it's because I don't know I'm trying.

. . .

I do enjoy writing, yes. A great deal. And I feel somewhat at a loss, aimless and foolishly sentimental, and disconnected, when I've finished one work and haven't yet become absorbed in another. All of us who write work out of a conviction that we are participating in some sort of communal activity. Whether my role is writing, or reading and responding, might not be very important. I take seriously Flaubert's statement that we must love one another in our art as the mystics love one another in God. By honoring one another's creation we honor something that deeply connects us all, and goes beyond us.

Of course writing is only one activity out of a vast number of activities that constitute our lives. It seems to be the one that some of us have concentrated on, as if we were fated for it. Since I have a great deal of faith in the processes and the wisdom of the unconscious, and have learned from experience to take lightly the judgments of the ego, and its inevitable doubts, I never find myself constrained to answer such questions. Life is energy, and energy is creativity. And even when we as individuals pass on, the energy is retained in the work of art, locked in it and awaiting release if only someone will take the time and the care to unlock it.

TONI MORRISON: I thought of myself as like the jazz musician: someone who practices and practices and practices in order to be able to invent and to make his art look effortless and graceful. I was always conscious of the constructed aspect of the writing process, and that art appears natural and elegant only as a result of constant practice and awareness of its formal structures. You must practice thrift in order to achieve that luxurious quality of wastefulness—that sense that you have enough to waste, that you are holding back—without actually wasting anything. You shouldn't overgratify, you should never satiate. I've always felt that that peculiar sense of hunger at the end of a piece of art—a yearning for more—is really very, very powerful. But there is at the same time a kind of contentment, knowing that at some other time there will indeed be more because the artist is endlessly inventive.

. . .

It's very important to me that my work be African-American; if it assimilates into a different or larger pool, so much the better. But I shouldn't be *asked* to do that. Joyce is not asked to do that. Tolstoy is not. I mean, they can all be Russian, French, Irish or Catholic, they write out of where they come from, and I do too. It just so happens that that space for me is African-American; it could be Catholic, it could be Midwestern. I'm those things too, and they are all important. I mean, could I have gone up to André Gide and said, "Yes, but when are you going to get serious and start writing about black people?" I don't think he would know how to answer that question. Just as I don't. He would say, "What?" "I will if I want" or "Who are you?" What is behind that question is, there's the center, which is white, and then there are these regional blacks or Asians, or any sort of marginal people. That question can only be asked from the center. Bill Moyers asked me that when-are-you-going-to-write-about question on television. I just said, "Well, maybe one day . . ." but I couldn't say to him, you know, you can only ask that question from the center. The center of the world! I mean he's a white male. He's asking a marginal person, "When are you going to get to the center? When are you going to write about white people?" I can't say, "Bill, why are you asking me that question?" or "As long as that question seems reasonable is as long as I won't, can't." The point is that he's patronizing; he's saying, "You write well enough. You could come on into the center if you wanted to. You don't have to stay out there on the margins." And I'm saying, "Yeah, well I'm gonna stay out here on the margin, and let the center look for me."

Maybe it's a false claim, but not fully. I'm sure it was true for the ones we think of as giants now. Joyce is a good example. He moved here and there, but he wrote about Ireland wherever he was, didn't care where he was. I am sure people said to him, "Why . . . ?" Maybe the French asked, "When you gonna write about Paris?"

IRIS MURDOCH: I think it is important to make a detailed plan before you write the first sentence. Some people think one should write— "George woke up and knew that something terrible had happened yesterday"—and then see what happens. I plan the whole thing in detail before I begin. I have a general scheme and lots of notes. Every chapter is planned. Every conversation is planned. This is, of course, a primary stage, and very frightening because you've committed yourself at this point. I mean, a novel is a long job, and if you get it wrong at the start you're going to be very unhappy later on. The second stage is that one should sit quietly and let the thing invent itself. One piece of imagination leads to another. You think about a certain situation and then some quite extraordinary aspect of it suddenly appears. The deep things that the work is about declare themselves and connect. Somehow things fly together and generate other things, and characters invent other characters, as if they were all doing it themselves. One should be patient and extend this period as far as possible. Of course, actually writing it involves a different kind of imagination and work.

JOYCE CAROL OATES: One must be pitiless about this matter of "mood." In a sense the writing will *create* the mood. If art is, as I believe it to be, a genuinely transcendental function—a means by which we rise out of limited, parochial states of mind—then it should not matter very much what states of mind or emotion we are in. Generally, I've found this to be true: I have forced myself to begin writing when I've been utterly exhausted, when I've felt my soul as thin as a playing-card, when nothing has seemed worth enduring for another five minutes . . . and somehow the activity of writing changes everything. Or appears to do so. Joyce said of the underlying structure of *Ulysses*—the Odyssean parallel and parody— that he really didn't care whether it was plausible, so long as it served as a bridge to get his "soldiers" across. Once they were across, what does it matter if the bridge collapses? One might say the same thing about the use of one's self as a means for the writing to get written. Once the soldiers are across the stream . . .

GRACE PALEY: You can't write without a lot of pressure. Sometimes the pressure comes from anger, which then changes into a pressure to write. It's not so much a matter of getting distance as simply a translation. I felt a lot of pressure writing some of those stories about women. Writers are lucky because when they're angry, the anger—by habit almost—I wouldn't say transcends but *becomes* an acute pressure to write, to tell. Some guy, he's angry, he wants to take a poke at someone—or he kicks a can, or sets fire to the house, or hits his wife, or the wife smacks the kid. Then again, it's not always violent. Some people go out and run for three hours. Some people go shopping. The pressure from anger is an energy that can be violent or useful or useless. Also the pressure doesn't have to be anger. It could be love. One could be overcome with feelings of life-time love or justice. Why not?

OCTAVIO PAZ: Writing is a painful process that requires huge effort and sleepless nights. In addition to the threat of writer's block, there is always the sensation that failure is inevitable. Nothing we write is what we wish we could write. Writing is a curse. The worst part of it is the anguish that precedes the act of writing—the hours, days or months when we search in vain for the phrase that turns the spigot that makes the water flow. Once that first phrase is written, everything changes: the process is enthralling, vital, and enriching, no matter what the final result is. Writing is a blessing!

S. J. PERELMAN: The old apothegm that easy writing makes hard reading is as succinct as ever. I used to know several eminent writers who were given to boasting of the speed with which they created. It's not a lovable attribute, to put it mildly, and I'm afraid our acquaintanceship has languished.

ROBERT PINSKY: Well, the point isn't performance. Poetry is a vocal art for me—but not necessarily a performative one. It might be reading to oneself or recalling some lines by memory. That physical tingle, that powerful, audible experience of poetry, has come to me not with poets projecting their own work powerfully to an audience, or with the John-Gielgud-reading-Shakespeare-sonnets records that friends have played for me on their stereos. It tends to be more intimate, less planned, than that. One is alone, or maybe with a friend or two.

Or it might even be in actual school. In my classes, I ask the students to find a poem they like and to get it by heart. To see someone in their late teens or early twenties, often by gender or ethnicity different from the author, shaping his or her mouth around those sounds created by somebody who is perhaps long dead, or perhaps thousands of miles away, and the students bringing their own experience to it, changing it with their own sensibility, so that they're both possessed and possessing—those moments have been very moving to me. Though the vocal performance may be crude, that crudeness just throws the essence of the poetry into higher relief. Whereas the effective personality of a poet giving a reading or the rich expert tones of an actor reading "When to the sessions of sweet silent thought" might muffle that essence by encasing it within the other art of performance.

PHILIP ROTH: Beginning a book is unpleasant. I'm entirely uncertain about the character and the predicament, and a character in his predicament is what I have to begin with. Worse than not knowing your subject is not knowing how to treat it, because that's finally everything. I type out beginnings and they're awful, more of an unconscious parody of my previous book than the breakaway from it that I want. I need something driving down the center of a book, a magnet to draw everything to it—that's what I look for during the first months of writing something new. I often have to write a hundred pages or more before there's a paragraph that's alive. Okay, I say to myself, that's your beginning, start there; that's the first paragraph of the book. I'll go over the first six months of work and underline in red a paragraph, a sentence, sometimes no more than a phrase, that has some life in it, and then I'll type all these out on one page. Usually it doesn't come to more than one page, but if I'm lucky, that's the start of page one. I look for the liveliness to set the tone. After the awful beginning come the months of freewheeling play, and after the play come the crises, turning against your material and hating the book.

JAMES SALTER: Isaac Babel is heroic to me. My idea of writing is of unflinching and continual effort, somehow trying to find the right words until you reach a point where you can make no further progress and you either have something or you don't. Babel was such a writer. He worked on manuscripts for a long time; there was a trunk full of them that just disappeared with work in it that he simply wasn't ready to have printed yet. His remarks, those that have been translated—various speeches or talks at symposiums between about 1930 and 1936—give you the impression of someone who is not without confidence, but by no means arrogant or proud. He said at one point that he wished he had never taken up anything as difficult as writing but instead had become a tractor salesman like his father. At the same time you know that in the final account it's not what he was going to do. He made a remark about Tolstoy that is very touching. He observed that Tolstoy only weighed three poods—a Russian weight measurement—but that they were three poods of pure genius.

ANNE SEXTON: It's a little mad, but I believe I am many people. When I am writing a poem, I feel I am the person who should have written it. Many times I assume these guises; I attack it the way a novelist might. Sometimes I become someone else and when I do, I believe, even in moments when I'm not writing the poem, that I am that person. When I wrote about the farmer's wife, I lived in my mind in Illinois; when I had the illegitimate child, I nursed it—in my mind—and gave it back and traded life. When I gave my lover back to his wife, in my mind, I grieved and saw how ethereal and unnecessary I had been. When I was Christ, I felt like Christ. My arms hurt, I desperately wanted to pull them in off the Cross. When I was taken down off the Cross, and buried alive, I sought solutions; I hoped they were Christian solutions.

NEIL SIMON: Sometimes I start laughing—and I've had moments in this office when I've burst into tears. Not that I thought the audience might do that. The moment had triggered a memory or a feeling that was deeply hidden. That's catharsis. It's one of the main reasons I write the plays. It's like analysis without going to the analyst. The play becomes your analysis. The writing of the play is the most enjoyable part of it. It's also the most frightening part because you walk into a forest without a knife, without a compass. But if your instincts are good, if you have a sense of geography, you find that you're clearing a path and getting to the right place. If the miracle happens, you come out at the very place you *wanted* to. But very often you have to go back to the beginning of the forest and start walking through it again, saying, "I went that way. It was a dead end." You cross out, cross over. You meet new friends along the way, people you never thought you'd meet. It takes you into a world you hadn't planned on going to when you started the play. The play may have started out to be a comedy, and suddenly you get into a place of such depth that it surprises you. As one critic aptly said, I wrote *Brighton Beach Memoirs* about the family I *wished* I'd had instead of the family I *did* have. It's closer to *Ah, Wilderness* than my reality.

WILLIAM STAFFORD: I remember when I was traveling in Pakistan someone asked, "Are you writing while you're traveling?" I said, "Yes." "Are you writing about Pakistan?" I was able to say yes, but I didn't want them to ask me more because at the time I was working on a poem about the patterns of cracks on the ceilings in hotel rooms in Pakistan. It was so immediate that it wasn't exotic. You know, there are cracks on the ceilings of hotel rooms in Cannon Beach, Oregon. So, I was at home. So much so that I wasn't a foreign traveler writing about an exotic place. I was a human being writing about his shelter for the night.

JOHN STEINBECK: Now let me give you the benefit of my experience in facing 400 pages of blank stock—the appalling stuff that must be filled. The following are some of the things I have had to do to keep from going nuts.

1. Abandon the idea that you are ever going to finish. Lose track of the 400 pages and write just one page for each day; it helps. Then when it gets finished, you are always surprised.

2. Write freely and as rapidly as possible and throw the whole thing on paper. Never correct or rewrite until the whole thing is down. Rewrite in process is usually found to be an excuse for not going on. It also interferes with flow and rhythm which can only come from a kind of unconscious association with the material.

3. Forget your generalized audience. In the first place, the nameless, faceless audience will scare you to death and in the second place, unlike the theater, it doesn't exist. In writing, your audience is one single reader.

I have found that sometimes it helps to pick out one person—a real person you know, or an imagined person—and write to that one.

4. If a scene or a section gets the better of you and you still think you want it—bypass it and go on. When you have finished the whole you can come back to it and then you may find that the reason it gave trouble is because it didn't belong there.

5. Beware of a scene that becomes too dear to you, dearer than the rest. It will usually be found that it is out of drawing.

6. If you are using dialogue—say it aloud as you write it. Only then will it have the sound of speech.

ROBERT STONE: It's goddamn hard. Nobody really cares whether you do it or not. You have to make yourself do it. I'm very lazy and I suffer as a result. Of course, when it's going well there's nothing in the world like it. But it's also very lonely. If you do something you're really pleased with, you're in the crazy position of being exhilarated all by yourself. I remember finishing one section of *Dog Soldiers*—the end of Hicks's walk—in the basement of a college library, working at night, while the rest of the place was closed down, and I staggered out in tears, talking to myself, and ran into a security guard. It's hard to come down from a high in your work—it's one of the reasons writers drink. The exhilaration of your work turns into the daily depression of the aftermath. But if you heal that with a lot of Scotch you're not fit for duty the next day. When I was younger I was able to use hangovers, but now I have to go to bed early.

WILLIAM STYRON: I guess like everybody I'm emotionally fouled up most of the time, but I find I do better when I'm relatively placid. It's hard to say, though. If writers had to wait until their precious psyches were completely serene there wouldn't be much writing done. Actually—though I don't take advantage of the fact as much as I should—I find that I'm simply the happiest, the placidest, *when* I'm writing, and so I suppose that that, for me, is the final answer. When I'm writing I find it's the only time that I feel completely self-possessed, even when the writing itself is not going too well. It's fine therapy for people who are perpetually scared of nameless threats as I am most of the time—for jittery people. Besides, I've discovered that when I'm not writing I'm prone to developing certain nervous tics, and hypochondria. Writing alleviates those quite a bit. I think I resist change more than most people. I dislike traveling, like to stay settled. When I first came to Paris all I could think about was going home,

home to the old James River. One of these days I expect to inherit a peanut farm. Go back home and farm them old peanuts and be real old Southern whiskey gentry.

JAMES THURBER: I never quite know when I'm not writing. Sometimes my wife comes up to me at a party and says, "Dammit, Thurber, stop writing." She usually catches me in the middle of a paragraph. Or my daughter will look up from the dinner table and ask, "Is he sick?" "No," my wife says. "He's writing something." I have to do it that way on account of my eyes. I still write occasionally—in the proper sense of the word—using black crayon on yellow paper and getting perhaps twenty words to the page. My usual method, though, is to spend the mornings turning over the text in my mind. Then in the afternoon, between 2 and 5, I call in a secretary and dictate to her. I can do about 2,000 words. It took me about 10 years to learn.

· · ·

Hervey Allen, you know, the author of the big best-seller *Anthony Adverse,* seriously told a friend of mine who was working on a biographical piece on Allen that he could close his eyes, lie down on a bed, and hear the voices of his ancestors. Furthermore there was some sort of angel-like creature that danced along his pen while he was writing. He wasn't balmy by any means. He just felt he was in communication with some sort of metaphysical recorder. So you see the novelists have all the luck. I never knew a humorist who got any help from his ancestors. Still, the act of writing is either something the writer dreads or actually likes, and I actually like it. Even rewriting's fun. You're getting somewhere, whether it seems to move or not. I remember Elliot Paul and I used to argue about re-writing back in 1925 when we both worked for the *Chicago Tribune* in Paris. It was his conviction you should leave the story as it came out of the typewriter, no changes. Naturally, he worked fast. Three novels he could turn out, each written in three weeks' time. I remember once he came to the office and said that a 60,000-word manuscript had been stolen. No carbons existed, no notes. We were all horrified. But it didn't bother him at all. He'd just get back to the typewriter and bat away again.

HELEN VENDLER: All good poets are terribly well-educated, otherwise they wouldn't be good poets. They have to have enormous linguistic command to write poetry well. Someone like Blake who never went to a university, someone like Whitman who never went to a university, who could say they were uneducated? Melville said the whaling ship was his Yale College and his Harvard; for Blake and Whitman, the printing press was a university.

. . .

I don't think poetry is killable. At one point, Ezra Pound wrote sardonically of "the filthy ... unkillable infants of the very poor." And I think of poetry as one of those. It will keep cropping up no matter what is done with it, because human beings feel such a perennial impulse to play with language. It's like any other kind of play ... play with notes, play with colors, play with line, play with rhythm. The human impulse to play with a given medium seems to be ineradicable.

EVELYN WAUGH: I don't find it easy. You see there are always words going round in my head; some people think in pictures, some in ideas. I think entirely in words. By the time I come to stick my pen in my ink pot these words have reached a stage of order which is fairly presentable.

EUDORA WELTY: Some things I let alone from first to last—the kernel of the story. You know enough not to touch something if it's right. The hardest thing for me is getting people in and out of rooms—the mechanics of a story. A simple act of putting on clothes is almost impossible for me to describe without many false starts. You have to be quick and specific in conveying that sort of action or fact, and also as neat and quiet about it as possible so that it doesn't obtrude. And I find that very challenging, especially to describe an action that I don't do very well myself, like sewing. I made Aunt Lexie in *Losing Battles* a poor sewer so that I wouldn't have to describe it too well. The easiest things to write about are emotions. For a writer those things are what you start with. You wouldn't have started a story without that awareness—that's what made you begin. That's what makes a character, projects the plot. Because you write from the inside. You can't start with how people look and speak and behave and come to know how they feel. You must know exactly what's in their hearts and minds before they ever set visible foot on the stage. You must know all, then not tell it all, or not tell too much at once; simply the right thing at the right moment. And the same character would be written about entirely differently in a novel as opposed to a short story. In a story you don't go into a character in order to develop him. He was born full grown, and he's present there to perform his part in the story. He's subservient to his function, and he doesn't exist outside it. But in a novel, he may. So you may have to allow for his growth and maybe hold him down and not tell everything you know, or else let him have his full sway—make room for a hero, even, in more spacious premises.

EDMUND WHITE: I wish I were more at home with writing. I can go a year or two or three without picking up my pen and I'm perfectly content. The minute I have to write I become neurotic and grouchy and ill; I become like a little wet, drenched bird, and I put a blanket over my shoulders and I try to write and I hate myself and I hate what I'm writing. Writing depends upon a fairly quiet life, whereas I am a sociable person. I think every writer goes back and forth on this question; it's a constant struggle to find the right balance between solitude and society and I don't think anyone ever does. I find it reassuring to read the complaints of Chekhov: "My country house is full of people, they never leave me alone; if only they would go away I could be a good writer." He's writing this close to the end of his life.

TENNESSEE WILLIAMS: When I write, everything is visual, as brilliantly as if it were on a lit stage. And I talk out the lines as I write.

When I was in Rome, my landlady thought I was demented. She told Frank (Merlo), "Oh, Mr. Williams has lost his mind! He stalks about the room talking out loud!"

Frank said, "Oh, he's just writing." She didn't understand *that*.

P. G. WODEHOUSE: I love writing. I never feel really comfortable unless I am either actually writing or have a story going. I could not stop writing.

ON REVISING: SELF-EVALUATION

Murder your darlings.   —G. K. CHESTERTON

My real judgment of my own work is that I have spoilt a
number of jolly good ideas in my time.
                                         —G. K. CHESTERTON

Run a moist pen through everything and start afresh.
                                         —CHARLES DICKENS

Let your literary compositions be kept from the public eye for
nine years at least.   —HORACE

Fall seven times, stand up eight.   —JAPANESE PROVERB

Read over your compositions and, when you meet a passage
which you think is particularly fine, strike it out.
                                         —SAMUEL JOHNSON

The players often mention it as an honor to Shakespeare that
in his writing, whatsoever he penned, he never blotted out a
line. My answer hath been, "Would he had blotted a thousand."
                                         —BEN JONSON

The wastepaper basket is the writer's best friend.
                                         —ISAAC BASHEVIS SINGER

This morning I took out a comma and this afternoon I put it
back again.   —OSCAR WILDE

CONRAD AIKEN: Occasionally I've discarded and then resurrected. I
would find a crumpled yellow ball of paper in the wastebasket, in the
morning, and open it to see what the hell I'd been up to; and occasionally
it was something that needed only a very slight change to be brought off,
which I'd missed the day before.

JOHN ASHBERY: I used to labor over what's done a great deal, but because of my strong desire to avoid all unnecessary work, I have somehow trained myself not to write something that I will either have to discard or be forced to work a great deal over. I like the idea of being as close to the original thought or voice as possible and not to falsify it by editing. Here is something I just read by Max Jacob, quoted by André Salmon in the notes to Jacob's book *La Défense de Tartuffe*. He talks about composing novels or stories in a notebook while taking long walks through Paris. I'll translate: "The ideas I found in this way seemed sacred to me and I didn't change a comma. I believe that prose which comes directly from meditation is a prose which has the form of the brain and which it is forbidden to touch."

JAMES BALDWIN: I do a lot of rewriting. It's very painful. You know it's finished when you can't do anything more to it, though it's never exactly the way you want it. . . . Most of the rewrite is cleaning. Don't describe it, show it. That's what I try to teach all young writers—take it out! Don't describe a purple sunset, make me see that it is purple. The hardest thing in the world is simplicity. And the most fearful thing, too. You have to strip yourself of all your disguises, some of which you didn't know you had. You want to write a sentence as clean as a bone. That is the goal.

JORGE LUIS BORGES: At first I did [revisions]. Then I found out that when a man reaches a certain age he has found his real tone. Nowadays, I try to go over what I've written after a fortnight or so and of course there are many slips and repetitions to be avoided, certain favorite tricks that should not be overworked. But I think that what I write nowadays is always on a certain level and that I can't better it very much nor can I spoil it very much either. Consequently I let it go, forget all about it, and think about what I'm doing at the time.

· · ·

We know that [Kafka] was very dissatisfied with his own work. Of course, when he told his friend, Max Brod, that he wanted his manuscripts to be burned, as Vergil did, I suppose he knew that his friend wouldn't do that. If a man wants to destroy his own work, he throws it into a fire, and there it goes. When he tells a close friend of his: "I want all the manuscripts to be destroyed," he knows that the friend will never do that, and the friend knows that he knows and that he knows that the other knows that he knows and so on and so forth.

RAYMOND CARVER: There's not much that I like better than to take a story that I've had around the house for a while and work it over again. It's the same with the poems I write. I'm in no hurry to send something off just after I write it, and I sometimes keep it around the house for months doing this or that to it, taking this out and putting that in. It doesn't take that long to do the first draft of the story, that usually happens in one sitting, but it does take a while to do the various versions of the story. I've done as many as twenty or thirty drafts of a story. Never less than ten or twelve drafts. It's instructive, and heartening both, to look at the early drafts of great writers. I'm thinking of the photographs of galleys belonging to Tolstoy, to name one writer who loved to revise. I mean, I don't know if he loved it or not, but he did a great deal of it. He was always revising, right down to the time of page proofs. He went through and rewrote *War and Peace* eight times and was still making corrections in the galleys. Things like this should hearten every writer whose first drafts are dreadful, like mine are.

JOHN DOS PASSOS: I do a lot of revising. Certain chapters six or seven times. Occasionally you can hit it right the first time. More often, you don't. George Moore rewrote entire novels. In my own case I usually write to a point where the work is getting worse rather than better. That's the point to stop and the time to publish.

LAWRENCE DURRELL: I suffer from terrible nausea about my own work, purely physical nausea. It sounds stupid, but the fact is I write at a terrific speed, and . . . you cross inner resistances like you cross a shoal of transmitters when you are fiddling with the dial on a radio. By the time the thing is in typescript, it is really with physical nausea that I regard it. When the proofs come back I have to take an aspirin before I can bring myself really to read it through. Occasionally when I'm asked to correct or edit a version, I always ask someone to do it for me. I don't know why. I just have a nausea about it. Perhaps when one day I get something I really do like, I won't have to take aspirin.

STANLEY ELKIN: My editor at Random House used to tell me, "Stanley, less is more." I had to fight him tooth and nail in the better restaurants to maintain excess because I don't believe that less is more. I believe that *more* is more. I believe that less is less, fat fat, thin thin, and enough is enough. There's a famous exchange between Fitzgerald and Thomas

Wolfe in which Fitzgerald criticizes Wolfe for one of his novels. Fitzgerald tells him that Flaubert believed in the *mot précis* and that there are two kinds of writers—the putter-inners and the taker-outers. Wolfe, who probably was not as good a writer as Fitzgerald but evidently wrote a better letter, said, "Flaubert me no Flauberts. Shakespeare was a putter-inner, Melville was a putter-inner." I can't remember who else was a putter-inner, but I'd rather be a putter-inner than a taker-outer.

WILLIAM FAULKNER: All of us failed to match our dream of perfection. So I rate us on the basis of our splendid failure to do the impossible. In my opinion, if I could write all my work again, I am convinced that I would do it better, which is the healthiest condition for an artist. That's why he keeps on working, trying again; he believes each time that this time he will do it, bring it off. Of course he won't, which is why this condition is healthy. Once he did it, once he matched the work to the image, the dream, nothing would remain but to cut his throat, jump off the other side of that pinnacle of perfection into suicide.

E. M. FORSTER: I am more interested in achievement than in advance on it and decline from it. And I am more interested in works than in authors. The paternal wish of critics to show how a writer dropped off or picked up as he went along seems to me misplaced. I am only interested in myself as a producer. What was it Mahler said?—"anyone will sufficiently understand me who will trace my development through my nine symphonies." This seems odd to me; I couldn't imagine myself making such a remark; it seems too uncasual. Other authors find themselves much more an object of study. I am conceited, but not interested in myself in this particular way. Of course I like reading my own work, and often do it. I go gently over the bits I think are bad.

CHRISTOPHER ISHERWOOD: What I tend to do is not so much pick at a thing but sit down and rewrite it completely. Both for *A Single Man* and *A Meeting by the River* I wrote three entire drafts. After making notes on one draft I'd sit down and rewrite it again from the beginning. I've found that's much better than patching and amputating things. One has to rethink the thing completely. They say D. H. Lawrence used to write second drafts and never look at the first.

WILLIAM KENNEDY: I presented my editor with *Legs,* which was then about one hundred pages. He bought it. Then it took me six years to finish it. I wrote it eight times and seven times it was no good. Six times it was especially no good. The seventh time out it was pretty good, though it was way too long. My son was six years old and so was my novel and they were both the same height. I was wounded many times in the writing of that novel.

JERZY KOSINSKI: I keep depressing my text, de-escalating the language. I count words the way Western Union does; often, I'm afraid my prose tends to resemble a night letter. Every word is there for a reason, and if not, I cross it out. I do rewrite—often entirely—my galley pages, even page proofs. The publishers complain, but I argue that every new draft keeps improving my own as well as their book. Still, I am never certain whether my English prose is sufficiently clear. Also, I rarely allow myself to use English in an unchecked, spontaneous way. I always have a sense of trembling—but so does a compass, after all.

ARCHIBALD MACLEISH: I formed the habit long ago of putting new poems into a desk drawer and letting them lie there to ripen (or the opposite) like apples. I suppose everyone else does the same thing. I learned early and by sad experience never to publish a green poem. Who in hell wrote that? Instead, I pull them out after a few weeks or months and say, "Well ... possibly ..." and start all over. Or consign the whole thing to the wood fire and hope the seed, whatever it was, will sow itself again. I doubt if it does. It's sick of me by that time.

BERNARD MALAMUD: First drafts are for learning what your novel or story is about. Revision is working with that knowledge to enlarge and enhance an idea, to re-form it. D. H. Lawrence, for instance, did seven or eight drafts of *The Rainbow*. The first draft of a book is the most uncertain—where you need guts, the ability to accept the imperfect until it is better. Revision is one of the true pleasures of writing. "The men and things of today are wont to lie fairer and truer in tomorrow's memory," Thoreau said.

HENRY MILLER: When I'm revising, I use a pen and ink to make changes, cross out, insert. The manuscript looks wonderful afterwards, like a Balzac. Then I retype, and in the process of retyping I make more changes. I prefer to retype everything myself, because even when I think I've made all the changes I want, the mere mechanical business of touching the keys sharpens my thoughts, and I find myself revising while doing the finished thing. In a way the machine acts as a stimulus; it's a cooperative thing.

MARIANNE MOORE: I don't approve of my "enigmas," or as somebody said, "the not ungreen grass."

I said to my mother one time, "How did you ever permit me to let this be printed?"

And she said, "You didn't ask my advice."

SAM SHEPARD: When I have a piece of writing that I think might be ready, I test it with actors, and then I see if it's what I imagined it to be. The best actors show you the flaws in the writing. They come to a certain place and there's nothing there, or they read a line and say, "Okay, now what?" That kind of questioning is more valuable than anything. They don't have to *say* anything. With the very best actors I can see it in the way they're proceeding. Sometimes I instinctively know that this little part at the end of scene two, act one is not quite there, but I say to myself, "Maybe we'll get away with it." A good actor won't let me. Not that he says, "Hey, I can't do this"; I just see that he's stumbling. And then I have to face up to the problem.

GEORGES SIMENON: I cut adjectives, adverbs, and every word which is there just to make an effect. Every sentence which is there just for the sentence. You know, you have a beautiful sentence—cut it. Every time I find such a thing in one of my novels it is to be cut. Sometimes I've changed the names while writing: a woman will be Helen in the first chapter and Charlotte in the second, you know; so in revising I straighten this out. And then, cut, cut, cut.

NEIL SIMON: *The Gingerbread Lady* was a flawed play, the producer was going to put up a closing notice in Boston. Maureen Stapleton, who was starring in the play, came to me and said, "If you close this play I'll never speak to you again." She said, "This is a potentially wonderful play. It needs work but don't walk away from it!" I thought, what a reasonable thing to say, because all it amounted to was more of my time. The producer said he wanted to close, to save me "from the slings and arrows of the critics in New York." I said, "I can take the slings and arrows. I've had enough success up to now. I'll *learn* from this one." What finally made up my mind, after reading three terrible reviews in Boston, was, while waiting at the airport for my plane, I picked up *The Christian Science Monitor,* and the review was a letter addressed to me. It said, "Dear Neil Simon, I know you're probably going to want to close this play, but I beg of you, don't do it. This is potentially the best play you have written. You're going into a whole new genre, a whole new mode of writing. Don't abandon it." So, I called the producer and said, "Please don't close the play. Let's run in Boston and see what happens." Then, I didn't want to get on a plane and arrive in New York an hour later; I wanted a four-hour trip on a train, so I could start the rewrite. By the time I got to New York I had rewritten fifteen pages of the play. I stayed in New York for a week and came back with about thirty-five new pages. And we went to work. The play was never a major success, but we did have a year's run, and sold it to the movies. Maureen Stapleton won the Tony Award, and Marsha Mason, who played the lead in the film version, got an Oscar nomination. So, something good came out of persevering.

SUSAN SONTAG: I revise as I go along. And that's quite a pleasurable task. I don't get impatient and I'm willing to go over and over something until it works. It's beginnings that are hard. I always begin with a great sense of dread and trepidation. Nietzsche says that the decision to start writing is like leaping into a cold lake. Only when I'm about a third of the way can I tell if it's good enough. Then I have my cards, and I can play my hand.

STEPHEN SPENDER: Occasionally, I can write a poem straight off. Usually I revise a great deal—a hundred or more rewritings. One good remark Virginia Woolf makes somewhere in her journals is that too much rewriting is symptomatic of a failure of imagination. *Mea culpa*. But if you put a poem aside, when you look at it again it tends to rewrite itself, because your remembered intention criticizes the failures of expression.

JAMES THURBER: My wife took a look at the first version of something I was doing not long ago and said: "Goddamn it, Thurber, that's high-school stuff." I have to tell her to wait until the seventh draft, it'll work out all right. I don't know why that should be so, that the first or second draft of everything I write reads as if it was turned out by a charwoman. I wrote a thing called *File and Forget* in one afternoon. But only because it was a series of letters just as one would ordinarily dictate. And I'd have to admit that the last letter of the series, after doing all the others that one afternoon, took me a week. It was the end of the piece and I had to fuss over it.

Brevity in any case—whether the work is supposed to be humorous or not—would seem to me to be desirable. Most of the books I like are short books: *The Red Badge of Courage, Turn of the Screw,* Conrad's short stories, *A Lost Lady,* Joseph Hergesheimer's *Wild Oranges,* Victoria Lincoln's *February Hill, The Great Gatsby.* . . . You know, Fitzgerald once wrote Thomas Wolfe: "You're a putter-inner and I'm a taker-outer." I stick with Fitzgerald. I don't believe, as Wolfe did, that you have to turn out a massive work before being judged a writer. Wolfe once told me at a cocktail party I didn't know what it was to be a writer. My wife, standing next to me, complained about that. "But my husband *is* a writer," she said. Wolfe was genuinely surprised. "He is?" he asked. "Why all I ever see is that stuff of his in *The New Yorker.*" In other words he felt that prose under 5,000 words was certainly not the work of a writer . . . it was some kind of doodling in words. If you said you were a writer, he wanted to know where the books were, the great big long books. He was really genuine about that.

EUDORA WELTY: I correct or change words, but I can't rewrite a scene or make a major change because there's a sense then of someone looking over my shoulder. It's necessary, anyway, to trust that moment when you were sure at last you had done all you could, done your best for that time. When it's finally in print, you're delivered—you don't ever have to look at it again. It's too late to worry about its failings. I'll have to apply any lessons this book has taught me toward writing the next one.

E. B. WHITE: I revise a great deal. I know when something is right because bells begin ringing and lights flash. I'm not at all sure what the "necessary equipment" is for a writer—it seems to vary greatly with the individual. Some writers are equipped with extra-sensory perception. Some have a good ear, like O'Hara. Some are equipped with humor—although not nearly as many as think they are. Some are equipped with a massive intellect, like [Edmund] Wilson. Some are prodigious. I do think the ability to evaluate one's own stuff with reasonable accuracy is a helpful piece of equipment. I've known good writers who've had it, and I've known writers who were utterly convinced that anything at all, if it came from their pen, was the work of genius and as close to being right as anything can be.

ELIE WIESEL: It is a struggle when I have to cut. I reduce nine hundred pages to one hundred sixty pages. I also enjoy cutting. I do it with a masochistic pleasure although even when you cut, you don't. Writing is not like painting, where you add. It is not what you put on the canvas that the reader sees. Writing is more like a sculpture where you remove, you eliminate in order to make the work visible. Even those pages you remove somehow remain. There is a difference between a book of two hundred pages from the very beginning, and a book of two hundred pages which is the result of an original eight hundred pages. The six hundred pages are there. Only you don't see them.

THORNTON WILDER: I forget which of the great sonneteers said: "One line in the fourteen comes from the ceiling; the others have to be adjusted around it." Well, likewise there are passages in every novel whose first writing is pretty much the last. But it's the joint and cement, between those spontaneous passages, that take a great deal of rewriting.

TOM WOLFE: You go to bed every night thinking that you've written the most brilliant passage ever done which somehow the next day you realize is sheer drivel. Sometimes it's six months later that it dawns on you that it doesn't work. It's a constant hazard. I can sympathize with Ken Kesey, who once said that he stopped writing because he was tired of being a seismograph—an instrument which measures rumblings from a great distance. He said he wanted to be a lightning rod—where it all happens at once, quick, and decisive. Perhaps this applies to painters, though I don't know. I suspect there are some awful dawns for them too.

On Editors

An editor should tell the author his writing is better than it is. Not a lot better, a little better.   —T. S. Eliot

I suppose some editors are failed writers—but so are most writers.   —T. S. Eliot

No author is a man of genius to his publisher.
                                        —Heinrich Heine

Manuscript: something submitted in haste and returned at leisure.   —Oliver Herford

Dear Herr Doctor:
    You are already 10 months behind with the manuscript of *Das Kapital,* which you have agreed to write for us. If we do not receive the manuscript within 6 months, we shall be obliged to commission another to do this work.
    —Letter to Karl Marx from his Leipzig publisher

We have read your manuscript with boundless delight. If we were to publish your paper, it would be impossible for us to publish any work of lower standard. And as it is unthinkable that in the next thousand years we shall see its equal, we are, to our regret, etc.   —Rejection slip from a Chinese economics journal, quoted in the *Financial Times*

No passion in the world is equal to the passion to alter someone else's draft.   —H. G. Wells

Ah! don't say you agree with me. When people agree with me I always feel that I must be wrong.   —Oscar Wilde

James Baldwin: I remember standing on a street corner with the black painter Beauford Delaney down in the Village waiting for the light to change, and he pointed down and said, "Look." I looked and all I saw was water. And he said, "Look again," which I did, and I saw oil on the water and the city reflected in the puddle. It was a great revelation to me. I can't explain it. He taught me how to see, and how to trust what I saw. Painters have often taught writers how to see. And once you've had that experience, you see differently.

ERSKINE CALDWELL: What gave me the courage to forget about poetry was a chap by the name of Louis Untermeyer. I had such admiration for him that I sent him some of my poems. He wrote to me and said that every young man is entitled to write poetry, but the sooner he gives it up, the better he's going to be as a man. So I took his advice.

JOHN CHEEVER: He [Harold Ross of *The New Yorker*] asked preposterous queries on a manuscript—everyone's written about that—something like thirty-six queries on a story. The author always thought it outrageous, a violation of taste, but Ross really didn't care. He liked to show his hand, to shake the writer up. Occasionally he was brilliant. In "The Enormous Radio" he made two changes. A diamond is found on the bathroom floor after a party. The man says, "Sell it, we can use a few dollars." Ross had changed "dollars" to "bucks," which was absolutely perfect. Brilliant. Then I had "the radio came softly" and Ross penciled in another "softly." "The radio came softly, softly." He was absolutely right. But then there were twenty-nine other suggestions like, "This story has gone on for twenty-four hours and no one has eaten anything. There's no mention of a meal." A typical example of this sort of thing was Shirley Jackson's "The Lottery," about the stoning ritual. He hated the story; he started turning vicious. He said there was no town in Vermont where there were rocks of that sort. He nagged and nagged and nagged. It was not surprising. Ross used to scare the hell out of me. I would go in for lunch. I never knew Ross was coming, until he'd bring in an egg cup. I'd sit with my back pressed against my chair. I was really afraid. He was a scratcher and a nose picker, and the sort of man who could get his underwear up so there was a strip of it showing between his trousers and his shirt. He used to hop at me, sort of jump about in his chair. It was a creative, destructive relationship from which I learned a great deal, and I miss him.

· · ·

Everyone keeps saying about my stories, "Oh, they're so sad." My agent, Candida Donadio, called me about a new story and said, "Oh, what a beautiful story, it's so sad." I said, "All right, so I'm a sad man." The sad thing about "The Brigadier and the Golf Widow" is the woman standing looking at the bomb shelter in the end of the story and then being sent away by a maid. Did you know that *The New Yorker* tried to take that out? They thought the story was much more effective without my ending. When I went in to look at page proofs, I thought there was a page missing. I asked where the end of the story was. Some girl said, "Mr. Shawn thinks it's better this way." I went into a very deep slow burn, took the train home, drank a lot of gin, and got one of the editors on the telephone. I was by then loud, abusive, and obscene. He was entertaining Elizabeth Bowen and Eudora Welty. He kept asking if he couldn't take this call in another place. Anyhow, I returned to New York in the morning. They had reset the whole magazine—poems, newsbreaks, cartoons—and replaced the scene.

· · ·

My definition of a good editor is a man I think charming, who sends me large checks, praises my work, my physical beauty, and my sexual prowess, and who has a stranglehold on the publisher and the bank.

MALCOLM COWLEY: These days there's a good deal more directed writing in which bright young publishers or editors dream up an idea for a book and then think of somebody to write it. Part of the creative process, at least in nonfiction, has moved over from the writer to the editor.... If an editor begins to let the concept of catering to the public weigh on him he becomes, to me, a bad editor. An editor should have an idea of what meets his own taste; that should provide the criterion. The whole notion of divining the public taste has been one of the deadliest ideas of publishing. When *True Confessions* was at the height of its success, a new fiction editor was picked every month. She would be one of the typists in the office, preferably the youngest, because it was felt that if she followed her own honest feeling about what was good, that was what the public wanted. After a month or so, she would become too sophisticated and then they would fire her as the fiction editor and take on another typist. That was cynicism carried to the extreme, but it may well have produced better results than an editor guessing at what the public might like.

ROBERT CREELEY: He [Ezra Pound] would send books at times which would be useful. *The History of Money* by Alexander Del Mar, which I read, and thought about. He was very helpful. It was very flattering to be taken at all seriously by him. [William Carlos] Williams was always much more specific. At times he would do things which would ... not *dismay* me—but my own ego would be set back. I remember one time I wrote him a very stern letter—some description about something I was going to do, or *this* was the way things were, *blah blah*. And he returned me the sheets of the letter and he had marked on the margin of particular sections, "Fine. Your style is tightening."

MICHAEL CRICHTON: In my experience of writing, you generally start out with some overall idea that you can see fairly clearly, as if you were standing on a dock and looking at a ship on the ocean. At first you can see the entire ship, but then as you begin work you're in the boiler room and you can't see the ship anymore. All you can see are the pipes and the grease and the fittings of the boiler room, and you have to *assume* the ship's exterior. What you really want in an editor is someone who's still on the dock, who can say, Hi, I'm looking at your ship, and it's missing a bow, the front mast is crooked, and it looks to me as if your propellers are going to have to be fixed.

T. S. ELIOT: He [Ezra Pound] was a marvelous critic because he didn't try to turn you into an imitation of himself. He tried to see what you were trying to do.

ROBERT FITZGERALD: There was, of course, Ezra Pound and his fondness for the *Odyssey*. He had helped W. H. D. Rouse. Rouse was trying to do a prose version and there was a correspondence between them. I always felt that Pound was really dissatisfied and disappointed in the end with what Rouse did. Before I went to Europe, I went to see Pound at St. Elizabeths. I wanted to tell him what I was going to try to do. I told him what I felt at the time—which was that there was no point in trying to do every line. I would do what I could. I'd hit the high spots. He said, "Oh no, don't do that. Let him say everything he wanted to say." So I had to re-think it and eventually I did let Homer say everything he wanted to say. I sent Pound the first draft of the first book when I got that done in Italy that fall. I got a postcard back, a wonderful postcard, saying, "Too much iambic will kill any subject matter." After that, I was very careful about getting singsong again. Keep the verse alive, that was the main thing.

RICHARD FORD: I've always had a lot of editing done on every book except the second one, *The Ultimate Good Luck*, which Donald Hall read when it was written in the first person. We met in New York in that little Irish bar next to the Algonquin, and he told me there that it wasn't any good. That was a horrible moment. We'd come into this little dark gloomy bar, and Donald put his hands on the table, looked at me and said, "I don't like your book." Whooh! You just have to take a deep breath and suck it up. I said, "Okay, okay, tell me what you can tell me." He told me all the things he didn't like about it and moreover told me he didn't know what the hell I was going to do with it, because it just wasn't any good this way.

I took it back, and I changed the point of view from first to third, and it got published, though not many people read it. It's in paperback now, and somebody's making a movie out of it—so it's gone on to have a life and a readership. Donald wasn't wrong. It wasn't a good book as I'd written it. But I changed the point of view, and in doing so, let the book admit a whole other wealth of material which the first person hadn't permitted. I didn't know what woes a change like that was going to impose on me, but it took then another year to reimagine in the third person.

ROBERT GOTTLIEB: The editor's relationship to a book should be an invisible one. The last thing anyone reading *Jane Eyre* would want to know, for example, is that I had convinced Charlotte Brontë that the first Mrs. Rochester should go up in flames. The most famous case of editorial intervention in English literature has always bothered me—you know, that Dickens's friend Bulwer-Lytton advised him to change the end of *Great Expectations:* I don't want to know that! As a critic, of course, as a literary historian, I'm interested, but as a reader, I find it very disconcerting.

· · ·

If you are a good editor, your relationship with every writer is different. To some writers you say things you couldn't say to others, either because they'd be angry or because it would be too devastating to them. You can't have only one way of doing things; on some instinctual level you have to respond not just to the words of the writer but to the temperament of the writer. That may be hard for some editors; I haven't found it hard, perhaps because I like to please people. Joe Heller and I, for instance, have never had a bad moment because he is perfectly detached. When you're editing a manuscript with him the two of you can look at it as though you were two surgeons examining a body stretched out upon a table. You just cut it open, deal with the offending organs, and stitch it up again. Joe is completely objective, he has that kind of mind, even immediately after finishing a book.

We worked like dogs on *Catch-22,* and then just before it went to press

I was reading it again, and I came to a chapter I'd always hated. I thought it was pretentious and literary. I said to Joe, You know, I've always hated this chapter, and he said, Well take it out. And out it went. He printed it many years later in *Esquire* as the lost chapter of *Catch-22*. That's Joe Heller. Now that doesn't mean he's better than Bob Caro. It means he has a completely different temperament in relation to his work. Joe is a pragmatist; Bob is a romantic.

Doris Lessing also has a very removed attitude to her writing. You can say to Doris exactly what you think without fear either of wounding her or overly influencing her. The day after she gave me the manuscript for *The Summer Before the Dark* we were walking in Queen Mary's rose garden in London; she asked me what I thought about the manuscript. I said I liked it very much and told her I was sure it was going to be her most successful book. She said, Now that's interesting, because it's by no means my *best* book. There are not many writers whose clarity and disinterestedness are such that they could say that about a book they had *just finished.*

ERNEST HEMINGWAY: Miss Stein wrote at some length and with considerable inaccuracy about her influence on my work. It was necessary for her to do this after she had learned to write dialogue from a book called *The Sun Also Rises.* I was very fond of her and thought it was splendid she had learned to write conversation. It was no new thing to me to learn from everyone I could, living or dead, and I had no idea it would affect Gertrude so violently. She already wrote very well in other ways. Ezra was extremely intelligent on the subjects he really knew. Doesn't this sort of talk bore you? This backyard literary gossip while washing out the dirty clothes of thirty-five years ago is disgusting to me. It would be different if one had tried to tell the whole truth. That would have some value. Here it is simpler and better to thank Gertrude for everything I learned from her about the abstract relationship of words, say how fond I was of her, reaffirm my loyalty to Ezra as a great poet and a loyal friend, and say that I cared so much for Max Perkins that I have never been able to accept that he is dead. He never asked me to change anything I wrote except to remove certain words which were not then publishable. Blanks were left, and anyone who knew the words would know what they were. For me he was not an editor. He was a wise friend and a wonderful companion. I liked the way he wore his hat and the strange way his lips moved.

JOHN HERSEY: One of the things that has been bad for American publishing was the invention of the person called a copy-editor, an expert who knows grammar and can spot inconsistencies: a technician of text. Many copy-editors are very good at what they do, but the creation of that function has taken away from the principal editor a basic interest in the text. Most editors, with some notable exceptions, have become packagers now, rather than close editors. And I think that publishers are more interested in acquisitions from their editors than they are in developing to the fullest extent the craft of each writer they deal with. Publishing has changed in my years. I've worked since the era of Alfred Knopf Sr., who had as contemporaries people like Alfred Harcourt, Horace Liveright, Charles Scribner Sr., all essentially book men. In the case of Knopf, he was dazzled by authorhood; he cared more about his relationship with authors than he did about his relationship with books. His concern was the full career of the writer. He lost many authors, he was crusty, many writers moved on to other firms. But Knopf's concern was always for the growth of the person as a craftsman. Now—again with some worthy exceptions—the heads of firms are more apt to be businessmen. That's been a loss, I think.

PHILIP LARKIN: I shouldn't normally show what I'd written to anyone: what would be the point? You remember Tennyson reading an unpublished poem to Jowett; when he had finished, Jowett said, "I shouldn't publish that if I were you, Tennyson." Tennyson replied, "If it comes to that, Master, the sherry you gave us at lunch was downright filthy." That's about all that can happen.

ROBERT LOWELL: I'd gone to call on Frost with a huge epic on the First Crusade, all written out in clumsy longhand on lined paper. He read a page of that and said, "You have no compression." Then he read me a very short poem of Collins, "How Sleep the Brave," and said, "That's not a great poem, but it's not too long." He was very kindly about it. You know his point about the voice coming into poetry: he took a very unusual example of that, the opening of *Hyperion;* the line about the Naiad, something about her pressing a cold finger to her cold lips, which wouldn't seem like a voice passage at all. And he said, "Now Keats comes alive here." That was a revelation to me; what had impressed me was the big Miltonic imitation in *Hyperion.* I don't know what I did with that, but I recoiled and realized that I was diffuse and monotonous.

TONI MORRISON: Good editors are really the third eye. Cool. Dispassionate. They don't love you or your work; for me that is what is valuable—not compliments. Sometimes it's uncanny: the editor puts his or her finger on exactly the place the writer knows is weak but just couldn't do any better at the time. Or perhaps the writer thought it might fly, but wasn't sure. Good editors identify that place, and sometimes make suggestions. Some suggestions are not useful because you can't explain everything to an editor about what you are trying to do. I couldn't possibly explain all of those things to an editor, because what I do has to work on so many levels. But within the relationship if there is some trust, some willingness to listen, remarkable things can happen. I read books all the time that I know would have profited from, not a copy editor, but somebody just talking through it. And it is important to get a great editor at a certain time, because if you don't have one in the beginning, you almost can't have one later. If you work well without an editor, and your books are well received for five or ten years, and then you write another one, which is successful but not very good, why should you then listen to an editor?

· · ·

I was an editor myself for a long while, and I have great difficulty explaining what was so gratifying about it. I suppose editing is almost maternal at times: you see yourself as being able to deliver something nurturing and corrective, and the benefit and the pleasure is in seeing the nurturing and the corrective show without your fingerprints. If it has your fingerprints on it, it's no good. It's like knowing you've been successful with your children when they don't need you.

VLADIMIR NABOKOV: By "editor" I suppose you mean proofreader. Among these I have known limpid creatures of limitless tact and tenderness who would discuss with me a semi-colon as if it were a point of honor—which, indeed, a point of art often is. But I have also come across a few pompous avuncular brutes who would attempt to "make suggestions" which I countered with a thunderous "stet!"

DOROTHY PARKER: He [Harold Ross of *The New Yorker*] was a professional lunatic, but I don't know if he was a great man. He had a profound ignorance. On one of Mr. Benchley's manuscripts he wrote in the margin opposite "Andromache," "Who he?" Mr. Benchley wrote back, "You keep out of this."

EZRA POUND: Apart from Fordie [Ford Madox Ford] rolling on the floor undecorously and holding his head in his hands, and groaning on one occasion, I don't think anybody helped me through my manuscripts. Ford's stuff appeared too loose then, but he led the fight against tertiary archaisms.

· · ·

Once out at Rapallo I tried for God's sake to prevent him [W. B. Yeats] from printing a thing. I told him it was rubbish. All he did was print it with a preface saying that I *said* it was rubbish.

V. S. PRITCHETT: AE [Russell] was a mystic and a comfortable old chap. He was immensely talkative, and he was then editing the *Irish States-man.* I sent him my first story, which was about a gypsy who gets into a fight and accidentally stabs his own donkey and kills him instead of his adversary. It was overwritten and florid—I had never been with gypsies—and oddly enough AE accepted it. He kept it for two years and finally didn't publish it. He said it got squeezed out by Irish politics! Later he did publish a story of mine, but he never paid me!

IRWIN SHAW: The editors I had at *The New Yorker* quietly helped me in peculiar, small ways. One thing they taught me was the value of cutting out the last paragraph of stories, something I pass down as a tip to all writers. The last paragraph in which you tell what the story is about is almost always best left out.

GEORGE STEINER: Mr. Whittaker, of the original *New Yorker,* whose nickname was Mr. Frimbo, was my editor for the first twenty years there. Mr. Whittaker regarded an imprecision, of syntax or punctuation, as being dirty in an almost moral sense. If a sentence wasn't absolutely precise, if it waffled, if you put a colon where there should have been a semicolon, you were doing dirt: on your reader, on the language and ultimately on yourself. This could lead to transatlantic calls which you simply wouldn't believe. He would say, "Mr. Steiner"—always Mr., of course—"I think what you really meant was . . ." And you'd say, "Well that's what it says," and he'd say, "No, no, not quite. Will you listen to it again?" And he'd read it again, and gradually you would realize that he was right, that it wasn't exactly what it said. Now that kind of love for the resources of the English language, for the inexhaustible nuance of English punctuation, is extraordinary. Mr. Whittaker was a superb teacher, and so was Mr. Shawn, whose care over detail became a legend in his lifetime. Those were true teachers to work with in harness.

Yes, I've been lucky. Let me paraphrase one of the many Hasidic parables and say that I hope I would have the courage and energy to go a long way barefoot to a man or woman who could teach me something.

JAMES THURBER: He [Harold Ross of *The New Yorker*] wasn't the man to develop a writer. He was an unread man. Well, he'd read Mark Twain's *Life on the Mississippi* and several other books he told me about—medical books—and he took the Encyclopaedia Britannica to the bathroom with him. I think he was about up to H when he died. But still his effect on writers was considerable. When you first met him you couldn't believe he was the editor of *The New Yorker* and afterwards you couldn't believe that anyone else could have been. The main thing he was interested in was clarity. Someone once said of *The New Yorker* that it never contained a sentence that would puzzle an intelligent 14-year-old or in any way affect her morals badly. Ross didn't like that, but nevertheless he was a purist and perfectionist and it had a tremendous effect on all of us: it kept us from being sloppy. When I first met him he asked me if I knew English. I thought he meant French or a foreign language. But he repeated, "Do you know English?" As Andy White mentioned in his obituary, Ross approached the English sentence as though it was an enemy, something that was going to throw him. He used to fuss for an hour over a comma. He'd call me in for lengthy discussions about the Thurber colon. And as for poetic license, he'd say, "Damn any license to get things wrong." In fact, Ross read so carefully that often he didn't get the sense of your story. I once said: "I wish you'd read my stories for pleasure, Ross." He replied he hadn't time for that.

REBECCA WEST: I never met anybody with whom I could have discussed books before or after. One doesn't have people on one's wavelength as completely as that. I very rarely found *The New Yorker* editors any good.

JOHN HALL WHEELOCK: Once or twice books were turned down by Mr. Scribner because he was jealous of keeping his imprint free from anything that seemed unworthy or tasteless. He was a man of great courage; he would take chances, but there were some things that he was adamant about. When Scott Fitzgerald's first book, *This Side of Paradise*, came in, Mr. Scribner, after reading it, simply did not want his imprint on it. Only our great determination—and that of some of the other editors—that the book should be published made Mr. Scribner change his mind, and only on the condition that Fitzgerald cut and rewrite the book in certain sections. Even then, Mr. Scribner was not quite sure.

The story of *The Sun Also Rises* is more striking. At a meeting in his office, Mr. Scribner said that he did not care to have his imprint on the book. There was a long silence. Max Perkins could be very silent and not feel that he had to talk, not even to relieve embarrassment. Max was standing. Mr. Scribner, who was seated at his desk, looked up at him and said: "Max, you haven't said anything. I'm turning the book down. Haven't you got something you'd like to say?" Max finally said, "Yes, I'd like to say this: That if we are going to turn down such a talent we might as well go out of the publishing business. We cannot go on publishing Richard Harding Davis, Thomas Nelson Page, George Cable, Henry Van Dyke, and other worthies. If we're going to be publishers, we have to move along with the talents of the time, even though they may offend . . . well, even though they might offend our kind of taste." Finally Mr. Scribner asked Max: "Will Hemingway change some of the four-letter words? Take them out?" Max said, "Yes, he will take some of them out, I'm quite sure." "Which words will he take out?" said Mr. Scribner. Whereupon Max hastened to his office, got a piece of paper, came back, and wrote down the words. Mr. Scribner looked at him (he had a very mischievous sense of humor) and he said: "Max— if Ernest knew that you couldn't say those words, that you had to write them down, he'd disown you!"

· · ·

Max, of course, saw more of Thomas Wolfe than I did. In fact, Wolfe absorbed so much of Max's time, and indeed of the time of everyone connected with the editorial department, that Mr. Scribner felt he'd have to let him go because other authors resented the excess attention Thomas Wolfe was getting. He slept in the office; he lived there, he was a tremendous talker; he would go from one office to another with this endless flow of language. He was an impetuous, impulsive man who in his normal state of mind, which was most of the time, could be very charming. But when he had a drink or two (and he was rather inclined to drink more as he tired from his tremendous labors), he could be really paranoiac, and almost manic. But the feeling that Max Perkins had for Wolfe as a writer was extraordinary. . . . I always felt there was more to the relationship: Max had no son; and he had a strange attitude about women which is hard to reconcile with his courtesy and his affection for his wife, but the fact was he regarded women as inferior, he seemed in some ways to resent them. He could be very severe with his wife. They had five daughters, so he sat down to breakfast with six women. He really longed for a son and he made Tom his son. As you know, Tom in the end betrayed him. Well, *betrayal* perhaps is the wrong word. But in his paranoiac state of mind, he conceived the idea that Max had ruined his books by playing so large a part in editing them and helping him. Max had objected to certain points-of-view in *Look Homeward, Angel* which reflected Tom's interest in communism ... involving Eugene, the hero of the book, in communist and liberal movements at a time when according to the background framework of the novel, no such things were going on. Because of this Tom got the idea that Max was an old Tory and was taming his book and had ruined it. He wrote letters to Max that were really dreadful. They were not found until after Max's death because Max was so ashamed of them he had hidden them in his desk. But, as you know, on his deathbed, Tom wrote that famous letter to Max which made all the difference. He admitted that Max was the one who had made his work possible, and he asked forgiveness and said: "Let's think of the day we walked over Brooklyn Bridge together, and the book had been published, and the first reviews were coming in, and the world with all its glory and beauty lay before us, and we were happy. That's the way I think of you now. I've met the dark man, and I don't think I was too afraid of him. But I know I have to go and I wanted you to get this before that happened."

On Publication: Success, Failure, etc.

Posterity—what you write for after being turned down by publishers. —George Ade

For several days after my first book was published I carried it about in my pocket, and took surreptitious peeps at it to make sure the ink had not faded. —Sir James M. Barrie

There is a great discovery still to be made in Literature, that of paying literary men by the quantity they do not write. —Thomas Carlyle

While we are asleep, we are all equal. —Miguel de Cervantes

If you aspire to the highest place it is no disgrace to stop at the second, or even the third. —Cicero

Success is a rare paint; hides all the ugliness. —Sir John Suckling

Success and failure are equally disastrous. —Tennessee Williams

W. H. Auden: A friend of mine, Dorothy Day, had been put in the women's prison at 6th Avenue and 8th Street, for her part in a protest. Well, once a week at this place, on a Saturday, the girls were marched down for a shower. A group were being ushered in when one, a whore, loudly proclaimed:

> Hundreds have lived without love,
> But none without water

A line from a poem of mine which had just appeared in *The New Yorker*. When I heard this I knew I hadn't written in vain!

SIMONE DE BEAUVOIR: In my time it was unusual to be published when you were very young. Of course, there were one or two examples, such as Radiguet, who was a prodigy. Sartre himself wasn't published until he was about thirty-five, when *Nausea* and *The Wall* were brought out. When my first more or less publishable book was rejected, I was a bit discouraged. And when the first version of *She Came to Stay* was rejected, it was very unpleasant. Then I thought that I ought to take my time. I knew many examples of writers who were slow in getting started. And people always spoke of the case of Stendhal, who didn't begin to write until he was forty.

SAUL BELLOW: I don't like to agree with the going view that if you write a best-seller it's because you betrayed an important principle or sold your soul. I know that sophisticated opinion believes this. And although I don't take much stock in sophisticated opinion, I have examined my conscience. I've tried to find out whether I had unwittingly done wrong. But I haven't yet discovered the sin. I do think that a book like *Herzog,* which ought to have been an obscure book with a total sale of 8000, has such a reception because it appeals to the unconscious sympathies of many people. I know from the mail I've received that the book described a common predicament. *Herzog* appealed to Jewish readers, to those who have been divorced, to those who talk to themselves, to college graduates, readers of paperbacks, autodidactics, to those who yet hope to live a while, etc.

JOHN BERRYMAN: You have to believe in your stuff—every day has to be the new day on which the new poem may be *it*. Well, fame supports that feeling. It gives self-confidence, it gives a sense of an actual, contemporary audience, and so on. On the other hand, unless it is sustained, it can cause trouble—and it is very seldom sustained. If your first book is a smash, your second book gets kicked in the face, and your third book, and lots of people, like Delmore [Schwartz], can't survive that disappointment. From that point of view, early fame is very dangerous indeed, and my situation, which was so painful to me for many years, was really in a way beneficial.

I overestimated myself, as it turned out, and felt bitter, bitterly neglected; but I had certain admirers, certain high judges on my side from the beginning, so that I had a certain amount of support. Moreover, I had a kind of indifference on my side—much as Joseph Conrad did. A reporter asked him once about reviews, and he said, "I don't read my reviews. I measure them." Now, until I was about thirty-five years old, I not only didn't read my reviews, I didn't measure them, I never even looked at them. That is so peculiar that close friends of mine wouldn't believe me when I told them. I thought that was indifference, but now I'm convinced that it was just that I had no skin on—you know, I was afraid of being killed by some remark. Oversensitivity. But there was an *element* of indifference in it, and so the public indifference to my work was countered with a certain amount of genuine indifference on my part, which has been very helpful since I became a celebrity. Auden once said that the best situation for a poet is to be taken up early and held for a considerable time and then dropped after he has reached the level of indifference.

Something else is in my head: a remark of Father Hopkins to Bridges. Two completely unknown poets in their thirties—fully mature—Hopkins, one of the great poets of the century, and Bridges, awfully good. Hopkins with no audience and Bridges with thirty readers. He says, "Fame in itself is nothing. The only thing that matters is virtue. Jesus Christ is the only true literary critic. But," he said, "from any lesser level or standard than that, we must recognize that fame is the true and appointed setting of men of genius." That seems to me appropriate. This business about geniuses in neglected garrets is for the birds. The idea that a man is somehow no good just because he becomes very popular, like Frost, is nonsense, also. There are exceptions, Chatterton, Hopkins, of course, Rimbaud, you can think of various cases, but on the whole, men of genius were judged by their contemporaries very much as posterity judges them. So if I were talking to a young writer, I would recommend the cultivation of extreme indifference to both praise and blame because praise will lead you to vanity, and blame will lead you to self-pity, and both are bad for writers.

JULIO CORTÁZAR: Ah, listen, I'll say something I shouldn't say because no one will believe it, but success isn't a pleasure for me. I'm glad to be able to live from what I write, so I have to put up with the popular and critical side of success. But I was happier as a man when I was unknown. Much happier. Now I can't go to Latin America or to Spain without being recognized every ten yards, and the autographs, the embraces. . . . It's very moving, because they're readers who are frequently quite young. I'm happy that they like what I do, but it's terribly distressing for me on the level of privacy. I can't go to a beach in Europe; in five minutes there's a photographer. I have a physical appearance that I can't disguise; if I were small I could shave and put on sunglasses, but with my height, my long arms, and all that, they discover me from afar. On the other hand, there are very beautiful things: I was in Barcelona a month ago, walking around the gothic quarter one evening, and there was an American girl, very pretty, playing the guitar very well and singing. She was seated on the ground singing to earn her living. She sang a bit like Joan Baez, a very pure, clear voice. There was a group of young people from Barcelona listening. I stopped to listen to her, but I stayed in the shadows. At one point, one of these young men who was about twenty, very young, very handsome, approached me. He had a cake in his hand. He said, "Julio, take a piece." So I took a piece and I ate it, and I told him, "Thanks a lot for coming up and giving that to me." He said to me, "But, listen, I give you so little next to what you've given me." I said, "Don't say that, don't say that," and we embraced and he went away. Well, things like that, that's the best recompense for my work as a writer. That a boy or a girl comes up to speak to you and to offer you a piece of cake, it's wonderful. It's worth the trouble of having written.

MALCOLM COWLEY: I keep hoping I'll be compensated in some way. Once I wrote a piece that tried to sum up the joys and vexations of being eighty, but I left out one of the worst vexations—which is to become a national scholarly resource. I never expected to become a national scholarly resource—but you can't escape the destiny of your dotage. Simply by having outlived your great contemporaries, you find that you have a field all to yourself; or if you don't have a field, at least you have a stable in one corner of the field. Hundreds of scholars then come into the field who are writing dissertations, monographs, biographies—all sorts of things—and for each one they want to have a little reinforcement, a little supplement; they want to have a word straight from the horse's mouth. So they come to me and say, "Well, you are the horse—won't you please share your memories? Won't you please answer this little questionnaire of five single-spaced typed pages?" or, "Won't you let us put your memories on tape?" There is no enrichment from this sort of thing. Not one of them thinks of filling the horse's feed-box with oats or of putting a little hay in the manger. They assume, I guess, that a horse can just forage for himself—if he has time; certainly nobody gives him an offer to earn an easy living by putting himself out to stud.

JAMES DICKEY: Luck plays an enormous part in it. It's not like business, though luck has a very strong place in business too. You can write one good poem by luck or hazard that's going to make people want your work. Whether or not you can produce anything good later on is not the important thing. It's that you struck it right then. It's the same with a novel—I wrote *Deliverance.* The movies bought it; it was serialized, written into a dozen languages; it's the best novel I can write, but there's also an enormous element of luck in it. I wrote the right book at the right time. People were caught up in a savage fable of decent men fighting for their lives and killing and getting away with it. My next novel could be a failure.

GABRIEL GARCÍA MÁRQUEZ: Fame invades your private life. It takes away from the time that you spend with friends, and the time that you can work. It tends to isolate you from the real world. A famous writer who wants to continue writing has to be constantly defending himself against fame. I don't really like to say this because it never sounds sincere, but I would really have liked for my books to have been published after my death, so I wouldn't have to go through all this business of fame and being a great writer. In my case, the only advantage in fame is that I have been able to give it a political use. Otherwise, it is quite uncomfortable. The problem is that you're famous for twenty-four hours a day and you can't say, "Okay, I won't be famous until tomorrow" or press a button and say, "I won't be famous here or now."

I was asked the other day if I would be interested in the Nobel Prize, but I think that for me it would be an absolute catastrophe. I would certainly be interested in deserving it, but to receive it would be terrible. It would just complicate even more the problems of fame. The only thing I really regret in life is not having a daughter.

LILLIAN HELLMAN: It [*The Days to Come*] was an absolute horror of a failure. I mean the curtain wasn't up ten minutes and catastrophe set in. It was just an awful failure. Mr. William Randolph Hearst caused a little excitement by getting up in the middle of the first act and leaving with his party of ten. I vomited in the back aisle. I did. I had to go home and change my clothes. I was drunk.

EUGÈNE IONESCO: I detest and despise success, yet I cannot do without it. I am like a drug addict—if nobody talks about me for a couple of months I have withdrawal symptoms. It is stupid to be hooked on fame, because it is like being hooked on corpses. After all, the people who come to see my plays, who create my fame, are going to die.

GARRISON KEILLOR: When *The New Yorker* rejected work, they did it in an elaborately polite way, apologizing for their shortsightedness, that undoubtedly it was their fault, but somehow, this story fell slightly short of your remarkably high standard. They had a way of rejecting my work that made me feel sorry for them, somehow.

ARCHIBALD MACLEISH: You get to the point where you realize that personal fame is not at all what you're concerned with really—that old Robert [Frost] was right when he said he hoped to leave half a dozen poems which would be hard to get rid of. Wonderful way of saying it. You begin to see that what is really going to happen is not that half a dozen but two, three, four poems, or maybe lines of poems, or fragments—some things may get shelved, shored up, or left behind. But left behind not alone but in a conjunction. So that you begin to think of yourself in terms of the others who were with you in this place—your contemporaries. "Oh living men, Remember me, Receive me among you." And you realize that's how you are really going to end up. You're going to be part of that, of them. And finally you begin to think, that's the way it ought to be. You ought to make the world fruitful that way. Rot! Leaving those fragments—those few poems that will be hard to get rid of.

. . .

I don't know if there is anything I can say about it, but by God something ought to be said. Let me begin with two people whom I knew, one very well and one quite well: Ernest Hemingway and Scott Fitzgerald. The tragedy—and it is a tragedy—of Hemingway's fame is that his life and his dramatization of himself have been built up, not by him, or let me say, not altogether by him, to such a point that the myth of the man is more important than the achievement—the work. And the same thing is true of Scott, Scott having done less about dramatizing himself, but having had more done for him. In each case the *Literary Figure*—capital "L", capital "F"—has been so blown up, so exaggerated, that the work has been diminished. You would know better than I how permanently, but in any case damage has been done. And the same thing is true of Robert Frost. Robert was himself the villain there, because, as anybody who knew him knows, he worked very hard at his own reputation even when he had no need to— when his greatness was acknowledged. This was damaging only to him. But the real question is what you do about this sort of thing. I don't know that pontificating about it does any good. My own conviction is that the literary person as such just doesn't count—doesn't matter. Some are interesting and some are dull. The only thing that matters is the work. And the amplification of the amplifying device, which is the man himself, is not good for the art of writing, is not good for the writer, is not good. Ernest used to love to come up and go to the nightclubs in New York. Why? To be recognized? But, for God's sake, he had been recognized in better ways before. I am not throwing off on Ernest. He is still the great prose stylist of the century. But if ever there was a cult of personality . . . ! Well, the one thing a young writer ought to swear to on his sword never to do is never to dramatize himself, whatever he may want to do about his work.

NORMAN MAILER: Booze, pot, too much sex, too much failure in one's private life, too much attrition, too much recognition, too little recognition, frustration. Nearly everything in the scheme of things works to dull a first-rate talent. But the worst probably is cowardice—as one gets older, one becomes aware of one's cowardice, the desire to be bold which once was a joy gets heavy with caution and duty. And finally there's apathy. About the time it doesn't seem too important anymore to be a great writer, you know you've slipped far enough to be doing your work now on the comeback trail.

FRANÇOIS MAURIAC: Almost all the works die while the men remain. We seldom read any more of Rousseau than his *Confessions,* or of Chateaubriand than his *Mémoires d'outre-tombe.* They alone interest us. I have always been and still remain a great admirer of Gide. It already appears, however, that only his journal and *Si le grain ne muert,* the story of his childhood, have any chance of lasting. The rarest thing in literature, and the only success, is when the author disappears and his work remains. We don't know who Shakespeare was, or Homer. People have worn themselves out writing about the life of Racine without being able to establish anything. He is lost in the radiance of his creation. That is quite rare.

JOHN MORTIMER: The first notice I got—and I don't like notices; they make me very frightened—was by a man called Daniel George who wrote in *The Daily Express,* "Not for fifteen years have I found so certain a touch." Now if I got that nowadays I would be absolutely delighted. But when I got that when I was twenty-three I was absolutely furious. I thought, "Who is this swine whom he read fifteen years ago who had such wonderful writing?"

PATRICK O'BRIAN: The writers of fan letters fall into four main classes: 1. Those who say "I love your books and I wish to thank you." 2. Poor lonely souls who just want to write to someone. 3. Those whose ancestors went to sea and who would like information about their careers, and 4. Those who point out my errors, sometimes real (I am a left-handed man and when I am writing I easily confuse right and left, east and west: this does not happen aboard, however) but more often, I am glad to say, imaginary. All four classes have grown so numerous these last years that I have had to beg my publishers to sieve them, because I am a slow, indifferent letter-writer and even half a dozen eat all the cream of my morning work, the best time by far. Yet they are sometimes extraordinarily encouraging: I think primarily of sick people who have found some relief in my books, but also of that splendid admiral who, dating his letter from the North Atlantic, told me that after a strenuous day of exercising his submarines he would submerge, sinking to the calmness of deep water, and there, in the ocean's bosom unespied, he would turn to my naval tales: or of that other gentleman whose thank you took the form of a wholly gratuitous offer of his 154-foot yacht with a numerous crew (including an excellent chef) and room for ourselves and six of our friends, to cruise for a fortnight in the Mediterranean or the Caribbean this coming spring or summer, himself making no appearance whatever. And if you do not call that handsome you must be very, very hard to please.

EDNA O'BRIEN: It is only by the grace of God, and perhaps willpower, that one comes through each time. Many wonderful writers write one or two books and then kill themselves. Sylvia Plath for instance. She was much younger than Virginia Woolf when she committed suicide, but if she had survived that terrible crisis, I feel she would have written better books. I have this theory that Woolf feared that the flame of her talent was extinguished or dwindling because her last book, *Between the Acts,* lacked the soaring genius of the others. When a writer, or an artist, has the feeling that he can't do it anymore, he descends into hell. So you must keep in mind that although it may stop, it can come back. When I was a child in

Ireland, a spring would suddenly appear and yield forth buckets of beautiful clear water, then just as suddenly it would dry up. The water-diviners would come with their rods and sometimes another spring would be found. One has to be one's own water-diviner. It is hard, especially as writers are always anxious, always on the run—from the telephone, from people, from responsibilities, from the distractions of this world. The other thing that can destroy talent is too much grief. Yeats said, "Too much sorrow can make a stone of the heart." I often wonder, if Emily Brontë had lived to be fifty, what kind of books would she have written? Her life was so penalizing—and Charlotte's too—utterly without sex. Emily was thirty when she wrote *Wuthering Heights.* I think the grinding suffering might have killed her talent later. It is not that you have to be happy—that would be asking too much—but if it gets too painful that sense of wonderment, or joy, dies, and with it the generosity so necessary to create.

FRANK O'CONNOR: Don't take rejection slips too seriously. I don't think they ought to send them out at all. I think a very amusing anthology might be gotten up of rejection letters alone. It's largely a question of remembering, when you send something out, that So-and-so is on the other end of this one, and he has certain interests. To give an example of what I mean on this rejection business, I had a story accepted by a magazine. So I wrote it over again as I always do, and sent it back. Well, someone else got it and I got this very nice letter saying that they couldn't use it, but that they'd be very interested in seeing anything else I wrote in the future.

CYNTHIA OZICK: One *must* avoid ambition *in order to* write. Otherwise something else is the goal: some kind of power beyond the power of language. And the power of language, it seems to me, is the only kind of power a writer is entitled to.

JAMES SALTER: I've never had a story in *The New Yorker;* everything has been rejected. At one point I came close. I had written a story called "Via Negativa," and I had a note from Roger Angell who said, please come in to talk about it. I sat in a little gray office with him, and he told me that he liked the story very much. He said, "This is really quite good, but I'm afraid we can't take it." I was stunned. I said, "Why is that?" He said, "At *The New Yorker* we have two rules we never violate. The first is that we never publish anything with obscenity in it. Second, we never publish any stories about writers or writing." I hardly knew what to say. "What about the Bech stories by Updike?" I asked. He said, "Well, that's another matter." A year or two later I was talking to Saul Bellow about this, and he said, "I tried to get them to publish a section of *The Victim,* but they didn't accept it. They said they had two rules that they never violated. One, they never published anything that had obscenity in it. Two, they never published anything about death or dying."

IRWIN SHAW: Failure is inevitable for the writer. Any writer. I don't care who he is, or how great he is, or what he's written. Sooner or later he's going to flop and everybody who admired him will try to write him off as a bum. He can't help it. He's bound to write something bad. Shakespeare wrote a few bad plays. Tolstoy was turning out some pretty dreadful stuff at the end of his life. Name me one great writer who hasn't had some failure. . . . Everybody forgets that a writer who has had success, even one who's made a lot of money on one book, may have waited fifteen years for that one book, and before he can produce another one, it may be another fifteen years, if ever. And I'm not only talking about commercial or critical failure. There's the kind of running failure that dogs a writer all his life—ideas that only get half-written, false beginnings, first drafts that suddenly go dead and have to be thrown away, even crucial paragraphs that stiffen under your hand and refuse to be revived. And then, whole books, even if they've been well-received, that nag you long after they've been published, because you see where you could have done something better with them. And then, American writers, more than any others, are haunted by the fear of failure, because it's such a common pattern in America. The ghost of Fitzgerald, dying in Hollywood, with his comeback book unfinished, and his best book, *Tender Is the Night,* scorned—his ghost hangs over every American typewriter. An absolutely necessary part of a writer's equipment, almost as necessary as talent, is the ability to stand up under punishment, both the punishment the world hands out and the punishment he inflicts upon himself. If he doesn't have the faith in himself, the energy, the ambition, to shake it off or absorb it and plow ahead, he'll wind up a one-book man or a two-book man, and hitting the bottle instead of the typewriter. Failure is more consistent—for everybody—than success. It's like living in a rainy belt—there are some sunny days, but most of the time it's wet outside and you'd better carry your umbrella. Anyway, failure is apt to produce self-pity and it's been my experience that self-pity can be very productive.

SAM SHEPARD: My father found out about a production of *Buried Child* that was going on at the Greer Garson Theater in New Mexico. He went to the show smashed, just pickled, and in the middle of the play he began to identify with some character, though I'm not sure which one, since all those characters are kind of loosely structured around his family. In the second act he stood up and started to carry on with the actors, and then yelled, "What a bunch of shit this is!" The ushers tried to throw him out. He resisted, and in the end they allowed him to stay because he was the father of the playwright.

NEIL SIMON: On the opening night of *Little Me*, Bob Fosse and I were standing in the back of the theater. The producers had allowed a black-tie audience to come from a dinner to the theater. They'd eaten, they'd had drinks, they all knew each other—that's the worst audience you can get. About three-quarters of the way through the first act, a man got up, so drunk he could hardly walk, and staggered up the aisle looking for the men's room. As he passed Bob and me, he said, "This is the worst piece of crap I've seen since *My Fair Lady!*" Go figure out what *that* means.

WILLIAM STAFFORD: I do feel at home in the world. I have genuinely felt throughout my life a sense that any acceptance of what I write is a bonus, a gift from other people. It's not something that's due me. When any editor has a place for some of my work, that's fine, but I always send that stamped return envelope. I'm genuinely ready for those rejections. I've always felt that an editor's role is to get the best possible material for the readers of the publication, not to serve the writer, not at all. If they don't want it, I don't want them to have it. So I never have felt that I needed to push this stuff into the world. If it's invited in, then it will come in. If it's not invited in, fine, it will live at home.

· · ·

This may sound brutal, but I don't cherish the poems that are done. I cherish the poems that are coming. I'd sacrifice all the poems of the past for whatever is coming up. It's not a feeling of either satisfaction, or progress, or defending them. As far as I'm concerned, they're in the world to make a living for themselves if they can do it. I'm not going to do anything for them.

TOM STOPPARD: One bull's-eye and you're rich and famous. The rich get more famous and the famous get richer. You're the talk of the town.

The taxi drivers have read about you and they remember you for a fortnight. You get to be photographed for *Vogue* with new clothes and Vuitton luggage, if that's your bag. If it's a new play, everyone owes the writer, they celebrate him—the theater owners, the producers, the actors. Even the stage doorman is somehow touched by the wand. The sense of so much depending on success is very hard to ignore, perhaps impossible. It leads to disproportionate anxiety and disproportionate relief or disappointment. The British are more phlegmatic about these things. You know about British phlegm.

P. L. TRAVERS: The other day two little boys accosted me in the street and said to me, "You are the lady who wrote *Mary Poppins,* aren't you?" And I admitted it, and said, "How do you know?" And they said, "Because we sing in the choir, and the vicar told us." So, clearly, they had thrown off their surplices and rushed after me to catch me. So I said, "Well, do you like her?" And they both nodded vigorously. I then said, "What is it you like about her?" And one of them said, "Well, she's so *ordinary* and then..." and having said "and then" he looked around for the proper word, and couldn't find it. And I said, "You don't have to say any more. That 'and then' says everything." And the other little boy said, "Yes, and I'm going to marry her when I grow up." And I saw the first one clench his fists and look very belligerent. I felt there might be trouble and so I said, "Well, we'll just have to see what *she* thinks about it, won't we? And in the meantime, my house is just there—come in and have a lemonade." So they did.

JOHN UPDIKE: I'm interviewed too much. I fight them off, but even one is too many. In any interview, you do say more or less than you mean. You leave the proper ground of your strength and become one more gassy monologist. Unlike Mailer and Bellow, I don't have much itch to pronounce on great matters, to reform the country, to get elected Mayor of New York, or minister to the world with laughter like the hero of "The Last Analysis." My life is, in a sense, trash, my life is only that of which the residue is my writing.

WENDY WASSERSTEIN: Fame is not about getting a restaurant reservation. It's about walking up Madison Avenue on the way to your therapist, and you're thinking, My God, I'm worthless, what am I doing with my life, I'm horrible. . . . Then some woman comes up to you and says, "You're Wendy Wasserstein. I can't tell you how much you mean to me."

I want to say to this person, "I'm glad I mean something to you because I mean nothing to me. Thank you very much." Then I think, What is wrong with me?

JESSAMYN WEST: A cousin of mine wrote to my professor of English at Whittier College and to my poor mother (who had been so proud that her daughter had a book published) to say, first of all, no Milhous had ever said "ain't." Second, it was degrading to the Quaker faith to have Jess pray louder than was necessary. Actually, he was not really shouting to God, you know, he was trying to make himself heard above the organ. Third, I often used dirty words. I said that a duck (and it was a Quaker duck too) deposited duck dung on the steps, and that Jess didn't like ducks for that reason. My cousin felt I could have found some other way to say it, in spite of the alliteration.

ON CRITICS

Critics are like eunuchs in a harem: they know how it's done, they've seen it done every day, but they're unable to do it themselves. —BRENDAN BEHAN

You know who critics are—the men who have failed in literature and art. —BENJAMIN DISRAELI

Monsieur Flaubert is not a writer.
—*LE FIGARO* on *Madame Bovary*

Some reviews give pain. That is regrettable, but no author has the right to whine. He was not obliged to be an author. He invited publicity, and he must take the publicity that comes along. —E. M. FORSTER

It's much more important to write than to be written about.
—GABRIEL GARCÍA MÁRQUEZ

It is advantageous to an author that his book should be attacked as well as praised. Fame is a shuttlecock. If it be struck at only one end of the room, it will soon fall to the ground. To keep it up, it must be struck at both ends. —SAMUEL JOHNSON

There be some men born only to suck out the poison of books.
—BEN JONSON

You do not publish your own verses, Laelius; you criticise mine. Pray cease to criticise mine, or else publish your own.
—MARTIAL

It is salutary to train oneself to be no more affected by censure than by praise. —W. SOMERSET MAUGHAM

It's a short walk from the hallelujah to the hoot.
—VLADIMIR NABOKOV

Book reviewers are little old ladies of both sexes.
—JOHN O'HARA

I love every bone in their heads. —EUGENE O'NEILL

A drama critic is a man who leaves no turn unstoned.
—GEORGE BERNARD SHAW

EDWARD ALBEE: Indeed it is true that a number of the movie critics of *Who's Afraid of Virginia Woolf?* have repeated the speculation that the play was written about four homosexuals disguised as heterosexual men and women. This comment first appeared around the time the play was produced. I was fascinated by it. I suppose what disturbed me about it was twofold: first, nobody has ever bothered to ask *me* whether it was true; second, the critics and columnists made no attempt to document the assertion from the text of the play. The facts are simple: *Who's Afraid of Virginia Woolf?* was written about two heterosexual couples. If I had wanted to write a play about four homosexuals, I would have done so. Parenthetically, it is interesting that when the film critic of *Newsweek* stated that he understood the play to have been written about four homosexuals, I had a letter written to him suggesting he check his information before printing such speculations. He replied, saying, in effect, two things: first, that we all know that a critic is a far better judge of an author's intention than the author; second, that seeing the play as being about four homosexuals was the only way that he could live with the play, meaning that he could not accept it as a valid examination of heterosexual life. Well, I'm sure that all the actresses from Uta Hagen to Elizabeth Taylor who've played the role of Martha would be absolutely astonished to learn they've been playing men.

TRUMAN CAPOTE: Before publication, and if provided by persons whose judgment you trust, yes, of course criticism helps. But after something is published all I want to read or hear is praise. Anything less is a bore, and I'll give you fifty dollars if you produce a writer who can honestly say he was ever helped by the prissy carpings and condescensions of reviewers. I don't mean to say that none of the professional critics are worth paying attention to . . . but few of the good ones review on a regular basis. Most of all, I believe in hardening yourself against opinion. I've had, and continue to receive, my full share of abuse, some of it extremely personal, but it doesn't faze me anymore. . . . I can read the most outrageous libel about myself and never skip a pulsebeat. And in this connection there is one piece of advice I strongly urge: never demean yourself by talking back to a critic, never. Write those letters to the editor in your head, but don't put them on paper.

JAMES DICKEY: I don't really read very many reviews of anything I write. If somebody comes up to me and says, "Jim, there's a fabulous review in the *Atlantic* and you must read it; he's crazy about the book," then I'll read it. If the guy says it's a horrible review and that I'm the anti-Christ himself, then I don't read it, because I don't want to go around filled with resentment against some stranger. That bleeds off your energies; you take them out in useless hatred. I need the energy for other things. I've known writers who are absolutely destroyed by adverse opinion, and I think this is a lot of shit. You shouldn't allow that to happen to yourself, and if you do, then it's *your* fault. My course is set; I know what I'm going to do. As Stephen Dedalus says, in *A Portrait of the Artist as a Young Man*, "I'm ready to make a lifelong mistake." I believe in making a lifelong mistake, but I don't believe in being guided by people who write about me. Why, there's not anything that could ever be said about a person either good or bad that hasn't been said about me. But it doesn't matter. I'm going to write my way, and if that doesn't agree with people's sensibilities or even their digestions, it doesn't make any difference to me. If it's a lifelong mistake, it won't be the first one that's been made.

J. P. DONLEAVY: Donoghue was someone who used to come into my rooms at Trinity and see something in the typewriter and glance at it. I'd ask him, "What do you think of that, Donoghue?" and he'd say, "It stinks!" This went on for days and days every time he'd come in trying to get food from me. And then—he was a classicist—one night I typed out some Plato and left it in my typewriter, and I had it ready for him as he popped in. And I said, "Okay, Donoghue, there is the typewriter. Now let's have your opinion on that." "That stinks too." "Look, Donoghue, I've tried awfully hard with this." He'd say, "Doesn't matter. You're never going to make it." I made him give it a second reading, but he said it still stunk. Then I revealed to him it was Plato. And that stopped him staring at my typewriter. He finally conceded, "What the hell, you work hard, maybe you'll make it."

JOHN DOS PASSOS: People sometimes send me articles about myself, and I bundle them off after a while to the University of Virginia for the professors to mull over. Occasionally I look at things, but I've generally managed to avoid stuff written about my work because there just isn't time to fuss with it. I don't think I've lost very much sleep by what you would call the critical reception of my work. I've been very fortunate in a way. If a thing is knocked in one place, somebody else may like it somewhere else. *The Great Days* was very much ignored in this country, but it went quite well in England and in Germany. I wouldn't have been able to make a living without the international market.

MARGARET DRABBLE: I find what they call "constructive" criticism helpful. Occasionally you come across somebody who says, "Why didn't she do so and so?" And you think, "God, why didn't I?" And he says, "Why doesn't she do so and so next time?" And you think, "Yes, why don't I?"

LAWRENCE DURRELL: [If I pay any attention to critics], I get blocks. I have discovered quite recently that the characteristic Freudian resistances to confessions of any sort, which are very well represented in all the writing blocks one goes through—the dizzy fits, the nauseas, and so on and so forth, which almost every writer has recorded—are a standard pattern for all kinds of creative things. They are simply forms of egotism. And egotism can be inflamed very easily by a good review, or a bad review for that matter, and you can get a nice tidy block which will cost you two days of work. And when you've got to get the money for the work, you can't afford it. So I don't read reviews unless they're sent to me. Usually they go to my agent because they help sell foreign rights. And it sounds very pompous, but really I think they have a bad influence on one, and even the good ones make you a bit ashamed. In fact I think the best regimen is to get up early, insult yourself a bit in the shaving-mirror, and then pretend you're cutting wood, which is really just about all the hell you are doing—if you see what I mean. But all the Jungian guilt about the importance of one's message, and all that sort of thing—well, you get a nice corpulent ego standing in the way there, telling you that you're so damn clever that you're almost afraid to write it down, it's so wonderful. And the minute you get that, where are your checks going to come from for next month's gas, light, and heat? You can't afford it.

ALDOUS HUXLEY: They've never had any effect on me, for the simple reason that I've never read them. I've never made a point of writing for any particular person or audience; I've simply tried to do the best job I could and let it go at that. The critics don't interest me because they're concerned with what's past and done, while I'm concerned with what comes next. I've never reread my early novels, for example. Perhaps I should read them one of these days.

JOHN IRVING: I have a friend who says that reviewers are the tickbirds of the literary rhinoceros—but he is being kind. Tickbirds perform a valuable service to the rhino and the rhino hardly notices the birds. Reviewers perform no service to the writer and are noticed too much. I like what Cocteau said about them. "Listen very carefully to the first criticism of your work. Note just what it is about your work that the reviewers don't like; it may be the only thing in your work that is original and worthwhile."

CYNTHIA OZICK: I was thirty-seven years old. I had the baby and the galleys together, and I sat at my desk—the same desk I use now, the same desk I inherited from my brother when I was eight years old—correcting the galleys with my right hand, and rocking the baby carriage with my left. I felt stung when the review in *Time*, which had a big feature on first novels that season, got my age wrong and added a year. I hated being so old; beginning when I thought I'd be so far along. I've had age-sorrow all my life.

V. S. PRITCHETT: I think the critic must first of all clear his own mind. Someone who has worked on a book, perhaps for years, and succeeded in getting it published, must have some quality. What is it? The critic has to sort him out and look for his merits. I always look for the real voice of a writer because most good writers have a distinctive voice. If he doesn't have a voice, however important the subject may be, the book is not interesting.

FRANÇOISE SAGAN: When the articles were agreeable I read them through. I never learned anything at all from them but I was astonished by their imagination and fecundity. They saw intentions I never had.

STEPHEN SPENDER: Auden himself had total self-confidence, of course. He just thought that he was cleverer than anyone else, but without arrogance really, just out of his own judgment, which may or may not have been right, but which nevertheless was never arrogant. He knew exactly what he was doing, and he was totally indifferent to what anyone said about it. And then being a "psychoanalyst" helped him a great deal. For instance, when he was so attacked by Randall Jarrell in 1947 or so, he said, "He must be in love with me; I can't think of any other explanation." Well, that isn't what one usually thinks about being attacked in print. He was genuinely puzzled. He didn't think it was a damaging attack in any way.

WILLIAM STYRON: From the writer's point of view, critics should be ignored, although it's hard not to do what they suggest. I think it's unfortunate to have critics for friends. Suppose you write something that stinks, what are they going to say in a review? Say it stinks? So if they're honest they do, and if you were friends you're still friends, but the knowledge of your lousy writing and their articulate admission of it will be always something between the two of you, like the knowledge between a man and his wife of some shady adultery. I know very few critics, but I usually read their reviews. Bad notices always give me a sense of humility, or perhaps humiliation, even when there's a tone of envy or sour grapes or even ignorance in them, but they don't help me much. When *Lie Down in Darkness* came out, my home-town paper scraped up the local literary figure to review the book, a guy who'd written something on hydraulics, I think, and he came to the conclusion that I was a decadent writer. Styron is a decadent writer, he said, because he writes a line like "the sea sucking at the shore," when for that depraved bit he should have substituted "the waves lapping at the shore." Probably his hydraulic background. No, I'm afraid I don't think much of critics for the most part, although I have to admit that some of them have so far treated me quite kindly. Look, there's only one person a writer should listen to, pay any attention to. It's not any damn critic. It's the reader. And that doesn't mean any compromise or sell-out. The writer must criticize his own work as a reader. Every day I pick up the story or whatever it is I've been working on and read it through. If I enjoy it as a reader then I know I'm getting along all right.

KURT VONNEGUT: *Slapstick* may be a very bad book. I am perfectly willing to believe that. Everybody else writes lousy books, so why shouldn't I? What was unusual about the reviews was that they wanted people to admit now that I had never been any good. The reviewer for the Sunday *Times* actually asked critics who had praised me in the past to now admit in public how wrong they'd been. All of a sudden, critics wanted me squashed like a bug. And it wasn't just that I had money all of a sudden, either. The hidden complaint was that I was barbarous, that I wrote without having made a systematic study of great literature, that I was no gentleman, since I had done hack writing so cheerfully for vulgar magazines—that I had not paid my academic dues. It was dishonorable enough that I perverted art for money. I then topped that felony by becoming, as I say, fabulously well-to-do. Well, that's just too damn bad for me and for everybody. I'm completely in print, so we're all stuck with me and stuck with my books.

THORNTON WILDER: The important thing is that you make sure that neither the favorable nor the unfavorable critics move into your head and take part in the composition of your next work.

P. G. WODEHOUSE: I always read them really carefully. You do get tips from them. Now that last Jeeves book of mine, *Jeeves and the Tie That Binds,* I forget which critic it was, but he said that the book was dangerously near to self-parody. I know what he meant. I had exaggerated Jeeves and Bertie. Jeeves always reciting some poetry or something. I'll correct that in the next one. I do think one can learn from criticism. In fact, I'm a pretty good critic of my own work. I know when it isn't as good as it ought to be.

PART II

TECHNICAL

MATTERS

On Beginnings and Endings

My way is to begin with the beginning.
— LORD BYRON, *Don Juan*

I always wanted to write a book that ended with the word
mayonnaise. — RICHARD BRAUTIGAN

My greatest trouble is getting the curtain up and down.
— T. S. ELIOT

A bad beginning makes a bad ending. — EURIPIDES, *Aeolus*

The only way round is through. — ROBERT FROST

Great is the art of beginning, but greater the art of ending.
— THOMAS FULLER, *Gnomologia*

The last thing one knows when writing a book is what to put
first. — BLAISE PASCAL

EDWARD ALBEE: As for curtain lines, well, I suppose there are playwrights who do build toward curtain lines. I don't think I do that. In a
sense, it's the same choice that has to be made when you wonder when to
start a play. And when to end it. The characters' lives have gone on before
the moment you chose to have the action of the play begin. And their lives
are going to go on after you have lowered the final curtain on the play, unless you've killed them off. A play is a parenthesis which contains all the
material you think has to be contained for the action of the play. Where
do you end that? Where the characters seem to come to a pause . . . where
they seem to want to stop—rather like, I would think, the construction of
a piece of music.

JOHN ASHBERY: A gag that's probably gone unnoticed turns up in the
last sentence of the novel I wrote with James Schuyler. Actually it's my
sentence. It reads: "So it was that the cliff dwellers, after bidding their
cousins good night, moved off towards the parking area, while the latter

bent their steps toward the partially rebuilt shopping plaza in the teeth of the freshening foehn." *Foehn* is a kind of warm wind that blows in Bavaria that produces a fog. I would doubt that many people know that. I liked the idea that people, if they bothered to, would have to open the dictionary to find out what the last word in the novel meant. They'd be closing one book and opening another.

JAMES BALDWIN: When you've finished a novel it means, "The train stops here, you have to get off here." You never get the book you wanted, you settle for the book you get. I've always felt that when a book ended there was something I didn't see, and usually when I remark the discovery it's too late to do anything about it.

E. M. FORSTER: Ends always give me trouble. Characters run away with you, and so won't fit on to what is coming.

JOHN GUARE: Moss Hart said the audience will give you all their attention in the play's first fifteen minutes; but in the sixteenth minute they will decide whether to go on the journey you want them to take. That first fifteen minutes draws up the contract of your agreement with the audience. You can subvert it or play with it, but you must set up the premises for the evening, whether the play is *Mother Courage* or *Getting Gertie's Garter*—well, maybe not *Getting Gertie's Garter*. I once gave a course at Yale on only the first fifteen minutes of a play. *The Homecoming. The Cherry Orchard. What the Butler Saw.* The information the audience receives in that opening movement, that musical statement, allows us to enter the world of that play.

JERZY KOSINSKI: I always start a novel by writing its first page and its last page, which seem to survive almost intact through all the following drafts and changes.

JOHN LE CARRÉ: The process is empathy, fear and dramatization. I have to put him into conflict with something, and that conflict usually comes from within. They're usually people who are torn in some way between personal and institutional loyalty. Then there's external conflict. "The cat sat on the mat" is not the beginning of a story, but "The cat sat on the dog's mat" *is.*

WILLIAM MAXWELL: Offhand I think of "None of them knew the color of the sky," which is *The Open Boat,* and "All the sisters lay dreaming of horses," which is *National Velvet.* And the wonderful first line of *Pride* *and Prejudice.* "It is a truth universally acknowledged, that a single man in possession of a good fortune must be in want of a wife."

HAROLD PINTER: It's pure instinct. The curtain comes down when the rhythm seems right—when the action calls for a finish. I'm very fond of curtain lines, of doing them properly.

KATHERINE ANNE PORTER: If I didn't know the ending of a story, I wouldn't begin. I always write my last lines, my last paragraph, my last page first, and then I go back and work towards it. I know where I'm going. I know what my goal is. And how I get there is God's grace.

· · ·

Any true work of art has got to give you the feeling of reconciliation—what the Greeks would call catharsis, the purification of your mind and imagination—through an ending that is endurable because it is right and true. Oh, not in any pawky individual idea of morality or some parochial idea of right and wrong. Sometimes the end is very tragic, because it needs to be. One of the most perfect and marvelous endings in literature—it raises my hair now—is the little boy at the end of *Wuthering Heights,* crying that he's afraid to go across the moor because there's a man and woman walking there.

SAM SHEPARD: I hate endings. Just detest them. Beginnings are definitely the most exciting, middles are perplexing, and endings are a disaster.

The temptation towards resolution, towards wrapping up the package, seems to me a terrible trap. Why not be more honest with the moment? The most authentic endings are the ones which are already revolving towards another beginning. That's genius. Somebody told me once that *fugue* means to flee, so that Bach's melody lines are like he's running away.

JOHN STEINBECK: I truly do not care about a book once it is finished. Any money or fame that results has no connection in my feeling with the book. The book dies a real death for me when I write the last word. I have a little sorrow and then go on to a new book which is alive. The rows of my books on the shelf are to me like very well embalmed corpses. They are neither alive nor mine. I have no sorrow for them because I have forgotten them, forgotten in its truest sense.

TOM STOPPARD: Curtain lines tend to be produced under the pressure of the preceding two or three acts, and usually they seem so dead right, to me anyway, that it really is as if they were in the DNA, unique and inevitable. Some of my favorite curtain lines are "The son of a bitch stole my watch" [from *The Front Page*]—I quote from memory—and "You that way; we this way" [from *Love's Labour's Lost*].

ON NAMES AND TITLES

The Ancient Mariner would not have taken so well if it had been called *The Old Sailor.* —SAMUEL BUTLER

EDWARD ALBEE: There was a saloon—it's changed its name now—on Tenth Street, between Greenwich Avenue and Waverly Place, that was called something at one time, now called something else, and they had a big mirror on the downstairs bar in this saloon where people used to scrawl graffiti. At one point back in about 1953, 1954 I think it was—long before any of us started doing much of anything—I was in there having a beer one night, and I saw "Who's Afraid of Virginia Woolf?" scrawled in soap, I suppose, on this mirror. When I started to write the play it cropped up in my mind again. And of course, who's afraid of Virginia Woolf means who's afraid of the big *bad* wolf . . . who's afraid of living life without false illusions. And it did strike me as being a rather typical university, intellectual joke.

SIMONE DE BEAUVOIR: I don't consider that very important. I chose the name Xavière in *She Came to Stay* because I had met only one person who had that name. When I look for names, I use the telephone directory or try to remember the names of former pupils.

HEINRICH BÖLL: I can't begin if I don't know the name. That's my problem at the moment. I have a plan in mind, something, a novel. I should have five or six names already that I don't have yet. Certainly I can help myself out—and that's not bad either—just by calling them all Schmitz, just to get going. But I can't think about names too much. It's an awkward mistake to try to make a name significant or characteristic of the person in question. The name of a person is really sacrosanct to me. A lot of things are ruined because I can't find a name. Sometimes I improvise on the typewriter, just as one improvises on the piano. I think, well, it starts with a D, then I put down an E, and then an N and so forth. So then he's named Denger or some such name.

. . .

The title comes afterwards, usually with considerable difficulty. I remember that *The Train Was on Time* had a totally different working title; it was called *Between Lemberg and Czernowitz.* The publisher said, "My God, two place names." I was persuaded to change it, but not against my will; I agreed to it then. A working title often changes.

JORGE LUIS BORGES: I have two methods: one of them is to work in the names of my grandfathers, great-grandfathers, and so on. To give them a kind of, well, I won't say immortality, but that's one of the methods. The other is to use names that somehow strike me. For example, in a story of mine, one of the characters who comes and goes is called Yarmolinsky because the name struck me—it's a strange word, no? Then another character is called Red Scharlach because Scharlach means *scarlet* in German and he was a murderer; he was doubly red, no? Red Scharlach: Red Scarlet.

JEAN COCTEAU: The name of the Angel Heurtebise, in the book of poems *L'Ange Heurtebise,* which was written in an unbroken automatism from start to finish, was taken from the name of an elevator stop where I happened to pause once. And I have named characters after designations on those great old-fashioned glass jars in a pharmacy in Normandy.

JOHN GARDNER: Sometimes I use characters from real life, and sometimes I use their real names—when I do, it's always in celebration of people that I like. Once or twice, as in *October Light,* I've borrowed other people's fictional characters. Naming is only a problem, of course, when you make the character up. It seems to me that every character—every person—is an embodiment of a very complicated, philosophical way of looking at the world, whether conscious or not. Names can be strong clues to the character's system. Names are magic. If you name a kid John, he'll grow up a different kid than if you named him Rudolph. I've used real characters in every single novel, except in *Grendel,* where it's impossible—

they didn't have our kinds of names in those days—but even in *Grendel* I used jokes and puns that give you clues to who I'm talking about. For instance there's a guy named Red Horse, which is really a sorrel, which is really George Sorel.

ERNEST HEMINGWAY: I make a list of titles *after* I've finished the story or the book—sometimes as many as a hundred. Then I start eliminating them, sometimes all of them.

ALDOUS HUXLEY: Yes, names are very important, aren't they? And the most unlikely names keep turning up in real life, so one must be careful. I can explain some of the names in *After Many a Summer.* Take Virginia Maunciple. That name was suggested to me by Chaucer's manciple— what is a manciple, anyhow? a kind of steward—it's the sort of a name that a movie starlet would choose, in the hope of being unique, custommade. She's called Virginia because she appears so virginal to Jeremy, and so obviously isn't, in fact; also because of her devotion to the Madonna. Dr. Sigmund Obispo: here the first name obviously refers to Freud, and Obispo I took from San Luis Obispo for local color and because it has a comical sound. And Jeremy Pordage. There's a story connected with that name. When I was an undergraduate at Oxford, Professor Walter Raleigh (who was a marvelous teacher) had me do a piece of research on the literature connected with the Popish Plot. One of the authors mentioned by Dryden under the name of "lame Mephibosheth" was called Pordage. His poetry, when I read it at the Bodleian, turned out to be unbelievably bad. But the name was a treasure. As for Jeremy, that was chosen for the sound: combined with Pordage it has a rather spinsterish ring. Propter came from the Latin for "on account of"—because, as a wise man, he is concerned with ultimate causes. Another reason why I chose the name was its occurrence in a poem of Edward Lear, "Incidents in the Life of My Uncle Arly." Let's see, how does it go now?

> Like the ancient Medes and Persians,
> Always by his own exertions
>   He subsisted on those hills;
> Whiles, by teaching children spelling,
> Or at times by merely yelling,
> Or at intervals by selling
>   "Propter's Nicodemus Pills."

Pete Boone doesn't mean anything in particular. It's just a straightforward American name that suits the character. Jo Stoyte, too—the name simply means what it sounds like.

GUILLERMO CABRERA INFANTE: The title always comes first, to me and to the reader. I've written many stories and articles just by doggedly following the title. Sometimes I use a working title, sometimes I find a title suitable for a given subject. Take my most recent novel, *La habana para un infante difunto* (1979). It had a different title when I began: *Las confesiones de agosto,* a clever allusion to confession and to Saint Augustine's *Confessions.* I had begun writing the book in August, so that was included as well. Then one day I heard a title, *La habana para un infante difunto,* just like that, the same way Saint Augustine heard the voice in the garden. With the new title in mind, I rewrote the whole book.

FRANÇOIS MAURIAC: I have been unwise enough to use names that are very well known in my part of the country, around Bordeaux. So far, I have been able to avoid the great embarrassments that this system could have caused me.

ANNE SEXTON: As I was writing the poem "Eighteen Days Without You"—the last poem in *Love Poems*—my husband said to me, "I can't stand it any longer, you haven't been with me for days." That poem originally was "Twenty-one Days Without You" and it became "Eighteen Days" because he had cut into the inspiration; he demanded my presence back again, into his life, and I couldn't take that much from him.

SUSAN SONTAG: I had the title; I can't write something unless I already know its title. I had the dedication; I knew I would dedicate it to my son. I had the *Così fan tutte* epigraph. And of course I had the story in some sense, and the span of the book. And what was most helpful, I had a very strong idea of a structure. I took it from a piece of music, Hindemith's *The Four Temperaments*—a work I know very well, since it's the music of one of Balanchine's most sublime ballets, which I've seen countless times. The Hindemith starts with a triple prologue, three very short pieces. Then come four movements: melancholic, sanguinic, phlegmatic, choleric. In that order. I knew I was going to have a triple prologue and then four sections or parts corresponding to the four temperaments—though I saw no reason to belabor the idea by actually labeling Parts I to IV "melancholic," "sanguinic," etc. I knew all of that, plus the novel's last sentence: "Damn them all." Of course, I didn't know who was going to utter it. In a sense, the whole work of writing the novel consisted of making something that would justify that sentence.

TENNESSEE WILLIAMS: Sometimes I'll come up with a title that doesn't sound good in itself, but it's the only title that really fits the meaning of the play. Like *A House Not Meant to Stand* isn't a beautiful title. But the house it refers to in the play is in a terrible state of disrepair, virtually leaking rain water everywhere. That house, and therefore the title, is a metaphor for society in our times. And, of course, the critics don't like that sort of thing, nor do they dare to openly approve it. They know who butters their bread.

Some titles come from dialogue as I write a play, or from the setting itself. Some come from poetry I've read. When I need a title I'll usually reread the poetry of Hart Crane. I take a copy of Crane's work with me when I travel. A phrase will catch my eye and seem right for what I'm writing. But there's no system to it. Sometimes a line from the play will serve as its title. I often change titles a number of times until I find one that seems right.

There is a Catholic church in Key West named "Mary, Star of the Sea." That would make a lovely title for a play.

TOM WOLFE: The title *The Bonfire of the Vanities* was in my mind for a long time. I once took an American Express bus tour of Florence. We reached the Piazza della Signoria, where there is a wonderful statue of Mercury by Cellini. The driver, who was also the guide, told the story of the "bonfires of the vanities," which had taken place there. At the end of the fifteenth century the Florentines had just been through a hog-wallowing, hog-stomping, baroque period, and when suddenly this ascetic monk, Savonarola, came forward and said, "Get rid of your evil ways, strip down, get rid of your vanities." A bonfire was built. Most of the things were thrown into the fire voluntarily. Some things weren't but most of them were—nonreligious paintings, books by Boccaccio, plus wigs and false eyelashes and all kinds of silver, gold. At first, the citizenry loved it. It's sort of like the granola period we're going into right now. They loved the asceticism of it. Then after two of these bonfires, they'd really gotten very bored with the whole process and besides the Pope was getting a little jealous of Savonarola, who was really running the city, and so he was the victim of the third bonfire. Anyway, this idea of a bonfire of the vanities stuck in my mind, intrigued me, and I said to myself how some day I'd write a book called that.

ON STYLE

The greatest masterpiece in literature is only a dictionary out of order. —JEAN COCTEAU

A work that aspires, however humbly, to the condition of art should carry its justification in every line.
—JOSEPH CONRAD, *The Nigger of the Narcissus,* Preface

All the fun's in how you say a thing. —ROBERT FROST

The most original authors of modern times are so, not because they create anything new, but only because they are able to say things in a manner as if they had never been said before.
—GOETHE

This is what I'd like to put in my letter: "Beautiful Marquise, your beautiful eyes make me die of love," but I'd like to put it in an elegant way, I want it prettily tuned. —MOLIÈRE

When we come across a natural style, we are surprised and delighted; for we expected an author, and we find a man.
—BLAISE PASCAL

Men should use common words to say uncommon things, but they do the opposite. —SCHOPENHAUER

Proper words in proper places make the true definition of a style. —JONATHAN SWIFT

When I read some of the rules for speaking and writing the English language correctly . . . I think
    —Any fool can make a rule
    And every fool will mind it.
—HENRY DAVID THOREAU

I never write *metropolis* for seven cents because I can get the same price for *city.* I never write *policeman* because I can get the same money for *cop.* —MARK TWAIN

The difference between the right word and the nearly right
word is the same as that between lightning and the lightning
bug.   —MARK TWAIN

CONRAD AIKEN: I never used a carbon because that made me self-
conscious. I can remember discussing the effect of the typewriter on our
work with Tom Eliot because he was moving to the typewriter about the
same time I was. And I remember our agreeing that it made for a slight
change of style in the prose—that you tended to use more periodic sentences, a little shorter, and a rather choppier style—and that one must be
careful about that. Because, you see, you couldn't look ahead quite far
enough, for you were always thinking about putting your fingers on the
bloody keys. But that was a passing phase only. We both soon discovered
that we were just as free to let the style throw itself into the air as we had
been writing manually.

NELSON ALGREN: Well, I haven't consciously tried to develop it. The
only thing I've consciously tried to do was put myself in a position to hear
the people I wanted to hear talk talk. I used the police line-up for I don't
know how many years . . . they finally stopped me . . . the card got ragged
as hell, pasted here and there, you couldn't read it . . . the detective who
sat at the door stopped me and said, "What happened, you mean you're
still looking for the guy?" This was like seven years later, and I said, "Hell
yes, I lost fourteen dollars," so he let me go ahead.

MARTIN AMIS: I would say that the writers I like and trust have at the
base of their prose something called the English sentence. An awful lot of
modern writing seems to me to be a depressed use of language. Once, I
called it "vow-of-poverty prose." No, give me the king in his counting-
house. Give me Updike. Anthony Burgess said there are two kinds of
writers: A-writers and B-writers. A-writers are storytellers, B-writers are
users of language. And I tend to be grouped in the Bs. Under Nabokov's
prose, under Burgess's prose, under my father's prose—his early rather
than his later prose—the English sentence is like a poetic meter. It's a
basic rhythm from which the writer is free to glance off in unexpected directions. But the sentence is still there. To be crude, it would be like say-

ing that I don't trust an abstract painter unless I know that he can do hands.

JORGE LUIS BORGES: When I began writing, I thought that everything should be defined by the writer. For example to say "the moon" was strictly forbidden; that one had to find an adjective, an epithet for the moon. (Of course, I'm simplifying things. I know it, because many times I have written "la luna," but this is a kind of symbol of what I was doing.) Well, I thought everything had to be defined and that no common terms of phrase should be used. I would never have said "So-and-so came in and sat down," because that was far too simple and far too easy. I thought I had to find out some fancy way of saying it. Now I find out that those things are generally annoyances to the reader. But I think the whole root of the matter lies in the fact that when a writer is young he feels somehow that what he is going to say is rather silly or obvious or commonplace, and then he tries to hide it under baroque ornament, under words taken from the seventeenth-century writers; or, if not, and he sets out to be modern, then he does the contrary: he's inventing words all the time, or alluding to airplanes, railway trains, or the telegraph and telephone because he's doing his best to be modern. Then as time goes on, one feels that one's ideas, good or bad, should be plainly expressed, because if you have an idea you must try to get that idea or that feeling or that mood into the mind of the reader. If, at the same time, you are trying to be, let's say, Sir Thomas Browne or Ezra Pound, then it can't be done. So that I think a writer always begins by being too complicated: he's playing at several games at the same time. He wants to convey a peculiar mood; at the same time he must be a contemporary and if not a contemporary, then he's a reactionary and a classic. As to the vocabulary, the first thing a young writer, at least in this country, sets out to do is to show his readers that he possesses a dictionary, that he knows all the synonyms; so we get, for example, in one line, *red,* then we get *scarlet,* then we get other different words, more or less, for the same color: *purple.*

Whenever I find an out-of-the-way word, that is to say, a word that may be used by the Spanish classics or a word used in the slums of Buenos Aires, I mean a word that is different from the others, then I strike it out and I use a common word. I remember that Stevenson wrote that in a well-written page all the words should look the same way. If you write an uncouth word or an astonishing or an archaic word, then the rule is broken;

and what is far more important, the attention of the reader is distracted by the word. One should be able to read smoothly in it, even if you're writing metaphysics or philosophy or whatever.

. . .

I think that Mark Twain was one of the really great writers but I think he was rather unaware of the fact. But perhaps in order to write a really great book, you *must* be rather unaware of the fact. You can slave away at it and change every adjective to some other adjective, but perhaps you can write better if you leave the mistakes. I remember what Bernard Shaw said, that as to style, a writer has as much style as his conviction will give him and not more. Shaw thought that the idea of a game of style was quite nonsensical, quite meaningless. He thought of Bunyan, for example, as a great writer because he was convinced of what he was saying. If a writer disbelieves what he is writing, then he can hardly expect his readers to believe it. In this country [Argentina], though, there is a tendency to regard any kind of writing—especially the writing of poetry—as a game of style. I have known many poets here who have written well—very fine stuff—with delicate moods and so on—but if you talk with them, the only thing they tell you is smutty stories or speak of politics in the way that everybody does, so that really their writing turns out to be a kind of sideshow. They had learned writing in the way that a man might learn to play chess or to play bridge. They were not really poets or writers at all. It was a trick they had learned and they had learned it thoroughly. They had the whole thing at their finger ends. But most of them—except four or five I should say—seemed to think of life as having nothing poetic or mysterious about it. They take things for granted. They know that when they have to write, then, well, they have to suddenly become rather sad or ironic.

HORTENSE CALISHER: To write in the first person seems the easiest. As all young journal-writers assume. Actually it may be hardest—there are so many hazards. Garrulity. Lack of shape, or proportion. Or even of judgment. On the other hand, when you're really riding that horse well, it can feel as if you're on Bucephalus. And you really feel the wind on you.

TRUMAN CAPOTE: I mean [by control] maintaining a stylistic and emotional upper hand over your material. Call it precious and go to hell, but I believe a story can be wrecked by a faulty rhythm in a sentence (especially if it occurs toward the end) or a mistake in paragraphing, even punctuation. Henry James is the maestro of the semi-colon. Hemingway is a first-rate paragrapher. From the point of view of ear, Virginia Woolf never wrote a bad sentence. I don't mean to imply that I successfully practice what I preach . . . I try, that's all.

. . .

What is style? And "what," as the Zen Koan asks, "is the sound of one hand clapping?" No one really *knows*; yet either you *know* or you don't. For myself, if you will excuse a rather cheap little image, I suppose style is the mirror of an artist's sensibility . . . more so than the *content* of his work. To some degree all writers have style. . . . Ronald Firbank, bless his heart, had little else, and thank God he realized it. But the possession of style, *a* style, is often a hindrance, a negative force, not as it should be, and as it is . . . with, say E. M. Forster and Colette and Flaubert and Mark Twain and Hemingway and Isak Dinesen, a reinforcement. Dreiser, for instance, has *a* style—but oh, Dio Buono! And Eugene O'Neill. And Faulkner, brilliant as he is. They all seem to me triumphs over strong but negative styles . . . styles that do not really add to the communication between writer and reader. Then there is the styleless stylist . . . which is very difficult, very admirable, and *always* very popular: Graham Greene, Maugham, Thornton Wilder, John Hersey, Willa Cather, Thurber, Sartre (remember, we're *not* discussing content), J. P. Marquand, and so on. But yes, there *is* such an animal as a nonstylist. Only they're not writers. They're typists. Sweaty typists blacking up pounds of Bond with formless, eyeless, earless messages. Well, who are some of the younger writers who seem to know that style exists? P. H. Newby, Françoise Sagan, somewhat. Bill Styron. Flannery O'Connor . . . she has some fine moments, that girl. James Merrill. William Goyen . . . if he'd stop being hysterical. J. D. Salinger . . . especially in the colloquial tradition. Colin Wilson? Another typist.

No, I don't think that style is consciously arrived at. Any more than one arrives at the color of one's eyes. After all, your style *is* you. At the end the personality of a writer has so much to do with the work. The personality has to be humanly there. Personality is a debased word, I know, but it's what I mean. The writer's individual humanity, his word or gesture toward the world, has to appear almost like a character that makes contact with the reader. If the personality is vague or confused or merely literary, *ça ne va pas*. Faulkner, McCullers—they project their personality at once.

CAMILO JOSÉ CELA: Well, there is nothing more undramatic than a writer who repeats himself, or who becomes a mere caricature of himself, not to mention the writer who transforms himself into his own death mask. When I published *The Family of Pascual Duarte* and the series of notes that describe my wanderings about Spain, *Los apuntes carpetovetónicos,* which contain a more or less conventional vision of Spain—*la España negra,* if you wish—it became obvious that I would always have been able to enjoy great success in following that style. But I simply couldn't persist in it. No, and I repeat, there is nothing more painful, more bitter, than to become your own death mask. A very important Italian painter became aware in his mature years that his paintings were not selling. He understood that people continued to look for the paintings he did as a youth. So he began to copy the style of his younger years. How bitter and appalling! I suppose it must be a terrifying feeling, and therefore to avoid it one must experiment with various paths. If one of these paths serves for someone who comes after you, then let them continue along it. After all, the paths belong to everyone; they're open to us all, no? All themes are fair game. I think it was Flaubert who one day was asked by a youth presuming to be a writer, "Maestro, if only I had a plot, I would be able to write a novel." "I will give you a plot," Flaubert said. "Let's see, a man and a woman love each other, period and end of story. Now develop it yourself. With talent, you will be able to come up with *The Charterhouse of Parma.* But you must put forth the talent." One day a writer, a young writer, approached me complaining that he didn't have the proper resources that would allow him to write. I told him, "I will give you one thousand pieces of paper and a fountain pen as a gift. If you have talent, you will write *Don Quixote* on one side and *The Divine Comedy* on the other. Now go ahead and write, and we'll see what happens, although you probably will not turn out such works." It's very dramatic, but also very true.

LAWRENCE DURRELL: I don't think anyone can, you know, develop a style consciously. I read with amazement, for example, of old Maugham solemnly writing out a page of Swift every day when he was trying to learn the job, in order to give himself a stylistic purchase as it were. It struck me as something I could never do. No. When you say "consciously," I mean it's like "Do you consciously dream?" One doesn't know very much about these processes at all. I think the writing itself grows you up, and you grow the writing up, and finally you get an amalgam of everything you have pinched with a new kind of personality which is your own, and then you are able to pay back these socking debts with a tiny bit of interest—which is the only honorable thing for a writer to do—at least a writer who is a thief like me.

LEON EDEL: He [Henry James] began dictating directly to the typewriter. It's a case of the medium being the message and with dictation he ran into longer sentences, and parenthetical remarks, and when he revised what he had dictated he tended to add further flourishes. In the old days when he wrote in longhand he was much briefer and crisper, but now he luxuriated in fine phrases and he was exquisitely baroque. It's a grand style but not to everyone's taste.

JOHN FOWLES: The notion that a perfect form, like a sort of god, hovers over all of us, which we either cling or pay lip service to, I dislike intensely. I think whatever form is chosen by each writer is "perfect" for him or her, however imperfect it may seem to those under the delusion of some general "perfect form" and its attainability. That sort of myth of a perfect form, applicable to all, seems to me one of those things modern art has sunk beyond resurrection. I certainly try to make the form I put things in suit their matter, but I agree totally with E. M. Forster that forcing matter into some supposed general idea of the form best suited to it is wrong. Novels in a sense are like new scientific theories. Of course there are ways in which they have to pay homage to the past, to high past standards; but they also have to disobey and question them, to break new ground. Nothing in their cultural pasts could have allowed for or predicted, say, *Tristram Shandy* or *Ulysses.*

GABRIEL GARCÍA MÁRQUEZ: After *The Evil Hour* I did not write anything for five years. I had an idea of what I always wanted to do, but there was something missing and I was not sure what it was until one day I discovered the right tone—the tone that I eventually used in *One Hundred Years of Solitude.* It was based on the way my grandmother used to tell her stories. She told things that sounded supernatural and fantastic, but she told them with complete naturalness. When I finally discovered the tone I had to use, I sat down for eighteen months and worked every day. What was most important was the expression she had on her face. She did not change her expression at all when telling her stories and everyone was surprised. In previous attempts to write *One Hundred Years of Solitude,* I tried to tell the story without believing in it. I discovered that what I had to do was believe in them myself and write them with the same expression with which my grandmother told them: with a brick face.

ROBERT GRAVES: Whoever thinks about the English language and tries to discover its principles, and also pulls a whole lot of writers to pieces to show how badly they write, can't afford to write badly himself. In 1959, I entirely rewrote *Goodbye to All That*—every single sentence— but no one noticed. Some said: "What a good book that is, after all. How well it's lasted." It hasn't lasted at all. It's an entirely new product. One of those computer analyses of style couldn't possibly decide that my historical novels were all written by the same hand. They're completely different in vocabulary, syntax, and language-level.

FRANCINE DU PLESSIX GRAY: We must all struggle against all that is curious, already-seen, fatigued, shopworn. I battle against what my admirable colleague William Gass calls "pissless prose," prose that lacks the muscle, the physicality, the gait of a good horse, for pissless prose is bodiless and has no soul. Of course this holds equally true for fiction as for essays, reporting, a letter to a friend, a book review, a decent contribution to art criticism—in sum I search for language in which faith intertwines with desire, faith that we can recapture, with erotic accuracy, that treasured memory or vision which is the object of our desire. I'm keen on the word "voluptuous," a word too seldom heard in this society founded on puritanical principles. I think back to a phrase of Julia Kristeva's, the most interesting feminist thinker of our time, who speaks of "the voluptuousness of family life." I would apply the same phrase to the prose I most admire, prose I can caress and nurture and linger on, diction which is nourished by the deep intimacy of familiar detail, and yet is constantly renewed by the force of the writer's love and fidelity to language.

HENRY GREEN: His [the writer's] style is himself, and we are all of us changing every day—developing, we hope! We leave our marks behind us like a snail.

ELIZABETH HARDWICK: The prose written by poets is one of my passions. I like the off-hand flashes, the absence of the lumber in the usual prose . . . the quickness, the deftness, confidence, and even the relief from spelling everything out, plank by plank. Here is a beautiful sentence, just right, inspired, a bit of prose I've memorized. It is by Pasternak. It goes:

"The beginning of April surprised Moscow in the white stupor of return-ing winter. On the seventh, it began to thaw for the second time, and on the fourteenth when Mayakovsky shot himself, not everyone had yet become accustomed to the novelty of spring." I love the rhythm of "the beginning of April . . . on the seventh . . . on the fourteenth" and the way the subject, Mayakovsky's suicide, is honored by the beauty of this introduction to the account. It's in *Safe Conduct,* Pasternak's autobiographical writing.

ERNEST HEMINGWAY: That is a long-term tiring question and if you spent a couple of days answering it you would be so self-conscious that you could not write. I might say that what amateurs call a style is usually only the unavoidable awkwardness in first trying to make something that has not heretofore been made. Almost no new classics resemble other pre-vious classics. At first people can see only the awkwardness. Then they are not so perceptible. When they show so very awkwardly people think these awkwardnesses are the style and many copy them. This is regrettable.

BERNARD MALAMUD: My style flows from the fingers. The eye and ear approve or amend.

FRANÇOIS MAURIAC: I have very seldom asked myself about the technique I was using. When I begin to write I don't stop and wonder if I am interfering too directly in the story, or if I know too much about my characters, or whether or not I ought to judge them. I write with complete naïveté, spontaneously. I've never had any preconceived notion of what I could or could not do. . . . I believe that my younger fellow novelists are greatly preoccupied with technique. They seem to think a good novel ought to follow certain rules imposed from outside. In fact, however, this preoccupation hampers them and embarrasses them in their creation. The great novelist doesn't depend on anyone but himself. Proust resem-bled none of his predecessors and he did not have, he could not have, any successors. The great novelist breaks his mold; he alone can use it. Balzac created the "Balzacian" novel; its style was suitable only for Balzac.

There is a close tie between a novelist's originality in general and the personal quality of his style. A borrowed style is a bad style. American nov-elists from Faulkner to Hemingway invented a style to express what they wanted to say—and it is a style that can't be passed on to their followers.

KATHERINE ANNE PORTER: I've been called a stylist until I really could tear my hair out. And I simply don't believe in style. The style is you. Oh, you can cultivate a style, I suppose, if you like. But I should say it remains a cultivated style. It remains artificial and imposed, and I don't think it deceives anyone. A cultivated style would be like a mask. Everybody knows it's a mask, and sooner or later you must show yourself—or at least, you show yourself as someone who could not afford to show himself, and so created something to hide behind. Style is the man. Aristotle said it first, as far as I know, and everybody has said it since, because it is one of those unarguable truths. You do not create a style. You work, and develop yourself; your style is an emanation from your own being.

EZRA POUND: I don't know about method. The *what* is so much more important than how.

WILLIAM STYRON: I used to spend a lot of time worrying over word order, trying to create beautiful passages. I still believe in the value of a handsome style. I appreciate the sensibility which can produce a nice turn of phrase, like Scott Fitzgerald. But I'm not interested anymore in turning out something shimmering and impressionistic—Southern, if you will—full of word-pictures, damn Dixie baby-talk, and that sort of thing. I guess I just get more and more interested in people. And story.

JOHN UPDIKE: It comes down to what is language? Up to now, until this age of mass literacy, language has been something spoken. In utterance there's a minimum of slowness. In trying to treat words as chisel strokes you run the risk of losing the quality of utterance, the rhythm of utterance, the happiness. A phrase out of Mark Twain—he describes a raft hitting a bridge and says that it "went all to smash and scatteration like a box of matches struck by lightning." The beauty of "scatteration" could only have occurred to a talkative man, a man who had been brought up among people who were talking and who loved to talk himself. I'm aware myself of a certain dryness of this reservoir, this backlog of spoken talk. A Rumanian once said to me that Americans are always telling stories. I'm not sure this is as true as it once was. Where we once used to spin yarns, now we sit in front of the T.V. and receive pictures. I'm not sure the younger generation even knows how to gossip. But, as for a writer, if he has something to tell, he should perhaps type it almost as fast as he could talk it. We must look to the organic world, not the inorganic world, for metaphors; and just as the organic world has periods of repose and periods of great speed and exercise, so I think the writer's process should be organically varied. But there's a kind of tautness that you should feel within yourself no matter how slow or fast you're spinning out the reel.

E. B. WHITE: I'm not familiar with books on style. My role in the revival of Strunk's book was a fluke—just something I took on because I was not doing anything else at the time. It cost me a year out of my life, so little did I know about grammar. I don't think [style] can be taught. Style results more from what a person is than from what he knows. But there are a few hints that can be thrown out to advantage. They would be the twenty-one hints I threw out in Chapter V of *The Elements of Style*. There was nothing new or original about them, but there they are, for all to read.*

---

*These are (1) Place yourself in the background; (2) Write in a way that comes naturally; (3) Work from a suitable design; (4) Write with nouns and verbs; (5) Revise and rewrite; (6) Do not overwrite; (7) Do not overstate; (8) Avoid the use of qualifiers; (9) Do not affect a breezy manner; (10) Use orthodox spelling; (11) Do not explain too much; (12) Do not construct awkward adverbs; (13) Make sure the reader knows who is speaking; (14) Avoid fancy words; (15) Do not use dialect unless your ear is good; (16) Be clear; (17) Do not inject opinion; (18) Use figures of speech sparingly; (19) Do not take shortcuts at the cost of clarity; (20) Avoid foreign languages; (21) Prefer the standard to the offbeat.

These are headings in Chapter V of *The Elements of Style* and are followed by explanatory texts.—Ed.

ON PLOT

What I am trying to achieve is a voice sitting by a fireplace telling you a story on a winter's evening. —TRUMAN CAPOTE

Writing is turning one's worst moments into money.
—J. P. DONLEAVY

The French writers do not burden themselves too much with plot, which has been reproached to them as a fault.
—JOHN DRYDEN

With me, it's story, story, story. —BERNARD MALAMUD

NELSON ALGREN: I've always figured the only way I could finish a book and get a plot was just to keep making it longer and longer until something happens ... you know, until it finds its own plot ... because you can't outline and then fit the thing into it. I suppose it's a slow way of working.

HEINRICH BÖLL: In my case, the work changes constantly, since I seldom have a firm plot or any idea at all about the ending. But there is a clear, almost mathematically conceptual idea that determines length— the length or brevity of a literary work being comparable to the size of the frame needed by a picture.

JOHN CHEEVER: I don't work with plots. I work with intuition, apprehension, dreams, concepts. Characters and events come simultaneously to me. Plot implies narrative and a lot of crap. It is a calculated attempt to hold the reader's interest at the sacrifice of moral conviction. Of course, one doesn't want to be boring ... one needs an element of suspense. But a good narrative is a rudimentary structure, rather like a kidney.

ISAK DINESEN: Yes, it is. I start with a tingle, a kind of feeling of the story I will write. Then come the characters, and they take over, they make the story. But all this ends by being a plot. For other writers, that seems an unnatural thing. But a proper tale has a shape and an outline. In a painting the frame is important. Where does the picture end? What details should one include? Or omit! Where does the line go that cuts off the picture? People always ask me, they say, "In 'The Deluge at Norderney,' were those characters drowned or saved at the end?" (You remember they are trapped in a loft during a flood and spend the night recounting their stories while awaiting rescue.) Well, what can I reply? How can I tell them? That's outside the story. I really don't know!

LAWRENCE DURRELL: It's like driving a few stakes in the ground; you haven't got to that point in the construction yet, so you run ahead fifty yards, and you plant a stake in to show roughly the direction your road is going, which helps to give you your orientation. But they are very far from planned in the exact sense.

E. M. FORSTER: The novelist should, I think, always settle when he starts what is going to happen, what his major event is to be. He may alter this event as he approaches it, indeed he probably will, indeed he probably had better, or the novel becomes tied up and tight. But the sense of a solid mass ahead, a mountain round or over or through which the story must somehow go, is most valuable and, for the novels I've tried to write, essential. There must be something, some major object towards which one is to approach. When I began *A Passage to India* I knew that something important happened in the Malabar Caves, and that it would have a central place in the novel—but I didn't know what it would be. The Malabar Caves represented an area in which concentration can take place. A cavity. Something to focus everything up: to engender an event like an egg.

JOHN GARDNER: When you teach creative writing, you teach people, among other things, how to plot. You explain the principles, how it is that fiction *thinks*. And to give the kids a sense of how a plot works, you just spin out plot after plot. In an hour session, you may spin out forty possible plots, one adhering to the real laws of energeia, each one a balance of the particular and general—and not one of them a story that you'd really want to write. Then one time, you hit one that catches you for some reason—you hit on the story that expresses your unrest. When I was teaching creative writing at Chico State, for instance, one of many plots I spun out was *The Resurrection*.

One plot will just sort of rise above all the others for reasons that you don't fully understand. All of them are interesting, all of them have interesting characters, all of them talk about things that you could talk about; but one of them catches you like a nightmare. Then you have no choice but to write it; you can't forget it. It's a weird thing. If it's the kind of plot you really don't want to do because it involves your mother too closely, or whatever, you can try to do something else. But the typewriter keeps hissing at you and shooting sparks, and the paper keeps wrinkling and the lamp goes off and nothing else works, so finally you do the one that God said you've got to do. And once you do it, you're grounded.

HENRY GREEN: As to plotting or thinking ahead, I don't in a novel. I let it come page by page, one a day, and carry it in my head. When I say carry I mean the proportions—that is, the length. This is the exhaustion of creating. Towards the end of the book your head is literally bursting. But try and write out a scheme or plan and you will only depart from it. My way you have a chance to set something living.

ELIZABETH HARDWICK: I don't have many plots and perhaps as a justification I sometimes think: if I want a plot I'll watch "Dallas." I think it's mood. No, I mean tone. Tone arrived at by language. I can't write a story or an essay until I can, by revision after revision, get the opening tone right. Sometimes it seems to take forever, but when I have it I can usually go on. It's a matter of the voice, how you are going to approach the task at hand. It's all language and rhythm and the establishment of the relation to the material, of who's speaking, not speaking as a person exactly, but as a mind, a sensibility.

ALDOUS HUXLEY: I have great difficulty in inventing plots. Some people are born with an amazing gift for storytelling; it's a gift which I've never had at all. One reads, for example, Stevenson's accounts of how all the plots for his stories were provided in dreams by his subconscious mind (what he calls the "Brownies" working for him), and that all he had to do was to work up the material they had provided. I've never had any Brownies. The great difficulty for me has always been creating situations.

· · ·

I work away a chapter at a time, finding my way as I go. I know very dimly when I start what's going to happen. I just have a very general idea, and then the thing develops as I write. Sometimes—it's happened to me more than once—I will write a great deal, then find it just doesn't work, and have to throw the whole thing away. I like to have a chapter finished before I begin on the next one. But I'm never entirely certain what's going to happen in the next chapter until I've worked it out. Things come to me in driblets, and when the driblets come I have to work hard to make them into something coherent.

JOHN IRVING: I have last chapters in my mind before I see first chapters, too. I usually begin with endings, with a sense of aftermath, of dust settling, of epilogue. I love plot, and how can you plot a novel if you don't know the ending first? How do you know how to introduce a character if you don't know how he *ends up?* You might say I back into a novel. All the important discoveries—at the end of a book—those are the things I have to know before I know where to begin. I knew that Garp's mother would be killed by a stupid man who blindly hates women; I knew Garp would be killed by a stupid woman who blindly hates men. I didn't even know which of them would be killed first; I had to wait to see which of them was the main character. At first I thought Jenny was the main character; but she was too much of a saint for a main character—in the way that Wilbur Larch is too much of a saint to be the main character of *The Cider House Rules.* Garp and Homer Wells are flawed; by comparison to Jenny and Dr. Larch, they're weak. They're main characters. Actors know how they end up—I mean how their *characters* end up—before they speak the opening lines. Shouldn't writers know at least as much about their characters as actors know? I think so.

P. D. JAMES: For myself I believe plot is necessary, although it would be easy to write a book without it. In the thirties, the so-called golden age of the detective story, plot was everything. Indeed what people wanted was ingenuity of plot. You couldn't have an ordinary murder, it had to be done with exceptional cunning. It was the age when corpses were found in locked rooms with locked windows, and a look of horror on their faces. With Agatha Christie ingenuity of plot was paramount—no one looked for subtlety of characterization, motivation, good writing. It was rather like a literary card trick. Today we've moved closer to the mainstream novel, but nevertheless we need plot. It takes me as long to develop the plot and work out the characters as to write the book. Sometimes longer. So once I've got the setting, I begin to get in touch with the people, as it were, and last of all the clues.

NORMAN MAILER: My plots are always rudimentary. Whatever I've accomplished certainly does not depend on my virtuosity with plot. Generally I don't even have a plot. What happens is that my characters engage in an action, and out of that action little bits of plot sometimes adhere to the narrative.

TONI MORRISON: I put the whole plot [of *Jazz*] on the first page. In fact, in the first edition the plot was on the cover, so that a person in a bookstore could read the cover and know right away what the book was about, and could, if they wished, dismiss it and buy another book. This seemed a suitable technique because I thought of the plot in that novel— the threesome—as the melody of the piece, and it is fine to follow a melody—to feel the satisfaction of recognizing a melody whenever the narrator returns to it. That was the real art of the enterprise for me: bumping up against that melody time and again, seeing it from another point of view, seeing it afresh each time, playing it back and forth. I wanted the story to be the vehicle which moved us from page one to the end, but I wanted the delight to be found in moving away from the story and coming back to it, looking around it, and through it, as though it were a prism, constantly turning.

JOHN MORTIMER: I've always enjoyed crime fiction. I think that much of the best writing being done today is in crime novels. The plot and discipline essential to a crime novel save it from the terrible traps of being sensitive and stream-of-consciousness and all of that stuff. You do need that discipline, I think, and plot! Life happens in plots all the time; life is absolutely composed of plots!

JAMES THURBER: I don't bother with charts and so forth. Elliot Nugent, on the other hand, was a careful constructor. When we were working on *The Male Animal* together, he was constantly concerned with plotting the play. He could plot the thing from back to front—what was going to happen here, what sort of a situation would end the first act curtain, and so forth. I can't work that way. Nugent would say: "Well, Thurber, we've got our problem, we've got all these people in the living room. Now what are we going to do with them?" I'd say that I didn't know and couldn't tell him until I'd sat down at the typewriter and found out. I don't believe the writer should know too much where he's going. If he does, he runs into old man blueprint . . . old man propaganda.

KURT VONNEGUT: I guarantee you that no modern story scheme, even plotlessness, will give a reader genuine satisfaction, unless one of those old-fashioned plots is smuggled in somewhere. I don't praise plots as accurate representations of life, but as ways to keep readers reading. When I used to teach creative writing, I would tell the students to make their characters want something right away—even if it's only a glass of water. Characters paralyzed by the meaninglessness of modern life still have to drink water from time to time. One of my students wrote a story about a nun who got a piece of dental floss stuck between her lower left molars, and who couldn't get it out all day long. I thought that was wonderful. The story dealt with issues a lot more important than dental floss, but what kept readers going was anxiety about when the dental floss would finally be removed. Nobody could read that story without fishing around in his mouth with a finger.

JESSAMYN WEST: I'll tell you what I think my greatest weakness is. I don't think I'm a very good plotter: I mean, of the mechanics of the story. I was in Hollywood for nine months during the making of *The Friendly Persuasion.* I remember Mr. William Wyler, who directed it, saying to me, "Jessamyn (actually, I think he said 'Miss West'), we've got to get one more 'will he? won't he?' into this." I tend not to do enough of that and I think this is what a reader wants.

REBECCA WEST: I do think modern novels are boring on the whole. Somebody told me I ought to read a wonderful thing about how a family of children buried Mum in a cellar under concrete and she began to smell. But that's the sole point of the story. Mum just smells. That's all that happens. It is not enough.

TENNESSEE WILLIAMS: What shouldn't you do if you're a young playwright? *Don't bore the audience!* I mean, even if you have to resort to totally arbitrary killing on stage, or pointless gunfire, at least it'll catch their attention and keep them awake. Just keep the thing going any way you can.

ON CHARACTER

A good novel tells us the truth about its hero; but a bad novel tells us the truth about its author.   —G. K. CHESTERTON

A novelist is a person who lives in other people's skins.
    —E. L. DOCTOROW

Human beings have their great chance in the novel.
    —E. M. FORSTER

You can never know enough about your characters.
    —W. SOMERSET MAUGHAM

I sometimes lose interest in the characters and get much more interested in the trees and animals.   —TONI MORRISON

CHINUA ACHEBE: Generally, I think I can say that the general idea is the first, followed almost immediately by the major characters. We live in a sea of general ideas, so that's not a novel, since there are so many general ideas. But the moment a particular idea is linked to a character, it's like an engine moves it. Then you have a novel underway. This is particularly so with novels which have distinct and overbearing characters like Ezeulu in *Arrow of God*. In novels like *A Man of the People,* or better still, *No Longer at Ease*, with characters who are not commanding personalities, there I think the general idea plays a stronger part at the initial stage. But once you pass that initial state, there's really no difference between the general idea and the character; each has to work.

Once a novel gets going, and I know it is viable, I don't then worry about plot or themes. These things will come in almost automatically because the characters are now pulling the story.

MARTIN AMIS: A bit of license, yes. But *I'm* the boss. I'm the boss but they're on the team. They're "my people," in the sense that a politician might have his people—his in-depth backup. I'm always willing to hear their ideas, although of course I retain the right of absolute veto; I slap them down but I want to hear what they've got to say.

· · ·

I'm very fond of quoting these two remarks. E. M. Forster said he used to line up his characters, as it were, at the starting line of the novel, and say to them, "Right. No larks." Nabokov used to say that his characters cringed as he walked past with his switch, and that he'd seen whole avenues of imagined trees lose their leaves in terror as he approached. I don't think I'm really like that. I think character is destiny within the novel as well as outside the novel . . . that characters you invent will contribute vitally to the kind of novel you're going to write. I feel that if they are alive in your mind, they're going to have ideas of their own and take you places you wouldn't perhaps have gone.

MAYA ANGELOU: Sometimes I make a character from a composite of three or four people, because the essence in any one person is not sufficiently strong to be written about. Essentially though, the work is true though sometimes I fiddle with the facts. Many of the people I've written about are alive today, and I have them to face. I wrote about an ex-husband—he's an African—in *The Heart of a Woman*. Before I did, I called him in Dar-es-Salaam and said, "I'm going to write about some of our years together." He said, "Now before you ask, I want you to know that I shall sign my release, because I know you will not lie. However, I am sure I shall argue with you about your interpretation of the truth."

LOUIS AUCHINCLOSS: I would not dare do what Forster does with his characters. He comes into his books sometimes and talks about them; he'll say, "So-and-so really was an ass." It's quite startling to hear Forster do that, but that's his particular thing. Thackeray was like that too.

· · ·

I remember a great tax lawyer, Norris Darrell, a very literal man with a marvelous mathematical mind, who accused me of putting him in a story. The story was about a passionate diarist. Eventually, the man comes to *live* for his diary; his whole life is oriented around seeking items for it. It is the tail wagging the dog. I asked Norris, "Why would you assume you were that character? Do *you* keep a diary?" He said, "Heavens no!" I asked: "Then what was it in the story that made you think you were the character?" He replied: "He was the senior tax partner in his firm." Well, that's usually the sort of thing a writer runs into.

ERSKINE CALDWELL: I have no influence over them. I'm only an observer, recording. The story is always being told by the characters themselves. In fact, I'm often critical, or maybe ashamed, of what some of them say and do—their profanity or their immorality. But I have no control over it.

JOHN CHEEVER: The legend that characters run away from their authors—taking up drugs, having sex operations, and becoming president—implies that the writer is a fool with no knowledge or mastery of his craft. This is absurd. Of course, any estimable exercise of the imagination draws upon such a complex richness of memory that it truly enjoys the expansiveness—the surprising turns, the response to light and darkness—of any living thing. But the idea of authors running around helplessly behind their cretinous inventions is contemptible.

JULIO CORTÁZAR: It's the characters who direct me. That is, I see a character, he's there, and I recognize someone I knew, or occasionally two who are a bit mixed together, but then that stops. Afterwards, the character acts on his own account. He says things . . . I never know *what* any of them are going to say when I'm writing dialogue. Really, it's up to them. Me, I'm just typing out what they're saying. Sometimes I burst out laughing, or I throw out a page and say, "There, there you've said silly things. Out!" And I put in another page and start over again with their dialogue.

MARGARET DRABBLE: I find it difficult to write about very stupid people. I'm aware that my characters tend to be not only intelligent, but intelligent about themselves. One of the things that I really admire is the ability to write with dignity and understanding about people who are not aware of themselves. I think most people are more intelligent than they are given credit for, but that they don't express themselves in a way people find accessible. I look at some people and I don't know what their minds contain. And that I find a problem.

And men. Writing about men. I used to find it difficult because I didn't trust myself to know what they were like. I still feel uneasy when I describe men's clothes and their offices. I have to do research, find out what they really look like, how they talk, and what kind of work pattern they have.

E. M. FORSTER: We all like to pretend we don't use real people, but one does actually. I used some of my family. Miss Bartlett was my Aunt Emily—they all read the book but they none of them saw it. Uncle Willie turned into Mrs. Failing. He was a bluff and simple character [*correcting himself*]—bluff without being simple. Miss Lavish was actually a Miss Spender. Mrs. Honeychurch was my grandmother. The three Miss Dickinsons condensed into two Miss Schlegels. Philip Herriton I modeled on Professor Dent. He knew this, and took an interest in his own progress. I have used several tourists.

In no book have I got down more than the people I like, the person I think I am, and the people who irritate me. This puts me among the large body of authors who are not really novelists, and have to get on as best they can with these three categories. We have not the power of observing the variety of life and describing it dispassionately. There are a few who have done this. Tolstoy was one, wasn't he?

A useful trick is to look back upon such a person with half-closed eyes, fully describing certain characteristics. I am left with about two-thirds of a human being and can get to work. A likeness isn't aimed at and couldn't be obtained, because a man's only himself amidst the particular circumstances of his life and not amid other circumstances. So that to refer back to Dent when Philip was in difficulties with Gino, or to ask one and one-half Miss Dickinsons how Helen should comport herself with an illegitimate baby would have ruined the atmosphere and the book. When all goes well, the original material soon disappears, and a character who belongs to the book and nowhere else emerges.

GABRIEL GARCÍA MÁRQUEZ: In every novel, the character is a collage: a collage of different characters that you've known, or heard about or read about. I read everything that I could find about Latin American dictators of the last century, and the beginning of this one. I also talked to a lot of people who had lived under dictatorships. I did that for at least ten years. And when I had a clear idea of what the character was going to be like, I made an effort to forget everything I had read and heard, so that I could invent, without using any situation that had occurred in real life. I realized at one point that I myself had not lived for any period of time under a dictatorship, so I thought if I wrote the book in Spain, I could see what the atmosphere was like living in an established dictatorship. But I found that the atmosphere was very different in Spain under Franco from that of a Caribbean dictatorship. So the book was kind of blocked for about a year. There was something missing and I wasn't sure what it was. Then overnight, I decided that the best thing was that we come back to the Caribbean. So we all moved back to Barranquilla in Colombia. I made a statement to the journalists which they thought was a joke. I said that I was coming back because I had forgotten what a guava smelled like. In truth, it was what I really needed to finish my book. I took a trip through the Caribbean. As I went from island to island, I found the elements which were the ones that had been lacking from my novel.

JOHN GARDNER: The first thing that makes a reader read a book is the characters. Say you're standing in a train station, or an airport, and you're leafing through books; what you're hoping for is a book where you'll like the characters, where the characters are interesting. To establish powerful characters, a writer needs a landscape to help define them; so setting becomes important. Setting is also a powerful vehicle of thematic concerns; in fact, it's one of the most powerful. If you're going to talk about the decline of Western civilization or at least the possibility of that decline, you take an old place that's sort of worn out and run-down. For instance, Batavia, New York, where the Holland Land Office was . . . the beginning of a civilization . . . selling the land in this country. It was, in the beginning, a wonderful, beautiful place with the smartest Indians in America around. Now it's this old, run-down town which has been urban-renewalized just about out of existence. The factories have stopped and the people are poor and sometimes crabby; the elm trees are all dead, and so are the oaks and maples. So it's a good symbol. You choose the setting that suits and illuminates your material.

NADINE GORDIMER: Henry James could have been a woman. E. M. Forster could have been. George Eliot could have been a man. I used to be too insistent on this point that there's no sex in the brain; I'm less insistent now—perhaps I'm being influenced by the changing attitude of women toward themselves in general? I don't think there's anything that women writers don't know. But it may be that there are certain aspects of life that they can deal with a shade better, just as I wonder whether any woman writer, however great, could have written the marvelous war scenes in *War and Peace.* By and large, I don't think it matters a damn what sex a writer is, so long as the work is that of a real *writer.* I think there *is* such a thing as "ladies' writing," for instance, feminine writing; there are "authoresses" and "poetesses." And there are men, like Hemingway, whose excessive "manliness" is a concomitant part of their writing. But with so many of the male writers whom I admire, it doesn't matter too much. There doesn't seem to be anything *they* don't know, either. After all, look at Molly Bloom's soliloquy. To me, that's the ultimate proof of the ability of either sex to understand and convey the inner workings of the other. No woman was ever "written" better by a woman writer. How did Joyce know? God knows how and it doesn't matter.

GRAHAM GREENE: One never knows enough about characters in real life to put them into novels. One gets started and then, suddenly, one can not remember what toothpaste they use; what are their views on interior decoration, and one is stuck utterly. No, major characters emerge: minor ones may be photographed.

LILLIAN HELLMAN: I don't think characters turn out the way you think they are going to turn out. They don't always go your way. At least they don't go my way. If I wanted to start writing about you, by page ten I probably wouldn't be. I don't think you start with a person. I think you start with the parts of many people. Drama has to do with conflict in people, with denials.

ERNEST HEMINGWAY: If I explained how that [the process of turning a real-life character into a fictional one] is sometimes done, it would be a handbook for libel lawyers.

ALDOUS HUXLEY: I try to imagine how certain people I know would behave in certain circumstances. Of course I base my characters partly on the people I know—one can't escape it—but fictional characters are oversimplified; they're much less complex than the people one knows.

JAMES JONES: By the time I'm done with them, they're not like anybody else but themselves. It would be better to say I use them as springboards. It's funny; I've been accused by various reviewers or critical writers of portraying myself—autobiographically—in nearly all of my characters. It's been said that I was Prewitt; it's been said that I was Warden; it's been said that I was Dave Hirsh. I couldn't be them all. I've actually had people, who of course romanticized Prewitt as a hero, flatly refuse to believe I didn't draw Prewitt from myself, even when I told them I hadn't. I guess it's true that when I was younger and more romantic, I would have liked to have been Prewitt, and Warden too for that matter. On the other hand, I certainly wouldn't want to be Dave Hirsh. But by and large I guess I take my characters from people I've known at one time or another. Sometimes, though, it's simply an event which strikes me and then I try to imagine a character who would fit into that event. For instance, the man who was killed by Fatso Judson in the Stockade, Blues Berry; I never knew him at all.

WILLIAM KENNEDY: When you begin to dwell on why he or she acted in this particular way—that is what moves you forward to the next page. That's the way it happens with me, because what's most interesting is not the plot. Who cares about the plot? Who? Forster in *The Art of the Novel* dismissed it as a faintly contemptible thing you have to have, somehow, but that's really not where the story exists. The character does something which is new, and then, the story begins to percolate. If I knew at the beginning how the book was going to end, I would probably never finish. I knew that Legs Diamond was going to die at the end of the book, so I killed him on page one.

NORMAN MAILER: I try to put the model in situations which have very little to do with his real situations in life. Very quickly the model disappears. His private reality can't hold up. For instance, I might take somebody who is a professional football player, a man let's say whom I know slightly, and make him a movie star. In a transposition of this sort, everything which relates particularly to the professional football player quickly disappears, and what is left, curiously, is what is *exportable* in his character. But this process while interesting in the early stages is not as exciting as the more creative act of allowing your characters to grow once they're separated from the model. It's when they become almost as complex as one's own personality that the fine excitement begins. Because then they are not really characters any longer—they're beings, which is a distinction I like to make. A character is someone you can grasp as a whole, you can have a clear idea of him, but a being is someone whose nature keeps shifting. Like a character of Forster's. In *The Deer Park* Lulu Myers is a being rather than a character. If you study her closely you will see that she is a different person in every scene. Just a little different. I don't know whether initially I did this by accident or purposefully, but at a certain point I made the conscious decision *not* to try to straighten her out, she seemed right in her change-ableness.

BERNARD MALAMUD: My characters run away but not far. Their guise is surprises.

FRANÇOIS MAURIAC: There is almost always a real person in the beginning, but then he changes so that sometimes he no longer bears the slightest resemblance to the original. In general, it is only the secondary characters who are taken directly from life.

TONI MORRISON: I never use anyone I know. In *The Bluest Eye* I think I used some gestures and dialogue of my mother in certain places, and a little geography. I've never done that since. I really am very conscientious about that. It's never based on anyone. I don't do what many writers do—this process of taking from something that's alive and using it for one's own purposes. You can do it with trees, butterflies or human beings. Making a little life for oneself by scavenging other people's lives is a big question, and it does have moral and ethical implications.

In fiction, I feel the most intelligent, and the most free, and the most excited, when my characters are fully invented people. That's part of the excitement. If they're based on somebody else, in a funny way it's an infringement of a copyright. That person *owns* his life, has a patent on it. It shouldn't be available for fiction. They are very carefully imagined. I feel as though I know all there is to know about them, even things I don't write—like how they part their hair. They are like ghosts. They have nothing on their minds but themselves and aren't interested in anything but themselves. So you can't let them write your book for you. I have read books in which I know that has happened—when a novelist has been totally taken over by a character. I want to say, "You can't do that. If those people could write books they would, but they can't. *You* can." So, you have to say, "Shut up. Leave me alone. I am doing this."

JOHN MORTIMER: I was reading E. M. Forster, who was writing about plot, and he said the awful thing is you create these wonderful characters and then they won't do anything; they won't be bothered to get involved in a plot!

IRIS MURDOCH: I would abominate the idea of putting real people into a novel, not only because I think it's morally questionable, but also because I think it would be terribly dull. I don't want to make a photographic copy of somebody I know. I want to create somebody who never existed, and who is at the same time a plausible person. I think the characteristics gradually gather together. The first image of the character may be very shadowy; one vaguely knows that he is a good citizen or a religious sort of chap. Perhaps he's puritanical, or hedonistic, and so on. I must have some notion of the troubles he's going to be in and his relationship to the other characters. But the details on which the novel depends, the details of his appearance, his peculiarities, his idiosyncrasies, his other characteristics, his mode of being, will come later—if one is lucky—and quite instinctively, because the more you see of a person the more a kind of coherence begins to evolve.

VLADIMIR NABOKOV: It was not he [E. M. Forster] who fathered that trite little whimsy about characters getting out of hand; it is as old as the quills, although of course one sympathizes with *his* people if they try to wriggle out of that trip to India or wherever he takes them. My characters are galley slaves.

EDNA O'BRIEN: Women are better at emotions and the havoc those emotions wreak. But it must be said that Anna Karenina is the most believable heroine. The last scene where she goes to the station and looks down at the rails and thinks of Vronski's rejection is terrible in its depiction of despair. Women, on the whole, are better at plumbing the depths. A woman artist can produce a perfect gem, as opposed to a huge piece of rock carving a man might produce. It is not a limitation of talent or intelligence, it is just a different way of looking at the world.

FRANÇOISE SAGAN: I've tried very hard and I've never found any resemblance between the people I know and the people in my novels. I don't search for exactitude in portraying people. I try to give to imaginary people a kind of veracity. It would bore me to death to put into my novels the people I know. It seems to me that there are two kinds of trickery: the "fronts" people assume before one another's eyes and the "front" a writer puts on the face of reality.

ROBERT STONE: It is very natural. You construct characters and set them going in their own interior landscape, and what they find to talk about and what confronts them are, of course, things that concern you most.

WILLIAM STYRON: E. M. Forster refers to "flat" and "round" characters. I try to make all of mine round. It takes an extrovert like Dickens to make flat characters come alive. But story as such has been neglected by today's introverted writers. Story and character should grow together; I think I'm lucky so far in that in practically everything I've tried to write these two elements have grown together. They must, to give an impression of life being lived, just because each man's life is a story, if you'll pardon the cliché.

WILLIAM TREVOR: Well, I think it does seem to me that the only way you can create a character is through observation. I don't think there is any other route. And what you observe is not quite like just meeting someone on a train, having a conversation, and then going away. I mean, really, a kind of adding up of people you notice. I think there's something *in* writers of fiction that makes them notice things and store them away all the time. Writers of fiction are collectors of useless information. They are the opposite of good, solid, wise citizens who collect good information and put it to good use. Fiction writers remember tiny little details, some of them almost malicious, but very telling. It's a way of endlessly remembering. A face comes back after years and years and years, as though you've taken a photograph. It's as though you have, for the moment, thought: "I know that person very well." You could argue that you have some extraordinary insight, but actually it's just a very hard-working imagination. It's almost like a stress in you that goes on, nibbling and nibbling, gnawing away at you, in a *very* inquisitive way, wanting to know. And of course while all that's happening you're stroking in the colors, putting a line here and a line there, creating something which moves further and further away from the original. The truth emerges, the person who is created is a different person altogether—a person in their own right.

ANGUS WILSON: Every character is a mixture of people you've known. Characters come to me—and I think this is behind the Madeleine business in Proust—when people are talking to me. I feel I have heard this, this tone of voice, in other circumstances. And, at the risk of seeming rude, I have to hold on to this and chase it back until it clicks with someone I've met before. The second secretary at the embassy in Bangkok may remind me of the chemistry assistant at Oxford. And I ask myself, what have they in common? Out of such mixtures I can create characters.

P. G. WODEHOUSE: I only intended to use him [Jeeves] once. His first entrance was: "Mrs. Gregson to see you, Sir," in a story called *Extricating Young Gussie*. He only had one other line, "Very good, Sir. Which suit will you wear?" But then I was writing a story, *The Artistic Career of Corky*, about two young men, Bertie Wooster and his friend Corky, getting into a lot of trouble, and neither of them had brains enough to get out of the trouble. I thought: Well, how can I get them out? And I thought: "Suppose one of them had an omniscient valet?" I wrote a short story about him, then another short story, then several more short stories and novels. That's how a character grows. I think I've written nine Jeeves novels now and about thirty short stories.

ON SYMBOLS

INTERVIEWER: What is the symbolic significance of the birds in so many of your sex scenes—the white bird that flies out of the gondola . . . ?

HEMINGWAY (shouting): You think you can do any better?

MARGARET DRABBLE: It's nearly always unintentional. I look back at it and think, "Oh, that relates to that." When you're writing in a certain vein, everything grows out of the same source. Occasionally it's more deliberate. I was very much aware when I got to the end of *The Ice Age* that it would be nice to have another bird. I had put a bird on the first page; it seemed obvious to put a bird on the last. And there were a lot of dead dogs in that book, but then there were just a lot of dead dogs around that year. It's a natural associative process, really. It's not exactly symbolism, it's just how life is. You notice one thing and then you notice the same thing again tomorrow.

STANLEY ELKIN: When I was about a hundred pages into *Boswell*, I suddenly discovered that I had Boswell in a lot of elevators, and because I had been trained in the New Criticism I decided, hey, this is pretty neat! Elevators. Makes a nice pattern. And so I was conscious of the elevator motif and kept moving him in and out of elevators. In a way it works because a great deal of novelistic fiction is about ascent. Since Boswell was a guy on the make and had this sort of excelsior personality, it was quite fitting for him to be in elevators, on up escalators, and to climb stairs. There's one scene in *Boswell* where he's in a Jewish community in Brooklyn, as I recall, to meet a miracle rabbi, and he can't get past the front door. He is not permitted to climb those stairs and is stalled. Sure, I'm conscious of symbols and patterns in my work. But this is something I've sometimes come on to only after the fact and then made the most of.

RALPH ELLISON: There are certain themes, symbols, and images which are based on folk material. For example, there is the old saying among Negroes: If you're black, stay back; if you're brown, stick around; if you're white, you're right. And there is the joke Negroes tell on themselves about their being so black they can't be seen in the dark. In my book this sort of thing was merged with the meanings which blackness and light have long had in Western mythology: evil and goodness, ignorance and knowledge, and so on. In my novel the narrator's development is one through blackness to light; that is, from ignorance to enlightenment: invisibility to visibility. He leaves the South and goes North; this, as you will notice in reading Negro folk tales, is always the road to freedom—the movement upward. You have the same thing again when he leaves his underground cave for the open.

It took me a long time to learn how to adapt such examples of myth into my work—also ritual. The use of ritual is equally a vital part of the creative process. I learned a few things from Eliot, Joyce, and Hemingway, but not how to adapt them. When I started writing, I knew that in both *The Waste Land* and *Ulysses* ancient myth and ritual were used to give form and significance to the material; but it took me a few years to realize that the myths and rites which we find functioning in our everyday lives could be used in the same way. In my first attempt at a novel—which I was unable to complete—I began by trying to manipulate the simple structural unities of *beginning, middle,* and *end,* but when I attempted to deal with the psychological strata—the images, symbols, and emotional configurations—of the experience at hand, I discovered that the unities were simply cool points of stability on which one could suspend the narrative line—but beneath the surface of apparently rational human relationships there seethed a chaos before which I was helpless. People rationalize what they shun or are incapable of dealing with; these superstitions and their rationalizations become ritual as they govern behavior. The rituals become social forms, and it is one of the functions of the artist to recognize them and raise them to the level of art.

I don't know whether I'm getting this over or not. Let's put it this way: Take the "Battle Royal" passage in my novel, where the boys are blindfolded and forced to fight each other for the amusement of the white observers. This is a vital part of behavior pattern in the South, which both Negroes and whites thoughtlessly accept. It is a ritual in preservation of caste lines, a keeping of taboo to appease the gods and ward off bad luck. It is also the initiation ritual to which all greenhorns are subjected. This passage states what Negroes will see I did not have to invent; the patterns were already there in society so that all I had to do was present them in a broader context of meaning. In any society there are many rituals of situation which, for the most part, go unquestioned. They can be simple or elaborate, but they are the connective tissue between the work of art and the audience.

ERNEST HEMINGWAY: I suppose there are symbols since critics keep finding them. If you do not mind I dislike talking about them and being questioned about them. It is hard enough to write books and stories without being asked to explain them as well. Also it deprives the explainers of work. If five or six or more good explainers can keep going why should I interfere with them? Read anything I write for the pleasure of reading it. Whatever else you find will be the measure of what you brought to the reading.

TED HUGHES: I don't know how to explain the birds as symbols. There are certain things that are just impressive, aren't there? One stone can be impressive, and the stones around it aren't. It's the same with animals. Some, for some reason, are strangely impressive. They just get into you in a strange way. Certain birds obviously have this extra quality which fascinates your attention. Obviously hawks have always been that for me, as for a great many others, not only impressive in themselves but also in that they've accumulated an enormous literature making them even more impressive. And crows too. Crows are the central bird in many mythologies. The crow is at every extreme, lives on every piece of land on earth, the most intelligent bird.

PABLO NERUDA: The dove signifies the dove and the guitar signifies a musical instrument called the guitar.

KATHERINE ANNE PORTER: I never consciously took or adopted a symbol in my life. I certainly did not say, "This blooming tree upon which Judas is supposed to have hanged himself is going to be the center of my story." I named "Flowering Judas" after it was written, because when reading back over it I suddenly saw the whole symbolic plan and pattern of which I was totally unconscious while I was writing. There's a pox of symbolist theory going the rounds these days in American colleges in the writing courses. Miss Mary McCarthy, who is one of the wittiest and most acute and in some ways the worst-tempered woman in American letters, tells about a little girl who came to her with a story. Now Miss McCarthy is an extremely good critic, and she found this to be a good story, and she told the girl that it was—that she considered it a finished work, and that she could with a clear conscience go on to something else. And the little girl said, "But Miss McCarthy, my writing teacher said, 'Yes, it's a good piece of work, but now we must go back and put in the symbols!' " I think that's an amusing story, and it makes my blood run cold.

ON DIALOGUE

Discourse, the sweeter banquet of the mind.
                                    —ALEXANDER POPE

KINGSLEY AMIS: Dialogue's a very powerful weapon, isn't it? Again, traditionally the novelist has to characterize people quite quickly by the way they talk: their various idioms, whether they talk plainly or in a flowery style. But I do find dialogue quicker to write than narrative—narrative I always find rather painful. Dialogue is more fun . . . but I always try over the phrases, fooling the reader into believing that this is how people actually talk. In fact, inevitably, it's far more coherent than any actual talk. I don't say I succeed all that often, but when in doubt I will repeat a phrase to myself seven or eight times, trying to put myself in the place of an actor speaking the part. And all these "I mean's" and "sort of's" and "you know's" are important because there are characters who find it difficult to lay their tongues on what they mean the first time, and I think this should be indicated.

DON DELILLO: Well, there are fifty-two ways to write dialogue that's faithful to the way people speak. And then there are times when you're not trying to be faithful. I've done it different ways myself and I think I concentrated on dialogue most deeply in *Players*. It's hyperrealistic, spoken by urban men and women who live together, who know each other's speech patterns and thought patterns and finish each other's sentences or don't even bother because it isn't necessary. Jumpy, edgy, a bit hostile, dialogue that's almost obsessive about being funny whatever the circumstances. New York voices.

JAMES JONES: Dialogue is almost too easy. For me. So much so that it makes me suspicious of it, so I have to be careful with it. I *could* find myself evading problems of true expression because dialogue's so easy for me to do. There are many important issues and points of sublety about people, about human behavior, that I want to make in writing, and it's easy to evade these—or do them superficially, do them halfway—by simply writing good dialogue. And it becomes increasingly easy as I get to know the people better. But good dialogue just isn't enough to explain the subtler ramifications of the characters and incidents which I'm trying to work out now. Not *realistic* dialogue, anyway. Perhaps if you used some kind of surrealistic dialogue, but then it would read like a dream episode. It wouldn't be real talk. For instance, it's obvious enough that in almost any conversation things are happening to the people in the conversation which they do not and cannot express. In a play it is possible for a good actor to imply that he is thinking something other than what he is saying. But it's pretty slipshod and half-assed, because he cannot convey what he's thinking *explicitly*. In prose, and especially in the novel form, this can be done. If the man is using a subterfuge, it can be explained explicitly, and why. Actually, in life, conversation is more often likely to be an attempt at deliberate evasion, deliberate confusion, rather than communication. We're all cheats and liars, really. And the novelist can show just how and why we are.

THOMAS McGUANE: Dialogue is very important to me because I've always loved it in novels. Lots of people read novels racing from dialogue to dialogue. In fact, I would like to really compress the prose in a novel, without getting too arch about it. Some people, like Manuel Puig, have written novels almost entirely in dialogue, but it gets to be a little too much sometimes since readers need to know where they are a bit. At any rate, writing dialogue is probably the best thing I do, and I'm always trying to work up an aesthetic for my fiction that will acknowledge that fact. Of course, Hemingway was really a great dialogue writer, it's one of the reasons we read him. Dialogue is a very useful tool to reveal things about people, and novels are about people and about what they do to each other. That's what novels are for. They're not pure text for deconstructionists. One day, that will be clear again.

FRANK O'CONNOR: If you're the sort of person that meets a girl in the street and instantly notices the color of her eyes and of her hair and the sort of dress she's wearing, then you're not in the least like me. I just notice a feeling from people. I notice particularly the cadence of their voices, the sort of phrases they'll use, and that's what I'm all the time trying to hear in my head, how people word things—because everybody speaks an entirely different language, that's really what it amounts to. I have terribly sensitive hearing and I'm terribly aware of voices. If I remember somebody, for instance, that I was very fond of, I don't remember what he or she looked like, but I can absolutely take off the voice. I'm a good mimic; I've a bit of the actor in me, I suppose, that's really what it amounts to. I cannot pass a story as finished unless I connect it myself, unless I know how everybody in it spoke, which, as I say, can go quite well with the fact that I couldn't tell you in the least what they looked like. If I use the right phrase and the reader hears the phrase in his head, he sees the individual.

V. S. PRITCHETT: It's hard to answer that. It comes naturally to me to write dialogue. I'm not a plot writer. I find it very difficult to invent a plot of any intricacy. Much more exciting to me is the intricacy, the plot form, of dialogue. The speaker is making up his drama as he goes along, and he doesn't know how good he is or how bad he is. It's natural, so therefore dialogue gets me out of any chip I have about not being able to think of a good plot. Dialogue is one of the things which I seem to be able to do, hit upon doing, and like. Dialogue is my form of poetry. I can't write poetry to save my life. Dialogue is the nearest I can come to the poetic.

SAM SHEPARD: I think an ear for stage dialogue is different from an ear for language that's heard in life. You can hear things in life that don't work at all when you try to reproduce them onstage. It's not the same; something changes.

It's being listened to in a direct way, like something overheard. It's not voyeuristic, not like I'm in the other room. I'm confronted by it, and the confrontational part of theater is the dialogue. We hear all kinds of fascinating things every day, but dialogue has to create a life. It has to be self-sustaining. Conversation is definitely not dialogue.

EUDORA WELTY: In its beginning, dialogue's the easiest thing in the world to write when you have a good ear, which I think I have. But as it goes on, it's the most difficult, because it has so many ways to function. Sometimes I needed to make a speech do three or four or five things at once—reveal what the character said but also what he thought he said, what he hid, what others were going to think he meant, and what they misunderstood, and so forth—all in his single speech. And the speech would have to keep the essence of this one character, his whole particular outlook in concentrated form. This isn't to say I succeeded. But I guess it explains why dialogue gives me my greatest pleasure in writing. I used to laugh out loud sometimes when I wrote it—the way P. G. Wodehouse is said to do. I'd think of some things my characters would say, and even if I couldn't use it, I would write the scene out just to let them loose on something—my private show.

. . .

Familiarity. Memory of the way things get said. Once you have heard certain expressions, sentences, you almost never forget them. It's like sending a bucket down the well and it always comes up full. You don't know you've remembered, but you have. And you listen for the right word, in the present, and you hear it. Once you're into a story everything seems to apply—what you overhear on a city bus is exactly what your character would say on the page you're writing. Wherever you go, you meet part of your story. I guess you're tuned in for it, and the right things are sort of magnetized—if you can think of your ears as magnets. I could hear someone saying—and I had to cut this out—"What, you never ate goat?" And someone answering, "Goat! Please don't say you serve *goat* at this reunion. I wasn't told it was *goat* I was served. I thought—" and so on, and then the recipe, and then it ended up with—I can't remember exactly now—it ended with, "You can do a whole lot of things with vinegar." Well, all these things I would just laugh about and think about for so long and put them in. And then I'd think, that's just plain indulgence. Take it out! And I'd take it out.

P. G. WODEHOUSE: Always get to the dialogue as soon as possible. I always feel the thing to go for is speed. Nothing puts the reader off more than a great slab of prose at the start. I think the success of every novel—if it's a novel of action—depends on the high spots. The thing to do is to say to yourself, "Which are my big scenes?" and then get every drop of juice out of them. The principle I always go on in writing a novel is to think of the characters in terms of actors in a play. I say to myself, if a big name were playing this part, and if he found that after a strong first act he had practically nothing to do in the second act, he would walk out. Now, then, can I twist the story so as to give him plenty to do all the way through? I believe the only way a writer can keep himself up to the mark is by examining each story quite coldly before he starts writing it and asking himself if it is all right *as a story.* I mean, once you go saying to yourself, "This is a pretty weak plot as it stands, but I'm such a hell of a writer that my magic touch will make it OK," you're sunk. If they aren't in interesting situations, characters can't be major characters, not even if you have the rest of the troop talk their heads off about them.

ON SEX

To enlarge or illustrate this power of effect of love is to set a
candle in the sun.   —ROBERT BURTON

Sex annihilates identity, and the space given to sex in
contemporary novels is an avowal of the absence of character.
                                            —MARY MCCARTHY

Cover that breast, it offends my eye.   —MOLIÈRE

Sex as an institution, sex as a general notion, sex as a problem,
sex as a platitude—all this is something I find too tedious for
words. Let's skip sex.   —VLADIMIR NABOKOV

The dirtiest book of all is the expurgated book.
                                            —WALT WHITMAN

KINGSLEY AMIS: I shy away from explicit sex mainly because it's so-
cially embarrassing. The comparison I usually draw is with being told
these things by an acquaintance—and after all, the novelist is only an acquaintance, isn't he, as far as the reader's concerned?—and to be told in detail what he's been up to for over half an hour—the equivalent of a chapter,
say—would be embarrassing, wouldn't it? *I* would find it embarrassing.

MARGARET ATWOOD: If by "sex" you mean just the sex act—"the
earth moved" stuff—well, I don't think I write those scenes much. They
can so quickly become comic or pretentious or overly metaphoric. "Her
breasts were like apples," that sort of thing. But "sex" is not just which part
of whose body was where. It's the relationship between the participants,
the furniture in the room or the leaves on the tree, what gets said before
and after, the emotions—act of love, act of lust, act of hate. Act of indifference, act of violence, act of despair, act of manipulation, act of hope?
Those things have to be part of it.
    Striptease has become less interesting since they did away with the cos-

tumes. It's become Newtonian. The movement of bodies through space, period. It can get boring.

ANTHONY BURGESS: My aversion to describing amorous details in my work is probably that I treasure physical love so highly I don't want to let strangers in on it. For, after all, when we describe copulation we're describing our own experiences. I like privacy. I think that other writers should do what they can do, and if they can spend—as one of my American girl students did—ten pages on the act of fellatio without embarrassing themselves, very good luck to them. But I think there's more artistic pleasure to be gained from the ingenious circumvention of a taboo than from what is called total permissiveness. When I wrote my first Enderby novel, I had to make my hero say "For cough," since "Fuck off" was not then acceptable. With the second book the climate had changed, and Enderby was at liberty to say "Fuck off." I wasn't happy. It was too easy. He still said "For cough," while others responded with "Fuck off." A compromise. Literature, however, thrives on taboos, just as all art thrives on technical difficulties.

JOHN DOS PASSOS: He [Hemingway] was *always* concerned with four-letter words. It never bothered me particularly. Sex can be indicated with asterisks. I've always felt that was as good a way as any.

JOHN FOWLES: I certainly think the erotic was very important for Hardy. The avoiding any direct contact with it (or expression of it), the slipping round it, plays an enormous part in his novels. He was obviously a shy and repressed man. He liked the tryst, that first secret meeting or instinctual attraction between lovers, so much more than the fully physical side, what we should call the sex. I suppose I am the same, that is, haunted, both ravished and tormented, by the erotic; yet happiest when it is left three quarters hidden, in secret. I spent a year of my life once writing an erotic novel, in common terms a pornographic one. One day, when it was virtually complete, I took it and all its drafts into the garden and burnt the lot. It would no doubt have made me a great deal of money, and I was rather proud of it, for what it was. It was not prudishness that made me burn; but much more a feeling of blasphemy, an error of bad taste. It broke that secret, bared the hidden part. That is why I dislike what I see as the unnecessary sexual explicitness in so much American fiction; it becomes infantile, destructive of the truly erotic, in the end.

Mantissa was meant to make fun of that, in part; and also of the poor novelists, like Hardy, Fournier, D. H. Lawrence, Henry Miller, and countless others, laboring under this monstrous erotic succubus they have to carry on their backs.

MARK HELPRIN: Why would dealing with sex in a novel be a problem? The trick, I believe, as with almost everything else in the world, is to keep it in proportion, to be honest about it, and to be modest. When a man and a woman feel love or infatuation, and the ethical codes by which they permit it, they express it physically. Of course it can get quite intense—hyperventilating and wall banging and that sort of thing—but when it's over it's over, and you go on to something else.

I think the failures to which you allude can be explained by various complementary theories. Quite simply, if one has no sexual outlet, one will think about sex a great deal. Writers work in isolation and are generally thoughtful people who do not live to satisfy their desires the way people do in, say, Brazil. In addition, the literary culture is also one of failed marriages, odd neuroses, and ill health. If you combine all these things you get less sex than biology might require, and so you get musings driven by heat. I find, for example, that I tend to write about food when I'm hungry: it's only natural.

Another reason may be that, without an intuitive sense of what art is, many people use sex as a—forgive me—prosthesis, just as they use politics, to fill the emptiness in their understanding. And, of course, it sells, doesn't it, so it elicits a Pavlovian response in writers. It's like a pigeon pressing the right button and causing food pellets to drop down a chute. Throw in a few tumescent penises and "breasts like upright cones" and you can put in that new swimming pool or make your annual contribution to The Cat Wilhelmina Guerilla Unit of the Animal Rights Liberation Army.

WILLIAM KENNEDY: I think writers should research sex in the same way they research historical characters. It's not difficult to write about. What is difficult to write about is the actual pornographic element of sex. That ceases to be interesting. What you need to do is find the surrounding elements. Yet another struggle of the genitals is hardly worth writing about. It's done on every streetcorner, fifty-five times a magazine. So that's not the point. On the contrary, it's when you discover a character like Kiki Roberts who is Legs Diamond's girlfriend and you look at her and discover this incredible beauty, obviously a great sex object for Diamond, who endangered his life many times for her. And she, reciprocating, constantly. She was a fugitive from justice with him. When you look at that woman, you can begin to imagine what it was about her that led him to behave that way. That was quite a pleasant thing for me—to reimagine Kiki Roberts.

HENRY MILLER: I've led a good rich sexual life, and I don't see why it should be left out.

TONI MORRISON: Sex is difficult to write about because it's just not sexy enough. The only way to write about it is not to write much. Let the reader bring his own sexuality into the text. A writer I usually admire has written about sex in the most off-putting way. There is just too much information. If you start saying "the curve of . . ." you soon sound like a gynecologist. Only Joyce could get away with that. He said all those forbidden words. He said *cunt,* and that was shocking. The forbidden word can be provocative. But after a while it becomes monotonous rather than arousing. Less is always better. Some writers think that if they use dirty words they've done it. It can work for a short period and for a very young imagination, but after a while it doesn't deliver.

REYNOLDS PRICE: In the seventies *Esquire* asked me to write an article about new sexual freedoms in fiction. It was really the time in American fiction when suddenly we began to realize, My God, I can say anything I want to, and even Jesse Helms can't stop me! I can portray any sexual act. I can indulge any private peculiarity in prose, and if I can convince a publisher to print it and send it to the bookshops of America, no one's going to clap me in jail. So I tried to look seriously at the question of how much sexual freedom a serious novelist really needs and can use.

For clarity's sake I tried to look back, rather than examining my contemporaries. I looked at *Anna Karenina,* and I said that essentially Tolstoy does not need to tell us any more about Anna's private sexual life than he does because it's not a book about sex. It's a book about something else—how the best of us may conspire with fate to end our lives and harm those near us. I said that Flaubert probably would have benefited had he been able to tell us more about what Emma's actual adulterous unions are like for her, because the whole subject of the novel is Emma's romantic and romantically poisonous delusions about sexual love. It was *Esquire* who gave it the title "What Did Madame Bovary Do in Bed?" Rather stunned and frantic, I would think. And I don't say it to be comic. I suspect stunned and frantic, breathless and shockingly cold to the touch.

JAMES THURBER: His [Harold Ross's of *The New Yorker*] idea was that sex is an incident. "If you can prove it," I said, "we can get it in a box on the front page of *The New York Times*." Now I don't want to say that in private life Ross was a prude. But as regards the theater or the printed page he certainly was. For example, he once sent an office memorandum to us in a sealed envelope. It was an order: "When you send me a memorandum with four-letter words in it, *seal it.* There are women in this office." I said, "Yah, Ross, and they know a lot more of these words than you do." When women were around he was very conscious of them. Once my wife and I were in his office and Ross was discussing a man and woman he knew much better than we did. Ross told us: "I have every reason to believe that they're *s-l-e-e-p-i-n-g* together." My wife replied: "Why, Harold Ross, what words you do spell out." But honest to goodness that was genuine. Women are either good or bad, he once told me, and the good ones must not hear these things.

P. L. TRAVERS: A great friend of mine at the beginning of our friendship (he was himself a poet) said to me very defiantly, "I have to tell you that I *loathe* children's books." And I said to him, "Well, won't you just read this just for my sake?" And he said grumpily, "Oh, very well, send it to me." I did, and I got a letter back saying: "Why didn't you *tell* me? Mary Poppins with her cool green core of sex has me enthralled forever."

REBECCA WEST: I would have thought that [the awkwardness in writing about sex] was completely true of Kafka, who couldn't write about sex or value its place in life. I think there's an awful lot of nonsense in Lawrence when he writes about Mexican sacrifices and sexual violence. Their only relevance was to the Mexicans' lack of protein, as in the South Sea Islands. Funny, that's a wonderful thing. I don't know why more people don't write about it: how the whole of life must have been different when four-footed animals came in. They had just a few deer before, but not enough to go round, and so they prevented the deer from becoming extinct by making them sacred to the kings. It's much more interesting to write about that than about sex, which most of your audience knows about.

On Experimental Writing

An original writer is not one who imitates nobody, but whom nobody can imitate.
                                                          —CHATEAUBRIAND

It's not wise to violate the rules until you know how to observe them.
                                                          —T. S. ELIOT

I'd just as soon play tennis with the net down.
                                                          —ROBERT FROST

Here lies that peerless paper peer Lord Peter,
Who broke the laws of God and man and metre.
                                                          —SIR WALTER SCOTT

Zounds! I was never so bethumped with words!
                                                          —WILLIAM SHAKESPEARE

JOHN CHEEVER: Fiction *is* experimentation; when it ceases to be that, it ceases to be fiction. One never puts down a sentence without the feeling that it has never been put down before in such a way, and that perhaps even the substance of the sentence has never been felt. Every sentence is an innovation.

JAMES LAUGHLIN: I don't think that [Gertrude Stein] moved on from her remarkable early work. She got deeper and deeper into automatic writing, which she was beginning at the time I worked for her. Automatic writing is a dead end. You go on writing "automatically" and what do you write? If you look at those later books that Yale published for her after she gave them her papers, they're pretty boring.

   I used to watch Gertrude at it. That last summer I spent in Savoie writing those press releases for *Lectures in America,* I'd watch her sitting in a bath chair on her terrace with a big notebook, writing just as fast as she could, the pen flying, no pauses whatsoever. No rewriting. And then Alice B. Toklas, sweet person—well, not all that sweet, *sort* of sweet—would be given these notebooks to type out. Her best work came early: *Three Lives, The Blood on the Dining-Room Floor,* parts of *The Making of Americans, Portrait of Mabel Dodge. Four Saints in Three Acts* was beautiful, and some of the other plays, the opera plays. She really needed someone like Virgil Thomson, whom she respected, to sit on her a bit and make her devise some plot. In the automatic writing pieces there's no plot movement; they just roll on and become tedious.

OCTAVIO PAZ: I did experiment with "automatic writing." It's very hard to do. Actually, it's *impossible.* No one can write with his mind blank, not thinking about what he's writing. Only God could write a real automatic poem because only for God are speaking, thinking, and acting the same thing. If God says, "A horse!" a horse immediately appears. But a poet has to *reinvent* his horse, that is, his poem. He has to think it, and he has to make it. All the automatic poems I wrote during the time of my friendship with the surrealists were thought and written with a certain deliberation. I wrote those poems with my eyes open. I was extremely fond of André Breton, who advocated this sort of thing, really admired him. It's no exaggeration to say he was a solar figure because his friendship emitted light and heat. Shortly after I met him, he asked me for a poem for a surrealist magazine. I gave him a prose poem, "*Mariposa de obsidiana*"—it alludes to a pre-Colombian goddess. He read it over several times, liked it, and decided to publish it. But he pointed out one line that seemed weak. I reread the poem, discovered he was right, and removed the phrase. He was charmed, but I was confused. So I asked him, "What about automatic writing?" He raised his leonine head and answered without changing expression: "That line was a journalistic intromission. . . ."

JOHN SIMON: I don't think there is such a thing as experimental theater. I think there is only theater that has something to say. The cheap way out is to say there's good theater and bad theater, but it's not quite that simple. There's theater that has something necessary to say—it may not even be good, but it has an insight it must express—and there's theater which may be very slick and accomplished but has nothing to say. That's the distinction. It is somewhat similar to good versus bad, but it's not synonymous.

So that's what I try to assess. And if it says it in an experimental way, fine. But what is experimental? Is Peter Sellars taking a boring six-hour opera by Olivier Messiaen and putting two hundred television sets on the stage experimental? Maybe it is, but it's still terrible. The Messiaen music has maybe half an hour of good stuff in it, and five and a half hours of boredom, and the television sets have nothing to say, and Peter Sellars has nothing to say. If that's experimental, I don't need it. But if somebody trying to write a new opera or play or movie says something in a different, difficult, subtle, roundabout, never before seen or heard way, fine. I'm all for it, and I don't care if it's downtown or uptown or out of town.

WALLACE STEGNER: I don't really aspire to write a novel that can be read backward as well as forward, that turns chronology on its head, has no continuity, no narrative, that, in effect, tries to create a novel by throwing all the pieces in a bag and shaking it. If a writer has to do *that* to be original, then I don't care about being original. In fact, I don't think the word "originality," as it's usually defined, is particularly useful. It usually seizes upon some innovation that often turns out to be frivolous or essentially unimportant. An awful lot of mutations, which is what these things are, turn out to be monsters that can't live. I'm content with the species, with turning out two-legged animals with one head.

· · ·

"No new ways to be new," as Frost said. I think that's a reasonably good statement. "There's nothing new under the sun," sayeth the Preacher. "All the rivers run into the sea, yet the sea is not full." I think more circularly than linearly. I don't think there are beginnings and destinations so much as circles which end by closing and starting over again. I can't think of any fiction that introduces new elements of what used to be called "Human Nature," nothing that isn't present, say, in *The Iliad* and *The Odyssey.* The qualities of character, the machinery of suspense and climax, of mounting action and falling action: I don't think we've seen anything new in that way. There are new clothes, because civilization can change, and we get out of armor and into doublet and hose, and then Brooks Brothers pants, but we're still the same people, and doing the same things essentially. I think it's a mistake to think originality amounts to that much.

I know people, for instance, including former students of mine, who got into the sexual revolution and thought they had opened up really new material for fiction. They felt like renaissance men and women discovering a new world with fifty-seven positions. But it's there in *One Thousand and One Nights,* it's there in the *Satyricon* of Petronius. There's nothing new about it. I doubt there's much Cain didn't know as soon as he got acquainted east of Eden. I don't think that's a way of getting anywhere: to pretend that there's anything new to be said. What's important is a larger understanding of what has always been.

WILLIAM TREVOR: No, I think all writing is experimental. The very obvious sort of experimental writing is not really more experimental than that of a conventional writer like myself. I experiment all the time but the experiments are hidden. Rather like abstract art: you look at an abstract picture, and then you look at a close-up of a Renaissance painting and find the same abstractions.

ROBERT PENN WARREN: What is "experimental writing"? James Joyce didn't do "experimental writing"—he wrote *Ulysses*. Eliot didn't do "experimental writing"—he wrote *The Waste Land*. When you fail at something you call it an "experiment," an elite word for flop. Just because lines are uneven or capitals missing doesn't mean experiment. Literary magazines devoted to experimental writing are usually filled with works by middle-aged or old people. Or young fogeys. In one way, of course, all writing that is any good *is* experimental; that is, it's a way of seeing what is possible—what poem, what novel is possible. Experiment—they define it as putting a question to nature, and that is true of writing undertaken with seriousness. You put the question to human nature—and especially your own nature—and see what comes out. It is unpredictable. If it is predictable—not experimental in that sense—then it will be worthless.

EVELYN WAUGH: Experiment? God forbid! Look at the results of experiment in the case of a writer like Joyce. He started off writing very well, then you can watch him going mad with vanity. He ends up a lunatic.

On Humor

Among all kinds of writing, there is none in which authors are more apt to miscarry than in works of humour, as there is none in which they are more ambitious to excel.

—Joseph Addison

Master, shall I begin with the usual jokes
That the audience always laugh at?

—Aristophanes

Aristotle said melancholy men of all others are most witty.

—Robert Burton

He deserves paradise who makes his companions laugh.

—The Koran

So long as there's a bit of a laugh going, things are all right. As soon as this infernal seriousness, like a greasy sea, heaves up, everything is lost.

—D. H. Lawrence

Make him [the reader] laugh and he will think you a trivial fellow, but bore him the right way and your reputation is assured.

—W. Somerset Maugham

'Tis a strange undertaking, to make the gentry laugh.

—Molière

Humor is emotional chaos remembered in tranquility.

—James Thurber

There are several kinds of stories, but only one difficult kind— the humorous.

—Mark Twain

The best way to cheer yourself up is to try to cheer somebody else up.

—Mark Twain

Kingsley Amis: There's one obvious one [pitfall]: you must never make one character laugh at what another says or does. Dornford Yates's

"Berry" novels, which are quite good fun in a sedate sort of way, are ruined by everybody collapsing with merriment whenever Berry shows up. The other pitfall is: you must never offer the reader anything simply *as* funny and nothing more. Make it acceptable as information, comment, narrative, et cetera, so that if the joke flops the reader has still got *something*. Wodehouse understood this perfectly, even better than Shakespeare did.

HEINRICH BÖLL: Humor is really one of the hardest things to define, very hard. And it's very ambiguous. You have it or you don't. You can't attain it. There are terrible forms of professional humor, the humorists' humor. That can be awful. It depresses me because it is artificial. You can't always be humorous, but a professional humorist must. That is a sad phenomenon.

ROBERTSON DAVIES: My pull is toward comedy. And I have a very high opinion of comedy: comedy is fully as revealing in its probing of human problems as is tragedy. The thing about comedy which I greatly value is that it is infinitely harder to fake than tragedy. It is extremely easy to be gloomy and to say, This is a terrible situation and everybody has got to be serious about it, and because I'm being serious about it, I am a writer of consequence. True, I have not often pulled out the *vox humana* and the *voix céleste* stops, but I know I have made quite a few people laugh a lot, and that is not the easiest thing to do. To see that life is funny and not to mock or jeer at somebody's predicament, cruelly and without understanding, simply because some aspects of it are funny—that takes a bit of doing. I saw an instance today on Fifth Avenue, a situation that was either comic or tragic depending on how you want to take it. This girl was sitting there in the rain begging, and she had a big sign which said what her trouble was. It was a quite ordinary tale of betrayal and misery and this, that, and the other—if it was true, and I don't know if it was true. But the person sitting in the rain looking wretched, even if she was not an honest beggar, was tragic. That someone of her age should be sitting on the sidewalk begging may mean not that she can't do something else, but that she has chosen to do that. It's tragic. You have to balance these two things against one another. Life is, as you said, a very rum thing.

STANLEY ELKIN: Inconsequential is the operative word there. Consequence to me is when the bone doesn't heal, when the germ does not do what the penicillin wants it to. Consequence is pain. There can be no consequences in comedy. Tom and Jerry chase each other; Tom falls off the Empire State Building and shatters like a dish. In the next loop he has reconstituted himself. Now, I don't laugh at Tom and Jerry, but in a simplistic way, that's the model for all comedy. Nothing bad may happen. There is safety in comedy.

HENRY GREEN: If you can make the reader laugh he is apt to get careless and go on reading. So you as the writer get a chance to get something on him.

EUGÈNE IONESCO: Georges Duhamel used to say that "Humor is the courtesy of despair." Humor is therefore very important. At the same time, I can understand people who can't laugh anymore. How can you, with the carnage that is going on in the world—in the Middle East, in Africa, in South America, everywhere? There is awfully little that is conducive to mirth.

GARRISON KEILLOR: When some people sit down to write humor, they adopt a giddy tone of voice, a whooping or comic warble, so that the reader will know it's funny. It's the writing equivalent of a clown suit. This does not wear well. Humor needs to come in under cover of darkness, in disguise, and surprise people. You don't want to get that *gdoing, gdoing, gdoing* sound in your writing. It makes the reader feel sorry for you.

PHILIP LARKIN: One uses humor to make people laugh. In my case, I don't know whether they in fact do. The trouble is, it makes them think you aren't being serious. That's the risk you take.

MARIO VARGAS LLOSA: I used to be "allergic" to humor because I thought, very naively, that serious literature never smiled; that humor could be very dangerous if I wanted to broach serious social, political, or cultural problems in my novels. I thought it would make my stories seem superficial and give my reader the impression that they were nothing more than light entertainment. That's why I had renounced humor, probably under the influence of Sartre, who was always very hostile to humor, at least in his writing. But one day, I discovered that in order to effect a certain experience of life in literature, humor could be a very precious tool. That happened with *Pantaleon and the Special Service*. From then on, I was very conscious of humor as a great treasure, a basic element of life and therefore of literature.

BERNARD MALAMUD: The funny bone is universal. I doubt humorists think of individual taste when they're enticing the laugh. With me humor comes unexpectedly, usually in defense of a character, sometimes because I need cheering up. When something starts funny I can feel my imagination eating and running. I love the distancing—the guise of invention— that humor gives fiction. Comedy, I imagine, is harder to do consistently than tragedy, but I like it spiced in the wine of sadness.

DOROTHY PARKER: I don't want to be classed as a humorist. It makes me feel guilty. I've never read a good tough quotable female humorist, and I never was one myself. I couldn't do it. A "smartcracker" they called me, and that makes me sick and unhappy. There's a hell of a distance between wisecracking and wit. Wit has truth in it; wisecracking is simply calisthenics with words. I didn't mind so much when they were good, but for a long time anything that was called a crack was attributed to me—and then they got the shaggy dogs.

S. J. PERELMAN: Well, it must be thoroughly apparent how many more people wrote humor for the printed page in the twenties. The form seems to be passing, and there aren't many practitioners left. The only magazine nowadays that carries any humor worthy of the name, in my estimation, is *The New Yorker*. Thirty years ago, on the other hand, there were *Judge, Life, Vanity Fair, College Humor,* and one or two others. I think the explanation for the paucity of written humor is simply that very few fledgling writers deign to bother with it. If someone has a flair for comedy, he usually goes into television or what remains of motion pictures. There's far more loot in those fields, and while it's ignominious to be an anonymous gagman, perhaps, eleven hundred dollars a week can be very emollient to the ego. The life of the freelance writer of humor is highly speculative and not to be recommended as a vocation. In the technical sense, the comic writer is a cat on a hot tin roof. His invitation to perform is liable to wear out at any moment; he must quickly and constantly amuse in a short span, and the first smothered yawn is a signal to get lost. The fiction writer, in contrast, has much more latitude. He's allowed to sideslip into exposition, to wander off into interminable byways and browse around endlessly in his characters' heads. The development of a comic idea has to be swift and economical; consequently, the pieces are shorter than conventional fiction and fetch a much smaller stipend.

· · ·

It may surprise you to hear me say—and I'll thank you not to confuse me with masters of the paradox like Oscar Wilde and G. K. Chesterton—that I regard my comic writing as serious. For the past thirty-four years, I have been approached almost hourly by damp people with foreheads like Rocky Ford melons who urge me to knock off my frivolous career and get started on that novel I'm burning to write. I have no earthly intention of doing any such thing. I don't believe in the importance of scale; to me the muralist is no more valid than the miniature painter. In this very large country, where size is all and where Thomas Wolfe outranks Robert Benchley, I am content to stitch away at my embroidery hoop. I think the form I work can have its own distinction, and I would like to surpass what I have done in it.

JOHN SIMON: I try to forget my bright sayings because they're the surest way to bore people at parties. I wouldn't be happy if a poet at a dinner party started reciting his latest poem even if it was good. Of course, sometimes, you can't forget them.

An English comedian, Norman Wisdom, came to Broadway in a play and I wrote, "If this be Norman Wisdom, give me Saxon folly." You see, I am as good as my word. You are asking me to remember and I can't.

NEIL SIMON: What was unique about writing for Sid Caesar's *Your Show of Shows* was that almost every one of the writers has gone on to do really major things: Mel Brooks's whole career . . . Larry Gelbart . . . Woody Allen . . . Joe Stein who wrote *Fiddler on the Roof* . . . Michael Stewart who wrote *Hello, Dolly* . . . it was a group of people only Sid Caesar knew how to put together. Maybe it was trial and error because the ones who didn't work fell out, but once we worked together it was the most excruciatingly hilarious time in my life. It was also one of the most painful because you were fighting for recognition, and there was no recognition. It was very difficult for me because I was quiet and shy, so I sat next to Carl Reiner and whispered my jokes to him. He was my spokesman, he'd jump up and say, "He's got it! He's got it!" Then Carl would say the line, and I would hear it, and I'd laugh because I thought it was funny. But when I watched the show on a Saturday night with my wife, Joan, she'd say, "That was your line, wasn't it?" and I'd say, "I don't remember." What I *do* remember is the screaming and fighting—a cocktail party without the cocktails, everyone yelling lines in and out, people getting very angry at others who were slacking off. Mel Brooks was the main culprit. We all came in to work at ten o'clock in the morning, but he showed up at one o'clock. We'd say, "That's it. We're sick and tired of this. Either Mel comes in at ten o'clock or we go to Sid and do something about it." At about ten to one, Mel would come in with a straw hat, fling it across the room and say "Lindy made it!" and everyone would fall down hysterical. He didn't need the eight hours we put in. He needed four hours. He is, maybe, the most uniquely funny man I've ever met. That inspired me. I wanted to be around those people. I've fooled around with this idea for a play. I even found a title for it, *Laughter on the Twenty-third Floor*, because I think the office was on the twenty-third floor. From that building we looked down on Bendel's and Bergdorf Goodman and Fifth Avenue, watching all the pretty girls go by through binoculars. Sometimes we'd set fire to the desk with lighter fluid. We should have been arrested, all of us.

JAMES THURBER: With humor you have to look out for traps. You're likely to be very gleeful with what you've first put down, and you think it's fine, very funny. One reason you go over and over it is to make the piece sound less as if you were having a lot of fun with it yourself. You try to play it down. In fact, if there's such a thing as a *New Yorker* style, that would be it—playing it down.

CALVIN TRILLIN: One person I read in college who I thought was funny was the very déclassé Max Shulman. I thought he was hilarious.

One time I was asked, by the New York Public Library, for a book put out in connection with some Literary Lion function, to submit a passage of prose that I particularly admired. A lot of writers were asked, and I suppose a lot of Proust found its way in there. It gave me the chance to quote Max Shulman.

I found this passage about Dobey's dog where his mother says, "Dobey you're going off to college and I'm no smarter than your old hound dog Edmund lying there in the corner." Dobey says, "Don't talk that way about Edmund, Mom. He's a smart dog." He whistles to him and says, "Play dead, Edmund. Look at how he obeys. All four feet sticking in the air." His mother says, "Dobey, I hadn't wanted to tell you. He's been dead since Friday. You ran over him with the car." It fit perfectly.

· · ·

I suppose that there is the necessity of some sort of structure in written humor that you can get away without in spoken humor by the use of timing and gesture. Everybody knows people who are funny just by the way they talk. Remember that comedian Jack Leonard—this big, fat guy who appeared on the Johnny Carson shows? He talked very fast. He would always say something like, "IjustwantyoutoknowJohnnyifyou-everneedafriendyouwon'tbeabletofindone." But if you listened to him carefully, after a while you realized a lot of things he said weren't funny at all. But he had a wonderful delivery. Or take the joke about the telegram that Trotsky sent to Stalin from exile in Mexico: "I was wrong. You were right. I should apologize." Somebody says to Stalin, "Trotsky's given up. He's asking forgiveness." Stalin says, "No, you don't understand: Trotsky's Jewish. What he's saying is, '*I* was wrong?? *You* were right?? *I* should apologize?!?' " So that's one thing. When you're writing, you are robbed of your delivery. People, particularly comedians, always say it's all in the timing. But in written humor, the reader has to do his own timing— you have to build in the timing for the reader, which is difficult.

E. B. WHITE: I find difficulty with the word "humor" and with the word "humorist" to peg a writer. I was taken aback, the other day, when I looked in *Who's Who* to discover Frank Sullivan's birthday and found him described as "humorist." It seemed a wholly inadequate summary of the man. Writing funny pieces is a legitimate form of activity, but the durable humor in literature, I suspect, is not the contrived humor of a funnyman commenting on the news but the sly and almost imperceptible ingredient that sometimes gets into writing. I think of Jane Austen, a deeply humorous woman. I think of Thoreau, a man of some humor along with his bile.

P. G. WODEHOUSE: I think character [makes a story funny] mostly. You know instinctively what's funny and what isn't if you're a humorous writer. I don't think a man can deliberately sit down to write a funny story unless he has got a sort of slant on life that leads to funny stories. If you take life fairly easily, then you take a humorous view of things. It's probably because you were born that way. Lord Emsworth and his pig—I *know* they're funny.

ON WRITER'S BLOCK

Facing it—always facing it—that's the way to get through it!
Face it! —JOSEPH CONRAD

Tom Birch is as brisk as a bee in conversation, but no sooner
does he take a pen in his hand, than it becomes a torpedo to
him, and benumbs all faculties. —SAMUEL JOHNSON

1ST WRITER (at a cocktail party): I'm working on my new novel.
2ND WRITER: Neither am I.
—CARTOON CAPTION IN *Private Eye*

If there is no wind, row. —LATIN PROVERB

If you are in difficulties with a book, try the element of
surprise: attack it at an hour when it isn't expecting it.
—H. G. WELLS

MARTIN AMIS: The common conception of how novels get written
seems to me to be an exact description of writer's block. In the common
view, the writer is at this stage so desperate that he's sitting around with a
list of characters, a list of themes and a framework for his plot, and ostensibly trying to mesh the three elements. In fact, it's never like that.
What happens is what Nabokov described as a throb. A throb or a glimmer, an act of recognition on the writer's part. At this stage the writer
thinks, Here is something I can write a novel about. In the absence of that
recognition I don't know what one would do. It may be that nothing about
this idea—or glimmer, or throb—appeals to you other than the fact that
it's your destiny, that it's your next book. You may even be secretly ap-
palled or awed or turned off by the idea, but it goes beyond that. You're
just reassured that there is another novel for you to write. The idea can be
incredibly thin—a situation, a character in a certain place at a certain
time. For *Money,* for example, I had an idea of a big fat guy in New York,
trying to make a film. That was all. Sometimes a novel can come pretty

consecutively and it's rather like a journey in that you get going and the plot, such as it is, unfolds and you follow your nose. You have to decide between identical-seeming dirt roads, both of which look completely hopeless, but you nevertheless have to choose which one to follow.

HEINRICH BÖLL: Inhibitions or blocks have recently become second nature with me. It has to do with the situation on earth. I live in a country which has the greatest concentration of atomic weapons on earth—and now more masses of new atomic weapons are to be added. That can take away your breath, and your enjoyment of life, and give you pause about whether writing makes any sense. For a time music, classical music, helped me to overcome a block—Beethoven's *breath,* for example, in which I sense something very West European and Rhinelike. The persistent problem with my writing is that I never know how something is going to come out; even when I write a short review, I always have to start all over. I have no mastery. But it's actually beneficial—it prevents things from becoming routine.

ERSKINE CALDWELL: You can always write something. You write limericks. You write a love letter. You do something to get you in the habit of writing again, to bring back the desire.

MALCOLM COWLEY: They tell me that success is a terrible test of people. Thank God I've never had to undergo it. But nationwide success with money pouring in will kill lots of writers. Ross Lockridge, who wrote *Raintree County,* and Thomas Heggen, the author of that novel about a ship, *Mister Roberts,* both committed suicide. It was always said that Gilbert Seldes's review of *The Great Gatsby,* which was ecstatic, probably damaged Scott Fitzgerald. The trouble is that after something like that, every work has to count . . . every word has to live up to this marvelous praise. The poor author gets stage fright.

WILLIAM GOYEN: Then, of course, she [Carson McCullers] was terribly affected by not being able to write. It was a murderous thing, a death blow, that block. She said she just didn't have anything to write. And really, it was as though she had never written. This happens to writers when there are dead spells. We die sometimes. And it's as though we're in a tomb; it's a death. That's what we all fear, and that's why so many of us become alcoholics or suicides or insane—or just no-good philanderers. It's amazing that we survive, though I think survival in some cases is kind of misgiven and it's a bore. It was written recently about Saul Bellow that one of the best things about him is that he survived, he didn't become an alcoholic, he didn't go mad and so forth. And that the true heroism of him lies simply in his endurance. That's the way we look at artists in America.

THOM GUNN: There are certain times when you are absolutely sterile, that is, when words seem to mean nothing. The words are there, the things in the world are there, you are interested in things in the same way and theoretically you can think up subjects for poems, but you simply can't write. You can sit down at your notebook with a good idea for a poem and nothing will come. It's as though there is a kind of light missing from the world. It's a wordless world, and it's somehow an empty and rather sterile world. I don't know what causes this, but it's very painful.

It might be that you have to go through dry periods so as in a sense to store things up. Maybe it's like a pregnancy. Sometimes I think it is and sometimes I don't. It'd be very nice to get up every day and write a new poem. I'm sure every poet would like to do that, but it's not possible. It may be that you've had some imaginative experience that's going to become a poem and it just has to become more a part of you. It has to stew, it has to cook until it's ready, and maybe there's nothing else to write about in-between. You've just got to cook away until it's ready to be taken out of the oven.

JIM HARRISON: I wonder, when a writer's blocked and doesn't have any resources to pull himself out of it, why doesn't he jump in his car and drive around the U.S.A.? I went last winter for 7000 miles and it was lovely. Inexpensive too. A lot of places—even good motels—are only twenty-five dollars in the winter, and food isn't much because there aren't any good restaurants. You pack along a bunch of stomach remedies and a bottle of whiskey.

TED HUGHES: The nearest I've ever felt to a block was a sort of unfitness, in the athletic sense: the need for an all-out sustained effort of writing simply to get myself into shape before starting on what I imagined would be the real thing. One whole book arrived like that, not a very long book, but one which I felt I needed to galvanize my inertia, break through the huge sloth I was up against. On the spur I invented a little plot: nine birds come to the fallen Adam urging him to get up and be birdlike. I wrote the whole as a bagatelle, to sweat myself out of that inertia—and to conjure myself to be a bit more birdlike. Then, suddenly there it was, a sort of book. *Adam and the Sacred Nine.* I'd written a book just trying to get to the point where I might begin to write something that might go into a book. Still, did it break through to the real thing? That's the question, isn't it? A block is when we can't get through to the real thing. Many writers write a great deal, but very few write more than a very little of the real thing. So most writing must be displaced activity. When cockerels confront each other and daren't fight, they busily start pecking imaginary grains off to the side. That's displaced activity. Much of what we do at any level is a bit like that, I fancy. But hard to know which is which. On the other hand, the machinery has to be kept running. The big problem for those who write verse is keeping the machine running without simply exercising evasion of the real confrontation. If Ulanova, the ballerina, missed one day of practice, she couldn't get back to peak fitness without a week of hard work. Dickens said the same about his writing—if he missed a day he needed a week of hard slog to get back into the flow.

WILLIAM MAXWELL: I've come close. There was a period after I left *The New Yorker* for the first time, when I thought I knew enough about writing stories to be able to make a living by it, but it turned out that every idea I had for a story was in some way too close to home. The stories I did write weren't bought. I began to feel that my hands were tied. I guess, though, I have always believed that if the material interested me enough to want to write about it, then it was all right; it wouldn't go away and so I should just keep working on it. Updike said once, riding in a taxi—he was talking about the reviewers, who had been scolding him for not writing what they thought he ought to be writing—"All I have to go on," he said, "is something I caught a glimpse of out of the corner of my eye." That seemed a very nice way of describing the way material comes to you. That glimpse, it's all you have. I don't think a writer's block is anything more than a loss of confidence. It certainly isn't a loss of talent.

EZRA POUND: Okay, I am stuck. The question is, am I dead, as Messrs. A.B.C. might wish? In case I conk out, this is provisionally what I have to do: I must clarify obscurities; I must make clearer definite ideas or dissociations. I must find a verbal formula to combat the rise of brutality—the principle of order versus the split atom. There was a man in the bughouse, by the way, who insisted that the atom had never been split.

An epic is a poem containing history. The modern mind contains heteroclite elements. The past epos has succeeded when all or a great many of the answers were assumed, at least between author and audience, or a great mass of audience. The attempt in an experimental age is therefore rash. Do you know the story: "What are you drawing, Johnny?"

"God!"

"But nobody knows what He looks like."

"They will when I get through!"

That confidence is no longer obtainable.

JOHN STEINBECK: It is usual that the moment you write for publication—I mean one of course—one stiffens in exactly the same way one does when one is being photographed. The simplest way to overcome this is to write it *to* someone, like me. Write it as a letter aimed at one person. This removes the vague terror of addressing the large and faceless audience and it also, you will find, will give a sense of freedom and a lack of self-consciousness.

JAMES THURBER: Well, the characteristic fear of the American writer is not so much that as it is the process of aging. The writer looks in the mirror and examines his hair and teeth to see if they're still with him. "Oh my God," he says, "I wonder how my writing is. I bet I can't write today." The only time I met Faulkner he told me he wanted to live long enough to do three more novels. He was 53 then, and I think he *has* done them. Then Hemingway says, you know, that he doesn't expect to be alive after sixty. But he doesn't look forward *not* to being. When I met Hemingway with John O'Hara in Costello's Bar 5 or 6 years ago we sat around and talked about how *old* we were getting. You see it's constantly on the minds of American writers. I've never known a woman who could weep about her age the way the men I know can.

Coupled with this fear of aging is the curious idea that the writer's inventiveness and ability will end in his fifties. And of course it often does. Carl Van Vechten stopped writing. The prolific Joseph Hergesheimer suddenly couldn't write anymore. Over in Europe that's never been the case.— Hardy, for instance, who started late and kept going. Of course Keats had good reason to write, *When I have fears that I may cease to be Before my pen has glean'd my teeming brain.* That's the great classic statement. But in America the writer is more likely to fear that his brain may cease to glean. I once did a drawing of a man at his typewriter, you see, and all this crumpled paper is on the floor, and he's staring down in discouragement. "What's the matter," his wife is saying. "Has your pen gleaned your teeming brain?"

ON ARTIFICIAL STIMULANTS

> I pray thee let me and my fellow have
> A hair of the dog that bit me last night.
> —JOHN HEYWOOD

> One of the disadvantages of wine is that it makes a man
> mistake words for thoughts.   —SAMUEL JOHNSON

> Some American writers who have known each other for years
> have never met in the daytime or when both were sober.
> —JAMES THURBER

CONRAD AIKEN: I've tried it long ago, with hashish and peyote. Fascinating, yes, but no good, no. This, as we find in alcohol, is an *escape* from awareness, a cheat, a momentary substitution, and in the end a destruction of it. With luck, someone might have a fragmentary Kubla Khan vision. But with no meaning. And with the steady destruction of the observing and remembering mind.

KINGSLEY AMIS: I find writing very nervous work. I'm always in a dither when starting a novel—that's the worst time. It's like going to the dentist, because you do make a kind of appointment with yourself. And this is one of the things I've learnt to recognize more and more with experience: that you realize it's got to be . . . next week. Not today—but if you don't sit down by the end of next week, it'll go off the boil slightly. Well, it can't be next Wednesday, because somebody from *The Paris Review* is coming to interview you, so it had better be Thursday. And then, quaking, you sit down at the typewriter. And that's when a glass of Scotch can be very useful as a sort of artistic icebreaker . . . artificial infusion of a little bit of confidence which is necessary in order to begin at all. And then each day's sitting down is still rather tense, though the tension goes away as the novel progresses, and when the end is even distantly in sight, the strain becomes small, though it's always there. So alcohol in moderate amounts and at a fairly leisurely speed is valuable to me—at least I think so. It could be that I could have written better without it . . . but it could also be true that I'd have written far less without it.

W. H. AUDEN: LSD? Nothing much happened, but I did get the distinct impression that some birds were trying to communicate with me.

J. G. BALLARD: Actually, there's no secret. One simply pulls the cork out of the bottle, waits three minutes, and two thousand or more years of Scottish craftsmanship does the rest.

WILLIAM BURROUGHS: The hallucinogens produce visionary states, sort of, but morphine and its derivatives decrease awareness of inner processes, thoughts, and feelings. They are painkillers, pure and simple. They are absolutely contraindicated for creative work, and I include in the lot alcohol, morphine, barbiturates, tranquilizers—the whole spectrum of sedative drugs. As for visions and heroin, I had a hallucinatory period at the very beginning of addiction, for instance, a sense of moving at high speed through space, but as soon as addiction was established, I had no visions—vision—at all and very few dreams.

JEAN COCTEAU: It is very useful to have some depressant, perhaps. Extreme fatigue can serve. Filming *Beauty and the Beast* on the Loire in 1945 immediately at the end of the war, I was very ill. Everything went wrong. Electricity failures nearly every day; planes passing over just at the moment of a scene. Jean Marais's horses made difficulties, and he persisted in vaulting onto them himself out of second floor windows, refusing a double, and risking his bones. And the sunlight changes every minute on the Loire. All these things contributed to the virtue of the film. And in "The Blood of a Poet" Man Ray's wife played a rôle; she had never acted. Her exhaustion and fear paralyzed her and she passed before the cameras so stunned she remembered nothing afterwards. In the rushes we saw she was splendid; with the outer part suppressed, she had been let perform.

MALCOLM COWLEY: One of the reasons why Hart, and many writers, turn into alcoholics is that early in their lives they find that getting drunk is part of the creative process, that it opens up visions. It's a terrible sort of creative device, because three out of four who involve themselves in it become alcoholics. But it does open up doors in the beginning. Hart

Crane would even make a first draft when he was drunk; he'd come out and read it, and say, "Isn't this the greatest poem *ever* written?" It wasn't. But then he would work over it patiently, dead sober, for several weeks, and it would amount to something. Not the greatest poem ever written, but still extraordinary.

MARGARET DRABBLE: I drink very strong coffee and very weak tea. Scenery can be a violent stimulant. Wordsworth, I think, was thinking of that. I love it. But rather like Wordsworth, I think too much of it isn't good for you. And I'm so susceptible to horror that reading the newspaper is enough for me; when I actually see the news on television it makes me feel terrible for days.

GABRIEL GARCÍA MÁRQUEZ: One thing that Hemingway wrote that greatly impressed me was that writing for him was like boxing. He took care of his health and his well-being. Faulkner had a reputation of being a drunkard, but in every interview that he gave he said that it was impossible to write one line when drunk. Hemingway said this too. Bad readers have asked me if I was drugged when I wrote some of my works. But that illustrates that they don't know anything about literature or drugs. To be a good writer you have to be absolutely lucid at every moment of writing and in good health. I'm very much against the romantic concept of writing which maintains that the act of writing is a sacrifice and that the worse the economic conditions or the emotional state, the better the writing. I think you have to be in a very good emotional and physical state. Literary creation for me requires good health, and the Lost Generation understood this. They were people who loved life.

ALLEN GINSBERG: What I do get is, say if I was in an apartment high on mescaline, I felt as if the apartment and myself were not merely on East Fifth Street but were in the middle of all space time. If I close my eyes on hallucinogens I get a vision of great scaly dragons in outer space, they're winding slowly and eating their own tails. Sometimes my skin and all the room seem sparkling with scales, and it's all made out of serpent stuff. And as if the whole illusion of life were made of reptile dream.

ROBERT GRAVES: I had two trips on the Mexican mushroom back in 1954 or so. None since. And never on LSD. First of all it's dangerous, and secondly ergot, from which LSD is made, is the enemy of mankind. Ergot is a minute black fungus that grows on rye, or did in the Middle Ages, and people who ate rye bread got manic visions, especially Germans. They now say that ergot affects the genes and might disorder the next generation. It occurs to me that this may explain the phenomenon of Nazism, a form of mass hysteria. Germans were rye-eaters, as opposed to wheat-eaters like the English. LSD reminds me of the minks that escape from mink-farms and breed in the forest and become dangerous and destructive. It has escaped from the drug factory and gets made in college laboratories.

THOM GUNN: When I came to write *Moly*, I took LSD. LSD certainly extends your awareness into other areas. It's chemical: it may be simply that you're not seeing round corners but you just think you are. You tend to think that these other areas are spiritual—and they may be. There's at least one poem, "The Messenger," in which I speak about angels: "Is this man turning angel as he stares / At one red flower...?" I was playing with the idea. I don't think I was being irresponsible. It is still a question, and it's not a question that I answer in the poem. The poem where I most overtly take up religious terms—spiritual terms would be better—is a poem called "At the Centre," which I now think is rather a pompous poem. This came out of my biggest acid trip. I took a colossal amount and stood with my friend Don Doody on a roof from which you could see the sign of a brewery, which had on the top of it a magnificent image in neon lights, even during the day, of a huge glass. The outline was permanently there, but it would fill up and drain with yellow lights, as if it were a filling-up glass of beer that would suddenly vanish and then fill up again from the bottom. This of course became a fantastic image for... Existence Itself! I think it comes into the poem with all the talk of flowing and stuff. And there I was indeed having, in that experience, a rather defiant conversation with a God whom I did not believe existed! There was one very funny thing happened during that day. I've only been able to admit it in recent years. (This was about 1968.) At one point, in this grandiloquent way that I had, I said to God: "What does it all mean?" Suddenly—this was a genuine hallucination—what seemed like a plastic bubble of shit crossed the sky. I did not admit this to my companion but I do remember saying: "No, oh no, not that. I do not want to believe that life is shit!" And I rejected that hallucination. But of course, the hallucination came from *me* in the first place. I'm not saying that the experiences in *Moly* were not genuine and I wouldn't disown anything in *Moly*. In fact, I still think of it as my best book, though few others have thought so. I think these experiences elicited my best poetry from me.

ALDOUS HUXLEY: I don't think there is any generalization one can make on this. Experience has shown that there's an enormous variation in the way people respond to lysergic acid. Some people probably could get direct aesthetic inspiration for painting or poetry out of it. Others I don't think could. For most people it's an extremely significant experience, and I suppose in an indirect way it could help the creative process. But I don't think one can sit down and say, "I want to write a magnificent poem, and so I'm going to take lysergic acid." I don't think it's by any means certain that you would get the result you wanted—you might get almost any result.

JOHN IRVING: They [Hemingway and Faulkner] should have gotten better as they got older; *I've* gotten better. We're not professional athletes; it's reasonable to assume that we'll get better as we mature—at least, until we start getting senile. Of course, some writers who write their best books early simply lose interest in writing; or they lose their concentration—probably because they want to do other things. But Hemingway and Fitzgerald really lived to write; their bodies and their brains betrayed them. I'm such an incapable drinker, I'm lucky. If I drink half a bottle of red wine with my dinner, I forget who I had dinner with—not to mention everything that I or anybody else said. If I drink more than half a bottle, I fall instantly asleep. But just think of what novelists do: fiction writing requires a kind of memory, a vigorous, invented memory. If I can forget who I had dinner with, what might I forget about my novel-in-progress? The irony is that drinking is especially dangerous to novelists; memory is vital to us. I'm not so down on drinking for writers from a moral point of view; but booze is clearly not good for writing *or* for driving cars. You know what Lawrence said: "The novel is the highest example of subtle interrelatedness that man has discovered." I agree! And just consider for one second what drinking does to "subtle interrelatedness." Forget the "subtle"; "interrelatedness" is what makes novels work—without it, you have no narrative momentum; you have incoherent rambling. Drunks ramble; so do books by drunks.

KEN KESEY: It's impossible for me to write on LSD—there are more important things to think about. Hunter Thompson can do it, but I can't.

It's like diving down to look at coral reefs. You can't write about what you've seen until you're back up in the boat. Almost every writer I know drinks to ease the burden of being out on the cliffs, so to speak. But writing under the influence of drugs is a little like a plumber trying to fix the pipes without being able to work the wrench.

ARTHUR KOESTLER: When I was under, I noticed that the nice English psychiatrist had a scar on his neck—from a mastoid operation perhaps. His face went green and the scar started gaping as a wound and for some reason I thought, "Now at last the Gestapo have got me." Or was it the KGB? It was one of the two. The psychiatrist had a standard lamp and the base of it suddenly developed bird's claws. Then I flipped for a moment into normality and told myself, "You are hallucinating, that's all—if you touch the claws they'll go away." So I touched them. But they didn't go away. Not only a visual but also a tactile hallucination. It was very frightening. So when you ask me what madness is—it is when your perceptions are dramatically deviating from reality. That is not a scientific definition, however. When I came back from this experience of induced schizophrenia, the aftereffects lasted for several months. Timothy Leary went round the bend, of course. I came to the opposite view to Huxley's. These things have no particular spiritual value but they might have clinical value. For example, I think every psychiatrist should have a session with mescaline or LSD in order to know what a psychosis is like, what hallucinations are like. It should be part of the psychiatrist's curriculum.

JAMES MERRILL: Liquor, in my parents' world, was always your reward at the end of a hard day—or an easy day, for that matter—and I like to observe that old family tradition. But I've never drunk for inspiration. Quite the contrary—it's like the wet sponge on the blackboard. I do now and then take a puff of grass, or a crumb of Alice Toklas fudge, when I've reached the last drafts of a poem. That's when you need X-ray eyes to see what you've done, and the grass helps. Some nice touches can fall into place.

RICHARD PRICE: I'm not Thomas de Quincey or Coleridge. I'm not William Burroughs. I don't feel anything creative for me can come out of writing under the influence of a drug. One danger is that cocaine gives you the illusion of being creative; you get into this vicious circle of feeling so inspired by this chemical in your system that you do write. Then you come down, and the next day you look at what you wrote and get depressed. What you see before you is yesterday's rush transformed into burbly bullshit, at which point you start to panic because now you're *really* behind your deadline or whatever and you better get cracking, but you're too depleted, physically and mentally, and therefore what you realize is, in order to jump-start yourself, maybe just a wee hair of the dog would be in order, so you go out and score again.

And here comes another day's worth of deluded flop-sweat trying to pass for art. I mean, you might be able to squeeze out a dazzling paragraph or two, but it's the law of diminishing returns. In the end, the coke will overwhelm the work. I got to the point where I had to do a line to write a line. You might do coke in order to write, but by the end you're writing in order to do coke.

I've never written anything good on coke. I mean, I've written good paragraphs and good pages, but if I were to write a story for one hundred days on coke, I might write one hundred good pages, but they wouldn't be pages that belonged together—one hundred pages for one hundred different books. Unfortunately, with a novel they're all supposed to be for the same story. Nobody can write well using cocaine. It's the worst drug of all for an artist.

Take marijuana: when you're stoned you know you're stoned and you stop smoking. When you're shooting heroin, you don't keep shooting. You don't think, "Maybe I should shoot some more." You're nodding. You stop. You put down the needle. When you're drinking, you can't drink endlessly. You're going to vomit or you're going to pass out. You stop. Cocaine is the only drug that you can take and take, and nothing stops you except running out of the stuff. And when you're blasted you don't realize that you've got garbage for brains.

One of Elmore Leonard's characters came across with the awful realization that addiction not only destroys your body and brain, but also dominates your consciousness. Twenty-four hours a day an addict is thinking about where they are in relation to their drug. They are thinking about how high they are. They're thinking about the fact that they're not high. They're thinking about scoring. They're thinking about cleaning up. They're thinking about cutting back, about getting better stuff. Endlessly thinking, 24-7-365. It simply dominates your thoughts around the clock.

ROBERT STONE: I happened to collide with Ken Kesey; he lived just a couple of streets away. That whole scene was just ready to take off. And I thought I knew all about peyote and drugs and such. It didn't bother me to experiment. Kesey had a job as an orderly in the Veteran's Hospital and he was involved in the first experiments that were being conducted in psychedelic drugs. He was a volunteer. They were doing all these crazy drugs on an experimental basis. Some of them worked, some of them did not. I can remember really off-the-wall things called IT290s; they didn't even have names they were so arcane. Whatever IT290 was, I remember walking through the woods and suddenly encountering this huge locomotive, a green locomotive with gold trim, a very detailed hallucination which I remember particularly well.

ANDREI VOZNESENSKY: Allen [Ginsberg] once gave me one he said was a little bit like LSD but something new. It was a white drug and I became very ill after. It was very strange. I took this drug when I was staying at the Chelsea Hotel; Allen gave me this drug and went away. I spent most of the day in a blackout. But I later had to get up and go read in Town Hall. I was a little high. I thought, "People will think I am drunk." I was in a strange mood. For the first time in my life I forgot my lines, and didn't know why I was there. But when I saw the audience and after Robert Lowell (I think) introduced me, my old reflexes began working again. I was like a reading machine. It was very difficult for me to come on to the music of poetry because of this drug experience. I read the first poem by instinct; the second poem was hard but then it got better and better as the poetry took over and the drug went away. And I forgot about the drug. One doctor told me that it was very good; I was destroyed after the reading; I was not longing for more drugs. Drugs don't help poetry. When you try to write on pot, you think it's very good, but you are false because you have no real feelings. You think it is very good, but later when you read it, it's bullshit.

PART III

DIFFERENT

FORMS

ON BIOGRAPHY

Read no history: nothing but biography, for that is life without theory.
                                    —BENJAMIN DISRAELI

I was day and night with Lincoln for years. I couldn't have picked a better companion.   —CARL SANDBURG

Just how difficult it is to write biography can be reckoned by anybody who sits down and considers just how many people know the truth about his or her love affairs.
                                    —REBECCA WEST

If Queen Elizabeth or Frederick the Great or Ernest Hemingway were to read their biographies, they would exclaim, "Ah, my secret is still safe." But if Natasha Rostov were to read *War and Peace* she would cry out as she covered her face with her hands: "How did he know, how did he know?"
                                    —THORNTON WILDER

LEON EDEL: The difference between a novelist and a biographer resides in the biographer's having to master a narrative of inquiry. Biography has to explain and examine the evidence. The story is told brushstroke by brushstroke like a painter, and the biographer often has to say he simply doesn't know—he cannot fill in the gaps. There's so much that can never be known, whereas the omniscient novelist can be—well, omniscient, something impossible in biography.

ELIZABETH HARDWICK: Biography cannot be fiction. I have said a novelist is free to do anything—the novel is as much a work of the imagination as the writer wants to make of it. The novelist creates the characters, supplies their background. Turgenev used to give each character a lengthy dossier as if the person had a police record. The biographer doesn't have that freedom. The characters are real. The dossiers have to be real. Lytton Strachey once gave Queen Elizabeth a jewel to wear at a great occasion, but when asked, he admitted he put the jewel there to add a touch to his picture. That was a piece of fictional "property" imported into the story. George Kennan once admitted that in one of his histories he put a goat into the landscape between Russia and Finland when he was describing the departure of some important diplomat or personage from Russia to Finland. This was historic license. But he did add that he had usually seen goats in that landscape even though he didn't know whether there was one there on that particular day. These of course are small details but they define the difference between fiction and history.

· · ·

Biography is a scrofulous cottage industry, done mostly by academics who get grants and have a good time going all over the place interviewing. How seldom it is that one has ever heard of the person writing the biography. What are the models, what are the qualifications? And it is not only the full-scale computer printout that these things are, but the books brought forth by lovers, friends from youth, cousins, whatever. I remember how horrified Dickens was when he met, in later life, the model for Dora in *David Copperfield*. Now Dora would hire a hack and write about Dickens.

On Children's Books

Good children's literature appeals not only to the child in the
adult but to the adult in the child.   —ANON.

To talk to a child, to fascinate him, is much more difficult than
to win an electoral victory. But it is also more rewarding.
                                                    —COLETTE

Don't set your wit against a child.   —JONATHAN SWIFT

P. L. TRAVERS: When I sat down to write *Mary Poppins* or any of the
other books, I did not know children would read them. I'm sure there
must be a field of "children's literature"—I hear about it so often—but
sometimes I wonder if it isn't a label created by publishers and book-
sellers who also have the impossible presumption to put on books such
notes as "from five to seven" or "from nine to twelve." How can they know
when a book will appeal to such and such an age?

If you look at other so-called children's authors, you'll see they never
wrote directly for children. Though Lewis Carroll dedicated his book to
Alice, I feel it was an afterthought once the whole was already committed
to paper. Beatrix Potter declared "I write to please myself!" And I think
the same can be said of Milne or Tolkien or Laura Ingalls Wilder.

I certainly had no specific child in mind when I wrote *Mary Poppins*. How
could I? If I were writing for the Japanese child who reads it in a land without staircases, how could I have written of a nanny that slides up the ban-
nister? If I were writing for the African child who reads the book in Swahili,
how could I have written of umbrellas for a child who has never seen or
used one?

But I suppose if there is something in my books that appeals to children, it is the result of my not having to go *back* to my childhood; I can, as
it were, turn *aside* and consult it (James Joyce once wrote, "My childhood
bends beside me"). If we're completely honest, not sentimental or nostal-

262 · *The Writer's Chapbook*

gic, we have no idea where childhood ends and maturity begins. It is one unending thread, not a life chopped up into sections out of touch with one another.

Once, when Maurice Sendak was being interviewed on television a little after the success of *Where the Wild Things Are,* he was asked the usual questions: Do you have children? Do you like children? After a pause, he said with simple dignity: "I was a child." That says it all.

But don't let me leave you with the impression that I am ungrateful to children. They have stolen much of the world's treasure and magic in the literature they have appropriated for themselves. Think, for example, of the myths or Grimm's fairy tales—none of which were written especially for them—this ancestral literature handed down by the folk. And so despite publishers' labels and my own protestations about not writing especially for them, I am grateful that children have included my books in their treasure trove.

E. B. WHITE: Anybody who shifts gears when he writes for children is likely to wind up stripping his gears. But I don't want to evade your question. There *is* a difference between writing for children and for adults. I am lucky, though, as I seldom seem to have my audience in mind when I am at work. It is as though they didn't exist.

Anyone who writes *down* to children is simply wasting his time. You have to write up, not down. Children are demanding. They are the most attentive, curious, eager, observant, sensitive, quick, and generally congenial readers on earth. They accept, almost without question, anything you present them with, as long as it is presented honestly, fearlessly, and clearly. I handed them, against the advice of experts, a mouse-boy, and they accepted it without a quiver. In *Charlotte's Web,* I gave them a literate spider, and they took that.

Some writers for children deliberately avoid using words they think a child doesn't know. This emasculates the prose and, I suspect, bores the reader. Children are game for anything. I throw them hard words, and they backhand them over the net. They love words that give them a hard time, provided they are in a context that absorbs their attention. I'm lucky again: my own vocabulary is small, compared to most writers, and I tend to use the short words. So it's no problem for me to write for children. We have a lot in common.

ON CRITICISM

Do not remove a fly from your friend's forehead with a hatchet.
—CHINESE PROVERB

There's more ado to interpret interpretations than to interpret things, and more books upon books than any other subject.
—MICHEL DE MONTAIGNE

This is not a novel to be tossed aside lightly. It should be thrown with great force.   —DOROTHY PARKER

I like criticism, but it must be my way.   —MARK TWAIN

There is no such thing as a moral or an immoral book. Books are well written or badly written.   —OSCAR WILDE

W. H. AUDEN: Unless one is a regular reviewer, or one is reviewing a book of reference where the facts are wrong—then it's one's duty to inform the public, as one would warn them of watered milk. Writing nasty reviews can be fun, but I don't think the practice is very good for the character.

JORGE LUIS BORGES: When somebody told me to write a review of a certain *History of Literature,* I found there were so many howlers and blunders, and as I greatly admire the author as a poet, I said: "No, I don't want to write about it, because if I write about it I shall write against it." I don't like to attack people, especially now—when I was a young man, yes, I was very fond of it—but as time goes on, one finds that it is no good. When people write in favor or against anybody that hardly helps or hurts them. I think that a man can be helped, well, the man can be done or undone by his *own* writing, not by what other people say of him, so that even if you brag a lot and people say that you are a genius—well, you'll be found out.

ELIZABETH HARDWICK: Criticism, analysis, reflection is a natural response to the existence in the world of works of art. It is an honorable and even an exalted endeavor. Without it, works of art would appear in a vacuum, as if they had no relation to the minds experiencing them. It would be a dismal, unthinkable world with these shooting stars arousing no comment, leaving no trace. But it is the mind of the critic, somehow, the establishment of his own thought and values, that counts; and that establishment is the authority of the voice, whether it comes from creative work in the arts or creative work in criticism. When I read a review, a mere short review, I am more interested at first in who is doing the reviewing than in the work under discussion. The name, what is attached to it by previous work, by serious thought, tells me whether it is likely to have any meaning or value for me. It is not a question of right or wrong specific opinions, but of the quality of the mind.

JOHN IRVING: I write only favorable reviews. A writer of fiction whose own fiction comes first is just too subjective a reader to allow himself to write a negative review. And there are already plenty of professional reviewers eager to be negative. If I get a book to review and I don't like it, I return it; I only review the book if I love it. Hence I've written very few reviews, and those are really just songs of praise or rather long, retrospective reviews of all the writer's works: of John Cheever, Kurt Vonnegut, and Günter Grass, for example. And then there is the occasional "younger" writer whom I introduce to readers, such as Jayne Anne Phillips and Craig Nova. Another thing about not writing negative reviews: grown-ups shouldn't finish books they're not enjoying. When you're no longer a child, and you no longer live at home, you don't have to finish everything on your plate. One reward of leaving school is that you don't have to finish books you don't like. You know, if I were a critic, I'd be angry and vicious, too; it *makes* poor critics angry and vicious—to have to *finish* all those books they're not enjoying. What a silly job criticism is! What unnatural work it is! It is certainly not work for a grown-up.

ANTHONY POWELL: I find [reviewing] extremely stimulating. I get two really pretty serious books a month—and I must say they're extremely good at trying to give me something that I like—and I really think it's rather good for you to have to review, say, a book about the organization of the Roman Army in the first half of the month and then the life of Christina Rossetti in the second. So far from being bad for you, I think it's very *educative* and it really makes your mind work. In fact, as I said before, I'm really rather lost now if I *don't* have something like that

that I've got to do. . . . But of course there *are* demoralizing forms of literary journalism, and I've done my stint of reviewing five novels in a column and so on. You know how it is: your friends say, "Are you mad saying this terrible book is quite good?" But you can't week in, week out keep saying this is all absolute rubbish.

JOHN SIMON: A critic has to get satisfaction not from being popular or liked or invited to parties, but from having done the bloody best he could, however imperfect it may be. If somebody throws a cocktail in your face at a party because of a bad review, you just have to take it. It has happened. The most famous case is Sylvia Miles throwing some steak tartare at me, which made her into a heroine. In fact, Andy Warhol said in one of his so-called books that she's famous for that and not much else. This incident was so welcomed by the Simon-hating press that the anecdote has been much retold. She herself has retold it ten thousand times. And this steak tartare has since metamorphosed into every known dish, from lasagna to chop suey. It's been so many things that you could feed the starving orphans of India or China with it.

GEORGE STEINER: What is our function? We are the pilot fish, those strange, tiny creatures, which go in front of the real thing, the great shark or the great whale, warning, saying to people, "It's coming." When I was in Africa, in a game reserve, we actually saw the beautiful little yellow birds that sit on the rhinoceros and chirp like mad to alert everyone that a rhino is coming. Now a good teacher, a good critic says, "This is the real thing. Here's why. Please read it, read it, come on and buy it. Go and get it."

I shall never forget my joy one day while teaching at Cambridge. A student was late for a tutorial, so I had a few minutes, and in the mail was a vast packet, a manuscript. *The New Yorker* usage is that I don't read manuscripts or endorse them in order to preserve full liberty as a reviewer, and I deeply respect that. So I was trying to get this huge package into the wastebasket and it wouldn't fit: the cardboard was too damn big. I read the first sentence of this manuscript and, Good God, I thought, something tremendous has landed on my desk. I phoned Mr. Shawn to ask whether I could review it, and he was very amused and he said that it would probably be a year and a half, two years before the book would be out but that yes, he would reserve it for me: *Zen & the Art of Motorcycle Maintenance.* I wrote the author and said, "You know, this is it." I did not tell him but I told my wife and wrote in my notes that I was afraid there would never be another book from this man worth reading. That was totally clear to me, which is a terrible thing, and I'm right, very sadly. But what I'm trying to emphasize here is my joy at being the chirp bird on the rhinoceros.

So I have been so lucky in being able quite often to say, "My God, this is wonderful." I'm still fighting. I believe England has had only one major novelist after Hardy: John Cowper Powys. Only a handful of people agree with me; I may be getting this completely wrong. I was able to get some of it into paperback, there is a following, but so far there's been no breakthrough. I believe *Glastonbury Romance, Porius* and *Wolf Solent* are the big ones. I write about him, I lecture, I tell people to go out and try it. So far, very few respond, and many have honestly tried and say I'm totally wrong, that he's unreadable. Fine. I would rather make those mistakes than keep my passions quiet.

Another case for which I've never been forgiven is Lawrence Durrell. Now let's be careful. Durrell is now mocked everywhere. I still believe that the first three volumes of the *Alexandria Quartet* are like nothing else. I admit the fourth one goes to a shambles, which is tragic, and that there is endless stuff after that. That doesn't matter. Suppose I was wrong, suppose I am wrong: hurrah! What interests me are errors of passion, errors which you stick your neck out on. Oh God, the attempt to be right! The attempt of our academic contemporaries to play it safe! For forty years I have been asking my students whose works they collect, which living writers they love so much that they want even their weaker books. If they don't collect any writer, I know they will not get anywhere in my trade, in my craft. Luckily, for Simenon I have Gide and everybody else on my side, so there's no courage in my saying he may be the most important of modern authors. But if somebody says Zane Grey is it, and lives that passion, and collects and studies, then I say, "Hurrah!" That is a soul that is safe for salvation. But the person who asks who the winners are, who the stock-market winners are, where they should invest: no, no, no! So yes, love is capital for me. It's been a bitter time, one of the bitterest times of cultural envy, and there have been very big men responsible for it. Every time Leavis opened his mouth, it was to say there were five classics, that the rest was damnable and vulgar and mustn't be read and wasn't worth the paper it was printed on. There have been hate critics in our time. There have been very powerful and influential teachers of hatred. These I have nothing in common with.

TOM STOPPARD: When I was a critic—on my local paper in Bristol and later for a magazine in London—I floundered between pronouncing what I hoped were magisterial judgments and merely declaring my own taste. If I might quote myself from a previous interview—"I was not a good critic because I never had the moral character to pan a friend. I'll rephrase that—I had the moral character never to pan a friend."

JOHN UPDIKE: I do it (a) when some author, like Spark or Borges, excites me and I want to share the good news, (b) when I want to write an essay, as on romantic love, or Barth's theology, (c) when I feel ignorant of something, like modern French fiction, and accepting a review assignment will compel me to read and learn.

HELEN VENDLER: Usually, I think there's nothing to be said about mediocre poetry. It's like being a talent scout for an opera company, when all you can say about the voice you hear is, "No, it has no carrying power, it hasn't any capacity to stay on pitch, it hasn't any sense of innate rhythm, it hasn't any expressive color, it hasn't interpretive power . . . it's just no, no, no." If you're a talent scout, what you like is to have a voice come along that not only has interpretive color, carrying power and musical intelligence, but is also distinctive in timbre. Then you can say a lot about the voice. When qualities are *not* there, it is very hard to describe, since you're describing absences. When the qualities *are* there you delight in showing how they're deployed.

. . .

I fear giving short shrift to something that is really very good, which I don't recognize at the time. We all know critics who have done that: the critics of Keats who told him to go back to his apothecary pots; the critics of Stevens who thought he was a dandy; the critics of *The Waste Land* who thought it was a hoax; and, perhaps, myself as a critic, say, of Pound, about whom I've never written, whom I think of as a minor poet of the fin de siècle and the early century. I don't admire the *Cantos;* perhaps that's a big blind spot in me since there are certainly many exquisitely gifted readers and writers who have admired the *Cantos.* But I can't. I've tried over and over. As Pound himself said later on, "I cannot make it cohere," and they don't cohere for me. Perhaps I'm missing a great body of work because of some defect in me. That's not how I see it, but it is how others see it.

ROBERT PENN WARREN: On this matter of criticism, something that appalls me is the idea going around now that the practice of criticism is opposed to the literary impulse. Is *necessarily* opposed to it. Sure, it *may* be a trap, it may destroy the creative impulse, but so may drink or money or respectability. But criticism is a perfectly natural human activity and somehow the dullest, most technical criticism may be associated with full creativity. Elizabethan criticism is all, or nearly all, technical—meter, how to hang a line together—kitchen criticism, how to make the cake. People deeply interested in an art are interested in the "how." Now I don't mean to say that this is the only kind of valuable criticism. Any kind is good that gives a deeper insight into the nature of the thing—a Marxist analysis, a Freudian study, the relation to a literary or social tradition, the history of a theme. But we have to remember that there is no *one, single, correct* kind of criticism, no *complete* criticism. You only have different kinds of perspectives, giving, when successful, different kinds of insights. And at one historical moment one kind of insight may be more needed than another.

EVELYN WAUGH: I think the general state of reviewing in England is contemptible—both slovenly and ostentatious. I used to have a rule when I reviewed books as a young man never to give an unfavorable notice to a book I hadn't read. I find even this simple rule is flagrantly broken now.

On Films

You can fake all the sincerity in Hollywood, place it in the navel of a fruit fly and still have room enough for three caraway seeds and a producer's heart. —FRED ALLEN

A film is a petrified fountain of thought. —JEAN COCTEAU

Why only twelve? Go out and get thousands!
—SAMUEL GOLDWYN, on restaging the Last Supper

Having your book made into a movie is like seeing your oxen turned into bouillon cubes. —JOHN LE CARRÉ

NELSON ALGREN: I didn't last long. I went out [to Hollywood] for a thousand a week, and I worked Monday, and I got fired Wednesday. The guy that hired me was out of town Tuesday.

ERSKINE CALDWELL: In the old days in Hollywood you couldn't be a writer unless you could dictate your story to a secretary, and I never could dictate to anybody. So I had to go home at night to write where nobody could see me. I used to write in secret.

. . .

It [*Tobacco Road*] had good actors, good actresses, a good screenwriter, and John Ford directing. It had everything in its favor. But then Darryl Zanuck came along and wanted a happy ending. So the characters go off to the poorhouse singing a folk song.

JOHN CHEEVER: I went to Hollywood to make money. It's very simple. The people are friendly and the food is good, but I've never been happy there, perhaps because I only went there to pick up a check. I do have the deepest respect for a dozen or so directors whose affairs are centered there and who, in spite of the overwhelming problems of financing films, continue to turn out brilliant and original films. But my principal feeling about Hollywood is suicide. If I could get out of bed and into the shower,

I was all right. Since I never paid the bills, I'd reach for the phone and order the most elaborate breakfast I could think of, and then I'd try to make it to the shower before I hanged myself. This is no reflection on Hollywood, but it's just that I seemed to have a suicide complex there. I don't like the freeways, for one thing. Also, the pools are too hot . . . 85 degrees, and when I was last there, in late January, in the stores they were selling yarmulkes for dogs—my God! I went to a dinner and across the room a woman lost her balance and fell down. Her husband shouted over to her, "When I told you to bring your crutches, you wouldn't listen to me." That line couldn't be better!

WILLIAM FAULKNER: I had just completed a contract at MGM and was about to return home. The director I had worked with said, "If you would like another job here, just let me know and I will speak to the studio about a new contract." I thanked him and came home. About six months later I wired my director friend that I would like another job. Shortly after that I received a letter from my Hollywood agent enclosing my first week's paycheck. I was surprised because I had expected first to get an official notice or recall and a contract from the studio. I thought to myself the contract is delayed and will arrive in the next mail. Instead, a week later I got another letter from the agent, enclosing my second week's paycheck. That began in November 1932 and continued until May 1933. Then I received a telegram from the studio. It said: *William Faulkner, Oxford, Miss. Where are you? MGM Studio.*

I wrote out a telegram: *MGM Studio, Culver City, California. William Faulkner.*

The young lady operator said, "Where is the message, Mr. Faulkner?" I said, "That's it." She said, "The rule book says that I can't send it without a message, you have to say something." So we went through her samples and selected I forget which one—one of the canned anniversary greeting messages. I sent that. Next was a long-distance telephone call from the studio directing me to get on the first airplane, go to New Orleans, and report to Director Browning. I could have got on a train in Oxford and been in New Orleans eight hours later. But I obeyed the studio and went to Memphis, where an airplane did occasionally go to New Orleans. Three days later one did.

I arrived at Mr. Browning's hotel about six p.m. and reported to him. A party was going on. He told me to get a good night's sleep and be ready for an early start in the morning. I asked him about the story. He said, "Oh, yes. Go to room so-and-so. That's the continuity writer. He'll tell you what the story is."

I went to the room as directed. The continuity writer was sitting in there alone. I told him who I was and asked him about the story. He said, "When you have written the dialogue I'll let you see the story." I went back to Browning's room and told him what had happened. "Go back," he said, "and tell that so-and-so—never mind, you get a good night's sleep so we can get an early start in the morning."

So the next morning in a very smart rented launch all of us except the continuity writer sailed down to Grand Isle, about a hundred miles away, where the picture was to be shot, reaching there just in time to eat lunch and have time to run the hundred miles back to New Orleans before dark.

That went on for three weeks. Now and then I would worry a little about the story, but Browning always said, "Stop worrying. Get a good night's sleep so we can get an early start tomorrow morning."

One evening on our return I had barely entered my room when the telephone rang. It was Browning. He told me to come to his room at once. I did so. He had a telegram. It said: *Faulkner is fired. MGM Studio.* "Don't worry," Browning said. "I'll call that so-and-so up this minute and not only make him put you back on the payroll but send you a written apology." There was a knock on the door. It was a page with another telegram. This one said: *Browning is fired. MGM Studio.* So I came back home. I presume Browning went somewhere too. I imagine that continuity writer is still sitting in a room somewhere with his weekly salary check clutched tightly in his hand. They never did finish the film. But they did build a shrimp village—a long platform on piles in the water with sheds built on it something like a wharf. The studio could have bought dozens of them for forty or fifty dollars apiece. Instead, they built one of their own, a false one. That is, a platform with a single wall on it, so that when you opened the door and stepped through it, you stepped right on off to the ocean itself. As they built it, on the first day, the Cajun fisherman paddled up in his narrow tricky pirogue made out of a hollow log. He would sit in it all day long in the broiling sun watching the strange white folks building this strange imitation platform. The next day he was back in the pirogue with his whole family, his wife nursing the baby, the other children, and the mother-in-law, all to sit all that day in the broiling sun to watch this foolish and incomprehensible activity. I was in New Orleans two or three years later and heard that the Cajun people were still coming in for miles to look at that imitation shrimp platform which a lot of white people had rushed in and built and then abandoned.

JIM HARRISON: The reason that writers get submerged in the film business is simply a result of ordinary human greed. There's nothing literary about it—it's just greed. Why should I blame Warner Brothers for my own greed? Faulkner always presented himself as this martyr to Hollywood. Well, bullshit. His family evolved such a high nut that he had to keep doing it, because he was supporting seventeen people—his brother's children, retainers, aunts, uncles, an alcoholic wife—and whether old Billy wanted to go to L.A. or not they stuck that sucker on the train and shot him out there to make some more money .

LILLIAN HELLMAN: When I first went out to Hollywood one heard talk from writers about whoring. But you are not tempted to whore unless you want to be a whore.

JOHN IRVING: Well, movies, movies, movies—they are our enemy, of course. Movies are the enemy of the novel because they are replacing novels. Novelists shouldn't write for the movies, unless, of course, they discover they're no good at writing novels. I like people who make movies, and I'm glad some of them, who are terribly smart, are not writing novels. There are enough people writing novels, God knows. Anyway, the main thing I learned by writing a screenplay of *Setting Free the Bears* was that screenwriting isn't really writing; it's carpentry. There's no language in it, and the writer is not in control of the pace of the story, or of the tone of the narration, and what else is there to be in control of? Tony Richardson told me that there *are* no screenwriters, so there is at least one director who agrees with me. It could be that it was the most valuable thing I ever did—to have my shot at writing a movie when I was so young, right after my first novel was published—because I was never tempted to do it again.

THOMAS MCGUANE: Screen writing made me rethink the role of a lot of the mnemonic things that most novelists leave in their books. The worst about these things is probably Faulkner, who frequently had his shit detector dialed down to zero. We all read Faulkner in a similar way: we move through these muddy bogs until we hit these wonderful streaks, and then we're back in the bogs again, right? Everyone agrees that Faulkner produced the greatest streaks in American literature from 1929 until 1935 but, depending on how you feel about this, you either admit that there's a lot of dead air in his works or you don't. After you've written screenplays for a while, you're not as willing to leave these warm-ups in there, those pencil sharpenings and refillings of the whiskey glasses and those sorts of trivialities. You're more conscious of dead time. Playwrights are even tougher on themselves in this regard. Twenty mediocre pages hardly hurt even a short novel but ten dead minutes will insure that a play won't get out of New Haven. Movies are like that: people just can't sit there, elbow-to-elbow with each other, and stand ten boring minutes in a movie. Oh, they will to a degree if they're prepared enough about the historical moment, if they're watching *Gandhi* or something, but not usually. At any rate, I think I go more for blood now, scene by scene in my writing, than maybe I would if I had never had that movie training. But basically it would be more appropriate to ask me if having to do my own grocery shopping has affected my writing. According to reviewers, I've spent the last ten years of my life in Hollywood, but to tell the truth I have logged less than thirty days in Los Angeles. Total. I do have one level of interest in movies, and that's that I like to read screenplays. They're little books. If I hear there's a wonderful new movie out and I can get my hands on the screenplay, I'll read that rather than go to see the movie itself. I enjoy shooting the movie in my mind. I love to read plays for the same reason.

DOROTHY PARKER: It's the people. Like the director who put his finger in Scott Fitzgerald's face and complained, "Pay *you*. Why, you ought to pay us." It was terrible about Scott; if you'd seen him you'd have been sick. When he died no one went to the funeral, not a single soul came, or even sent a flower. I said, "Poor son of a bitch," a quote right out of *The Great Gatsby*, and everyone thought it was another wisecrack. But it was said in dead seriousness. Sickening about Scott. And it wasn't only the people, but also the indignity to which your ability was put. There was a picture in which Mr. Benchley had a part. In it Monty Woolley had a scene in which he had to enter a room through a door on which was balanced a bucket of water. He came into the room covered with water and muttered to Mr. Benchley, who had a part in the scene, "Benchley? Benchley of *Harvard*?" "Yes," mumbled Mr. Benchley and he asked, "Woolley? Woolley of *Yale*?"

. . .

Hollywood money isn't money. It's congealed snow, melts in your hand, and there you are. I can't talk about Hollywood. It was a horror to me when I was there and it's a horror to look back on. I can't imagine how I did it. When I got away from it I couldn't even refer to the place by name. "Out there," I called it. You want to know what "out there" means to me? Once I was coming down a street in Beverly Hills and I saw a Cadillac about a block long, and out of the side window was a wonderfully slinky mink, and an arm, and at the end of the arm a hand in a white suede glove wrinkled around the wrist, and in the hand was a bagel with a bite out of it.

S. J. PERELMAN: I worked there sporadically from 1931 to 1942, and I can say in all sincerity that I would have spent my time to better advantage on Tristan da Cunha. The mere mention of Hollywood induces a condition in me like breakbone fever. It was a hideous and untenable place when I dwelt there, populated with few exceptions by Yahoos, and now that it has become the chief citadel of television, it's unspeakable. The closest analogy I can draw to describe the place is that it strikingly resembled the Sargasso Sea—an immense, turgidly revolving whirlpool in which literary hulks encrusted with verdigris moldered until they sank. It was really quite startling, at those buffet dinners in Beverly Hills, to encounter some dramatist or short-story writer out of your boyhood, or some one-shot lady novelist who'd had a flash success, who was now grinding out screenplays about the Cisco Kid for Sol Wurtzel. I remember, one day on the back lot at MGM, that a pallid wraith of a man erupted from a row of ramshackle dressing rooms and embraced me as though we had encountered each other in the Empty Quarter of Arabia. He was a geezer I'd known twelve years before on *Judge* magazine, a fellow who ran some inconsequential column full of Prohibition jokes. When I asked him what he was doing, he replied that he had been writing a screenplay of "Edwin Drood" for the past two years. He confessed quite candidly that he hadn't been able as yet to devise a finish, which, of course, wasn't too surprising inasmuch as Charles Dickens couldn't do so either.

RICHARD PRICE: Every screenwriter loves to trash screenwriting. It's like shooting fish in a barrel. They trash the calculatedness, the cynicism, the idiocy, the pandering. But if they're really honest, they'll also admit they love the action, the interaction. Depending on whom you're working with, screenwriting is fun up to a point. And movies have such an impact on people. Thomas Keneally once told me about a time he was with the guerrillas in Eritrea during the civil war in Ethiopia. They were sitting on the cusp of the desert under the moon. They all had their muskets; they were about to attack some place. Wanting to chill out before they mobilized, they watched *The Color of Money* on video. So every once in a while the hugeness of Hollywood gets to you—the number of people who see a movie compared to the number of people who read a book. So as a screenwriter you keep hoping against hope, "Just because they screwed me the last time doesn't mean they're going to screw me this time." Well, of course they will. They're just going to screw you in a way you haven't been screwed before.

The first draft is the most creative, the most like real writing because it's just you and the story. The minute they get a hold of that first draft it ceases to be fun because it's all about making everybody happy. Raymond Chandler said that the danger of Hollywood for a writer is that you learn to put everything you've got into your first draft and then you steel yourself not to care what happens because you know you're going to be powerless after that. If you do that time and time again, the heart goes out of you.

IRWIN SHAW: You get an interesting technical exercise there—writing in handcuffs—which might one day be of considerable use in your own things.

TENNESSEE WILLIAMS: In the 1940s I had a glorious time in Hollywood because I was fired almost at once from the project I was working on and they had to continue to pay me. That was in my contract. For six months they had to pay me $250 a week. This was in 1943, when $250 was equivalent to about $1000 now, I would guess. They had to pay me whether I had an assignment or not.

First they put me on *Marriage Is a Private Affair* for Lana Turner. Well, they expressed great delight with my dialogue, and I think it was good. But they said, "You give Miss Turner too many multisyllable words!" So I said,

"Well, some words *do* contain more than one syllable!" And Pandro Berman, who loved me very much—Lana Turner just happened to be his girlfriend at the time—he said to me, "Tennessee, Lana can tackle two syllables, but I'm afraid if you go into three you're taxing her vocabulary!"

Then they asked me if I'd like to write a screenplay for a child star, one named Margaret O'Brien. I said, "I'd sooner shoot myself!" By that time I knew I'd get the $250 regardless.

So I lived out in Santa Monica and had a ball until the money ran out.

ON JOURNALISM

Literature is the art of writing something that will be read twice; journalism what will be grasped at once.
                                        —CYRIL CONNOLLY

Journalism is concerned with events, poetry with feelings. Journalism is concerned with the look of the world, poetry with the feel of the world.   —ARCHIBALD MACLEISH

Journalism is the ability to meet the challenge of filling space.
                                        —REBECCA WEST

The difference between journalism and literature is that journalism is unreadable and literature is not read.
                                        —OSCAR WILDE

MARTIN AMIS: Journalism, particularly book reviewing, brings with it another magnitude of difficulty. Fiction writing is basically what I want to do when I get up in the morning. If I haven't done any all day, then I feel dissatisfied. If I wake up knowing that I have some journalism to write, then it's with a heavy tread that I go to the bathroom—without relish, for many and obvious reasons. You're no longer in complete control.

But I think you have a duty to contribute, to go on contributing to what Gore Vidal calls "book chat." For certain self-interested reasons, you want to keep standards up so that when your next book comes out, it's more likely that people will get the hang of it. I have no admiration for writers who think at a certain point they can wash their hands of book chat. You should be part of the ongoing debate.

ROBERTSON DAVIES: It's influenced my writing immeasurably more than I could possibly define. When I was a boy, my father was a newspaperman, my two brothers were newspapermen, my mother was intensely interested in newspaper work, and I heard newspaper talk at every meal. In a newspaper family you learn not only all the news that's fit to print, but all the news that is *not* fit to print and you acquire an insight into human nature and the essence of a community which is very hard to acquire, I think, in any other way. I was the editor of a newspaper for twenty years. During that time I had to deal with not only the recorded news, but the news I knew about which might be supportive of the recorded news but some of which could not possibly be printed because it was so extraordinarily damaging and often wounding. You find out what people are like, and how they live, and what they're up to at night, and what goes on behind the lace curtains. The world you report is rarely more than half the world you know.

GABRIEL GARCÍA MÁRQUEZ: I don't think there is any difference. The sources are the same, the material is the same, the resources and the language are the same. *The Journal of the Plague Year* by Daniel Defoe is a great novel and [John Hersey's] *Hiroshima* is a great work of journalism. In journalism just one fact that is false prejudices the entire work. In contrast, in fiction one single fact that is true gives legitimacy to the entire work. That's the only difference and it lies in the commitment of the writer. A novelist can do anything he wants so long as he makes people believe in it.

．　．　．

The writer's very attempt to portray reality often leads him to a distorted view of it. In trying to transpose reality he can end up losing contact with it, in an ivory tower, as they say. Journalism is a very good guard against that. That's why I have always tried to keep on doing journalism because it keeps me in contact with the real world, particularly political journalism and politics.

ERNEST HEMINGWAY: On the [Kansas City] *Star,* you were forced to learn to write a simple declarative sentence. This is useful to anyone. Newspaper work will not harm a young writer and could help him if he gets out of it in time. This is one of the dustiest clichés there is and I apologize for it. But when you ask someone old tired questions you are apt to receive old tired answers.

JOHN HERSEY: Journalism allows its readers to witness history; fiction gives its readers the opportunity to live it.

AMOS OZ: I write articles not because I'm asked to, but because I'm filled with *rage*. I feel I have to tell my government what to do and, sometimes, where to go. Not that they listen. Then I drop everything and write an essay, which is always published here first, then picked up by *The New York Times*, or England's *Guardian* or another publication. You see, I'm not a political analyst or commentator. I write from a sense of injustice and my revolt against it. I have never written a story or a novel to make people change their minds about anything—not once. When I need to do this, I write an essay, or an article. I even use two different pens, as a symbolic gesture: one to tell stories, the other to tell the government what to do with itself.

JAMES SALTER: It happened that one of the first pieces of journalism I did was an interview with Nabokov. They said, first of all, he only gives written interviews. You must send in your questions in advance. So I sat down and wrote ten we assume penetrating questions, which I wouldn't like to see again, and sent them to him. No response, of course. But it was arranged that if I went to Europe I would be able to meet and talk to him. I reached Europe and was in Paris, it was in the winter, and I was in one of those hotels where they still had telephones with a separate piece you held to your ear, the old French phones. I got hold of the *Time* man in Geneva who had arranged the meeting with Nabokov, and he gave me the distressing news that the interview was called off. Nabokov had changed his mind. I said, "How can he do that? I've come to Europe." "Well, he's called it off." I didn't know what to do. He said, "Why don't you call him?" The idea was unthinkable. It was like somebody saying why don't you call the Pope? There seemed to be no alternative, so I called. A voice said, "Montreux Palace Hotel," and I said, "Mr. Nabokov, please." The phone was ringing and, of course, I didn't know what I was going to say. A woman answered. It was Vera Nabokov. I explained who I was and what had happened. She said, "Oh no, my husband can't do an interview. He's not well. You must submit your questions in writing." I told her I had done that but there had been no response, and she repeated that he answered only in writing. "I must tell you," she said, "my husband does not ad lib." Nevertheless, I asked if she would not, since I had come to Europe, be good enough to see if he wouldn't give me a few moments, merely so I had a physical impression, some description to add to the answers. She put the phone down, and I pictured her just looking out the window for a moment and then picking it up again and saying, "I'm sorry, he can't." But she surprised me by coming back and saying, "My husband will meet you at five o'clock on Sunday afternoon in the Green Bar of the Montreux Palace." She repeated the date and time to be sure it was understood.

At five o'clock on Sunday, the elevator door opened, and out stepped a tall, blazered, gray-trousered man whom I instantly recognized, and a white-haired woman in a handsome Rodier suit. It was the Nabokovs. They came to the table. I was a little nervous. I was not an accomplished journalist; I knew Nabokov did not ad lib; I was unable to bring a tape recorder because of that, and I would be unable to take notes, I knew, for the same reason. I had as my only source of strength the, I am certain, fabrication of Truman Capote that he had spent a night drinking and talking with Marlon Brando in Tokyo and the next day had written down the entire conversation exactly. It appeared in *The New Yorker.* I thought if Capote could do it for an entire night while drinking I could certainly do thirty abstemious minutes with Nabokov. I summoned all my powers and said I'm going to concentrate on everything he says, listen and not think of being clever or what I should say; I simply want to listen to him. It turned out to be about forty-five minutes. We were getting along quite well, and finally he said, "Shall we have another julep?" He was referring whimsically to scotch and soda. But I was afraid that one more drink might begin to obliterate the text. So I excused myself. I had the distinct impression we could have gone on and had dinner, but I was afraid to. I apologized for having taken up so much time and immediately went to the railroad station where I wrote down everything I remembered. It wasn't in order, of course, but it was four or five pages, and from it I constructed an interview. It was all fairly exact, I must say. I missed the train but I cherish the memory.

ISAAC BASHEVIS SINGER: I think that journalism is a healthier occupation for a writer than teaching, especially if he teaches literature. By teaching literature, the writer gets accustomed to analyze literature all the time. One man, a critic, said to me, "I could never write anything because the moment I write the first line I am already writing an essay about it. I am already criticizing my own writing."

It's not good when the writer is both a critic and a writer. It doesn't matter if he writes a review once in a while or even an essay about criticism. But if this kind of analyzing goes on all the time and it becomes his daily bread, it may one day become a part of his writing: it is very bad when the writer is half-writer and half-critic. He writes essays about his heroes instead of telling a story.

ELIE WIESEL: It's a different kind of recording. Journalism is too immediate, too monotonous and superficial. A chronicler is alone in his room and writes. A journalist is rarely alone. He writes about other people, and the essential is always missed. I was a journalist long enough to know. You write only of the fleeting moment—the most dramatic, the most visible, not the underlying reasons.

TOM WOLFE: The newspaper is, in fact, very bad for one's prose style. That's why I gravitated towards feature stories, where you get a little more leeway in the writing style. When I started writing magazine pieces for *Esquire* I had to unlearn newspaper restraints and shortcuts. Working on newspapers, you're writing to a certain length, often very brief pieces; you tend to look for easy forms of humor: "Women can't drive," things like that. That's about the level of a lot of newspaper humor. It becomes a form of laziness. But I wouldn't give anything for the years I spent on newspapers because it forces you, it immerses you, in so many different sides of life. I did try to cut up as much as I could; I think I was a lively newspaper writer, but that's a long way from being a good writer.

ON POTBOILERS

Commissions suit me. They set limits. Jean Marais dared me to write a play in which he would not speak in the first act, would weep for joy in the second and in the last would fall backwards down a flight of stairs.
—JEAN COCTEAU

A cow is very good in a field, but we turn her out of a garden.
—SAMUEL JOHNSON

KINGSLEY AMIS: I've always been interested in these less respectable forms of writing—the adventure story, the thriller, science-fiction, and so on—and this is why I've produced one or two examples myself. I read somewhere recently somebody saying: "When I want to read a book, I write one." I think that's very good. It puts its finger on it, because there are never enough books of the kind one likes: one adds to the stock for one's own entertainment.

JOHN CHEEVER: I was asked to do an interview with Sophia Loren by the *Saturday Evening Post*. I did. I got to kiss her. I've had other offers but nothing as good.

LAWRENCE DURRELL: I've done hundreds and thousands of words of feature articles, all buried in remote periodicals. Some under my own name, some under initials. In Cairo I ran a comic column. And then I've written millions of words of Foreign Office dispatches—a much harder job than any foreign correspondent's because I was the buffer state between, say, four and four hundred correspondents in a situation where a statement of policy was expected on a split-second basis and so watertight that it wouldn't fall apart under analysis. Of course, to make that kind of statement you have to have a policy, and in most of the places where I worked we didn't. In fact, I was selling a pig in a poke most of the time, living on my wits. Or, as Sir Henry Wotton said, "lying abroad for my country." But I mean it's an incomparable training, and by rubbing shoulders with a vast variety of journalists I learned most of the tricks of the trade—most of them rather shabby tricks, mind you, and magpie tricks and easy to learn. But one of the lessons, writing as you do under pressure in the journalistic world, is that you learn concision, which is invaluable, and you also learn to work for a deadline. Whenever the deadline is you've got to do it and you've got to have the will to do it. Well, you do it. Of course, the element of luck is very great. I might have written all my things and not had a publisher, or I might not have written them well enough to sell them.... I have to admit in my heart of hearts that I could have written books twice as good as the quartet and not have sold three hundred copies. The element of luck is absolutely mixed up with the whole thing.

. . .

I have had to do a lot of potboiling in my career. Let me say this: if one stays absolutely sincere and honest towards a form—even when I'm writing this Antrobus nonsense, I'm writing it with a reverence to P. G. Wodehouse. I mean every form thoroughly exploited and honestly dealt with is not shameful. So that potboiling as an idea of someone writing with a typewriter in his cheek or something—I can't say I do that. I mean I put as much hard work into a dull Antrobus story, which may or may not come off, as I put into the next chapter of the book I have to get on with.

HENRY GREEN: It's impossible for a novelist not to look out for other media nowadays. It isn't that everything has been done in fiction—truly nothing has been done as yet, save Fielding, and he only started it all. It is simply that the novelist is a communicator and must therefore be interested in any form of communication. You don't dictate to a girl now, you use a recording apparatus; no one faints anymore, they have blackouts; in Geneva you don't kill someone by cutting his throat, you blow a poisoned dart through a tube and *zing,* you've got him. Media change. We don't have to paint chapels like Cocteau, but at the same time we must all be ever on the lookout for the new ways.

MARY McCARTHY: I once started a detective story to make money— but I couldn't get the murder to take place! At the end of three chapters I was still describing the characters and the milieu, so I thought, this is not going to work. No corpse!

EZRA POUND: I was never too good a hand at writing for the magazines. I once did a satirical article for *Vogue,* I think it was. On a painter whom I did not admire. They thought I had got just the right tone and then Verhaeren died and they asked me to do a note on Verhaeren. And I went down and said, "You want a nice bright snappy obituary notice of the gloomiest man in Europe."

"What, gloomy cuss, was he?"

"Yes," I said. "He wrote about peasants."

"Peasants or pheasants?"

"Peasants."

"Oh, I don't think we ought to touch it."

That is the way I crippled my earning capacity by not knowing enough to keep quiet.

ON SHORT STORIES

Not that the story need be long, but it will take a long while to make it short. —HENRY DAVID THOREAU

LAWRENCE DURRELL: The length worries me. There are two things which feel uncomfortable and awkward to me ... like a wooden leg. One is the short story of about four thousand words, and the other is the feature for the *Times*. I could easily give them five thousand words or eight thousand words, but I'm damned if I can do anything under one thousand. So what I have to do is overwrite, give them eight thousand, and let them cut it down to their required size. As for the short story, I've done, as I say, several, but I've never felt happy in the form. Either I've felt it should be another forty pages, in which case it becomes a junior novel, a concertina novel, or else I've felt it should be two pages ... O. Henry and finish, you know. I admire the form, but it doesn't come easily to me.

FRANK O'CONNOR: The short story is the nearest thing I know to lyric poetry—I wrote lyric poetry for a long time, then discovered that God had not intended me to be a lyric poet, and the nearest thing to that is the short story. A novel actually requires far more logic and far more knowledge of circumstances, whereas a short story can have the sort of detachment from circumstances that lyric poetry has.... My own experience with the novel is that it was always too difficult for me to do. At least to do a novel like *Pride and Prejudice* requires something more than to be a failed B. A. or a failed poet or a failed short-story writer, or a failed anything else. Creating in the novel a sense of continuing life is the thing. We don't have that problem in the short story, where you merely suggest continuing life.

. . .

Short stories and plays go together in my mind. You take a point in time and develop it from there; there is no room for development backwards. In a novel I also take a point in time, but feel every room for development backwards. All fiction for me is a kind of magic and trickery—a confidence trick, trying to make people believe something is true that isn't. And the novelist, in particular, is trying to convince the reader that he is seeing society as a whole. . . . You can't do this sort of thing with short stories. They have a kind of immediate ethical text. Many of mine have punning titles. I take a platitude—"the wrong set," for example: the point is that no one knows what the wrong set is, and one person's wrong set is another's right set. And you get the pay-off, which is something I like. A play is rather like this, but has more depth. And plays and short stories are similar in that both start when all but the action has finished.

KATHERINE ANNE PORTER: I always write a story in one sitting. I started "Flowering Judas" at seven p.m. and at one-thirty I was standing on a snowy windy corner putting it in the mailbox. And when I wrote my short novels, two of them, I just simply took the manuscript, packed a suitcase, and departed to an inn in Georgetown, Pennsylvania, without leaving any forwarding address! Fourteen days later I had finished *Old Mortality* and *Noon Wine*.

V. S. PRITCHETT: I think I really wanted to be a short-story writer because I thought I was a man of short breath. I haven't got the breath to write novels. Long stories I think are admirable. I like those. That is quite another matter because you have your central theme, which is sustained and helps you along. But a novel is like an enormous tree with so many branches going off from it in all directions. At least the nineteenth-century novel is like that, and that's what I was brought up on. That's no good to me, but the short story and the long short story are. I've written quite a lot of them. I think it's been a question of speeding up. You may fall in love too much with certain conceits, and elaborations. The thing is to keep it running well, keep it lightly clad. *Athletic* is the word; I think that's a good word to describe my attitude to stories.

IRWIN SHAW: The form of the short story is so free as to escape restriction to any theory. Theories just don't seem to hold up. I had a theory when I began and I know I haven't been able to follow it out. I wanted to write stories in each one of which the style and shape would be dictated, as far as possible, not by me but by the material itself. That is, I wanted to make the attempt to cut the umbilical cord between the creator and the character. The Promethean writer would be the one who sounded like a Russian artillery officer when he was writing "The Cossacks," a Dublin lush when he was writing "Counterparts," and a German professor when he was writing "Disorder and Early Sorrow." I know it's impossible, but some damned interesting writing might come out of the attempt.

WILLIAM TREVOR: I think it is the art of the glimpse. If the novel is like an intricate Renaissance painting, the short story is an Impressionist painting. It *should* be an explosion of truth. Its strength lies in what it leaves out just as much as what it puts in, if not more. It is concerned with the total exclusion of meaninglessness. Life, on the other hand, is meaningless most of the time. The novel imitates life, where the short story is bony, and cannot wander. It is essential art.

. . .

Stories begin in all kinds of ways. With a remembered schoolteacher, or someone who might later have had something to do with your life, or some unimportant occurrence. You begin to write and in the process of writing it is often the case that whatever it was that started you off gets lost. On other occasions, stories simply come out of nowhere: you never discover the source. I remember being on a train and I was perhaps walking down to the bar when I noticed a woman and a boy traveling together. He was in his school uniform and she was clearly in charge of him. I can remember now the fatigue on her face. Afterwards—probably years afterwards—I wrote a story called *Going Home.*

P. G. WODEHOUSE: I think I'd sooner write short stories than novels. I feel really happy with a short story. I like the sense of completing something. The only trouble is that if I do get a good idea, I rather want to work it into a novel. I mean, I'm rather wasting a novel if I write a short story.

ON THEATER

Be patient. Our playwright may show in some fifth act what
this wild drama means.　　　　　—ALFRED, LORD TENNYSON

Some writers take to drink, others take to audiences.
　　　　　　　　　　　　　　　　　　　—GORE VIDAL

T. S. ELIOT: There is all the difference in the world between writing a
play for an audience and writing a poem, in which you're writing primarily for yourself—although obviously you wouldn't be satisfied if the poem
didn't mean something to other people afterward. With a poem you can
say, "I got my feeling into words for myself. I now have the equivalent in
words for that much of what I have felt." Also in a poem you're writing for
your own voice, which is very important. You're thinking in terms of your
own voice, whereas in a play from the beginning you have to realize that
you're preparing something which is going into the hands of other people, unknown at the time you're writing it. Of course I won't say there
aren't moments in a play when the two approaches may not converge,
when I think ideally they should. Very often in Shakespeare they do, when
he is writing a poem and thinking in terms of the theater and the actors
and the audience all at once. And the two things are one. That's wonderful when you can get that. With me it only happens at odd moments.

JOHN GUARE: I love the part of playwrighting that is a craft to be
learned continually, the -wright part, like *shipwright* or *wheelwright* or
cartwright. Whether Aeschylus or George S. Kaufman, a playwright is a
writer who understands the technical aspects of knowing how to deliver
exposition, how to get a character on and offstage, where to place the in-
termission, how to bring down a curtain. How to have all the characters'

stories end up simultaneously. That's craft, and craft can be taught by emulation. You figure out how your playwright of the moment accomplishes those facts of the theater. You learn to study those playwrights technically, the way a musician does a score, breaking the work down to learn how its composer achieved certain effects. And then, having learned a technique, one can use it oneself.

LILLIAN HELLMAN: There shouldn't be any difference between writing for the theater and writing for anything else. Only that one has to know the theater. Know it. To publish a novel or a poem one doesn't have to know print types or the publishing world. But to do a play, no matter how much one wishes to stay away from it, one has to *know* the theater. Playwrights have tried to stay away, including Shaw and Chekhov, but in the end, they were involved. Chekhov used to send letters of instructions and angry notes. A play is not only on paper. It is there to share with actors, directors, scene designers, electricians.

EUGÈNE IONESCO: The theater chose me. As I said, I started with poetry, and I also wrote criticism and dialogue. But I realized that I was most successful at dialogue. Perhaps I abandoned criticism because I am full of contradictions, and when you write an essay you are not supposed to contradict yourself. But in the theater, by inventing various characters, you can. My characters are contradictory not only in their language, but in their behavior as well.

DAVID MAMET: Drama has to do with circumstance, tragedy has to do with individual choice. The precipitating element of a drama can be a person's sexuality, their wealth, their disease . . . A tragedy can't be about any of those things. That's why we identify with a tragic hero more than with a dramatic hero: we understand the tragic hero to be ourselves. That's why it's easier for the audiences initially to form an affection for the drama rather than the tragedy. Although it seems that they're exercising a capacity for identification—"Oh, yes, I understand. So-and-so is in a shitload of difficulty and I identify with them, and I see where the going's bad and I see where the hero is good"—in effect they're distancing themselves, because they'll say, "Well, shit, I couldn't get into that situation because I'm not gay, or because I am gay, because I'm not crippled or because I am crippled . . ." They're distanced. Because I can go on with drama. A tragedy has to be the attempt of one specific person to obtain one specific goal, and when he either gets it or doesn't get it, then we know the play is over, and we can go home and put out the baby-sitter.

IRIS MURDOCH: The theater is such a different game. Writers of fiction, of novels, are pleased when they can see something of their work on the stage and hear people uttering their lines and so on. But a play is made of lines, and it's got to be ... I mean, the miracle about the theater is why people stay there. Why don't they get up and go? It's not at all easy to write a play. There's a special kind of magic involved. My first adventure in the theater was a very pleasant one because I worked with J. B. Priestley on making a play out of a novel of mine called *A Severed Head.* He said to me, "Duckie, this is a difficult game; a very few people can succeed at it. If it was all that easy everybody would be doing it." It is very difficult to compress the reflections of one's characters and the great pattern of a novel into drama where it is a matter of lines and short speeches and actual actors and so on. The forms are so different that they can't possibly be compared. A play is much more like a poem.

IRWIN SHAW: Young novelists come a dime a dozen, but the playwright must be older, more experienced, and in more complete control of his craft. The scope of the novel is such that mistakes can be made, even serious mistakes, without impairing the value of the work. But the theater audience is hypercritical, and the form of the play is extremely exacting and one mistake and you're through. I've had a hard time with the theater. I've always been anxious to write plays. I read all kinds of plays and books on the theater and books about how to write plays but all I learned was that playwriting is something nobody can teach you.

JOHN UPDIKE: I've never much enjoyed going to plays myself; they always seem one act too long, and I often can't hear. The last play I went to, I remember, was "A Delicate Balance"; I sat next to the wall and trucks kept shifting gears on the other side of it and I missed most of the dialogue. The unreality of painted people standing on a platform saying things they've said to each other for months is more than I can overlook. Also, I think the theater is a quicksand of money and people with push. Harold Brodkey, a splendid writer my age, disappeared for five years into a play that was never produced. From Twain and James to Faulkner and Bellow, the history of novelists as playwrights is a sad one. A novelist is no more prepared to write for the stage than a good distance runner is equipped for ballet. A play is verbal ballet, and I mean to include in that equation some strong reservations about ballet. Less than perfectly done, it's very tiresome. A play's capacity for mimesis is a fraction of a novel's. Shakespeare, and to a lesser extent Shaw, wrote their plays as "turns" and exercises for actors they knew—without Will Kempe, no Falstaff. Without this kind of intimacy, the chances of life creeping into a play are slight. On both sides of the footlights, I think the present American theater mainly an excuse for being sociable.

THORNTON WILDER: A dramatist is one who believes that the pure event, an action involving human beings, is more arresting than any comment that can be made upon it. On the stage it is always *now;* the personages are standing on that razor-edge, between the past and the future, which is the essential character of conscious being; the words are rising to their lips in immediate spontaneity. A novel is what *took place;* no self-effacement on the part of the narrator can hide the fact that we hear his voice recounting, recalling events that are past and over, and which he has selected—from uncountable others—to lay before us from his presiding intelligence. Even the most objective novels are cradled in the authors' emotions and the authors' assumptions about life and mind and the passions. Now the paradox lies not so much in the fact that you and I know that the dramatist equally has selected what he exhibits and what the characters will say—such an operation is inherent in any work of art— but that all the greatest dramatists, except the very greatest *one,* have precisely employed the stage to convey a moral or religious point of view concerning the action. The theater is supremely fitted to say: "Behold! These things are." Yet most dramatists employ it to say: "This moral truth can be learned from beholding this action."

The Greek tragic poets wrote for edification, admonition, and even for our political education. The comic tradition in the theater carries the intention of exposing folly and curbing excess. Only in Shakespeare are we free of hearing axes ground. . . . I regard the theater as the greatest of all art forms, the most immediate way in which a human being can share with another the sense of what it is to be a human being. This supremacy of the theater derives from the fact that it is always "now" on the stage. It is enough that generations have been riveted by the sight of Clytemnestra luring Agamemnon to the fatal bath, and Oedipus searching out the truth which will ruin him; those circumambient tags about "Don't get prideful" and "Don't call anybody happy until he's dead" are incidental concomitants. The theater *is* so vast and fascinating a realm that there is room in it for preachers and moralists and pamphleteers. But as to the highest function of the theater, I rest my case with Shakespeare—*Twelfth Night* as well as *Macbeth*.

. . .

All excellence is equally difficult, but, considering sheer métier, I would always advise any young writer for the theater to do everything—to adapt plays, to translate plays, to hang around theaters, to paint scenery, to become an actor, if possible. Writing for TV or radio or the movies is all part of it. There's a bottomless pit in the acquisition of how to tell an imagined story to listeners and viewers.

PART IV

THE WRITER'S LIFE

ON SOCIAL LIFE: WRITERS' COLONIES, SALONS, LITERARY COMMUNITIES, ETC.

Writing is a dog's life, but the only life worth living.
—GUSTAVE FLAUBERT

One more drink and I'll be under the host.
—DOROTHY PARKER

Desperate writers, who once by their cries of agony wrung tears from tender-hearted readers, come to prefer the glittering smiles of hostesses as hard as their marble mantelpieces.
—LOGAN PEARSALL SMITH

W. H. AUDEN: I've told people I'm a medieval historian, when asked what I do. It freezes conversation. If one tells them one's a poet, one gets these odd looks which seem to say, "Well, what's he living off?" In the old days a man was proud to have in his passport, Occupation: Gentleman. Lord Antrim's passport simply said, Occupation: Peer—which I felt was correct. I've had a lucky life, I had a happy home, and my parents provided me with a good education. And my father was both a physician and a scholar, so I never got the idea that art and science were opposing cultures—both were entertained equally in my home. I cannot complain. I've never had to do anything I really disliked. Certainly I've had to do various jobs I would not have taken on if I'd had the money; but I've always considered myself a worker, not a laborer. So many people have jobs they don't like at all. I haven't, and I'm grateful for that.

ELIZABETH BISHOP: I went to Yaddo [the writers' colony] twice, once in the summer for two weeks, and for several months the winter before I went to Brazil. I didn't like it in the summer because of the incessant coming and going, but the winter was rather different. There were only six of us and just by luck we all liked each other and had a very good time. I wrote one poem, I think, in that whole stretch. The first time I liked the horse races, I'm afraid. In the summer—I think this still goes on—you can walk through the Whitney estate to the tracks. A friend and I used to walk there early in the morning and sit at the track and have coffee and blueberry muffins while they exercised the horses. I loved that. We went to a sale of yearlings in August and that was beautiful. The sale was in a big tent. The grooms had brass dustpans and brooms with brass handles and they'd go around after the little colts and sweep up the manure. That's what I remember best about Yaddo.

PAUL BOWLES: I was never aware of wanting to become part of a community, no. I wanted to meet them. I suppose I simply felt that I was taking pot shots at clay pipes. Pop! Down goes Gertrude, down goes Jean Cocteau, down goes André Gide. I made a point of those things—meeting Manuel de Falla, for example—for no reason at all. I went to Granada, found his door, knocked, went in, and spent the afternoon. He had no idea who I was. Why I did that, I don't know. Apparently I thought such encounters were important or I wouldn't have bothered, because it involved a lot of work and sometimes a sacrifice of something I cared about. But exactly how I felt I can't remember, because it wasn't an intellectual thing. It was "unthought," and it's hard for me to recall the reason for it. Of course, I've never been a thinking person. A lot seems to happen without my conscious knowledge.

WILLIAM GOYEN: My closest friends are theater people. Painters were once closest to me. For some years I lived among painters. But that changed. Now it's either performers or directors. I love theater people, they give me a great deal. I don't particularly like writers, and I am not prone to talk about writing. Since they're solitary workers, writers tend to *act out* in public, I believe. They seem to carry more hostility, maybe because they are responsible to more people (their characters), to a whole world—like God—than painters or actors. Maybe it's because writers are caught in the English language, which sometimes seems like a sticky web you can't pull your antennae out of, like insects I've watched in webs, and are, in public and when they're with other people, still thrashing about in an invisible web. It is *enraging* to work in words, sometimes; no wonder writers are often nervous and crazy: paint seems to be a more benevolent, a more soothing and serene-making medium.

Musicians always want to play for you, which is wonderful and wordless; painters seem to want to talk only about sex or point out to you the hidden genital configurations in their canvas! Since the writer is truly a seminal person (he spits out his own web, as Yeats said, and then, as I just said, gets caught in it), the truly creative writer, I mean, he's full of the fear and the pride that a maker of *new* things feels.

FRANCINE DU PLESSIX GRAY: Here's a major point of tension in most writers' lives: How can we rub enough with the world to nourish our writing, while keeping the world enough at bay to safeguard our creative energies? I like living where I do, in southern New England, because I can better control my impulsive, innate gregariousness. It's easier to resist temptations here and yet I can get into New York in two and a half hours, a few times a month, to sample that week's *Zeitgeist*. In a similar manner, teaching offers me a form of human contact which I find deeply satisfying yet less draining than most other social engagements. Listening to students' problems, inciting them to read Plato or Colette, the heatedness and fun of class discussions—that's one of the most nourishing and inspiring things I know. And the sheer boredom of most other traditional social contacts, the literary party circuit in the Hamptons or the Vineyard for instance, could lead me to the loony bin in the space of a weekend. The vapid tiddlywinks conversation, and the tedium of the endless cocktail hours! Cocktails is one American custom I continue to find loathsome; I can't abide dining with anyone who'll make me wait more than twenty-five minutes for dinner. There's a lot of the pedant in me; my idea of a good time is to sit under a tree with some close friends over a picnic of bread and cheese and wine and talk about Ficino's influence on Titian's concept of love, or chew over some new insights into William James. Now that's the *greatest* fun. So teaching is something born into me which I love deeply, and it's the form of fraternizing which I find least draining, most inspiring and nourishing.

JOSEPH HELLER: I don't think writers are comfortable in each other's presence. We can talk, of course, for five minutes or so, but I don't think we want to socialize. There's always an acute status consciousness relating to how high or low a writer exists in the opinion of the person he's talking to. I've noticed that the opening gambit in conversation between two writers—and I'm always very uncomfortable hearing it—is, "I like your work." I've heard it so often. It's so condescending. What if the person had not done any work?: he would not be spoken to at all. This sort of relationship is peculiar to writers—after all, our status is never challenged by anyone else, one's jeweler, or a dress-manufacturer. No, I don't think two novelists who have enjoyed a high measure of success can exist into their middle years living close to each other if both continue writing—I don't believe human nature can accept such a situation.

ALDOUS HUXLEY: I don't believe there is an ideal occupation for the writer. He could write under almost any circumstance, even in complete isolation. Why, look at Balzac: locked up in a secret room in Paris, hiding from his creditors, and producing the *Comédie Humaine.* Or think of Proust in his cork-lined room (although of course he had plenty of visitors). I suppose the best occupation is just meeting a great many different kinds of people and seeing what interests them. That's one of the disadvantages of getting older; you're inclined to make intimate contacts with fewer people.

EUGÈNE IONESCO: The Collège de Pataphysique was an enterprise dedicated to nihilism and irony, which in my view corresponded to Zen. Its chief occupation was to devise commissions, whose job it was to create subcommissions, which in turn did nothing. There was one commission which was preparing a thesis on the history of latrines from the beginning of civilization to our time. The members were students of Dr. Faustrol, who was an invented character, and the prophet of Alfred Jarry. So the purpose of the Collège was the demolition of culture, even of Surrealism, which they considered too organized. But make no mistake, these people were graduates of the École Normale Supérieure and highly cultured. Their method was based on puns and practical jokes—*le canular.* There is a great tradition of puns in Anglo-Saxon literature—Shakespeare, *Alice in Wonderland*—but not in French. So they adopted it. They believed that the science of sciences is the *pataphysique* and its dogma, *le canular.* The Collège was organized with great precision: there was a hierarchy, grades, a pastiche of Freemasonry. Anybody could join, and the first grade was that of *Auditeur Amphitéote.* After that, you became a *Regent,* and finally a *Satrap.* The satrap was entitled to be addressed as *Votre Transcendence,* and when you left his presence you had to walk backwards. Our principal activity was to write pamphlets and to make absurd statements, such as "Jean Paulhan does not exist!" Our meetings took place in a little café-restaurant in the Latin Quarter, and we discussed nothing, because we believed—and I still do—that there is no reason for anything, that everything is meaningless. Our God was Alfred Jarry, and, apart from our meetings, we made pilgrimages to his grave near Paris. As you know, Jarry had written *Ubu Roi,* which was a parody of *Macbeth.* Much later I wrote a play based on *Macbeth* too. Anyway, the Collège gave decorations, the most important of which was *La Gidouille,* which was a large turd to be pinned on your lapel. At the premiere of *The Bald Soprano,* twenty to thirty of them turned up wearing their *gidouilles* on their lapels. The audience was shocked at the sight of so many big turds, and thought they were members of a secret cult.

. . .

Literary salons don't exist any longer in Paris, but in those days there were two. The first was the salon of Madame Dézenas—a rich lady who liked literature and the arts. All sorts of celebrities came there: Stravinsky, Etiemble, young Michel Butor, Henri Michaux. . . . The second salon was la Vicomtesse de Noailles's. I went there once and met Jean-Louis Barrault. I remember how a ripple of excitement, a *frisson,* ran through the gathering when Aragon and Elsa Triolet were announced. "Here come the Communists!" they all said. Aragon was in a dinner jacket and Elsa was covered in jewelry. But *I* went there to drink whiskey and to meet friends, not out of worldliness.

PHILIP LARKIN: I'm somewhat withdrawn from what you call "the contemporary literary community," for two reasons: in the first place, I don't write for a living, and so don't have to keep in touch with literary editors and publishers and television people in order to earn money; and in the second, I don't live in London. Given that, my relations with it are quite amicable.

. . .

I've never been to America, nor to anywhere else, for that matter. Does that sound very snubbing? It isn't meant to. I suppose I'm pretty unadventurous by nature, partly that isn't the way I earn my living—reading and lecturing and taking classes and so on. I should hate it.

And of course I'm so deaf now that I shouldn't dare. Someone would say, What about Ashbery, and I'd say, I'd prefer strawberry, that kind of thing. I suppose everyone has his own dream of America. A writer once said to me, If you ever go to America, go either to the East Coast or the West Coast: the rest is a desert full of bigots. That's what I think I'd like: where if you help a girl trim the Christmas tree you're regarded as engaged, and her brothers start oiling their shotguns if you don't call on the minister. A version of pastoral.

ARCHIBALD MACLEISH: From any point of view, the decade of the twenties was a terrible decade: it was self-indulgent, it was fat, it was rich, it was full of the most loathsome kinds of open and flagrant money-making. All the worst aspects of the French came out as the franc dropped. And yet that decade in Paris was perfect. I suppose it was the right period for *us*. Because of the war, I was a lot older than I should have been to do what I was doing—trying to learn an art. But I was trying to do it alone, which is the best way to try to do it, and I was living in a city where you could *be* alone without ever being lonely, and I had Ada with me. She—I don't need to tell *you*—was a singer. A lovely singer with a beautiful, clear, high voice, and a superb musician. She was going great guns singing new songs for Stravinsky and Poulenc and Copland. So we were right in the middle of the most exciting period in almost a century of music. Also, the people who drifted along—Ernest, Dos, Scott, Gerald Murphy, above all, the Murphys—were people of extraordinary interest who were also—or became, most of them—close friends. I can see why this still interests *me*—I love to go back to it in my mind—but why anybody else forty, fifty, sixty years younger should be interested in it, I just don't understand. I can only answer for myself—what *I* saw and heard. Everyone was aware, I think, that work was being produced in Paris which was magnificent by any standard. This was true of all the arts—the arts generally—the arts as practiced by artists of many nationalities: French, Spanish, Russian, Irish, German, Greek, Austrian. We knew we belonged to a great, a greatly creative, generation—that we lived in a generative time. Everything seemed possible—*was* possible. To be young in a time like that was incredible luck—to be young and in Paris. That much is certain: the witnesses are innumerable. But when you narrow the circle to the American the answers are not so easy. American letters at the turn of the century had reached something which looked to my generation like rock bottom, and the achievements of Eliot and Pound during and after the First World War, though they had raised our hearts, had not wholly persuaded us that *we* belonged in this great resurgence of all the arts which was evident in Paris—this world resurgence of great art. So our excitement, real enough, was a little hesitant, a little tentative. Hemingway's *In Our Time* was the first solid American proof to appear on the Seine—

proof that a master of English prose had established himself and that this master was indubitably American, American not only by blood but by eye and ear. But *In Our Time* was a collection of short stories. Would there be a great novel? A great *American* novel? We didn't know in Paris in the twenties. We only knew anything was possible.

I met Hemingway a year or so after we got to Paris and Gerald Murphy about the same time . . . Dos, Estlin Cummings, Bishop, Scott . . . but there was no "community" in the sense in which you, I think, are using the word. No Americans-in-Paris community. That notion is a myth concocted after the event by critics with fish to fry. There was the literary-tourist world of the Dôme and the Rotonde but no work came out of that. The real "community" was, of course, Paris—the Paris of Valéry and Fargue and Larbaud—the world center of art which had drawn Picasso from abroad, and Juan Gris and Stravinsky and all the rest of that great international generation including, first and foremost, Joyce. The world center of poetry which held Alexis Léger down at the Quai d'Orsay in his anonymity as St.-J. Perse. That community—real community—drew and sustained the young Americans who lived in Paris in those years, but they didn't belong to it nor did they communicate with it, except to watch and wonder like the rest of the world. I knew Fargue and Larbaud, and Jules Romains through Adrienne Monnier. Alexis Léger became a close friend many years afterward, when all this was gone and Paris was a Nazi slum. I knew Joyce and marveled at him. But I was not part of *that* Paris nor were any Americans I knew, with the possible exceptions of Tom Eliot and Ezra Pound, who sometimes appeared. In a touching letter toward the end of his life, Scott speaks of "the last American season" in Paris. If there ever was an "American season" in Paris in the twenties, Paris was not aware of it. Nor, I think, was anyone else.

CZESLAW MILOSZ: I worked for many years in a state of nearly total obscurity. My years in Berkeley were a time when I had practically no audience here, and very few people in America on whose judgment I could rely. I had a couple of friends in Paris and Poland, so correspondence played an enormous role for me: letters received from a few friends were my only sustaining force. I was publishing my books of verse in Polish. They had to be smuggled into Poland so I did not know the reactions of readers in Poland.

I knew who I was, and I knew my worth, but I was completely unknown to almost all my colleagues at Berkeley except, of course, the Slavic languages professors. I was an obscure professor in an obscure department. I became well known to students only when I started to teach Dostoyevsky. There is a story which summarizes those years. I was at a literary dinner at Stanford with Jerzy Kosinski and, of course, he was quite famous. There was a woman, a fan of Kosinski's, who was my neighbor at the table. She felt obliged to be polite and asked, "What do you do?" And I said, "I write poetry." She snapped in reply: "Everybody writes poetry." I didn't mind that much but it still hurt. It represented my situation for years, the sufferings of ambition.

WALKER PERCY: Mine has been a happy marriage—thanks mainly to my wife. Who would want to live with a novelist? A man underfoot in the house all day? A man, moreover, subject to solitary funks and strange elations. If I were a woman, I'd prefer a traveling salesman. There is no secret, or rather the secrets are buried in platitudes. That is to say, it has something to do with love, commitment and family. As to the institution, it is something like Churchill's description of democracy: vicissitudinous yes, but look at the alternatives.

· · ·

Novelists don't talk much about each other. Maybe this is because novelists secrete a certain B.O. which only other novelists detect, like certain buzzards who emit a repellent pheromone detectable only by other buzzards, which is to say that only a novelist can know how neurotic, devious, underhanded a novelist can be.

PHILIP ROTH: I recently heard the critic George Steiner, on English television, denouncing contemporary Western literature as utterly worthless and without quality, and claiming that the great documents of the human soul, the masterpieces, could only arise from souls being crushed by regimes like those in Czechoslovakia. I wonder then why all the writers I know in Czechoslovakia loathe the regime and passionately wish that it would disappear from the face of the earth. Don't they understand, as Steiner does, that this is their chance to be great? Sometimes one or two writers with colossal brute strength do manage, miraculously, to survive and, taking the system as their subject, to make art of a very high order out of their persecution. But most of them who remain sealed up inside totalitarian states are, as writers, destroyed by the system. That system doesn't make masterpieces; it makes coronaries, ulcers, and asthma, it makes alcoholics, it makes depressives, it makes bitterness and desperation and insanity. The writers are intellectually disfigured, spiritually demoralized, physically sickened, and culturally bored. Frequently they are silenced completely. Nine-tenths of the best of them will never do their best work just because of the system. The writers nourished by this system are the party hacks. When such a system prevails for two or three generations, relentlessly grinding away at a community of writers for twenty, thirty, or forty years, the obsessions become fixed, the language grows stale, the readership slowly dies out from starvation, and the existence of a national literature of originality, variety, vibrancy (which is very different from the brute survival of a single powerful voice) is nearly impossible. A literature that has the misfortune of remaining isolated underground for too long will inevitably become provincial, backwards, even naïve, despite the fund of dark experience that may inspire it. By contrast, our work here hasn't been deprived of authenticity because as writers we haven't been stomped on by a totalitarian government. I don't know of any Western writer, aside from George Steiner, who is so grandiosely and sentimentally deluded about human suffering—and "masterpieces"—that he's come back from behind the Iron Curtain thinking himself devalued because he hasn't had to contend with such a wretched intellectual and literary environment.

MAY SARTON: I don't like writers. I don't like seeing writers. I'm not good at it. It upsets me. It's been too hard a struggle. I'm very competitive, and that side comes out. I'm uncomfortable with writers. I love painters and sculptors.

ISAAC BASHEVIS SINGER: When I lived in Poland, I used to hang out at the writers' club. I'd be there every day. But there is nothing quite like that in America. I know practically no other writers. Once in a while I meet some writers at a cocktail party, and I like them: they are very fine people. But somehow it never goes beyond a superficial meeting. I am sorry about this. I would like to be friendly with more writers.

JESSAMYN WEST: I don't know that those marriages work out well . . . whether it's two literary people or two movie actors, maybe even two school superintendents. My husband, Max, is not a literary person. If he were a terribly literary person who wanted to look at everything I wrote, I might not be able to stomach it. I cannot stomach it even when my editor shows tendencies in that direction. There are examples. Virginia Woolf had a literary husband and they worked together in the Hogarth Press. But then you have someone like Scott Fitzgerald and Zelda where there was such competition. So it's worked out for me. Max reads an occasional novel, but mostly ones that I say, "Hey, you're going to miss something if you don't read this." He reads books about schoolwork, about farming, investments. I think maybe if he had a different wife, he might never have bought anything but a practical book.

TENNESSEE WILLIAMS: I think it [being single] made it possible for me to practice my profession as a writer. You know what happened to poor Norman Mailer. One wife after another, and all that alimony. I've been spared all that. I give people money, yes. But I couldn't have afforded alimony, not to all those wives. I would've had to behead them!

P. G. WODEHOUSE: Ethel has always been wonderful in that way. You've got to be alone quite a bit when you're writing. She doesn't mind that at all. I've always had great luck with the things that really matter in life. I should imagine an unhappy marriage would simply kill a man.

On Security: Grants, Prizes, Honors, etc.

Anythin' for the quiet life, as the man said when he took the sitiviation at the lighthouse.   —Charles Dickens

The Nobel is a ticket to one's own funeral. No one has ever done anything after he got it.

—T. S. Eliot, on winning it

One of the things which makes me happier today is that I will never be a Nobel Prize candidate again.

—Gabriel García Márquez, on winning it

Nothing is so silly as the expression of a man who is being complimented.   —André Gide

There's no money in poetry, but then there's no poetry in money.   —Robert Graves

The only happy author in this world is he who is below the care of reputation.   —Washington Irving

I know at last what distinguishes man from animals: financial worry.   —Jules Renard

A writer who takes political, social, or literary positions must act only with the means that are his. These means are the writer's words.

—Jean-Paul Sartre, on refusing the Nobel Prize

I turned down the National Institute of Arts and Letters when I was elected to it in 1976 on the grounds that I was already in the Diner's Club.   —Gore Vidal

I don't expect you'll hear me writing any poems to the greater glory of Ronald and Nancy Reagan.

—Robert Penn Warren, on being named
poet laureate

I would love to be the poet laureate of Coney Island.

—THORNTON WILDER

A. R. AMMONS: I detest government support of the arts. I detest it on many grounds, but three first. And the first is that the government gouges money from people who may need it for other purposes. Second, the money forced from needy average citizens is then filtered through the sieve of a bureaucracy, which absorbs much of the money into itself and distributes the rest incompetently—since how could you expect the level of knowledge and judgment among such a cluster to be much in advance of the times? At the same time the government attaches strings to the money, not theirs in the first place, to those who gave it in the first place. And third, I detest the averaging down of expectation and dedication that occurs when thousands of poets are given money in what is really waste and welfare, not art at all. Artists should be left alone to paint or not to paint, write or not to write. As it is, the world is full of trash. The genuine is lost, and the whole field wallops with political and social distortions.

Everybody who loves the arts should have the liberty to sustain the particular arts he loves, whenever, wherever. If the love and money go to the popular arts, that's the way it should be. If there is an outcry for symphonic performances of the great Bs, then that is what should be addressed. High arts that hang on almost vestigial in a culture should be addressed in their own scope, and I think they would not perish but that genius and energy would burst out whenever it's not already stifled by some blank, some holding grant, some template that just keeps blocking itself out.

ELIZABETH BISHOP: We lived on top of a mountain peak [in Brazil]—really way up in the air. I was alone in the house with Maria, the cook. A friend had gone to market. The telephone rang. It was a newsman from the American Embassy and he asked me who it was in English and of course it was very rare to hear someone speak in English. He said, "Do you know you've won the Pulitzer Prize?" Well, I thought it was a joke. I said, "Oh, come on." And he said, "Don't you hear me?" The telephone connection was very bad and he was shrieking. And I said, "Oh, it can't be." But he said it wasn't a joke. I couldn't make an impression on Maria with this news, but I felt I had to share it, so I hurried down the mountain a half-mile or so to the next house but no one was at home. I thought I should do something to celebrate, have a glass of wine or something. But all I could find in that house, a friend's, were some cookies from America, some awful chocolate cookies—Oreos, I think—so I ended up eating two of those. And that's how I celebrated winning the Pulitzer Prize.

The next day there was a picture in the afternoon paper—they take such things very seriously in Brazil—and the day after that my Brazilian friend went to market again. There was a big covered market with stalls for every kind of comestible, and there was one vegetable man we always went to. He said, "Wasn't that Doña Elizabetchy's picture in the paper yesterday?" She said, "Yes, it was. She won a prize." And he said, "You know, it's amazing! Last week Señora (Somebody) took a chance on a bicycle and *she* won! My customers are so lucky!"

HORTENSE CALISHER: I don't think artists can compete—except as to money and prizes, and, of course, status. Which may be temporary. But not on the page. Or the canvas or the stone. Or the musical score. All you can hope to be is worthy of the company you respect.

BLAISE CENDRARS: My dear sir, in the Belle Epoque space-writers were paid one sou a line in the papers and an Apollinaire had to wait months and years before he could sign his articles and count on steady employment with regular pay. That was why he published pornography, to earn his bread. You can't imagine how solidly closed all doors were to us. I have the impression that today you're much better received, I run into young writers everywhere, on the papers, the radio, in the picture studios. Before 1914 those who wanted a job stood in line at the door, or at an employment window that never opened. The others contented themselves with playing the buffoon, the wild bull, in the streets. To hell with a job and a decent living. We laughed. The Paris girls were pretty.

WILLIAM FAULKNER: The writer doesn't need economic freedom. All he needs is a pencil and some paper. I've never known anything good in writing to come from having accepted any free gift of money. The good writer never applies to a foundation. He's too busy writing something. If he isn't first rate he fools himself by saying he hasn't got time or economic freedom. Good art can come out of thieves, bootleggers, or horse swipes. People really are afraid to find out just how much hardship and poverty they can stand. They area afraid to find out how tough they are. Nothing can destroy the good writer. The only thing that can alter the good writer is death. Good ones don't have time to bother with success or getting rich. Success is feminine and like a woman; if you cringe before her, she will override you. So the way to treat her is to show her the back of your hand. Then maybe she will do the crawling.

ROBERT FITZGERALD: I'm reminded of Eugenio Montale's great piece on the encouragement of poetry, particularly by the state—National Endowments and things like that. He was very skeptical about the utility of encouraging poetry on a grand scale. Is encouragement what a poet needs? Open question. Maybe he needs *dis*couragement. In fact, quite a few of them need more discouragement, the most discouragement possible.

WILLIAM GADDIS: Well, I almost think that if I'd gotten the Nobel Prize when *The Recognitions* was published I wouldn't have been terribly surprised. I mean that's the grand intoxication of youth, or what's a heaven for. And so the book's reception was a sobering experience, quite a humbling one. When finally help did come along, recognition as you say, a Rockefeller Foundation grant, a Guggenheim Fellowship, the National Endowment for the Arts, they came in difficult times and allowed and encouraged me to keep on with the second book and start the third. Without them, I wonder if I might not just have dropped the whole damned business, though God knows what else I might have done, too late even to be any of the things I never wanted to be. There's always the talk about feeding at the public trough, disdaining grants because you've never been given one. I mean we'd all wish to come out with the fierce integrity of Samuel Butler, say, who never wrote simply to publish or published everything he wrote—*The Way of All Flesh* was posthumous after all—and that has been the luxury of the MacArthur. But then I never was a fellow to rush into print.

SEAMUS HEANEY: Receiving the Nobel Prize was a bit like being caught in a mostly benign avalanche. You are totally daunted, of course, when you think of previous writers who received the prize. And daunted when you think of the ones who didn't receive it. Just confining yourself to Ireland you have Yeats, Shaw and Beckett in the first group and James

Joyce in the second. So you soon realize you'd better not think too much about it at all. Nothing can prepare you for it. Zeus thunders and the world blinks twice and you get to your feet again and try to keep going.

MARK HELPRIN: With financial security, as with everything else, you're ruined by either too much or too little. The question remains, how do you define what is too much or too little? One of the most beautiful phrases in the Hebrew liturgy is *Daienu*, which is pronounced "die-ainu." It means "enough (for us)," and in the song that is sung at Passover, the idea is that God has given much more than we require. Among other things, this allows us not to waste our lives in continual pursuit of *more*, and suggests that we should decide what it is that we truly need and then learn to stop wanting.

DAVID IGNATOW: Well, I'm not a Buddha in the sense of I can sit under a tree for a thousand years. Who can? The climate doesn't allow for it, anyway. So we need money. We need money for houses and for comfort. To relax.

PHILIP LARKIN: I was brought up to think you had to have a job, and write in your spare time, like Trollope. Then, when you started earning enough money by writing, you phase the job out. But in fact I was over fifty before I could have "lived by my writing"—and then only because I had edited a big anthology—and by that time you think, Well, I might as well get my pension, since I've gone so far.

· · ·

Poetry and sovereignty are very primitive things. I like to think of their being united in this way, in England. On the other hand, it's not clear what the Laureate is, or does. Deliberately so, in a way: it isn't a job, there are no duties, no salary, and yet it isn't quite an honor, either, or not just an honor. I'm sure the worst thing about it, especially today, is the publicity it brings, the pressure to be involved publicly with poetry, which must be pretty inimical to any real writing.

Of course, the days when Tennyson would publish a sonnet telling Gladstone what to do about foreign policy are over. It's funny that Kipling, who is what most people think of as a poet as national spokesman, never was Laureate. He should have had it when Bridges was appointed, but it's typical that he didn't—the post isn't thought of in that way. It really is a genuine attempt to honor someone. But the publicity having anything to do with the Palace is so fierce these days, it must be really more of an ordeal than an honor.

NAGUIB MAHFOUZ: The news [about the Nobel Prize] came across the tickers at Al-Ahram and they called my house. My wife woke me up to tell me, but I thought she was joking and wanted to go back to sleep. Then she told me Al-Ahram was on the phone. I picked up to hear someone saying, "Congratulations!" It was Mr. Basha. Now Mr. Basha sometimes plays jokes on me, so I didn't take him seriously. I went into the living room in my pyjamas and was just sitting down when the doorbell rang. Someone came in whom I assumed was a journalist, but he turned out to be the Swedish ambassador! So I excused myself to change . . . and that's how it happened.

EDNA O'BRIEN: I have never written anything in order to make money. A story comes to me, is given me, as it were, and I write it. But perhaps the need to earn a living and my need to write coincided. I know that I would still write if tomorrow I was given a huge legacy, and I will always be profligate.

FRANK O'CONNOR: Now, that's something I can't understand about America. It's a big, generous country, but so many students of mine seemed to think they couldn't let anyone else support them. A student of mine had this thing about you mustn't live on your father and I argued with him. I explained that a European writer would live on anybody, would live on a prostitute if he had to—it didn't matter—the great thing was to get the job done. But he didn't believe in this, so he rang up his father and told him he'd had a story refused by *The New Yorker,* and his father said, "I can keep you for the next forty years, don't you think you can get a story in *The New Yorker* in forty years?" Now, I felt the father was a man I understood and sympathized with, a decent man. But the boy felt he mustn't be supported by his father, so he came down to New York and started selling office furniture.

DOROTHY PARKER: Being in a garret doesn't do you any good unless you're some sort of a Keats. The people who lived and wrote well in the twenties were comfortable and easy-living. They were able to find stories and novels, and good ones, in conflicts that came out of two million dollars a year, not a garret. As for me, I'd like to have money. And I'd like to be a good writer. These two can come together, and I hope they will, but if that's too adorable, I'd rather have money. I hate almost all rich people, but I think I'd be darling at it. At the moment, however, I like to think of Maurice Baring's remark: "If you would know what the Lord God thinks of money, you have only to look at those to whom he gives it." I realize that's not much help when the wolf comes scratching at the door, but it's a comfort.

. . .

The art of the country so immeasurably adds to its prestige that if you want the country to have writers and artists—persons who live precariously in our country—the state must help. I do not think that any kind of artist thrives under charity, by which I mean one person or organization giving him money. Here and there, this and that—that's no good. The difference between the state giving and the individual patron is that one is charity and the other isn't. Charity is murder and you know it. But I do think that if the government supports its artists, they need have no feeling of gratitude—the meanest and most sniveling attribute in the world—or baskets being brought to them, or apple-polishing. Working for the state—for Christ's sake, are you grateful to your employers? Let the state see what its artists are trying to do—like France with the Académie Française. The artists are a part of their country and their country should recognize this, so both it and the artists can take pride in their efforts.

KATHERINE ANNE PORTER: Even Saint Teresa said, "I can pray better when I'm comfortable," and she refused to wear her haircloth shirt or starve herself. I don't think living in cellars and starving is any better for an artist than it is for anybody else; the only thing is that sometimes the artist has to take it, because it is the only possible way of salvation, if you'll forgive that old-fashioned word. So I took it rather instinctively. I was inexperienced in the world, and likewise I hadn't been trained to do anything, you know, so I took all kinds of laborious jobs. But, you know, I think I could probably have written better if I'd been a little more comfortable.

PHILIP ROTH: Recently, the first American novelist to receive a special Congressional Gold Medal for his "contribution to the nation" was Louis L'Amour. It was presented to him at the White House by the President. The only other country in the world where such a writer would receive his government's highest award is the Soviet Union. In a totalitarian state, however, *all* culture is dictated by the regime; fortunately we in America live in Reagan's and not Plato's Republic, and aside from their stupid medal, culture is almost entirely ignored. And that is preferable by far. As long as those on top keep giving the honors to Louis L'Amour and couldn't care less about anything else, everything will be just fine.

GEORGE SEFERIS: I should from the beginning tell you quite bluntly—if I can say it in English—that the Nobel Prize is an accident, no more than an accident. It's not an appointment. And I have no feeling that I have been appointed to any sort of function. It is just an accident which one has to try and forget as soon as possible. Otherwise, if you are overdazzled by that sort of thing, you get lost and founder. At the time I won the prize, there was a sort of—how can I put it in English?—a sort of Cassandra-like critic who wrote that Seferis should be very careful because he's going to be completely dried up as far as his work is concerned and even die from various illnesses since that sort of thing happens to people who have that kind of success. He was just exaggerating the one side of it, without considering, after all, what showed in the way I reacted to the prize. For example, I said in Stockholm to my judges (or whatever they are): "Gentlemen, I thank you"—this at the end of a sort of lecture I gave there—"for allowing me, after a long effort, to be *nobody*, to be unnoticed, as Homer says of Ulysses." And I was quite sincere. After all, I don't recognize the right of anybody to take you by the back of your neck and throw you into a sort of ocean of empty responsibilities. Why, that's scandalous after all.

MARY LEE SETTLE: As for money, I think that for serious writers, it's a matter of luck. Some have that luck, some don't. There is a danger in trying too hard to control it. It simply lands on people. Peter Ustinov once suggested a parlor game in London. Everyone was supposed to tell what they would do if they had a hundred thousand pounds. When it was J. B. Priestley's turn, he slowly drew on his pipe, thinking. Then he said, in his Yorkshire accent, "Ah 'ave 'undred thasand pounds."

IRWIN SHAW: When I started out, in the early 1930s, there were a great many magazines that published short stories. And writers of fiction, when they begin, are more likely to try the short form. At that time there was a great market for it, greater interest in the short story, and the young writer had a chance to practice his craft, to get criticism and meet with editors. Since that time, unfortunately, the short-story market has dwindled to almost nothing, and that form of expression has become almost obsolete for all writers in America except those who are willing to publish in small magazines or those writers who have enough of a reputation that they can use the limited space in two or three magazines throughout the country. However, from the point of view of finances, getting started as a writer has become more feasible. Although the number of newspapers has dwindled—and that used to be a field where a lot of beginning writers could serve their apprenticeship—there are many other forms that are lucrative. The chief one is television, which devours huge amounts of the written word, as does advertising and industry. The demand for quality in the writing in magazines like *Time, Newsweek,* et cetera, is attractive to bright young people of talent, and the proliferation of special-interests magazines offers a multitude of opportunities for financial security. However, those are dangerous places for writers to start in with, because the money is good and the writing quickly falls into a routine and people who had started out as serious are very likely to find themselves in a financial as well as an artistic bind, since working in those mediums is an all-day, all-week job. And they are liable to find themselves artistically exhausted when they want to work on something of their own. On the other hand, in my experience I've found that if you're young enough, *any* kind of writing you do for a short period of time—up to two years, perhaps—is a marvelous apprenticeship. I told my son, who wanted to be a writer, that his newspaper experience—he was lucky enough to get four years of newspaper experience under demanding editors on the U.P.I. and *The Washington Post*—could only help him. But you must avoid giving hostages to fortune, like getting an expensive wife, an expensive house, and a style of living that never lets you afford the time to take the chance to write what you wish. So that, while writers in general can make a living much more easily than when I first started in the 1930s, the serious writer who doesn't want to compromise at all finds it much more difficult. Still, we're fortunate enough. The other day I got a contract from a magazine in Budapest. To reprint a short story of mine they agreed to pay me fifty dollars, out of which there would be deducted a thirty percent tax, a ten percent agent's fee, and furthermore I was required to send at my own expense two books to some bureaucratic organization of the Hungarian government. You can imagine how well writers are doing in Budapest.

W. D. SNODGRASS: It's really easy to fantasize about all the things you'd like to have, you'd like to do. Then suddenly you can be all those things. You could do all the terrible things you fantasized about. There are women knocking on your door at night, lining up outside taking a number; you have money enough to live on for a change, and you can influence what books publishers take, who gets awards; you have a lot of weight to throw around. Also, you know that nobody will like your having got this. In particular, your friends, the people you counted on, are going to hate you for it. The very people you would have thought would be pleased are not. They're upset *they* didn't get it. You no longer have your lover, your wife, your best friends. They're all upset. And you know everybody hates you, because you remember how much you hated the people who got prizes before.

WENDY WASSERSTEIN: I was home, and Mark Thibodeux, the press agent for *The Heidi Chronicles,* called up and said, "You won the Pulitzer." I said, "That's not funny." He said, "No, no, I'm serious. You won the Pulitzer." I kept saying, "You're the Queen of Romania, Mark, don't do this to me." He told me to call my mother, so I did, because I thought, This woman's going to hear my name on the radio and think I died or something. I called her. She asked me, "Is that as good as a Tony?" I thought, That's my mother, undermine it, don't say congratulations, just pull the rug out from under me. I wasn't in the mood, so I said, "Why don't you just call my brother and he'll explain it to you." Then the phone started ringing off the hook, it was like the phone went up and started spinning around the room. I went out that afternoon and had champagne at the Four Seasons with my brother Bruce and sister Sandra and Walter Shapiro and André Bishop. Then I went to the theater. Edward Albee was there. He told me to go on stage and take a bow. I said I was too shy. He said that I never knew when it was going to happen again. So I did it.

MARGUERITE YOURCENAR: The Dutch have kindly elected me to their Academy, the Erasmus Institute for the Arts and Letters. Unlike its French counterpart it includes a substantial prize, half of which one has to donate to a charity. I gave mine to the World Wildlife Organization. They protested at first, saying that the Institute was for the promotion of the Arts and Letters, not lions and birds! But I said that I would have to refuse the prize unless I could make my gift, and they accepted. How sincere are the Green and Ecology parties, and how much of it is political posturing, I simply do not know. But something has to be done before it is too late. It is almost too late already, with the acid rain destroying Europe's forests and the defoliation of the tropical forests in South America.

ON READINGS: SEMINARS, CONFERENCES, ETC.

> It's a sad fact about our culture that a poet can earn much
> more money writing or talking about his art than he can by
> practicing it.
> —W. H. AUDEN

> "The time has come," the Walrus said,
> "To talk of many things:"
> —LEWIS CARROLL

> The Wedding-Guest sat on a stone:
> He cannot choose but hear.
> —SAMUEL TAYLOR COLERIDGE

ELIZABETH BISHOP: I'm not very fond of poetry readings. I'd much rather read the book. I know I'm wrong. I've only been to a few poetry readings I could *bear*. Of course, you're too young to have gone through the Dylan Thomas craze. . . .

When it was somebody like Cal Lowell or Marianne Moore, it's as if they were my children. I'd get terribly upset. I went to hear Marianne several times and finally I just couldn't go because I'd sit there with tears running down my face. I don't know, it's sort of embarrassing. You're so afraid they'll do something wrong.

Cal thought that the most important thing about readings was the remarks poets made in between the poems. The first time I heard him read was years ago at the New School for Social Research in a small, grey auditorium. It was with Allen Tate and Louise Bogan. Cal was very much younger than anybody else and had published just two books. He read a long, endless poem—I've forgotten its title*—about a Canadian nun in

---

* "Mother Marie Therese" in *The Mills of the Kavanaughs*.

New Brunswick. I've forgotten what the point of the poem is, but it's very, very long and it's quite beautiful, particularly in the beginning. Well, he started, and he read very badly. He kind of droned and everybody was trying to get it. He had gotten about two-thirds of the way through when somebody yelled, "Fire!" There was a small fire in the lobby, nothing much, that was put out in about five minutes and everybody went back to their seats. Poor Cal said, "I think I'd better begin over again," so he read the whole thing all over again! But his reading got much, much better in later years.

JAMES DICKEY: It sure killed off poor Dylan Thomas. He didn't write even *one* poem in the last six years of his life. Everybody adored him, paid him a lot of money; why should he write another book of *poems,* and maybe give the critics a shot at him that would lower his reading fee? Everybody *loved* him; he was screwing all the coeds in America, drinking all the whiskey, and he'd get up there and read his poems, and then he'd go on and read them somewhere else. He got a lot of dough for it. I mean, what incentive for him to write *was* there? To survive, a poet has to find some way of maintaining his original enthusiasm for *poetry,* not for the by-products of poetry, not for the fringe benefits of poetry, but for *it.*

ELIZABETH HARDWICK: I do remember saying once [at a reading] that maybe the greatest female novelist in English was Constance Garnett. Sometimes I try to lighten the gloom of discussions but I notice that no one laughs. Instead you see a few people writing down the name.

PHILIP LARKIN: I don't give readings, no, although I have recorded three of my collections, just to show how *I* should read them. Hearing a poem, as opposed to reading it on the page, means you miss so much— the shape, the punctuation, the italics, even knowing how far you are from the end. Reading it on the page means you can go your own pace, taking it in properly; hearing it means you're dragged along at the speaker's own rate, missing things, not taking it in, confusing "there" and "their" and things like that. And the speaker may interpose his own personality between you and the poem, for better or worse. For that matter, so may the audience. I don't like hearing things in public, even music. In fact, I think poetry readings grew up on a false analogy with music: the text is the "score" that doesn't "come to life" until it's "performed." It's false because people can read words, whereas they can't read music. When you write a poem, you put everything into it that's needed: the reader should "hear" it just as clearly as if you were in the room saying it to him. And of course this fashion for poetry readings has led to a kind of poetry that you *can* understand first go: easy rhythms, easy emotions, easy syntax. I don't think it stands up on the page.

JAMES LAUGHLIN: Eliot told someone that when he gave a poetry reading he always felt it was a kind of indecent exposure.

DORIS LESSING: Oh, Germany last year, my God! That was the most disastrous trip. It was at some academic institution in Germany. I said to them, "Look, I want to do what I always do. I'll read the story and then I'll take questions." They said, the way they always do, "Oh, you can't expect the Germans to ask questions." I said, "Look, just let me handle this, because I know how." Anyway, what happened was typical in Germany: we met at four o'clock in order to discuss the meeting that was going to take place at eight. They cannot stand any ambiguity or disorder—no, no! Can't bear it. I said, "Look, just leave it." The auditorium was very large and I read a story in English and it went down very well, perfectly okay. I said, "I will now take questions." Then this bank of four bloody professors started to put questions to me, these immensely long academic questions of such tedium that finally the audience started to get up and drift out. A young man, a student sprawled on the gangway—as a professor finished something immensely long—called out, "BLAH, BLAH, BLAH, BLAH, BLAH." So with total lack of concern for the professors' feelings I said, "Look, I will take questions in English from the audience." So they all came back and sat down, and it went well . . . perfectly lively questions! The professors were absolutely furious. So that was Germany. Germany's the worst, it really is; the end.

MARIANNE MOORE: During the French program at Mount Holyoke one afternoon Wallace Stevens had a discourse, the one about Goethe dancing, on a packet-boat in black wool stockings. My mother and I were there; and I gave a reading with commentary. Henry Church had an astoundingly beautiful Panama hat—a sort of pork-pie with a wide brim, a little like Bernard Berenson's hats. I have never seen as fine a weave, and he had a pepper-and-salt shawl which he draped about himself. This lecture was on the lawn.

Wallace Stevens was extremely friendly. We should have had a tape recorder on that occasion, for at lunch they seated us all at a kind of refectory table and a girl kept asking him questions such as, "Mr. Stevens have you read the—*Four—Quartets?*"

"Of course, but I can't read much of Eliot or I wouldn't have any individuality of my own."

PABLO NERUDA: I remember that Federico García Lorca was always asking me to read my lines, my poetry, and yet in the middle of my reading, he would say, "Stop, stop! Don't go on, lest you influence me!"

WILLIAM STAFFORD: Recently I've come to realize that for many people the reading of their own poems to a group is a kind of breakthrough. It's a kind of achievement of participation in society. Apparently that's important. I didn't feel it myself, partly because readings didn't become popular until after I'd been writing for a long time. By then my pattern was already set, and I didn't feel elation about reading. I just felt that if they were ready to hear it, I was ready to read it. If they want to pay me, great; it means I'll travel well.

P. L. TRAVERS: One day the head of Administration House asked me if I would give a talk to the Indians. And I said, "How could I talk to them, these ancient people? It is they who could tell me things." He said, "Try." So they came into what I suppose was a clubhouse, a big place with a stage, and I stood on the stage and the place was full of Indians. I told them about England, because she was at war then, and all that was happening. I said that for me England was the place "Where the Sun Rises" because, you see, England is east of where I was. I said, "Over large water." And I told them about the children who were being evacuated from the cities and some of the experiences of the children. I put it as mythologically as I could, just very simple sayings.

At the end there was dead silence. I turned to the man who had introduced me and said, "I'm sorry. I failed. I haven't got across." And he said, "You wait. You don't know them as well as I do." And every Indian in that big hall came up and took me silently by the hand, one after another. That was their way of expressing feeling with me.

DEREK WALCOTT: It was at the Guggenheim. I was staying at the Chelsea Hotel, and that day I felt I needed a haircut, so, foolishly, I went around the corner and sat down. The barber took the electric razor and gave me one of the wildest haircuts I think I've ever had. It infuriated me, but you can't put your hair back on. I even thought of wearing a hat. But I went on anyway, my head looked like hell. I had gotten some distance into the reading—I was reading "A Far Cry from Africa"—when suddenly there was the sound of applause from the auditorium. Now I had never heard applause at a poetry reading before. I don't think I'd ever given a formal poetry reading, and I thought for some reason that the applause was saying it was time to stop, that they thought it was over. So I walked off the stage. I felt in a state of shock. I actually walked off feeling the clapping was their way of saying, "Well, thank you, it's been nice." Someone in charge asked me to go back and finish the reading, but I said no. I must have sounded extremely arrogant, but I felt that if I went back out there it would have been conceited. I went back to Trinidad.

RICHARD WILBUR: Every now and then there are certain people to whom I show poems, and who show poems to me: Bill Meredith, Bill Smith, John Brinnin, and Cal Lowell, when he's around—we aren't in the same place at present. But that's just one-on-one. The last time I found myself involved in anything groupy was about seven years ago when Stephen Spender was staying at Wesleyan and certain people on the Wesleyan faculty were interested in reading poems to each other. Stephen, with his usual generosity—of course this wasn't part of any deal he'd signed on to do—joined the group. I suppose there were five or six meetings. We'd go around in a circle and everybody would read at least one poem.

One evening Stephen invited I. A. Richards to come, and Richards had not understood the character of the invitation. He hadn't realized he was going to have to listen to a lot of people read poems, one after the other, and then discuss them. And as soon as that became clear, he did the most glorious thing. He simply stood up and said, "Oh no, no, no. I'm sorry, no, I'm sorry, I can't. Good night! Good night!" and out he went. He didn't have any evidence that any particular, horrible poem was going to be read, but he thought the chances were pretty good and he didn't see why, at his age, he had to sit and listen to it.

ON POLITICS

King Louis Philippe once said to me that he attributed the great success of the British nation in political life to their talking politics after dinner.　—BENJAMIN DISRAELI

Nothing is more dangerous to the state than persons who try to govern kingdoms according to maxims drawn from books.
　　　　　　　　　　　　　　　　　　　　　　　—RICHELIEU

For a country to have a great writer is like having a second government. That is why no regime has ever loved great writers, only minor writers.　—ALEXANDER SOLZHENITSYN

If you ask me what I have come to do in the world, I who am an artist, I will reply: "I am here to live aloud."
　　　　　　　　　　　　　　　　　　　　　　　—ÉMILE ZOLA

CHINUA ACHEBE: I don't lay down the law for anybody else. But I think writers are not only writers, they are also citizens. They are generally adults. My position is that serious and good art has always existed to help, to serve, humanity. Not to indict. I don't see how art can be called art if its purpose is to frustrate humanity. To make humanity uncomfortable, yes. But intrinsically to be against humanity, that I don't take. This is why I find racism impossible, because this is against humanity. Some people think, Well, what he's saying is we must praise his people." For God's sake! Go and read my books. I don't praise my people. I am their greatest critic. Some people think my little pamphlet, *The Trouble with Nigeria*, went too far. I've got into all kinds of trouble for my writing. Art should be on the side of humanity. I think it was Yevtushenko talking about Rimbaud, the Frenchman who went to Ethiopia and came back with all kinds of diseases. Yevtushenko said of him that a poet cannot become a slave trader. When Rimbaud became a slave trader, he stopped writing poetry. Poetry and slave trading cannot be bedfellows. That's where I stand.

W. H. AUDEN: I have had very little contact with [politicians]. I knew some undergraduates, of course, while I was at Oxford, who eventually made it—Hugh Gaitskell, Crossman, and so forth. I think we should do very well without politicians. Our leaders should be elected by lot. The people could vote their conscience, and the computers could take care of the rest. Writers seldom make good leaders. They're self-employed, for one thing, and they have very little contact with their customers. It's very easy for a writer to be unrealistic. I have not lost my interest in politics, but I have come to realise that, in cases of social or political injustice, only two things are effective: political action and straight journalistic reportage of the facts. The arts can do nothing. The social and political history of Europe would be what it has been if Dante, Shakespeare, Michelangelo, Mozart, et al., had never lived. A poet, *qua* poet, has only one political duty, namely, in his own writing to set an example of the correct use of his mother tongue which is always being corrupted. When words lose their meaning, physical force takes over. By all means, let a poet, if he wants to, write what is now called an "*engagé*" poem, so long as he realizes that it is mainly himself who will benefit from it. It will enhance his literary reputation among those who feel the same as he does.

JOHN BARTH: I don't think that as a group we'd be any better at running the world than the people who are botching it up. Poetry makes nothing happen. Politically committed artists like Gabriel García Márquez give honest voice to their political passion at no great cost to the quality control of their art. But do they really change the world? I doubt it, I doubt it, Abraham Lincoln's remark to Harriet Beecher Stowe notwithstanding: "So you're the little woman who wrote the book that made this great war!" Well, she didn't. No: without sounding too terribly decadent about it, I much prefer the late Vladimir Nabokov's remark about what he wanted from his novels: "aesthetic bliss." Well, that *does* sound too decadent. Let me change masters for a moment and say that I prefer Henry James's remark that the first obligation of the writer—which I would also regard as his last obligation—is to be interesting, *to be interesting.* To be interesting in one beautiful sentence after another. To be interesting, not to change the world.

SIMONE DE BEAUVOIR: Hemingway was never deeply committed, so he thinks that what is eternal in literature is what isn't dated, isn't committed. I don't agree. In the case of many writers, it's also their political stand which makes me like or dislike them. There aren't many writers of former times whose work was really committed. And although one reads Rousseau's *Social Contract* as eagerly as one reads his *Confessions,* one no longer reads *The New Héloïse.*

JAMES DICKEY: A poet is only a professional sensibility. His opinion in politics is no better than anyone else's ninety-nine percent of the time. But they're always being interviewed and always being asked their political opinion: what should we do with the military, what should we do with the economy, with government spending, et cetera. Poets don't know anything about that. If they did, they wouldn't be poets. This is not to say that they are precluded from knowing anything about it at *all;* it is to say, however, that just because they are poets their opinions should not be paid any more attention to than anybody else's. It does not give them any privilege or any insight or any clairvoyance as to the political and economic and military future of America.

. . .

Poetry *can* speak on topical things eloquently. Look at Yeats on the riots of 1916, for example. But we should not be led into the corner of assuming that poetry is no good which does not speak on news items. If a man wants to write about the circle that's made in the water when a fish jumps, he should be able to write about that and should not be charged off as irrelevant because he's not writing about the Vietnam riots. You should have the whole gamut: political action, the jump of the fish, or the space program. You should have anything you want.

JOHN DOS PASSOS: Recently, I've been calling my novels contemporary chronicles, which seems to fit them rather better. They have a strong political bent because after all—although it isn't the only thing—politics in our time has pushed people around more than anything else. I don't see why dealing with politics should harm a writer at all. Despite what he said about politics in the novel being "the pistol shot at the opera," Stendhal also wrote contemporary chronicles. Or look at Thucydides. I don't think his history was at all damaged by the fact that he was a political writer. A lot of very good writing has been more or less involved in politics, although it's always a dangerous territory. It's better for some people to keep out unless they're willing to learn how to observe. It is the occupation of a special kind of writer. His investigation—using blocks of raw experience—must be balanced. Sartre in his straight, plain reporting was wonderful. I can't read him now. A writer in this field should be both engaged and disengaged. He must have passion and concern and anger—but he must keep his emotions at arm's length in his work. If he doesn't, he's simply a propagandist and what he offers is a "preachment."

CARLOS FUENTES: We have to do more things in our culture than American writers do in theirs. They can have more time for themselves and for their writing, whereas we have social demands. Pablo Neruda used to say that every Latin American writer goes around dragging a heavy body, the body of his people, of his past, of his national history. We have to assimilate the enormous weight of our past so we will not forget what gives us life. If you forget your past, you die. You fulfill certain functions for the collectivity because they are obligations you have as a citizen, not as a writer. Despite that, you reserve your esthetic freedom and your esthetic privileges. This creates a tension, but I think it is better to have the tension than to have no tension at all, as sometimes happens in the United States.

SEAMUS HEANEY: I think the poet who didn't feel the pressure at a politically difficult time would be either stupid or insensitive. I take great comfort in this regard from a formulation of Robert Pinsky's in his essay on the responsibility of the poet. He relates the word *responsibility* to its origin in *response* and then to its Anglo-Saxon equivalent in the word *answer*. Pinsky says that as long as you feel the need to answer you are being responsible, because it's in the ground of one's answering being that the responsibility of the poet is lodged. How you actually deliver the answer, of course, is something else. There's a temperament involved. And there's the crucial matter of artistic ability whether you are artistically fit to take on what is often recalcitrant subject matter.

I do think politics can be affected. I think there's far too much mealy-mouthedness about that. Auden's remark that poetry makes nothing happen is used too often to foreclose the question. I do believe, for example, that Robert Lowell had a political effect. I'm not saying that because of the thematic content of his work, but because he had established a profile and an authority as a poet. Lowell manifested a kind of *gravitas*. His enemies might say he represented portentousness, but that's neither here nor there. There was a sense that he stood for something. When he intervened in public matters, when he decided to decline an invitation from the White House, say, that had a political effect. And when he took part in the march on the Pentagon, it had meaning because of the regard in which he was held, as poet and patrician. Come to think of it, Philip Larkin had a definite political influence also. He fortified a certain kind of recalcitrant Englishness. His masquerade encouraged a strain of xenophobia and a strain of philistinism in English life. I'm not saying there's anything philistine about his melodies. But there was nothing admirable in his pronouncements about art and life, all those statements to the effect of, "Oh, I don't know. I just love Margaret Thatcher. I don't read poetry in translation and I would never dream of going abroad." That kind of lowest-common-denominator stuff, that kind of thing actually works itself into the culture. Larkin's antiheroics and his absconding from anything visionary or bold did have its effect. And I would say that Hugh MacDiarmid had an effect too—very different—in Scotland. Norman MacCaig once said that the Scottish nation should observe two minutes of pandemonium every year on the anniversary of MacDiarmid's death. In Ireland, of course, we observe two weeks of summer school every year in memory of Yeats. And rightly so.

MARK HELPRIN: You can imagine how well I and my work are received in academic circles, when I assert plainly and without apology that deconstructionism, like Nazism or Stalinism, is less a system of thought than a sign of mental illness. In 1975, I went to visit Roger Rosenblatt at *The New Republic* in Washington. He had been one of my teachers at Harvard, and Marty Peretz had been a tutor in Kirkland House, where I had lived briefly a decade before. Roger reintroduced me to Marty by saying, "You remember Helprin, don't you? From the asylum?"

He was making a joke that then came true. I had always wondered what would happen to people who spent six to ten years laboring on a five-hundred-page tome entitled *Vaginal Motifs in Etruscan Beekeeping,* and now I know. They go stark raving mad, and then they get tenure. In an accident of history, the American university system mistakenly modeled itself after the German rather than the English and then distorted even that. The greatest sin in American academia is to make a generalization. That's why Oxford and Cambridge seem so civilized in comparison: there, they recognize that life, history, even the deeper currents of science, are terms of art. Here, on the other hand, you spend the best years of your life grinding away at vaginal motifs in Etruscan beekeeping, and when it comes time for independent thinking you're about as ready as the lid of a garbage can.

I don't want to beat a dead horse to death, and I do want to return to your line of inquiry, so let me say in summary that relativism and politicization have so smothered the universities and the world of publishing that to state, as I do, that it is possible to serve universal ideals and appeal, nonpolitically, to the fundamental needs of human nature by addressing its fundamental questions, is perceived as heresy. The end and the beginning of it is that I dissent from the dominant orthodoxies that cradle the profession I practice, that, despite what some assert, I have never been shy about it, and that, therefore, I find myself not only out of the mainstream, but playing the role, at times, of moving target. As I have an activist nature, I fire back. I confess, even, that I have often opened fire before being fired upon, as I would, for example, were I to come upon a platoon of the SS or terrorists about to attack a school.

ERNEST HEMINGWAY: Everyone has his own conscience, and there should be no rules about how a conscience should function. All you can be sure about in a political-minded writer is that if his work should last you will have to skip the politics when you read it. Many of the so-called politically enlisted writers change their politics frequently. This is very exciting to them and to their political-literary reviews. Sometimes they even have to rewrite their viewpoints ... and in a hurry. Perhaps it can be respected as a form of the pursuit of happiness.

MARIO VARGAS LLOSA: A writer cannot put literature and politics on an equal footing without failing as a writer and perhaps also as a politician. We must remember that political action is rather ephemeral whereas literature is in for the duration. You don't write a book for the present day; in order for a work to exert influence over the future, time must play its role, which is never or rarely the case for political actions. However, even as I say this, I never stop passing judgments on the political climate or implicating myself by what I write and what I do. I believe that a writer cannot avoid political involvement, especially in countries like mine where the problems are difficult and the economic and social situation often has dramatic aspects. It's very important that writers act in one way or another, by offering criticism, ideas, by using their imagination in order to contribute to the solution of the problems. I think it's crucial that writers show—because like all artists, they sense this more strongly than anyone—the importance of freedom for the society as well as for the individual. Justice, which we all wish to rule, should never become disassociated from freedom; and we must never accept the notion that freedom should at certain times be sacrificed in the name of social justice or national security, as totalitarians from the extreme left and reactionaries from the extreme right would have us do. Writers know this because every day they sense the degree to which freedom is necessary for creation, for life itself. Writers should defend their freedom as a necessity like a fair salary or the right to work.

But while I think it's important that writers participate, make judgments, and intervene, also they should not let politics invade and destroy the literary sphere, the writer's creative domain. When that happens, it kills the writer, making him nothing more than a propagandist. It is therefore crucial that he put limits on his political activities without renouncing or stripping himself of his duty to voice his opinion.

PABLO NERUDA: What I would never advise [young poets] to do is to begin with political poetry. Political poetry is more profoundly emotional than any other—at least as much as love poetry—and cannot be forced because it then becomes vulgar and unacceptable. It is necessary first to pass through all other poetry in order to become a political poet. The political poet must also be prepared to accept the censure which is thrown at him—betraying poetry, or betraying literature. Then, too, political poetry has to arm itself with such content and substance and intellectual and emotional richness that it is able to scorn everything else. This is rarely achieved.

GEORGE SEFRIS: I don't like people who try to express worldviews in writing poetry. I remember once I had a reading in Thessalonik, and a philosopher stood up and asked: "But what, after all, Mr. Seferis, is your worldview?" And I said: "My dear friend, I'm sorry to say that I have no worldview. I have to make this public confession to you that I am writing without having any world view. I don't know, perhaps you find that scandalous, sir, but may I ask you to tell me what Homer's world view is?" And I didn't get an answer.

GARY SNYDER: The whole history of Chinese poetry is full of great poets who played a role in their society. Indeed, I do too. I am on committees in my county. I have always taken on some roles that were there for me to take in local politics, and I believe deeply in civic life. But I don't think that as a writer I could move on to a state or national scale of politics and remain a writer. My choice is to remain a writer.

STEPHEN SPENDER: Always at the beginning of a war thére is a demand from editors that poets should write war poetry. This comes from a recognition that, in a situation in which patriotic feelings are required, poetry may stimulate those feelings. I imagine the sonnets of Rupert Brooke at the beginning of the First World War probably did make some people join up to fight the Germans. During the Spanish Civil War, the poetry that was written probably helped the International Brigade. Then in a much wider sense poetry can be politically effective as well. Surely one can trace the sources of the movement for Italian unity to the fact that Dante decided to write *The Divine Comedy* in idiomatic Italian and not in Latin, which would have been the correct thing for him to have done. And Goethe, who created, really all by himself, modern German literature, also contributed greatly to the idea of German unity through doing this. He created a German culture and taught Germans that they could respect themselves in relation to France, especially, and other countries.

But I think it is wrong to believe that poetry is really very effective in politics. And politics can certainly be very bad for poetry. I was discussing this with Denise Levertov when she was here. She read a political poem, which was based on her visiting Hanoi and being taken 'round by the North Vietnamese to see damage done to hospitals by American aircraft. Of course she had extremely strong feelings about this, and I don't want to call it just a propaganda operation on the part of the North Vietnamese, but somehow to enter almost as a tourist into that kind of suffering and to make propaganda out of it is not what a poet should be doing. For a journalist it's all right, but a poet has to go in for an act of the imagination, which is on a deeper level. I mean, if you penetrate to the depths of the suffering, you see that it is not just inflicted by one side; it's something that human beings do to one another. Also if you write what one has to call propaganda poetry, you lay yourself open to a kind of argument which is all right in politics but which oughtn't to occur in poetry. Someone will say, "Well, if the North Vietnamese had had airplanes, they'd have done the same thing," which you can't really dispute. I don't think that poets ought to get themselves into that kind of argument.

There are, of course, political situations so absolutely unspeakable that they become quite literally unimaginable. It would be impertinent, for example, to imagine what was happening in the concentration camps during the 1930s and 1940s. The only way to know that suffering was to be a part of it, but if you became a part of it, you were destroyed. As a matter of fact, at the end of the concentration camp era, when various poets, particularly in Poland, emerged from the camps, they hated poetry. They regarded poetry as the greatest betrayal because it always in some way offers pleasure. It would therefore have to extract some kind of comfort, something pleasurable, from all these horrors. And so they started writing what they called anti-poetry.

WILLIAM STYRON: It seems to me that only a great satirist can tackle the world problems and articulate them. Most writers write simply out of some strong interior need, and that I think is the answer. A great writer, writing out of this need, will give substance to and perhaps even explain all the problems of the world without even knowing it, until a scholar comes along a hundred years after he's dead and digs up some symbols. The purpose of a young writer is to write, and he shouldn't think too much. He shouldn't think that after he's written one book he's God Almighty and air all his immature opinions in pompous interviews.

ON TEACHING: ADVICE, WRITING
COURSES, ETC.

You shouldn't pay very much attention to anything writers say. They don't know why they do what they do. They're like good tennis players or good painters, who are just full of nonsense, pompous and embarrassing, or merely mistaken, when they open their mouths. —JOHN BARTH

The wise may be instructed by a fool. —RABELAIS

Everyone who does not *need* to be a writer, who thinks he can do something else, ought to do something else.
—GEORGES SIMENON

Don't offer me advice. Offer me money. —SPANISH PROVERB

Agassiz *does* recommend authors to eat fish, because the phosphorus in it makes brains. But I cannot help you to a decision about the amount you need to eat. Perhaps a couple of whales would be enough. —MARK TWAIN

Teaching has ruined more American novelists than drink.
—GORE VIDAL

JOHN ASHBERY: I try to avoid the well-known cliché that you learn from your students. Neither do I believe that there's something ennobling for a writer to teach, that it's narcissistic to spend time wallowing in your writing when you could be out helping in the world's work. Writers should write, and poets especially spend altogether too much time at other tasks such as teaching. However, since so many of us have to do it, there are certain things to be said for it. You are forced to bring a critical attention into play when you are reading students' work that you would not use otherwise, and that can help when you return to your own writing. And being immersed in a group of young unproven writers who are fiercely serious about what they are doing can have a chastening effect sometimes on us blasé oldsters. Besides, they may be writing great poetry, only nobody knows it because nobody has seen it yet. I sometimes think that the "greatness" my friends and I used to see in each other's poetry when we were very young had a lot to do with the fact that it was unknown. It could turn out to be anything; the possibilities were limitless, more so than when we were at last discovered and identified and pinned down in our books.

W. H. AUDEN: If I had to "teach poetry," which, thank God, I don't, I would concentrate on prosody, rhetoric, philology, and learning poems by heart. I may be quite wrong, but I don't see what can be learned except purely technical things—what a sonnet is, something about prosody. If you did have a poetic academy, the subjects should be quite different—natural history, history, theology, all kinds of other things. When I've been at colleges, I've always insisted on giving ordinary academic courses—on the Eighteenth Century, or Romanticism. True, it's wonderful what the colleges have done as patrons of the artists. But the artists should agree not to have anything to do with contemporary literature. If they take academic positions, they should do academic work, and the further they get away from the kind of thing that directly affects what they're writing, the better. They should teach the Eighteenth Century, or something that won't interfere with their work and yet earn them a living. To teach Creative Writing—I think that's dangerous. The only possibility I can conceive of is an apprentice system like those they had in the Renaissance—where a poet who was very busy got students to finish his poems for him. Then you'd *really* be teaching, and you'd be responsible, of course, since the results would go out under the poet's name.

JAMES BALDWIN: If you are going to be a writer there is nothing I can say to stop you; if you're not going to be a writer nothing I can say will help you. What you really need at the beginning is somebody to let you know that the effort is real.

J. G. BALLARD: A lifetime's experience urges me to utter a warning cry: do anything else, take someone's golden retriever for a walk, run away with a saxophone player. Perhaps what's wrong with being a writer is that one can't even say "good luck"—luck plays no part in the writing of a novel. No happy accidents as with the paint pot or chisel. I don't think you can say anything, really. I've always wanted to juggle and ride a unicycle, but I dare say if I ever asked the advice of an acrobat he would say, "All you do is get on and start pedaling. . . ."

JOHN BARTH: I happen to think there's some justification for having courses in so-called creative writing. I know from happy experience with young writers that the muses make no distinction between undergraduates and graduate students. The muses know only expert writers and less expert writers. A beginner—such as I was when, with the swamp still on my shoes, I came into Johns Hopkins as an undergraduate—needs to be taught that literature is there; here are some examples of it, and here's how the great writers do it. That's teaching. In time, a writer, or any artist, stops making mistakes on a crude, first level, and begins making mistakes on the next, more elevated level. And then finally you begin to make your mistakes on the highest level—let's say the upper slopes of slippery Parnassus—and it's at that point you need coaching. Now sometimes coaching means advising the skier to come down off the advanced slope and back to the bunny hill for a while, back to the snowplow. One must be gentle about it. To shift metaphors violently, one must understand that the house of fiction has many windows; you don't want to defenestrate your young apprentices. But sometimes such a simple thing as suggesting to a student that perhaps realism instead of fantasy may be a more sympathetic genre, or humor instead of the opposite, or the novel rather than the short story—sometimes a simple suggestion like that can be the one that makes things click. It doesn't always.

· · ·

As an undergraduate I had a couple of tutors in writing who were not themselves writers. They were simply good coaches. I've thought of that in a chastened way since. Dealing with my own students, many of whom are very skillful, advanced apprentice writers, I often wonder whether it's a good idea for them to have, at the other end of the table, somebody who's already working at a certain level of success and notoriety. Is that not perhaps intimidating? I just don't know, but I suspect the trade-off is fair enough. I might have learned some things faster had I been working with an established writer rather than a very sympathetic coach.

DONALD BARTHELME: I've just read an article that strongly implies that teaching writing is a dismal racket, an impoverishing fraud, and maybe it is as practiced in some venues, but I'd hate this to be taken as generally true. At City College, where I teach a graduate workshop, the writing students are fully the equals in seriousness and accomplishment of the other graduate students. Maybe writing can't be taught, but editing *can* be taught—prayer, fasting, and self-mutilation. Notions of the lousy can be taught. Ethics.

All of this is new in universities, didn't exist when I was in school, but it's hardly a racket.

JOHN BERRYMAN: It depends on the kind of teaching you do. If you teach creative writing, you get absolutely nothing out of it. Or English— what are you teaching? People you read twenty years ago. Maybe you pick up a little if you keep on preparing, but very few people keep on preparing. Everybody is lazy, and poets, in addition to being lazy, have another activity which is very demanding, so they tend to slight their teaching. But I give courses in the history of civilization, and when I first began teaching here I nearly went crazy. I was teaching Christian origins and the Middle Ages, and I had certain weak spots. I was O.K. with *The Divine Comedy* and certain other things, but I had an awful time of it. I worked it out once, and it took me nine hours to prepare a fifty-minute lecture. I have learned much more from giving these lecture courses than I ever learned at Columbia or Cambridge. It has forced me out into areas where I wouldn't otherwise have been, and since I am a scholar, these things are connected I make myself acquainted with the scholarship. Suppose I'm lecturing on Augustine. My Latin is very rusty, but I'll pay a certain amount of attention to the Latin text in the Loeb edition, with the English across the page. Then I'll visit the library and consult five or six old and recent works on St. Augustine, who is a particular interest of mine, anyway. Now all that becomes part of your equipment for poetry, even for lyric poetry. The Bradstreet poem is a very learned poem. There is a lot of theology in it, there is a lot of theology in *The Dream Songs*. Anything is useful to a poet. Take observation of nature, of which I have absolutely none. It makes possible a world of moral observation for Frost, or Hopkins. So scholarship and teaching are directly useful to my activity as a writer.

HAROLD BLOOM: I suppose that they [creative writing courses] do more good than harm, and yet it baffles me. Writing seems to me so much an art of solitude. Criticism is a teachable art, but like every art it too finally depends upon an inherent or implicit gift. I remember remarking somewhere in something I wrote that I gave up going to the Modern Language Association some years ago because the idea of a convention of twenty-five or thirty thousand critics is every bit as hilarious as the idea of going to a convention of twenty-five thousand poets or novelists. There *aren't* twenty-five thousand critics. I frequently wonder if there are *five* critics alive at any one time. The extent to which the art of fiction or the art of poetry is teachable is a more complex problem. Historically, we know how poets become poets and fiction writers become fiction writers. They read. They read their predecessors, and they learn what is to be learned. The idea of Herman Melville in a writing class is always distressing to me.

CAMILO JOSÉ CELA: I don't give advice to anyone; let each person make his own mistakes.

AMY CLAMPITT: If you had to construct a poet out of whole cloth, I think it goes without saying that you'd start with someone who refused to grow up. I don't know exactly why that's important, except that if you're totally grown up, you're somehow set in your emotional ways so that you're not surprised in the kinds of ways that poets tend to be.

GABRIEL GARCÍA MÁRQUEZ: If I had to give a young writer some advice I would say to write about something that has happened to him; it's always easy to tell whether a writer is writing about something that has happened to him or something he has read or been told. Pablo Neruda has a line in a poem that says "God help me from inventing when I sing." It always amuses me that the biggest praise for my work comes for the imagination while the truth is that there's not a single line in all my work that does not have a basis in reality. The problem is that Caribbean reality resembles the wildest imagination.

JOHN GARDNER: When you teach creative writing, you discover a great deal. For instance, if a student's story is really wonderful, but thin, you have to analyze to figure out why it's thin; how you could beef it up. Every discovery of that kind is important. When you're reading only classical and medieval literature, all the bad stuff has been filtered out. There are no bad works in either Greek or Anglo-Saxon. Even the ones that are minor are the very best of the minor, because everything else has been lost or burned or thrown away. When you read this kind of literature, you never really learn how a piece can go wrong, but when you teach creative writing, you see a thousand ways that a piece can go wrong. So it's helpful to me. The other thing that's helpful when you're teaching creative writing is that there are an awful lot of people who at the age of seventeen or eighteen can write as well as you do. That's a frightening discovery. So you ask yourself, what am I doing? Here I've decided that what I'm going to be in life is to be this literary artist, at best; I'm going to stand with Tolstoy, Melville, and all the boys. And there's this kid, nineteen, who's writing just as well. The characters are vividly perceived, the rhythm in the story is wonderful. What have I got that he hasn't got? You begin to think harder and harder about what makes great fiction. That can lead you to straining and over-blowing your own fiction, which I've done sometimes, but it's useful to think about.

· · ·

I hate nihilistic, cynical writing. I hate it. It bothers me and worse yet bores me. But if I have a student who writes with morbid delight about murder, what I'll have to do (though of course I'll tell him I don't like this kind of writing, that it's immoral, stupid, and bad for civilization) is say what is successful about the work and what is not. I have to swallow every bit of my moral feelings to help the writer write his way, his truth. It may be that the most moral writing of all is writing which shows us how a murderer feels, how it happens. It may be it will protect us from murderers someday.

· · ·

Working with intelligent undergraduate and graduate students—and working alongside intelligent teachers—I have a clear idea of my audience, or anyway of a hypothetical audience. I don't think a writer can write well without some such notions. One may claim one writes for oneself, but it's a paltry claim. One more word on all this, I'm obviously convinced that my scholarly career has made me a better writer than I would have been without it, but I'm no longer concerned—as I was in my tempestuous, ego-maddened youth—with proving myself the greatest writer of all time. What I notice now is that all around me there are first-rate writers, and in nearly every case it seems to me that what makes them first-rate is their similar involvement in teaching and scholarship. There are exceptions—maybe William Gaddis, I'm not sure. (A brilliant writer, though I disapprove of him.) Perhaps the most important exception is

John Updike, who, unlike John Hawkes, Bill Gass, Stanley Elkin and Saul Bellow and so on, is not a teacher. But the exception means nothing, because, teacher or not, he's the most academic of all.

WILLIAM GASS: I resent spending a lot of time on lousy stuff. If somebody is reading a bad paper in a seminar, it is nevertheless on Plato, and it is Plato we can talk about. Whereas if somebody is writing about their hunting trip—well—where can one go for salvation or relief? Creative-writing teachers, poor souls, must immerse themselves in slop and even take it seriously. Since I can't bear it, resent it, I shouldn't teach it. It is probably impossible to teach anyone to be a good writer. You can teach people how to read, possibly.

I am also aware of how little I can tolerate other people telling me how to write. So why should I do it to my students? I do not invite or accept this sort of personal criticism. I usually have poor to absent relations with editors because they have a habit of desiring changes and I resist changes. So why should I tell students to make changes? I also remember how bad I was. I wrote far worse stuff than I see from students. What can I fairly say to them?

WILLIAM GOYEN: Teaching writing is draining too, of course. Especially the way I do it. You see, I believe that everybody can write. And in believing and teaching this, what happens, of course, is enormous productivity on the part of many students. One's students produce so much that he is followed down the street by the mass of stuff he's encouraged! I mean, he's overtaken by it. And there's that much more work to do and more conferences to hold, and it's a depleting and exhausting thing. Just as exhausting as editing.

SEAMUS HEANEY: There is something perilous about teaching if you are a poet. You are cushioned from a certain exhilarating exposure to risk when you have a salary and a "situation in life." But it's better to recognize that and get on with the job than to live on the cushion and still go around pretending that you are somehow a free bohemian spirit. Some writers within the academy have this *nous autres, les écrivains* attitude, taking their big stipend and all their freebies and travel grants and Guggenheims but manifesting a kind of *mauvaise foi* by not admitting that their attachment to the academy is their own decision, as it were, and instead just going around mocking this dreary milieu they have opted for. It's an understandable defense mechanism, but it gets on my nerves. It's a sign that they have fallen for the myth of their own creativity. And that they're too anxious about that public perception you ask about—since the myth prescribes the garret rather than the Guggenheim.

ERNEST HEMINGWAY: Let's say that he [an apprentice] should go out and hang himself because he finds that writing well is impossibly difficult. Then he should be cut down without mercy and forced by his own self to write as well as he can for the rest of his life. At least he will have the story of the hanging to commence with.

JOHN HERSEY: There's long been argument among writers about whether they should let themselves be captured by the academic world, whether they don't stultify there, and so on. I have always had the view that it really doesn't matter what a writer does; the argument that you should go out and meet raw life, work on the crew of a freighter, take part in revolutions and what not, doesn't seem to me valid. What matters is how a writer responds to the life around him. When I arrived in Pierson that first term, I had thought of the university [Yale] as an ivory tower, and had been afraid that if I was incarcerated there I would stagnate. But in the very first term we had every human manifestation that I could think of except for murder. And we almost had that, from time to time. We did have violent death, and suicide, and rape, and everything in degrees up to those traumas. So the life is around you wherever you are, whatever you do, and it's a matter of how keenly and sensitively you respond to what's happening.

JOHN HOLLANDER: You can teach the *writing* of verse—like prose, an instrument—and the *recognition* of true poetry. The rest, writers must teach themselves. Before there were any creative writing courses, people set their own exercises. Look at Keats's or Blake's juvenilia, for example— exercises in verse forms, in order to discover their own private relationships with form, scheme, and mythology. Now that self-help has been discouraged by the culture as a whole, I try to teach writers how to teach themselves. But not workshops—wasn't it Kingsley Amis who said that most of the terrible things that had happened to the world since 1945 had come out of a workshop?

JOHN IRVING: I was not necessarily "taught" anything there [Iowa Writers Workshop] as a student, although I was certainly encouraged and helped—and the advice of Vance Bourjaily, Kurt Vonnegut, and José Donoso clearly saved me some valuable time; that is, they told me things about my writing and about writing in general that I would probably have figured out for myself, but time is precious for a young writer. I always say that this is what I can "teach" a young writer: something he'll know for himself in a little while longer; but why wait to know these things? I am talking about technical things, the only things you can presume to teach, anyway.

JAMES JONES: Most of the desultory courses that I've taken in literature have had a peculiar snobbism about them. An adulation of certain writers is inculcated in the student by the instructor (who is probably a frustrated writer anyway), to the point where the student finds himself asking whether he has anything to say that Tolstoy or James hasn't already said better. Moreover, most of the instruction seems to be concerned with writings rather than with how to write, which is impossible to teach anyway.

WILLIAM KENNEDY: In Puerto Rico, where he was teaching, I met Saul Bellow over a period of a semester. It was very important. I took his criticism very seriously and he was very helpful. He would explain to me that my writing was "fatty." I was saying everything twice and I had too many adjectives. He said it was also occasionally "clotty"—a kind of imprecision that he was talking about, an effort to use a word that wasn't quite precise enough and so just screwed up the clause or sentence. When he would point that out to me, I would go back through the whole book and slash—it turned me into a real fiction editor of my own copy, and it later helped when *I* became a teacher. If I was that ruthless with my own stuff, why shouldn't I be with everybody else's? Bellow also talked about being prodigal. He said that a writer shouldn't be parsimonious with his work, but "prodigal, like nature." He said, just think of nature and how many billions of sperm are used when only one is needed for creating life. And that principle was, it seemed, at the heart of *Augie March*. I mean, he just exploded with language and ideas. I never became that kind of writer, exactly, but I think the effusion, the principle, was important, and I was never afraid of writing too much or thinking that just because you've written a sentence it means something or that it's a good sentence just because you've written it.

PHILIP LARKIN: The academic world has worked all right for me, but then, I'm not a teacher. I couldn't be. I should think that chewing over other people's work, writing I mean, must be terribly stultifying. Quite sickens you with the whole business of literature. But then, I haven't got that kind of mind, conceptual or ratiocinative or whatever it is. It would be death to me to have to think about literature as such, to say why one poem was "better" than another, and so on.

JOHN LE CARRÉ: I would give to a composite writer all the virtues I have not got, but the trouble is, I am not sure he would be able to write. I would give him clarity of vision, independence of public acclaim, the early experience of happy heterosexual love between two good parents and a voracious appetite for other people's writing. Then I would fall asleep.

PETER LEVI: Steer clear of the writing departments of universities. Steer clear of English. Learn foreign, preferably dead languages, but learn them properly. Do not be a wastrel, don't just hang about the world. Poetry is about life. The quality of your poetry will be the quality of your life. And you can't regulate that by a knob. Read. Get or get near a very good library. Take more notice of Randall Jarrell than you do of any academic critic. Don't spend time attacking other writers. Dig to the bottom of your mind, and don't give two damns about publications.

Writing is like breathing or it ought to be. One's got to write poems. Like one has to go to church. Not out of social duty, or because there's any pressure on one to do so. Not even out of reaction to people who say one shouldn't do so. But just because of some decent, natural good behavior. One might as well go on with it.

PHILIP LEVINE: [John Berryman] liked me a lot personally, and he worked very hard with me. He seemed to feel I had something genuine, but that I wasn't doing enough with it, wasn't demanding enough from my work. He kept directing me to poetry that would raise my standards. He knew an enormous body of poetry, and he wanted me to open myself to it. He was very sure of himself, very confident, and I think I caught some of that confidence and some of the confidence he had in me. Another very nice thing: when the semester ended, he said to me, "I'll let you send me some poems, four or five poems. I'll read them and comment on them and send them back. And that'll be that." So about a year and a half later I sent him four poems. He made his comments, and once again he let me know this was the last time. He was right, absolutely right. Out of the nest, into the world.

· · ·

By not going to Paris to study at the foot of Gertrude Stein or going to Harvard to study with Harry Levin or Walter Jackson Bate or Archibald MacLeish, I stayed at home and studied with my equals, people of my own age, which may have been right for me. I was better off with my equals. What was I going to write about Gertrude Stein?

I met a woman once who lived in a house here in New York with Emma Goldman, with whom she was in tutelage. I asked her what Emma was like. She said, "Well, first thing, she never taught me anything because she didn't like women, so she never really talked to me." I said, "She didn't like women?" She said, "No, she didn't think women were serious." She said, "My main remembrance of her was that in the morning she had a little glass bell; when she awakened she rang it. And we would bring her breakfast up to her." I thought, my God, this great freedom fighter for anarchism and the rights of women and workers and everything else! Isn't it marvelous. Who would have guessed?

ROBERT LOWELL: I'd wanted to be a football player very much, and got my letter but didn't make the team. Well, that was satisfying but crushing too. I read a good deal, but had never written. So this was a recoil from that. Then I had some luck in that Richard Eberhart was teaching there.

He was a young man about thirty. I never had him in class, but I used to go to him. He'd read aloud and we'd talk, he was very pleasant that way. He'd smoke honey-scented tobacco, and read Baudelaire and Shakespeare and Hopkins—it made the thing living—and he'd read his own poems. I wrote very badly at first, but he was encouraging and enthusiastic. That probably was decisive, that there was someone there whom I admired who was engaged in writing poetry.

· · ·

Almost all the poets of my generation, all the best ones, teach. I only know one, Elizabeth Bishop, who doesn't. They do it for a livelihood, but they also do it because you can't write poetry all the time. They do it to extend themselves, and I think it's undoubtedly been a gain to them. Now the question is whether something else might be more of a gain. Certainly the danger of teaching is that it's much too close to what you're doing—close and not close. You can get expert at teaching and be crude in practice. The revision, the consciousness that tinkers with the poem—that has something to do with teaching and criticism. But the impulse that starts a poem and makes it of any importance is distinct from teaching.

I think you have to tear it apart from that. Teaching may make the poetry even more different, less academic than it would be otherwise.

. . .

I'm sure that writing isn't a craft, that is, something for which you learn the skills and go on turning out. It must come from some deep impulse, deep inspiration. That can't be taught, it can't be what you use in teaching. And you may go further afield looking for that than you would if you didn't teach. I don't know, really; the teaching probably makes you more cautious, more self-conscious, makes you write less. It may make you bolder when you do write.

WILLIAM MAXWELL: I expect you can be taught to write a clean, decent sentence.

TONI MORRISON: I've always thought the public schools needed to study the best literature. I always taught *Oedipus Rex* to all kinds of what they used to call remedial or development classes. The reason those kids are in those classes is that they're bored to death; so you can't give them boring things. You have to give them the best there is to engage them.

VLADIMIR NABOKOV: My method of teaching precluded genuine contact with my students. At best, they regurgitated a few bits of my brain during examinations. Every lecture I delivered had been carefully, lovingly handwritten and typed out, and I leisurely read it out in class, sometimes stopping to rewrite a sentence and sometimes repeating a paragraph—a mnemonic prod, which, however, seldom provoked any change in the rhythm of wrists taking it down. I welcomed the few shorthand experts in my audience, hoping they would communicate the information they stored to their less fortunate comrades. Vainly I tried to replace my appearances at the lectern by taped records to be played over the college radio. On the other hand, I deeply enjoyed the chuckle of appreciation in this or that warm spot of the lecture hall at this or that point of my lecture. My best reward comes from those former students of mine who ten or fifteen years later write to me to say that they now understand what I wanted of them when I taught them to visualize Emma Bovary's mistranslated hairdo or the arrangement of rooms in the Samsa household or the two homosexuals in *Anna Karenina*. I do not know if I learned anything from teaching but I know I amassed an invaluable amount of exciting information in analyzing a dozen novels for my students. My salary as you happen to know was not exactly a princely one.

. . .

A first-rate college library with a comfortable campus around it is a fine milieu for a writer. There is of course the problem of fellow readers. I remember how once, between terms, not at Cornell, a student brought a transistor set with him into the reading room. He managed to state that 1) he was playing "classical" music; that 2) he was doing it "softly"; and that 3) "there were not many readers around in summer." I was there, a one-man multitude.

CYNTHIA OZICK: I was taking a course with Lionel Trilling and wrote a paper for him with an opening sentence that contained a parenthesis. He returned the paper with a wounding reprimand: "Never, never begin an essay with a parenthesis in the first sentence." Ever since then, I've made a point of starting out with a parenthesis in the first sentence. Years later, Trilling was cordial and very kind to me, and I felt redeemed, though it took two decades to earn his approval.

. . .

When I've taught those classes, I always say, "Forget about 'Write about what you know.' Write about what you don't know." The point is that the self is limiting. The self—subjectivity—is narrow and bound to be repetitive. We are, after all, a species. When you write about what you don't know, this means you begin to think about the world at large. You begin to think beyond the home-thoughts. You enter dream and imagination.

GRACE PALEY: The best training is to read and write, no matter what. Don't live with a lover or roommate who doesn't respect your work. Don't lie, buy time, borrow to buy time. Write what will stop your breath if you don't write.

. . .

It's helpful to have money. I don't think writers have to suffer to starve to death. One of the first things I tell my classes is, if you want to write, keep a low overhead. If you want to live expansively you're going to be in trouble because then you have to start thinking very hard about whom you're writing to, who your audience is, who the *editor* thinks your audience is, who he *wants* your audience to be?

EZRA POUND: I went to London because I thought Yeats knew more about poetry than anybody else. I made my life in London by going to see Ford in the afternoons and Yeats in the evenings. By mentioning one to the other one could always start a discussion. That was the exercise. I went to study with Yeats and found that Ford disagreed with him. So then I kept on disagreeing with *them* for twenty years.

REYNOLDS PRICE: American writing teachers are much too kind generally, too kind to the point of perjury. Flannery O'Connor, in her sidewinder way, said a dead-true thing: "Everywhere I go I'm asked if I think the universities stifle writers. My opinion is that they don't stifle enough of them." She apparently meant more or less the same thing that I mean by saying "Quit if you can. Don't take this up at all lightly." If the person persists and starts sending me his or her published books, then I'm often interested and try to like the work and say that I do. Writing is a fearsome but grand vocation—potentially healing but likewise deadly.

RICHARD PRICE: You can't teach talent anymore than you can teach somebody to be an athlete. But maybe you help the writer find their story, and that's 99 percent of it. Oftentimes, it's a matter of lining up the archer with the target. I had a student in one of my classes. He was writing all this stuff about these black guys in the South Bronx who were on angel dust . . . the most amoral thrill-killers. They were evil, evil. But it was all so over-the-top to the point of being silly. He didn't know what he was talking about. I didn't know this stuff either, but I knew enough to know that this wasn't it.

I said to the kid, "Why are you writing this? Are you from the Bronx?"

He says, "No. From New Jersey."

"Are you a former angel-dust sniffer? Do you run with a gang?"

He says, "No. My father's a fireman out in Toms River."

"Oh, so he's a black fireman in suburban New Jersey? Christ! Why don't you write about that? I mean, nobody writes about black guys in the suburbs." I said, "Why are you writing this other stuff?"

He said to me, "Well, I figure people are expecting me to write this stuff."

"What if they do? First of all, they don't. Second, even if they did, which is stupid, why should I read you? What do you know that I don't know?"

He turned out to be one of these kids in the early eighties who was bombing trains with graffiti—one of these guys who was part of the whole train-signing subculture, you know, *Turk 182.* He wrote a story, over a hundred pages long, about what it was like to be one of these guys—fifteen pages alone on how to steal aerosol cans from hardware stores. He could describe the smell of spray paint mixing with that rush of tunnel air when someone jerked open the connecting door on a moving train that you were "decorating." He wrote about the Atlantic Avenue station in Brooklyn where all the graffiti-signers would hang out, their informal clubhouse, how they all kept scrapbooks of each other's tags. Who would know that stuff except somebody who really knew? And, it was great. The guy was bringing in the news. Now, whether it's art or not depends on how good he is. But he went from this painful chicken scratch of five-page bullshit about angel-dust killers to writing stuff that smacked of authenticity and intimacy.

That is the job of the writing teacher: what do you think you should be writing about? At Yale I had the same problem. They'd write ten pages of well-worded this or that, but where's the story? I finally came up with an assignment. I hate giving assignments. I hated getting them, and I hate giving them. But—the last of the good assignments—I made them all find a photograph of their family taken at least one year before the writer was born. I said, "All right. Write me a story that starts the minute these people break this pose. Where did they go? What did they do?" We all have stories about our family, most of them are apocryphal, but whether you love or hate your family, they're yours, and these are your stories. On the other hand, Tom McGuane once said, "I've done a lot of horrible things in my life but I never taught creative writing."

ANNE SEXTON: He [Robert Lowell] was formal in a rather awkward New England sense. His voice was soft and slow as he read the students' poems. At first I felt the impatient desire to interrupt his slow, line-by-line readings. He would read the first line, stop, and then discuss it at length. I wanted to go through the whole poem quickly and then go back. I couldn't see any merit in dragging through it until you almost hated the damned thing, even your own poems, especially your own. At that point, I wrote to Snodgrass about my impatience, and his reply went this way, "Frankly,

I used to nod my head at his every statement, and he taught me more than a whole gang of scholars could." So I kept my mouth shut, and Snodgrass was right. Robert Lowell's method of teaching is intuitive and open. After he had read a student's poem, he would read another evoked by it. Comparison was often painful. He worked with a cold chisel, with no more mercy than a dentist. He got out the decay, but if he was never kind to the poem, he was kind to the poet.

KARL SHAPIRO: I've never encouraged *anybody* to do that [to adopt writing as a way of life]. I think it's not only presumptuous, it's dangerous. When I first started teaching, I encouraged a few students in a couple of cases. But you can change the whole course of their career—a terrible responsibility. I wouldn't do it now. But if I ran across a talented student, I'd encourage him or her as much as I could. I used to try to direct those writing students to a job or a profession. I had a student at Davis who was very good, who said to me one day, "I'm going to go to the Academy of the Merchant Marine and be a ship's captain." I said, "Gee, that's wonderful! That'll be terrific for your poetry." Well, he went and he's still a captain of a ship somewhere. I haven't seen any more poetry from him. That still may be better than hanging around the academy all one's life.

W. D. SNODGRASS: If you can, get out. Everything else in the world pays better. Everything else in the world costs less, not only in terms of money but in terms of damage to your life. Everything else in the world is more justly rewarded. If you can be happy doing something else, the chances are you will be happier doing something else.

WILLIAM STAFFORD: The sixties changed my life because it made poets very popular; poets traveled around the country. It enhanced the kind of popularity that had been growing. Economically, my life has greatly benefited from the popularity of writers and readings and workshops. The flourishing is manifested at workshops too. Many people come, having realized that writing is an access route to their deeper selves. I've felt and heard others talk about this fact, that many people who come to workshop sessions are like refugees from that world out there— the reverberating world.

ROBERT STONE: A creative writing class can at least be good for morale. When I teach writing, I do things like take classes to bars and race tracks to listen to dialogue. But that kind of thing has limited usefulness.

There's no body of technology to impart. But that doesn't mean classes can't help. The idea that young writers ought to be out slinging hash or covering the fights or whatever is bullshit. There's a point where a class can do a lot of good. You know, you throw the rock and you get the splash.

GORE VIDAL: This business of taking novels apart in order to show bored children how they were put together—there's a madness to it. Only a literary critic would benefit, and there are never more than ten good critics in the United States at any given moment. So what is the point to these desultory autopsies performed according to that little set of instructions at the end of each text? Have you seen one? What symbols to look for? What does the author mean by the word "white"? I look at the notes appended to my own pieces in anthologies and know despair.

KURT VONNEGUT: In a creative writing class of twenty people anywhere in this country, six students will be startlingly talented. Two of those might actually publish something by and by.

They will have something other than literature itself on their minds. They will probably be hustlers, too. I mean that they won't want to wait passively for somebody to discover them. They will insist on being read.

EUDORA WELTY: A lady had decided she'd write a novel and got along fine till she came to the love scene. "So," she told my friend, "I thought, there's William Faulkner, sitting right up there in Oxford. Why not send it to William Faulkner and ask him?" So she sent it to him, and time went by, and she didn't ever hear from him, and so she called him up. Because there he was. She said, "Mr. Faulkner, did you ever get that love scene I sent you?" He said yes, he had got it. And she said, "Well, what did you think of it?" And he said, "Well, honey, it's not the way I'd do it—but you go *right ahead.*" Now, wasn't that gentle of him?

ELIE WIESEL: I never taught creative writing courses. I believe in creative reading. That's what I am trying to teach—creative reading. I'd assign the Scripture and Midrash, Ovid and Kafka, Thomas Mann and Camus, Plato and André Schwarz-Bart. A writer must first know how to read. You can see whether a person is a writer by the way he reads a text, by the way he deciphers a text. I'd also say to a young writer, if you can choose not to write, don't. Nothing is as painful. From the outside, people think it's good; it's easy; it's romantic. Not at all. It's much easier not to write than to write. Except if you are a writer. Then you have no choice.

RICHARD WILBUR: About the same way golf can be taught. A pro can point out obvious flaws in your swing. I did that well, I think, at the University of Iowa for two years. Gail Godwin and John Irving and Jonathan Penner and Bruce Dobler and John Casey and Jane Casey were all students of mine out there. They've all published wonderful stuff since then. I taught creative writing badly at Harvard—because my marriage was breaking up, and because I was commuting every week to Cambridge from New York. I taught even worse at City College a couple of years ago. I had too many other projects going on at the same time. I don't have the will to teach any more. I only know the theory.

It was stated by Paul Engle—the founder of the Writers Workshop at Iowa. He told me that, if the Workshop ever got a building of its own, these words should be inscribed over the entrance: "Don't take it all so seriously."

. . .

I think the best part of teaching from the point of view of the teacher-writer, writer-teacher, is that it makes you read a good deal and makes you be articulate about what you read. You can't read passively because you have to be prepared to move other people to recognitions and acts of analysis. I know a few writers who don't teach and who, in consequence, do very little reading. This doesn't mean that they are bad writers, but in some cases I think they might be better writers if they read more. As for the experience of the classroom, I enjoy it; I am very depressed by classes which don't work, and rather elated by classes which do. I like to see if I can express myself clearly enough to stick an idea in somebody's head. Of course there are also disadvantages, one of which is that the time one spends teaching could be spent writing. Another involves this very articulateness of which I've been speaking. It uses the same gray cells, pretty much, that writing does, and so one can come to the job of writing with too little of a sense of rediscovery of the language. That is one reason I like to live out here in the country and lead a fairly physical life—play a lot of tennis, raise a lot of vegetables, go on a lot of long walks. I do things which are non-verbal so that I can return to language with excitement and move toward language from kinds of strong awareness for which I haven't instantly found facile words. It is good for a writer to move into words out of the silence, as much as he can.

THORNTON WILDER: I think all are unfavorable to the writer. If by day you handle the English language either in the conventional forms, which are journalism and advertising, or in the analysis, which is teaching English in school or college, you will have a double, a quadruple difficulty in finding *your* English language at night and on Sundays. It is proverbial that every newspaper reporter has a half-finished novel in his bureau drawer. Reporting—which can be admirable in itself—is poles apart from shaping concepts into imagined actions and requires a totally different ordering of mind and language. When I had to earn my living for many years, I taught French. I should have taught mathematics. By teaching math or biology or physics, you come refreshed to writing.

ON PEERS: PORTRAITS

Writers seldom wish other writers well.　　—SAUL BELLOW

"Sir," said Mr. Tupman, "you're a fellow." "Sir," said Mr.
Pickwick, "you're another!"　　—CHARLES DICKENS

There is no denying the fact that writers should be read but
not seen. Rarely are they a winsome sight.　　—EDNA FERBER

W. H. AUDEN

GRACE PALEY: He was giving a class on the history of English literature. At one point he said, "Are there any poets who would like to speak
to me or who want me to look at their work?" There were 250 people in
the room, and maybe five people put up their hands. I was one of them.
Nowadays 240 would have raised their hands. That I even put my hand up
was amazing to me, since I'd just gone through high school without raising it once. And then he said, "Meet me in Stewart's Cafeteria." So the
next week, I went to meet him at Stewart's Cafeteria and he wasn't there.
I immediately called up this boy I had begun to go around with (and later
married) and bawled, "He wasn't there, he was fooling."

It turned out there were *two* Stewart's Cafeterias on Twenty-third
Street—one east and one west—he was in the other one. So the next week
he said, "Where were you, Grace Goodside?" Then I did meet him. He
read my poems—which were exactly like his.

I mean, I really wrote in his style. I was crazy about him. I loved his
poems so much that I was using this British language all the time—I was
saying *trousers* and *subaltern* and things like that. You understand I was a
Bronx kid. We went through a few poems, and he kept asking me, do you
really *talk* like that? And I kept saying, "Oh yeah, well, sometimes." That
was the great thing I learned from Auden: that you'd better talk your own

language. Then I asked him what young writers now ask me—and I always tell them this story—I said to Auden, "Well, do you think I should keep writing?" He laughed and then became very solemn. "If you're a writer," he said, "you'll keep writing no matter what. That's not a question a writer should ask." Something like that, not exactly, but close.

DJUNA BARNES

JAMES LAUGHLIN: We were planning a special hardbound edition of *Nightwood*. Barnes insisted she had to have paper that would last a thousand years. We asked the paper dealers, and they said, "No, it's impossible. You can't unless you go to an Italian or French handmade paper, which would be exorbitant. We cannot *produce* a paper that we will guarantee for more than five hundred years." So we finally printed the book on Curtis Rag, which the manufacturer guaranteed for five hundred years, but Djuna was never happy about it.

SAMUEL BECKETT

BARNEY ROSSET: He knew that I played Ping-Pong, or more properly table tennis, and that I was good at it. Perhaps I told him. Anyway one day we walked up the Boulevard St. Germain looking for a place to play. We couldn't find one. Finally we ended up in a billiard parlor on the corner of St. Germain and the Boulevard St. Michel. Up on the second floor. I'd played pool, but I didn't know how to play billiards. Billiards was a big thing of Beckett's. We played. He put a good face on it, being sweet, nice, and trying to show me what to do, but it was a disaster.

He was a fine athlete. I have photographs of him as a stalwart member of his prep school cricket team. In the fifties he was troubled with cataracts. He would stagger around on the street because he wasn't seeing well. People used to think he was drunk. They took it for granted: "Well, he's had too much." Eventually he had a successful operation.

But he was a great enthusiast. I remember we went to Roland Garros to watch what turned out to be one of the greatest tennis matches I ever saw—a semifinal in a professional tournament between Lew Hoad and Pancho Gonzales. The umpire was a Basque whom Beckett knew; they waved at each other as we came in. At one point in the match Gonzales got very upset at the umpire, threw his racquet up into the stands and said he wouldn't continue unless they threw the umpire out. So they did this, and as he left the stadium the umpire waved up at Beckett. You would have thought someone in a situation like that would have something else on his mind than to wave at a friend. Oh yes, a lot of sports people knew Beckett. One of his favorite places was a bar/restaurant called the Ile de Matisse, a seafood place with photographs of sports figures on the wall. Beckett's was up there next to Sugar Ray Robinson's.

He tried to teach me how to play chess, at which he was also very good. He played chess with friends by mail—in Yugoslavia, in Germany. He failed as miserably teaching me chess as he had billiards.

Eventually we played Ping-Pong. He found a place with a table—an inn near his house outside Paris. We drove out there in his Citroën deux chevaux—that crazy sardine-can automobile with its front wheels turned inward so that it swayed like being in a ship, and he was driving, and of course he couldn't see. It was like being in a Beckett novel.

I was better at Ping-Pong than he was. First of all I could see, and I'm pretty good at table tennis. I've played a lot. I think he wanted to find a game he knew I could really play because he had beaten me so badly at billiards and then chess. He had just humiliated me. He wanted to make me feel better.

He took to being beaten as well as he took to winning at billiards. Beckett was a gentleman; I think they may have invented the word for him—a gentle, sweet human being who some people thought was unfriendly because he didn't say anything. Beckett was an intense listener. He listened to you as if you were the only human being in the world. With each person he was like a deep lover. Sometimes it was disconcerting, especially to those who didn't know him. Richard Avedon, I remember, got almost hysterical because he thought Beckett was being hostile. In his nervousness he began telling crazy stories about photographing snakes in Texas. He went rambling on and on, Beckett sitting there listening very intently, along with me and my two children. Avedon was very upset. Well, anyway, that's the way it was.

BRENDAN BEHAN

J. P. DONLEAVY: Behan always wore his shirt open to the navel; he never had shoelaces and the tongues of his shoes would always hang out. You could see his bare ankles and the heels of his shoes were always so worn away that his ankles leaned over and he waddled around. Every year or so he'd buy himself a new suit, and as soon as he walked into the pub someone would say, "Behan, you've got a new suit!" He'd say, "Oh, you think it's new," and he'd immediately get off the bar stool, walk outside, and roll up and down in the gutter, then he'd come back in. If someone said, "Well, Behan, jeez, you've washed your hair!" he'd take his pint of Guinness and pour it over his head.

MAXWELL BODENHEIM

CONRAD AIKEN: He was a fascinating talker, in spite of the stammer, and he knew everybody. He was a great friend of Bill Williams. You must have heard the story of his broken arm? He called up Williams at Rutherford and said, "I've broken my arm. Can I come and stay with you till it heals?" Bill said, "Certainly." About a month or two went by and Max did nothing about having the cast examined or changed, so finally Bill insisted on looking at it and discovered that there had never been any broken arm.

JOYCE CARY

V. S. PRITCHETT: I didn't know him very well, but I did know him. A most extraordinary man, a very strange man. He used to live in Oxford, and I went to see him there. He seemed far too accomplished; he seemed to have everything. He'd been a very distinguished civil servant in Africa. He'd been a great book collector and was a rather able painter—not a genius, but he painted better than most of us. His background was very amusing. He had a rather wild Anglo-Irish background, which was immediately recognizable to anyone who knew Ireland at that time. He was very serious. Oxford made him seem a bit solemn, but he wasn't really solemn. He was very restless. For example, when we were talking at Oxford, suddenly there was a noise at the front door. He clapped his hands and said, "That's my cutlet! That's my dinner! Dear old so-and-so's dropped me in my cutlet!" Someone had dropped some meat in through the letter drop. He rushed to the door, picked it up, opened the door, and said, "Oh, she's gone." I heard him shout down the street, "Thank you! Thank you! Thank you!" He was very excitable.

LOUIS-FERDINAND CÉLINE

JAMES LAUGHLIN: Céline I met. I once went out to see him when he was living in Meudon, an industrial suburb of Paris near the Renault plant. He had a small house, and outside it there was a high barbed-wire fence. He had two very fierce dogs that barked at me when I rang the gate bell. He had to come out and tie up the dogs. This was because Denöel, his publisher, had been murdered on a street in Paris. Denöel had been a collaborator, too. Céline was rather paranoid, but he was friendly to me. I had had contact with his wife, who was a ballet dancer. While they were in exile in Denmark during the war, she couldn't get ballet shoes for her practice. So she used to write to me and I'd go down to Capezio in New York to buy her ballet shoes and air-mail them over to her.

E. E. CUMMINGS

JOHN CHEEVER: I was in doubt that I could make something of myself as a writer until I met two people who were very important to me: one was Gaston Lachaise and the other was E. E. Cummings. Cummings I loved, and I love his memory. He did a wonderful imitation of a woodburning locomotive going from Tiflis to Minsk. He could hear a pin falling in soft dirt at the distance of three miles. Do you remember the story of Cummings's death? It was September, hot, and Cummings was cutting kindling in the back of his house in New Hampshire. He was sixty-six or -seven or something like that. Marion, his wife, leaned out the window and asked, "Cummings, isn't it frightfully hot to be chopping wood?" He said, "I'm going to stop now, but I'm going to sharpen the ax before I put it up, dear." Those were the last words he spoke. At his funeral Marianne Moore gave the eulogy. Marion Cummings had enormous eyes. You could make a place in a book with them. She smoked cigarettes as though they were heavy, and she wore a dark dress with a cigarette hole in it. And Lachaise? I'm not sure what to say about him. I thought him an outstanding artist, and I found him a contented man. He used to go to the Metropolitan— where he was not represented—and embrace the statues he loved.

T. S. ELIOT

CONRAD AIKEN: Eliot and I must have met at the end of my freshman year, when I was elected to the *Harvard Advocate*. We saw a great deal of each other, in spite of the fact that we were a year apart, and remained very close.

Of course, at the beginning, on the *Advocate,* we talked chiefly about poetry, or literature in general. But as the friendship, or kinship, developed—for in a way I became his younger brother—it widened to take in everything. And we met on very, very many quite frivolous occasions. Sports, comics, everything. We developed a shorthand language of our own which we fell into for the rest of our lives whenever we met, no holds barred—all a matter of past reference, a common language, but basically *affection,* along with humor, and appreciation of each other's minds, and of Krazy Kat. Faced with England, and the New World, and Freud and all, we always managed to *relax,* and go back to the kidding, and bad punning, and drinking, to the end. It really was marvelous. When he paid his infrequent visits here, we invariably met to get drunk together. There was a splendid occasion when he and I and our wives dined at "The Greeks' " after he'd received a silver bowl from the Signet Society; he was wearing a cowboy hat, and we all got plastered. We went on to the Red Lion Grill, after many drinks at the Silver Dollar Bar, the two toughest and *queerest* joints in Boston. He couldn't walk, for his ankles were crossed, so Valerie *lifted* him into the taxi.

ROBERT FITZGERALD: I got to know him earlier, when I was in England in '31–'32. Vachel Lindsay had written to him, and he wrote me at Cambridge to invite me, saying, "Do drop in." You know, at Faber and Faber. I did. I went to see him and we talked about Cambridge, where I was working in philosophy. He was familiar with the people at Cambridge who were then my teachers or lecturers, C. D. Broad and G. E. Moore. This, of course, was a continuing interest in his life. He had, after all, done his dissertation on Bradley. Had he gone on in that direction, he would have been a philosopher in the philosophy department here at Harvard. I think on the second or third of my visits I had the courage to hand him a poem. He looked at the poem for a long time. Great silence. He studied it, then he looked up and said, "Is this the best you can do?" *Whoo!* Quite a thing to say! I didn't realize then what I realized later—that it was an editor's question: "Shall I publish this or shall I wait until he does something that shows more confidence?" What I thought at the time, and there was also this about it, was that it was fraternal. Just talking to me as one craftsman to another. A compliment, really.

PHILIP LARKIN: Once I was in the Faber offices—the old ones, "24, Russell Square," that magic address!—talking to Charles Monteith, and he said, "Have you ever met Eliot?" I said no, and to my astonishment he stepped out and reappeared with Eliot, who must have been in the next room. We shook hands, and he explained that he was expecting someone to tea and couldn't stay. There was a pause, and he said, "I'm glad to see you in this office." The significance of that was that I wasn't a Faber author—it must have been before 1964 when they published *The Whitsun Weddings*—and I took it as a great compliment. But it was a shattering few minutes: I hardly remember what I thought. I met Auden once at Stephen Spender's house, which was very kind of Spender, and in a sense he was more frightening than Eliot. I remember he said, Do you like living in Hull? and I said, I don't suppose I'm unhappier there than I should be anywhere else. To which he replied, Naughty, naughty. I thought that was very funny.

W. S. MERWIN: Eliot was a very kind man. In those days I smoked and liked French cigarettes, and people used to give him French cigarettes, which he no longer smoked. So whenever I went to see him he would open a drawer and hand me a whole bunch. That was a big thing in London in the early fifties, and I was touched that he remembered. We used to sit and reminisce about America. There was a side of Eliot that was very homesick for the States, and I was feeling homesick in London, too. We had several wonderful conversations—about the Ohio River and about his family out on the Mississippi in St. Louis and about the riverboats. It's very strange to think of him having any connection with that world. He talked about the *Delta Queen,* that steamboat that went up and down the river until a few years ago. He really wanted to take a trip on that. I wanted to write verse plays in those days, when I was in my early twenties. But, after a while, I came to feel that the plays weren't going very well and that the verse certainly wasn't helping them. As long as I had this fixation about verse plays, I wasn't learning anything about writing plays. I talked to him about that. I said I was thinking of abandoning writing them in verse altogether and trying to write them in prose. "Well," he said, "I've thought of doing that, too, but if I were to write my plays in prose, there are so many other people who could do it better."

REBECCA WEST: I didn't like him a bit. He was a poseur. He was married to this woman who was very pretty. My husband and I were asked to see them, and my husband roamed around the flat and there were endless photographs of T. S. Eliot and bits of his poetry done in embroidery by pious American ladies, and only one picture of his wife, and that was when she was getting married. Henry pointed it out to me and said, "I don't think I like that man."

WILLIAM FAULKNER

S. J. PERELMAN: Sometimes, of a Sunday morning, he used to stroll by a house I occupied in Beverly Hills. I noticed him only because the sight of anybody walking in that environment stamped him as an eccentric, and indeed, it eventually got him into trouble. A prowl car picked him up and he had a rather sticky time of it. The police were convinced he was a finger man for some jewelry mob planning to knock over one of the fancy residences.

FORD MADOX FORD

MALCOLM COWLEY: Ford was a character; he was a liar, not for his own profit, but just because he had a very faint hold on actuality. He told beautiful stories of English literary life, in which he knew everybody, had a hand in everything, and his hand grew larger as he told the story. He had a roving eye for younger women, whom he especially liked to fascinate. He came to this country after the breakup of his marriage to Stella Bowen. I can remember on one occasion he came up to Robber Rocks—a place back in the woods near the New York–Connecticut line which was the country headquarters for Allen Tate, Hart Crane, and others—where a lot of young wives were around at the party. They would be fondled by Ford, and then escape him up the stairs. Ford, heavy and wheezing by that time, would follow them to the head of the narrow stairs, and the door would close in his face. He would wheeze back down, and a while later he'd follow another young woman until she took refuge behind a locked door.

ROBERT FROST

JAMES DICKEY: I don't care much for Robert Frost and have never been able to understand his reputation. He says a good thing now and then, but with a strange way of averting his eyes while saying it which may be profound and may be poppycock. If it were thought that anything I wrote was influenced by Robert Frost, I would take that particular work of mine, shred it, and flush it down the toilet, hoping not to clog the pipes.

STEPHEN SPENDER: I met him only two or three times. He had a number of sides to his nature, as we know, including a very black one. He showed me his vain side. I had to give a dinner party for him, and had someone bellow in his ear the names of all the other people and had all their place names written out very large so he could see them at the table. He sat next to E. M. Forster, and asked, "And what magazine do you write for?" He just didn't take these people seriously, and didn't bother to find out who they were.

ALLEN GINSBERG

JACK KEROUAC: Allen Ginsberg asked me when he was nineteen years old, should I change my name to Allen Renard? You change your name to Allen Renard I'll kick you right in the balls! Stick to Ginsberg . . . and he did. That's one thing I like about Allen. *Allen Renard!!!*

ANDREI VOZNESENSKY: Yes, I like his "Howl." I love "Howl" and "Kaddish." He [Ginsberg] came to see me in the Soviet Union, and people thought he was mad. He went to Mayakovsky's grave and fell down crying and weeping and praying to him. He is very interesting. I feel he is a type of guru. We had a very good reading together on a ferryboat in New York. I read my poems and he read translations. But I'm very sad that at another reading, somebody I don't know personally said, "Please don't ask Allen to come to the stage, because so-and-so will be upset, they don't approve of him." I was upset and I repeated this to Allen, who said, "Oh, Andrei, don't start anything please. I'll be here in the hall, in the auditorium. I'll be happy." But I like to read together with him, because he is a great performer. We read in a church once, for Bangladesh.

FRANK HARRIS

JAMES THURBER: I can remember calling on Frank Harris—he was about seventy then—when I was on the *Chicago Tribune*'s edition in Nice. In his house he had three portraits on the wall—Mark Twain, Frank Harris, and I think it was Hawthorne. Harris was in the middle. Harris would point up to them and say, "Those three are the best American writers. The one in the middle is the best." Harris really thought he was wonderful. Once he told me he was going to live to be a hundred. When I asked him what the formula was, he told me it was very simple. He said: "I've bought myself a stomach pump and one half hour after dinner I pump myself out." Can you imagine that? Well, it didn't work. It's a wonder it didn't kill him sooner.

A. E. HOUSMAN

W. H. AUDEN: Yes, and later I knew him quite well. He [Housman] told me a very funny story about Clarence Darrow. It seems that Darrow had written him a very laudatory letter, claiming to have saved several clients from the Chair with quotes from Housman's poetry. Shortly afterwards, Housman had a chance to meet Darrow. They had a very nice meeting, and Darrow produced the trial transcripts he had alluded to. "Sure enough," Housman told me, "there were two of my poems—both misquoted!" These are the minor headaches a writer must live with. My pet peeve is people who send for autographs but omit putting in stamps.

CHRISTOPHER ISHERWOOD

TENNESSEE WILLIAMS: I met him in the forties in California. At the time he was into Vedanta, an Eastern religious thing. He was living in a monastery. They had periods of silence and meditation, you know. The night I met him, through a letter from Lincoln Kirstein, I arrived during one of these silent periods. The monk who opened the door handed me a pencil and paper to write what my business was and who I'd come to see. I wrote, "Christopher Isherwood," and they regarded me with considerable suspicion from that point on.

In this big room in the monastery, everyone was sitting in . . . what do they call it? The lotus position? Including Christopher. All strictly observing the vow of silence. I didn't dig the scene.

I suddenly made some reference out loud about the Krishna. I didn't know who the hell he was, I was only trying to break the silence. Christopher got up, and wrote on a piece of paper, "I'll call you tomorrow." He was very polite, and he took me to the door.

JAMES JOYCE

FRANK O'CONNOR: An extraordinarily handsome man! He gave the impression of being a great surgeon but not a writer at all. And he was a surgeon, he was not a writer. He used to wear white surgeon's coats all the time and that increased the impression and he had this queer, ax-like face with this enormous jaw, the biggest jaw I have ever seen on a human being. I once did a talk on Joyce in which I mentioned that he had the biggest chin I had ever seen on a human being and T. S. Eliot wrote a letter saying that he had often seen chins as big as that on other Irishmen. Well, I didn't know how to reply to that.

JACK KEROUAC

RUSSELL BANKS: Yes, I met Kerouac. It must have been 1967—a year or two, at most, before he died. I got a call from a pal in a bar in town, the Tempo Room, a local hangout: "Jack Kerouac is in town with a couple of other guys, and he wants to have a party." I said, "Yeah, sure, right." He said, "No, really." I was the only guy in this crowd with a regular house. So Jack Kerouac showed up with a troupe of about forty people he had gathered as he went along, and three guys who he insisted, and I think they indeed were, Micmac Indians from Quebec. Kerouac, like a lot of writers of the open road, didn't have a driver's license; he needed a Neil Cassady just to get around. This time he had these crazy Indians, who were driving him to Florida to be with his mother. They all ended up crashing for the weekend. He had just received his advance for what turned out to be his last book and was spending it like a sailor on leave. He brought with him a disruptiveness and wild disorder, and moments of brilliance, too. I could see how attractive he must have been when he was young, both physically and intellectually. He was an incredibly beautiful man. But at that age (he was about forty-seven), the alcohol had wreaked such destruction that it left him beautiful only from the neck up. Also, you could see why they called him Memory Babe: he would switch into long, beautiful twenty-minute recitations of Blake or the Upanishads or Hoagy Carmichael song lyrics. Then he would phase out and turn into an anti-Semitic, angry, fucked-up, tormented old drunk, a real Know-Nothing. It was comical, but sad. There was a lot of argument back and forth, then we would realize, No, he's just a sad, old drunk, I can't take this stuff seriously. Then he would realize it himself and he would back off and turn himself into a senior literary figure and say, I can't take that stuff seriously either. Every time he came forward, he would switch personas, and you would go bouncing back off him. It was a very strange and strenuous weekend. And very moving. It was the first time I had seen one of my literary heroes seem fragile and vulnerable.

D. H. LAWRENCE

ALDOUS HUXLEY: We saw the Lawrences often during those last four years; they stayed with us in Paris, then we were together in Switzerland, and we visited them at the Villa Mirenda near Florence. My wife typed out the manuscript of *Lady Chatterley's Lover* for him, even though she was a bad typist and had no patience with English spelling—she was a Belgian, you know. Then she didn't always appreciate the nuances of the language she was typing. When she started using some of those four-letter words in conversation, Lawrence was profoundly shocked.

SINCLAIR LEWIS

BLAISE CENDRARS: It was in 1930, in Rome. He'd already been widely discussed in Italy, where he was trailing about with a squadron of jolly New York girls who were causing a scandal. One fine day he landed in Rome, where I was making a movie. He let me know that he urgently wanted to meet me. I asked him to come to the studio, but he answered that he had a cold, he didn't like movies, and anyway he didn't have the time because he was leaving Rome the next morning for Stockholm to collect the Nobel Prize. So I went to his hotel, where I found half a dozen American girls completely drunk, making a gigantic cocktail in a soup tureen full of whipped cream, into which—while quarreling with each other about how much to put in—they were pouring two, three liters of vermouth. I didn't think I could join this scene of madwomen right away—one of them held out some scissors to me and dared me to cut her hair—so I thought I'd take a little stroll. But I changed my mind and decided to search the apartment for the master of the séance, whom I hadn't seen yet. The door of the bathroom was half-open, and boiling water was coming out. I went in. The bathtub was overflowing and the faucets were wide open. Two feet, dressed in polished dancing pumps, hung out of the tub, and at the bottom a man in a tuxedo was drowning. It was my Sinclair Lewis. I pulled him out of his unfortunate position, and that was how I saved his life so he could take the train the next morning for Stockholm and his prize.

The next day I put him on the train—he didn't even buy me a drink. It's true he had a hangover and probably didn't want to drink, or maybe he'd sworn never to drink again. But a drunk's oaths don't hold, you know.

ROBERT LOWELL

W. D. SNODGRASS: Lowell had been an enormous help. When we looked at poems, his responses were incredibly rich. For example, I took a Greek poetry workshop taught jointly by him and Gerald Else, who was then probably the nation's leading classicist. We did the *Iliad*, six lines a day. The whole class was made up of poets. For the first forty-five minutes every day, Lowell would talk about these six lines, just throwing out the most incredible and marvelous ideas. Then for the second forty-five minutes, Gerald Else would tell us what they were *really* about, and it was always quite different, but also wonderful. We learned what constituted an adequate response to a work of art, and that our own responses, up to that point, had never been adequate.

A friend of mine said that when Lowell did a poem in the workshop, it was like having an octopus come and sit down on the thing: it would send out one arm and grab—Philosophy. And it would send out another arm and grab—Mythology. Another would haul in Sociology. One after another he'd pull in all these different fields. You'd think, "This man is as crazy as they told me. My poor little poem doesn't have anything to do with all this." And then he'd start tying them all together, and you would see he was right. You'd walk out of there just staggered. Then you'd meet him on the street two days later, and he would sort of hover over you and say, "Listen, I've been thinking about that poem of yours. You know the one with the rather grand language—" (that was description, not praise; that meant it was maybe a little pretentious) "—I was all wrong about that. Here's what it's really about." And he'd be off again with a whole new set of theories. When the man's mind was working, it was just unbelievable. I'd never been around a mind, such a gigantic piece of machinery as that. It was just marvelous. But that didn't mean he was right all the time.

PETER TAYLOR: It's a long story, part of it very funny. Allen Tate had called me from Chicago and said, "Cal is not himself at all," and that he and Caroline Gordon had just put him on a train! Well, of course I was furious—Allen had no business putting him on a train. But I also knew that Allen had a great dramatic sense, and I thought he must be exaggerating. I didn't think it was true when he said that Cal was beside himself, behaved strangely, frightened a child at the station, and that he had picked up Allen and carried him down the platform. True, Allen was very small! Anyhow, Allen said I was to meet Cal with the police at the railroad station! Anyway, as soon as Cal stepped off the train I could see he was out of his head. He wasn't the Lowell I knew. He was dirty and disheveled. So I took him to the faculty club and put him up there instead of taking him home. We had a new baby and I told him the baby was not well. But while we were having dinner in this place he began to sniff, and said, "Do you smell that?" I said no, and he said, "I know what it is, it's brimstone. He's over there behind the fern." I took him to his room and went to my house. But a few minutes later I was called by the people at the club. They said he had come out of his room and run through the kitchen terrorizing the cooks, and then rushed out into the streets. I spent the early part of the night searching for him, going through the streets calling, "Lowell, Lowell," at the top of my voice. In the meantime he'd gone up to a movie house and stolen a roll of tickets—just reached in and grabbed the tickets and run off down the street! By now the police were looking for him, too. We were all running around the town—Bloomington is not a big town!—and finally he knocked on a door that happened to be a policeman's house, and they took him in. For me the most traumatic part of it all was the next morning. I was just beside myself because we had been the closest friends—roommates and all—and I thought it was the end. I never thought he would be sane again. So the next morning I went down there to the jail, and he was in a block of cells, and there was nobody there with him. They let me in and locked the gate, and I went into the cell with him. I was scared to death. Finally I said, "Cal, let's pray," and he said, "Let's get down here and pray together to get out of this place." And I said—because I was scared—"Cal, I never could pray in the same room with anybody." So I went into the next cell, and we got down on our knees and prayed in adjoining cells. But then time went by and they changed guards. The new guard hadn't been told I wasn't also an inmate! I was in there four hours with him. I would call for them to let me out, and Cal would say, "That's not Christian. You call for them to let me out and I'll call for them to let you out!"

DEREK WALCOTT: Lowell and Elizabeth Hardwick were on a tour going to Brazil and they stopped off in Trinidad. I remember meeting them at Queen's Park Hotel and being so flustered that I called Elizabeth Hardwick Edna St. Vincent Millay. She said, "I'm not that old yet." I was just flabbergasted. And then we became very friendly. My wife, Margaret, and I took them up to the beach. Their daughter, Harriet, was there. I remember being up at this beach house with Lowell. His daughter and his wife, I think, must have gone to bed. We had gas lanterns. *Imitations* had just come out, and I remember that he showed me his imitations of Hugo and Rilke and asked me what I thought about them. I asked him if two of the stanzas were from Rilke, and he said, "No, these are mine." It was a very flattering and warm feeling to have this fine man with this great reputation really asking me what I thought. He did that with a lot of people, very honestly, humbly, and directly. I cherish that memory a lot. When we went back to New York, Cal and Lizzy had a big party for us with a lot of people there, and we became very close. Cal was a big man in bulk but an extremely gentle, poignant person, and very funny. I don't think any of the biographies have caught the sort of gentle, amused, benign beauty of him when he was calm. He kept a picture of Peter, my son, and Harriet for a long time in his wallet, and he'd take it out and show it to me. He was sweetly impulsive. Once I went to visit him and he said, "Let's call up Allen Ginsberg and ask him to come over." That's so cherishable that it's a very hard thing for me to think of him as not being around. In a way, I can't separate my affection for Lowell from his influence on me. I think of his character and gentleness, the immediacy that was part of knowing him. I loved his openness to receive influences. He was not a poet who said, "I'm an American poet, I'm going to be peculiar, and I'm going to have my own voice which is going to be different from anybody's voice." He was a poet who said, "I'm going to take in everything." He had a kind of multifaceted imagination; he was not embarrassed to admit that he was influenced even in his middle-age by William Carlos Williams, or by François Villon, or by Boris Pasternak, all at the same time. That was wonderful.

W. SOMERSET MAUGHAM

REBECCA WEST: He couldn't write for toffee, bless his heart. He wrote conventional short stories, much inferior to the work of other people. But they were much better than his plays, which were too frightful. He was an extremely interesting man though, not a bit clever or cold or cynical. I know of many affectionate things he did. He had a great capacity for falling in love with the wrong people. His taste seemed to give way under him so extraordinarily sometimes. He fascinated me by his appearance; he was so neatly made, like a swordstick that fits just so. Occasionally his conversation was beautifully funny and quite unmalicious. I object strongly to pictures of Maugham as if he were a second-rate Hollywood producer in the lavish age. His house was very pleasant and quiet and agreeable.

P. G. WODEHOUSE: We got along on just sort of "how do you do" terms. I remember walking back from a cricket match at Lords in London, and Maugham came along on the other side. He looked at me and I looked at him, and we were thinking the same thing: Oh, my God, shall we have to stop and talk? Fortunately, we didn't.

CARSON McCULLERS

WILLIAM GOYEN: I had first known her in this nest that Linscott had up there for these little birdlings of writers. Carson had great vitality and she was quite beautiful in that already decaying way. She was like a fairy. She had the most delicate kind of tinkling, dazzling little way about her . . . like a little star. Like a Christmas, she was like an ornament of a kind. She had no mind and she could make no philosophical statements about anything; she didn't need to. She said far-out, wonderfully mad things, that were totally disarming and for a while people would say, "I'll go wherever you go." She'd knock them straight out the window. She had a devastating crush on Elizabeth Bowen. She actually got to Bowen's Court: she shambled over there to England and spent a fortnight. I heard from Elizabeth that Carson appeared at dinner the first night in her shorts, tennis shorts; that poor body, you know, in tennis shorts and she came down the stairs; that was her debut. It didn't last long. But that was Carson.

THOMAS MERTON

JAMES LAUGHLIN: He was so nice, so jolly. He wasn't a dour monk at all. He was a kind friend and interested in everything. I often went down to visit him at the monastery in Kentucky. The Abbot would give him a day off, and I'd rent a car. Tom would get an old bishop's suit out of the storeroom and start out in that. Then we would stop in the woods and he'd change into his farmworker's blue jeans and a beret to hide his tonsure. Then we'd hit the bars across Kentucky. He loved his beer, and he loved that smoked ham they have down there. He was a wonderful person. He wanted to read contemporary writers, but the books were often confiscated, so we had a secret system. I sent the books he wanted to the monastery psychiatrist in Louisville, who would get them to Merton. I sent him everyone he wanted to read: Sartre and Camus, Rexroth and Pound, Henry Miller and many more. We talked a great deal about the Oriental religions. He was very ecumenical. We talked about his situation and why he stuck it out in the monastery. Once I asked, "Tom, why do you stay here? You could get out and be a tremendous success in the world." He answered that the monastery was where God wanted him to be. He would have been misplaced if he hadn't been so determined to get what he wanted in the monastery—his own hermitage among the hills. He couldn't stand the "social life" in the monastery with all the monks talking sign language, having to go to church six times a day, going to chapter, and making cheese. He finally did persuade the Abbot to build him a hermitage. Tom was a shrewd operator. He got out of sleeping in the communal dormitory by learning how to snore so loudly that the other monks got together at chapter and said, "Father Louis has got to leave the dormitory." So Tom was allowed to use one of the old bishop's rooms. He believed that the old monastic tradition was so strict that it could no longer foster true spirituality.

HENRY MILLER

EUDORA WELTY: Henry Miller came one time. We had him for three days. I got two or three boyfriends to help me with him and drive the car and protect me from God only knew what my mother thought. They were going to give him a glass automobile, from which he could see out and they could see in. He didn't come in a glass automobile, but he came anyway.

He never looked at anything. I guess he was bored by being in Mississippi. That day they were going to move the hospital for the insane down on North State Street to the next county, to a bigger place. The patients were helping move themselves. I thought that that would be a funny sight for Mr. Miller, especially since the superintendent was named Love. Superintendent Love, moving the insane hospital patients from Jackson to across the river. It meant absolutely nothing to him.

It's not every day there's something like that in Jackson to offer anyone. These poor old crazy people carrying their own beds out, and putting them in a truck and driving away. Don't you like that?

He had written a letter suggesting I write pornography. He really was doing it out of kindness. He thought it was a way to make a little extra money. I guess he had different people he knew that were doing this. Some of his friends. I was so astonished that I told my mother about it when I read the letter, and she was shocked. She said, That man can never enter my house. I think he was planning to do so. We took him out to dine. There was only one good restaurant in Jackson then. We took him to it every night. There were different entrances. Afterwards, he said, "How is it that a hole like Jackson, Mississippi, has three good restaurants?" We didn't ever tell him it was just one.

MARIANNE MOORE

DONALD HALL: I had lunch with her twice in Brooklyn. The first time she took me up the hill to the little Viennese restaurant where she took everybody. Like everybody else I fought with her for the check and lost. She was tiny and frail and modest, but oh so powerful. I think she must have been a weightlifter in another life—or maybe a middle linebacker. Whenever you're in the presence of extreme modesty or diffidence, *always* look for great degrees of reticent power, or a hugely strong ego. Marianne Moore as editor of the *Dial* was made of steel. To wrestle with her over a check was to be pinned to the mat.

Another time when I came to visit, her teeth were being repaired so she made lunch at her apartment. She thought she looked dreadful and wouldn't go outside the house without a complete set of teeth. Lunch was extraordinary! On a tray she placed three tiny paper cups and a plate. One of the cups contained about two teaspoons of V-8 juice. Another had about eight raisins in it, and the other five and a half Spanish peanuts. On the plate was a mound of Fritos, and when she passed them to me she said, "I like Fritos. They're so good for you, you know." She was eating health foods at the time, and I'm quite sure she wasn't being ironic. She entertained some notion that Fritos were a health food. What else did she serve? Half a cupcake for dessert, maybe? She prepared a magnificent small cafeteria for birds.

PABLO NERUDA

MARIO VARGAS LLOSA: Neruda adored life. He was wild about everything—painting, art in general, books, rare editions, food, drink. Eating and drinking were almost a mystical experience for him. A wonderfully likeable man, full of vitality—if you forget his poems in praise of Stalin, of course. He lived in a near-feudal world, where everything led to his rejoicing, his sweet-toothed exuberance for life. I had the good fortune to spend a weekend on Isla Negra. It was wonderful! A kind of social machinery worked around him: hordes of people who cooked and worked—and always quantities of guests. It was a very funny society, extraordinarily alive, without the slightest trace of intellectualism. Neruda was exactly the opposite of Borges, the man who appeared never to drink, smoke, or eat, who one would have said had never made love, for whom all these things seemed completely secondary, and if he had done them it was out of politeness and nothing more. That's because ideas, reading, reflection, and creation were his life, the purely cerebral life. Neruda comes out of the Jorge Amado and Rafael Alberti tradition that says literature is generated by a sensual experience of life.

I remember the day we celebrated Neruda's birthday in London. He wanted to have the party on a boat on the Thames. Fortunately, one of his admirers, the English poet Alastair Reid, happened to live on a boat on the Thames, so we were able to organize a party for him. The moment came and he announced that he was going to make a cocktail. It was the most expensive drink in the world with I don't know how many bottles of Dom Perignon, fruit juices, and God knows what else. The result, of course, was wonderful, but one glass of it was enough to make you drunk. So there we were, drunk every one of us, without exception. Even so, I still remember what he told me then; something that has proven to be a great truth over the years. An article at the time—I can't remember what it was about—had upset and irritated me because it insulted me and told lies about me. I showed it to Neruda. In the middle of the party, he prophesied: "You are becoming famous. I want you to know what awaits you: the more famous you are, the more you will be attacked like this. For every praise, there will be two or three insults. I myself have a chest full of all the insults, villainies, and infamies a man is capable of withstanding. I wasn't spared a single one: thief, pervert, traitor, thug, cuckold . . . everything! If you become famous, you will have to go through that."

Neruda told the truth; his prognosis came absolutely true. I not only have a chest, but several suitcases full of articles that contain every insult known to man.

SYLVIA PLATH

TED HUGHES: Sylvia and I met because she was curious about my group of friends at university and I was curious about her. I was working in London but I used to go back up to Cambridge at weekends. Half a dozen or so of us made a poetic gang. Our main cooperative activity was drinking in the Anchor and our main common interest, apart from fellow feeling and mutual attraction, was Irish, Scottish and Welsh traditional songs—folk songs and broadsheet ballads. We sang a lot. Recorded folk song was rare in those days. Our poetic interests were more mutually understood than talked about. But we did print a broadsheet of literary comment. In one issue, one of our group, our Welshman, Dan Huws, demolished a poem that Sylvia had published, "Caryatids." He later became a close friend of hers, wrote a beautiful elegy when she died. That attack attracted her attention. Also, she had met one of our group, Lucas Myers, an American, who was an especially close friend of mine. Luke was very dark and skinny. He could be incredibly wild. Just what you hoped for from Tennessee. His poems were startling to us—Hart Crane, Wallace Stevens vocabulary, zany. He interested Sylvia. In her journals she records the occasional dream in which Luke appears unmistakably. When we published a magazine full of our own poems, the only issue of *St. Botolph's*, and launched it at a big dance party, Sylvia came to see what the rest of us looked like. Up to that point I'd never set eyes on her. I'd heard plenty about her from an English girlfriend who shared supervisions with her. There she suddenly was, raving Luke's verses at Luke and my verses at me.

Once I got to know her and read her poems, I saw straight off that she was a genius of some kind. Quite suddenly we were completely committed to each other and to each other's writing. The year before, I had started writing again, after the years of the devastation of university. I'd just written what have become some of my more anthologized pieces— "The Thought Fox," the Jaguar poems, "Wind." I see now that when we met, my writing, like hers, left its old path and started to circle and search. To me, of course, she was not only herself: she was America and American literature in person. I don't know what I was to her. Apart from the more monumental classics—Tolstoy, Dostoyevsky and so on—my background reading was utterly different from hers. But our minds soon became two parts of one operation. We dreamed a lot of shared or complementary dreams. Our telepathy was intrusive. I don't know whether our verse exchanged much, if we influenced one another that way—not in the early days. Maybe others see that differently. Our methods were not the same. Hers was to collect a heap of vivid objects and good words and make a pattern; the pattern would be projected from somewhere deep inside, from her very distinctly evolved myth. It appears distinctly evolved to a reader now—despite having been totally unconscious to her then. My method was to find a thread end and draw the rest out of a hidden tangle. Her method was more painterly, mine more narrative, perhaps. Throughout our time together we looked at each other's verses at every stage—up to the *Ariel* poems of October 1962, which was when we separated.

EZRA POUND

MALCOLM COWLEY: I went to see him a couple of times, but I was a little uneasy with him. Pound always had some new discovery or enthusiasm; he was always finding the lowdown on something. On one of my visits to his little apartment, he announced loudly, "I've got the lowdown on the Elizabethan drama! It was all cribbed from these books," and he carried out two huge volumes of the Venetian State Papers. Well, it *was* a real discovery: the plots of several Elizabethan plays *did* come out of the Venetian State Papers.

ROBERT FROST: [I met Pound] through Frank Flint, the early Imagist and translator. He was a friend of Pound and belonged in that little group there. He met me in a book store, said, "American?" And I said, "Yes. How'd you know?" He said, "Shoes." It was the Poetry Book Shop, Harold Monroe's, just being organized. He said, "Poetry?" And I said, "I accept the omen." Then he said, "You should know your fellow countryman, Ezra Pound." And I said, "I've never heard of him." And I hadn't. I'd been skipping literary magazines—I don't ever read them very much—and the gossip, you know, I never paid much attention to. So he said, "I'm going to tell him you're here." And I had a card from Pound afterwards. I didn't use it for two or three months after that. Just said, "At home, sometimes." Just like Pound. So I didn't feel that that was a very warm invitation. Then one day walking past Church Walk in Kensington, I took his card out and went in to look for him. And I found him there, a little put out that I hadn't come sooner, in his Poundian way. And then he said, "Flint tells me you have a book." And I said, "Well, I ought to have." He said, "You haven't seen it?" And I said, "No." He said, "What do you say we go and get a copy?" He was eager about being the first one to talk. That's one of the best things you can say about Pound: he wanted to be the first to jump. Didn't call people up on the telephone to see how they were going to jump. He was all silent with eagerness. We walked over to my publisher; he got the book. Didn't show it to me—put it in his pocket. We went back to his room. He said, "You don't mind our liking this?" in his British accent, slightly. And I said, "Oh, go ahead and like it." Pretty soon he laughed at something, and I said I knew where that was in the book, what Pound would laugh at. And then pretty soon he said, "You better run along home, I'm going to review it." And I never touched it. I went home without my book and he kept it. I'd barely seen it in his hands.

. . .

He admired at that time, when I first met him, Robinson and de La Mare. He got over admiring de La Mare anyway, and I think he threw out Robinson too. We'd just bring up a couple of little poems. I was around with him quite a little for a few weeks. I was charmed with his ways. He cultivated a certain rudeness to people that he didn't like, just like Willy Whistler. I thought he'd come under the influence of Whistler. They cultivated the French style of boxing. They used to kick you in the teeth. You know the song, the nasty song: "They fight with their feet—" Among other things, what Pound did was show me Bohemia. He'd take me to restaurants and things. Showed me jujitsu in a restaurant. Threw me over his head. Wasn't ready for him at all. I was just as strong as he was. He said, "I'll show you, I'll show you. Stand up." So I stood up, gave him my hand. He grabbed my wrist, tipped over backwards, and threw me over his head. Everybody in the restaurant stood up. He used to talk about himself as a tennis player. I never played tennis with him. And then he'd show you all these places with these people that specialized in poets that dropped their aitches and things like that. Not like the "beatniks," quite. I remember one occasion they had a poet in who had a poem in *The English Review* on Aphrodite, how he met Aphrodite at Leatherhead.* He was coming in and he was a navvy. I don't remember his name, never heard of him again— may have gone on and had books. But he was a real navvy. Came in with his bicycle clips on. Tea party. Everybody horrified in a delighted way, you know. Horror, social horror. Rednecked, thick, heavy-built fellow, strong fellow, you know, like John L. Lewis or somebody. But he was a poet. And then I saw poets made out of whole cloth by Ezra. Ezra thought he did that. Take a fellow that had never written anything and think he could make a poet out of him. We won't go into that.

JAMES LAUGHLIN: I went up to Paris, lived in a tiny room in an insurance office which I rented for seven dollars a month, and after a while, I wrote to Ezra, not expecting a reply, really, just asking if I could come down to Rapallo to see him . . . and to my astonishment he sent me a telegram: "Visibility high." So I went down then to Rapallo. Ezra and I hit it off immediately. He found me an eager student, and certainly he was the thwarted professor. He found a room for me in the flat of an old German lady, and I was enrolled in what he called the "Ezuversity." No tuition.

The Ezuversity instruction was mostly a monologue about the mail he'd received that morning. His mornings were devoted to his correspondence. He used to say that postage was his highest living expense. Then we'd have lunch in the dining room of the Albergo Rapallo, and then after the snooze he'd take, we would go swimming or play tennis. One of the wonderful

---

*Frost is thinking of a poet named John Helston, author of "Aphrodite at Leatherhead," which took up fourteen pages of *The English Review* for March 1913. Frost's recollection gives a special flavor, if one is needed, to the note appended to the poem by the editors of the magazine: "Without presuming to 'present' Mr. Helston after the manner of fashionable actors, we think it will interest the public to know that he was for years a working mechanic—turner, fitter, etc.—in electrical, locomotive, motor-car, and other workshops."

things about those monologues was his mimetic ability. He could imitate Joyce, how he talked, or how Yeats talked. His stories were endless, and very funny, and what I remember about them—over all those years—was that I never heard him tell an off-color story.

Oh, you could never predict what he was going to do—even from the very first. I remember that one summer we drove up to Salzburg—Ezra, Olga Rudge, and my Harvard classmate John Slocum—to the *Festspielhaus,* where Toscanini was conducting Beethoven's *Fidelio.* Ezra didn't think much of Beethoven. After about twenty minutes into the opera, Ezra rose up and said in a very clear voice, "No wonder! The man had syphilis!" He started out, and all of us, of course, felt we had to file out with him. Toscanini was absolutely unfazed. He continued to conduct.

W. S. Merwin: I was staying with friends in Washington, at Easter vacation, when I went over to see Pound. He received me in this open ward, with people wandering around, flushing imaginary toilets. He sat in a deep chair and held forth. I was eighteen—I didn't have much to say to Pound—and he told me all about how, when the Hundredth Canto was finished, the whole thing was all going to fall into place and so on. It would be like putting the keystone in the arch, or the lintel on the doorposts. He was also wonderfully generous and wrote me postcards afterwards. "Read seeds, not twigs E.P.," he wrote. And he gave me a bit of advice about translating, about taking translating seriously as a kind of practice, about learning languages and trying to get as close as possible to the sense and the form of the original. I didn't know what he meant about a lot of those things until I had been practicing for a while, until I had been trying to do it.

MARCEL PROUST

Jean Cocteau: Marcel combatted those things in his own way. He would circle among his victims collecting his "black honey," his *miel noir,* and then he wrote, "I beg of you, Jean, since you live in the rue d'Anjou in the same building with Mme. de Chevigné, of whom I've made the Duchess de Guermantes; I entreat you to get her to read my book. She won't read me; and she says she stubs her foot in my sentences. I beg you—" I told him that was as if he asked an ant to read Fabre. You don't ask an insect to read entomology.

GERTRUDE STEIN

LILLIAN HELLMAN: Miss Stein arrived in America and said that there were two people that she wanted to meet. They were both in California at that minute—Chaplin and Dash [Dashiell Hammett]. And we were invited to dinner at the house of a friend of Miss Stein; Charlie Chaplin, Dash and myself, Paulette Goddard, Miss Toklas, our host and hostess and another man. There was this magnificent china and lace tablecloth. Chaplin turned over his coffee cup, nowhere near Stein, just all over this beautiful cloth, and the first thing Miss Stein said was, "Don't worry, it didn't get on me." She was miles away from him. She said it perfectly seriously. Then she told Dash he was the only American writer who wrote well about women. He was very pleased.

JAMES LAUGHLIN: She was going on her famous lecture tour through America, and somebody had suggested that in each city where she was scheduled she should hand out a press release explaining what she was going to be talking about. That was my job—to take these lectures and produce a one-page presentation for each. It was not easy at all. The *Lectures in America* are philosophical and dense. To try to identify their central themes and translate them from Steinese into American newspaperese was quite a task. I would try, carrying my attempts to her, and she would say, "No, no, you've missed the entire point. Go back and try again." That's why I stayed there a month. It took me that long to get these releases done to her satisfaction. The two of us sat out on the terrace in the mornings, working. Then in the afternoon we'd tour the countryside in her little Ford with Gertrude, who drove, sitting in the front seat with Alice B. Toklas, while I sat in the back with those two awful dogs—Basket, who was a white poodle, and Pepe, who was a nasty little black Mexican nipper. Trying to control the pair of them back there, I saw very little of the Savoie countryside. That part of the Savoie is a favorite place for hikers. They'd lose nails out of their hiking boots, and almost invariably the little Ford's tires would get a puncture. Gertrude would pull off to the side of the road and she and Alice B. Toklas would take out their picnic things from the car and find a nice cozy spot to overlook it all. They'd sit and chat and eat while I would change the tire, harassed, as you can imagine, by Basket and Pepe.

Gertrude had great natural charm, tremendous charisma. Marvelous head. Those wonderful flashing eyes. A deep, firm voice. So I couldn't help but be very much impressed by her at times, except that often she'd erupt with crazy ideas. She thought Hitler was a great man ... this *before* the war, of course, but how a Jewess could be attracted to such a notion at *any* time is difficult to understand. She was certainly a woman of strong opinions—indeed to the point of megalomania. She felt she had influenced everyone. We had a big fight one day when I mentioned I was reading Proust. She said, "How can you read junk like that? Don't you know, J., that Proust and Joyce both copied their work from *The Making of Americans?*" She finally cooled on me. I simply didn't accept everything she said. That was disrespectful.

· · ·

You know how Gertrude and Bill [Williams] broke up? One evening at her place in Paris she took out a big stack of her manuscripts and asked Bill what to do with them. Bill replied in his "Billyums" way, "I'd pick out the best one and throw the rest away." This was an impossible thing to tell Gertrude, who believed her every word was Great Art. Alice B. Toklas showed the Williamses to the door.

IGOR STRAVINSKY

CHRISTOPHER ISHERWOOD: I always think of Stravinsky in a very physical way. He was physically adorable; he was cuddly—he was so little, and you wanted to protect him. He was very demonstrative, a person who—I suppose it was his Russianness—was full of kisses and embraces. He had great warmth. He could be fearfully hostile and snub people and attack his critics and so forth, but personally, he was a person of immense joy and warmth. The first time I came to his house, he said to me: "Would you like to hear my Mass before we get drunk?" He was always saying things like that. He seemed to me to have a wonderful appreciation for all the arts. He spoke English fluently, but it astonished me what an appreciation he had of writing in the English language, although he was really more at home in German or French—after Russian. When I was seeing a great deal of him, I was usually drinking a great deal, too, because he had these wonderful drinks. I recall a fatal, beautiful liquid called Marc—Marc de Bourgogne—made out of grape pits, colorless but powerful beyond belief. I used to think to myself, Goddamit, I'm drunk again, and here's Igor saying these marvelous things, and I won't remember one of them in the morning. When I think of those days, I really seem to have behaved very oddly. I remember once I'd actually passed out on the floor, and, looking up, I saw at an immense altitude above me, Aldous Huxley, who was very tall, standing up and talking French to Stravinsky, who never seemed to get overcome, however much he drank. And Aldous, who I think was very fond of me, was looking at me rather curiously, as much as to say, "Aren't you going a little far?" It's not like me to behave like that, or so I imagine. Perhaps it is. But I suddenly realized how relaxed I felt, how completely at home. It didn't matter if I blotted my copy book. The Stravinskys projected the most astonishing coziness. Because Vera Stravinsky was a part of it, she had enormous charm and style, and she's very amusing. Going out with them was always an experience. We drove up once to the sequoia forest, and I remember Stravinsky, so tiny, looking up at this enormous giant sequoia and standing there for a long time in meditation and then turning to me and saying: "That's serious."

DYLAN THOMAS

JAMES LAUGHLIN: It was difficult, because he always wanted to drink. I went on one bender with him in London which lasted for two days and three nights. We ended up sleeping on the floor of some lady's apartment and neither of us knew who she was. He always wanted to drink, but I'm not such a great drinker. When he came to New York he'd come in the office at ten o'clock in the morning and say, "Let's go to the White Horse Tavern." I'd say, "Dylan, I've got work to do." So he'd go off to the White Horse and meet various cronies and sycophants. Sometimes I'd join him late in the evening. He was a sad case, Dylan; he was basically a nice person, and when he started boozing he was very amusing, but he would never stop; he'd go on and on. It's very hard to get close to a drinker. There was always that thing between us, the boozing. He was a great talker, too; he was a wonderful talker, but I had work to do. When Dylan drank he wanted people to be with him, to listen to him. It was a method of attracting people. But he was very indiscriminate about whom he would attract. He had a bunch of hangers-on in New York, such as that jerk Oscar Williams, who were crumbs. That was a barrier, because he'd be with such crummy characters. You couldn't really have a conversation with Dylan when he was drinking. It wore me down. John Davenport had a good name for Dylan. He called him "Old Messy." He was. He was messy because of the drinking. You couldn't count on him. If you wanted to do something you couldn't count on his turning up sober or on time.

EUDORA WELTY

RICHARD FORD: I didn't meet Miss Welty until 1981, when she came to Princeton, where I was teaching, to give a reading. I had only published one book. I had a feeling she probably knew about it, that it was full of dirty words and sex and violence. And when I met her it didn't seem to have registered that I was from Jackson and had written a novel. I remember saying to her, "Miss Welty, I'm Richard Ford, and I'm from Jackson, Mississippi." She has a wonderful way about her; she said, "Oh, you are?"—but nothing else. And I thought, Gee, what that means is that she hates my book. I felt horrible about it. And I then published another book full of sex and violence, and I thought, Well, I'm just out of the Eudora Welty sweepstakes here. We're never going to be friends. Then I wrote *The Sportswriter* and did a book-signing at Lemuria Books in Jackson. I was sitting there at my little table signing books, and I looked up and here was Miss Welty. She said, "Well, I had to come pay my respects." I felt beatified. I felt, Finally I've written a book you aren't too embarrassed by to come and meet me. I've gone on to be wonderful friends with her. I see her often. In addition to being a great writer she's also one of the wittiest people I've ever been around. She does voices, she mimics, she has a sensitivity to the absurdities of language. She also has a vivid memory for song lyrics. She's a performer who simply didn't choose to perform upon a conventional stage. Her work often doesn't seem funny, but then is funny under the surface—sometimes even quite grave stories. I remember one time I was walking with her into a bookstore. They had prepared a big celebration for her birthday. Somebody was standing beside a helium cylinder and was filling balloon after balloon. Each time, the little machine would give off a kind of *ssshoou* sound, and Eudora said, "Oh, I thought it was someone sighing at my arrival."

VIRGINIA WOOLF

MAY SARTON: I had left my first book of poems at her door, with some flowers, and the darling maid opened the door just then and said, "Oh, won't you come up?" I said, "Oh, no, I wouldn't think of it." I just left the book.

Elizabeth Bowen knew that I wanted to meet Virginia Woolf desperately, so she invited the two of us and a couple of other people to dinner.

That was when I first met her. She walked in, in a "robe de style," a lovely, rather eighteenth-century-looking, long dress with a wide collar, and she came into the room like a dazzled deer and walked right across—this was a beautiful house on Regent's Park—to the long windows and stood there looking out. My memory is that she was not even introduced at that point, that she just walked across, very shyly, and stood there looking absolutely beautiful. She was much more beautiful than any of the photographs show. And then she discovered that I was the person who had left the poems.

She was very canny . . . she answered my gift of that book with a lovely note, which is now in the Berg collection, just saying: "Thank you so much, and the flowers came just as someone had given me a vase, and were perfect, and I shall look forward to reading the poems." In other words, never put yourself in a position of having to judge. So she never said a word about the poems. But she was delighted to find out that I was the person who had left them.

Then, later, we talked—Elizabeth and Virginia Woolf and I. The gentlemen were having their brandy and cigars in the other room. We talked about hairdressers. It was like something in *The Waves*! We all talked like characters in a Virginia Woolf novel. She had a great sense of humor. Very malicious. She liked to tease people, in a charming way, but she was a great tease.

But she put me at ease and I saw her quite often after that. Every time I was in England I would have tea with her, which was a two-hour talk. She would absolutely ply me with questions. That was the novelist. I always felt the novelist at work. Where did I buy my clothes? Whom was I seeing? Whom was I in love with? Everything. So it was enrapturing to a young woman to be that *interesting* to Virginia Woolf. But I think it was her way of living, in a sense. Vicariously. Through people.

She was never warm. That's true. There was no warmth. It was partly physical, I think. She was a physically unwarm person. I can't imagine kissing her, for instance, I mean on the cheek. But she was delightful and zany, full of humor and laughter. Never did you feel a person on the brink of madness. That has distorted the image, because she was so in control.

W. B. YEATS

JOHN BERRYMAN: I remember the taxi ride over. The taxi was left over from the First World War, and when we arrived in Pall Mall—we could see the Atheneum—the driver said he didn't feel he could get in. Finally I decided to abandon ship and take off on my own. So I went in and asked for Mr. Yeats. Very much like asking, "Is Mr. Ben Jonson here?" And he came down. He was much taller than I expected, and haggard. Big, though, big head, rather wonderful looking in a sort of a blunt, patrician kind of way, but there was something shrunken also. He told me he was just recovering from an illness. He was very courteous, and we went in to tea. At a certain point, I had a cigarette, and I asked him if he would like one. To my great surprise he said yes. So I gave him a Craven-A and then lit it for him, and I thought, Immortality is mine! From now on it's just a question of reaping the fruits of my effort. He did most of the talking. I asked him a few questions. He did not ask me any questions about myself, although he was extremely courteous and very kind. At one point he said, "I have reached the age when my daughter can beat me at croquet," and I thought, Hurrah, he's human! I made notes of the interview afterwards, which I have probably lost. One comment in particular I remember. He said, "I never revise now"—you know how much he revised his stuff— "but in the interest of a more passionate syntax." Now that struck me as a very good remark. I have no idea what it meant and still don't know, but the longer I think about it, the better I like it.

EZRA POUND: Mostly reading aloud to him. Doughty's *Dawn in Britain,* and so on. And wrangling, you see. The Irish like contradiction. He tried to learn fencing at forty-five, which was amusing. He would thrash around with the foils like a whale. He sometimes gave the impression of being even a worse idiot than I am.

STEPHEN SPENDER: I met Yeats, I think probably in 1935 or 1936, at Lady Ottoline Morrell's. Ottoline asked me to tea alone with Yeats. He was very blind and—I don't know whether he was deaf, but he was very sort of remote, he seemed tremendously old. He was only about the age I am now, but he seemed tremendously old and remote. He looked at me and then he said, "Young man, what do you think of the Sayers?" I hadn't the faintest idea what he was talking about—I thought perhaps he meant Dorothy Sayers' crime stories or something—I became flustered. What he meant was a group of young ladies who chanted poems in chorus. Ottoline got very alarmed and rushed out of the room and telephoned to Virginia Woolf, who was just around the corner, and asked her to come save the situation. Virginia arrived in about ten minutes' time, tremendously amused, and Yeats was very pleased to meet her because he'd just been reading *The Waves*. He also read quite a lot of science—I think he read Eddington and Rutherford and all those kinds of things—and so he told her that *The Waves* was a marvelous novel, that it was entirely up to date in scientific theory because light moved in waves, and time, and so on. Of course Virginia, who hadn't thought of all this, was terribly pleased and flattered. And then I remember he started telling her a story in which he said, "And as I went down the stairs there was a marble statue of a baby and it started talking in Greek to me"—that sort of thing. Virginia adored it all, of course. . . . I remember his telling the story of his trip to Rapallo to show the manuscript of *The Tower* to Ezra Pound. He stayed at the hotel and then went around and left the manuscript in a packet for Pound, accompanied by a letter saying I am an old man, this may be the last poetry I'll ever write, it is very different from my other work—all that kind of thing—and what do you think of it? Next day he received a postcard from Ezra Pound with on it the one word "putrid." Yeats was rather amused by that. Apparently Pound had a tremendous collection of cats, and Yeats used to say that Pound couldn't possibly be a nasty man because he fed all the cats of Rapallo. I once asked him how he came to be a modern poet, and he told me that it took him thirty years to modernize his style. He said he didn't really like the modern poetry of Eliot and Pound. He thought it was static, that it didn't have any movement, and for him poetry had always to have the romantic movement. He said, "For me poetry always means 'For we'll go no more a-roving / By the light o' the moon.' " So the problem was how to keep the movement of the Byron lines but at the same time enlarge it so that it could include the kind of material that he was interested in, which was to do with everyday life—politics, quarrels between people, sexual love, and not just the frustrated love he had with Maud Gonne.

REBECCA WEST: He wasn't a bit impressive, and he wasn't my sort of person at all. He boomed at you like a foghorn. He was there one time when Philip Guedella and two or three of us were all very young and were talking nonsense about murderers in Shakespeare and whether a third murderer ever became a first murderer by working hard or were they, sort of, hereditary slots? Were they like Japanese specialists and one did one kind of murder, another did another? It was really awfully funny. Philip was very funny to be with. Then we started talking about something on the Western Isles but Yeats wouldn't join in, until we fussed round and were nice to him. But we were all wrong; what he liked was solemnity and, if you were big enough, heavy enough, and strong enough, he loved you. He loved great big women. He would have been mad about Vanessa Redgrave.

ON THE FUTURE

Light tomorrow with today.
—ELIZABETH BARRETT BROWNING

It is a mistake to think that books have come to stay. The human race did without them for thousands of years and may decide to do without them again.   —E. M. FORSTER

JOHN BERRYMAN: I have a tiny little secret hope that, after a decent period of silence and prose, I will find myself in some almost impossible life situation and will respond to this with outcries of rage, rage and love, such as the world has never heard before. Like Yeats's great outburst at the end of his life. This comes out of a feeling that endowment is a very small part of achievement. I would rate it about fifteen or twenty percent. Then you have historical luck, personal luck, health, things like that, then you have hard work, sweat. And you have ambition. The incredible difference between the achievement of A and the achievement of B is that B *wanted* it, so he made all kinds of sacrifices. A could have had it, but he didn't give a damn. The idea that everybody wants to be President of the United States or have a million dollars is simply not the case. Most people want to go down to the corner and have a glass of beer. They're very happy. In *Henderson the Rain King,* the hero keeps on saying, "I want. I want." Well, I'm that kind of character. I don't know whether that is exhausted in me or not. I can't tell.

But what I was going on to say is that I do strongly feel that among the greatest pieces of luck for high achievement is ordeal. Certain great artists can make out without it, Titian and others, but mostly you need ordeal. My idea is this: The artist is extremely lucky who is presented with the worst possible ordeal which will not actually kill him. At that point, he's in business. Beethoven's deafness, Goya's deafness, Milton's blindness, that kind of thing. And I think that what happens in my poetic work in the future will probably largely depend not on my sitting calmly on my ass as I think, "Hmm, hmm, a long poem again? Hmm," but on being knocked in the face, and thrown flat, and given cancer, and all kinds of other things short of senile dementia. At that point, I'm out, but short of that, I don't know. I hope to be nearly crucified. I'm scared, but I'm willing. I'm sure this is a preposterous attitude, but I'm not ashamed of it.*

HAROLD BLOOM: I'm reminded of that great trope of Wallace Stevens's in "The Auroras of Autumn," when he speaks of a "Great shadow's last embellishment." There's always a further embellishment. It looks like a last embellishment and then it turns out not to be—yet once more, and yet once more. One is always saying farewell to it, it is always saying farewell to itself, and then it perpetuates itself. One is always astonished and delighted. When I introduced John Ashbery, at one of the poetry readings in the old days at Yale, I heard, for the first time, "Wet Casements." How it ravished my heart away the moment I heard it! Certainly when I recite that poem to myself and remember the original experience of hearing him deliver it, it's hard to see how any poem could be more adequate. Clearly it is not a diminished or finished art form as long as a poem like "Wet Casements" is still possible.

WILLIAM BURROUGHS: I think that words are an around-the-world, ox-cart way of doing things, awkward instruments, and they will be laid aside eventually, probably sooner than we think.

CARLOS FUENTES: I was talking a few months ago in Mexico with one of the great filmmakers of our time, Luis Buñuel. He was eighty years old, and I was asking how he looked back on his career and on the destiny of the film. He said, "I think films are perishable, because they depend too much on technology, which advances too quickly and the films become old-fashioned, antiques. What I hope for is that technology advances to the point that films in the future will depend on a little pill which you take; then you sit in the dark, and from your eyes you project the film you want to see on a blank wall."

ROBERT GRAVES: I realize from time to time that certain poems were written for the wrong reasons, and feel obliged to remove them; they give

*Delusion.—J. B., March 1971

me a sick feeling. Only the few necessary poems should be kept. There's no mystery about them: if one is a poet, one eventually learns which they are. Though of course a perfect poem is impossible. Once it had been written, the world would end.

JERZY KOSINSKI: Reading novels—serious novels, anyhow—is an experience limited to a very small percentage of the so-called enlightened public. Increasingly, it's going to be a pursuit for those who seek unusual experiences, moral fetishists perhaps, people of heightened imagination, the troubled pursuers of the ambiguous self.

Today, people are absorbed in the most common denominator, the *visual*. It requires no education to watch TV. It knows no age limit. Your infant child can watch the same program you do. Witness its role in the homes of the old and incurably sick. Television is everywhere. It has the immediacy which the evocative medium of language doesn't. Language requires some inner triggering; television doesn't. The image is ultimately accessible, i.e., extremely attractive. And, I think, ultimately deadly, because it turns the viewer into a bystander. Of course, that's a situation we have always dreamt of . . . the ultimate hope of religion was that it would release us from trauma. Television actually does so. It "proves" that you can always be an observer of the tragedies of others. The fact that one day you will die in front of the live show is irrelevant—you are reminded about it no more than you are reminded about real weather existing outside the TV weather program. You're not told to open your window and take a look; television will never say that. It says, instead, "The weather today is . . ." and so forth. The weatherman never says, "If you don't believe me, go find out."

From way back, our major development as a race of frightened beings has been towards how to avoid facing the discomfort of our existence, primarily the possibility of an accident, immediate death, ugliness, and the ultimate departure. In terms of all this, television is a very pleasing medium: one is always the observer. The life of discomfort is always accorded to others, and even *this* is disqualified, since one program immediately disqualifies the preceding one. Literature does not have this ability to soothe. You have to evoke, and by evoking, you yourself have to provide your own inner setting. When you read about a man who dies, part of you dies with him because you have to re-create his dying inside your head.

ROSAMOND LEHMANN: People have been saying the novel is dead for as far back as I can remember. The novel will never die, but it will keep changing and evolving and taking different shapes. Storytelling, which is the basis of the novel, has always existed and always will. Nowadays, there are too many books and not enough good ones. Something will have to happen, but I don't think it will come from Britain or America. Things have gone too far in sophisticated countries; the intensity of emotion, the moral conflicts, all that was the basis of great novels has gone. The change will come from somewhere quite unexpected. But it will happen—human beings have infinite resources of renewal.

BERNARD MALAMUD: I'm not saying it [the novel] will disappear, just entertaining the idea. Assume it does; then someday a talented writer writes himself a long heartfelt letter and the form reappears. The human race needs the novel. We need all the experience we can get. Those who say the novel is dead can't write them.

FRANÇOIS MAURIAC: Even the great characters that have survived in novels are found now more in handbooks and histories, as though in a museum. As living creatures they get worn out, and they grow feeble. Sometimes we even see them die. Madame Bovary seems to me to be in poorer health than she used to be. . . . Yes, and even Anna Karenina, even the Karamazovs. First, because they need readers in order to live and the new generations are less and less capable of providing them with the air they need to breathe.

EDNA O'BRIEN: These are more careless times. Literature is no longer sacred, it is a business. There is an invisible umbilical cord between the writer and his potential reader, and I fear that the time has gone when readers could sink into a book the way they did in the past, for the *pace* of life is fast and frenetic. The world is cynical: the dwelling on emotions, the perfection of style, the intensity of a Flaubert is wasted on modern sensibility. I have a feeling that there is a *dying,* if not a *death,* of great literature. Some blame the television for it. Perhaps. There is hardly any distinction between a writer and a journalist—indeed, most writers *are* journalists. Nothing wrong with journalism any more than with dentistry, but they are worlds apart! Whenever I read the English Sunday papers I notice that the standard of literacy is high—all very clever and hollow—but no dues to literature. They care about their own egos. They synopsize the book, tell the plot. Well, fuck the plot! That is for precocious schoolboys. What matters is the imaginative *truth,* and the perfection and care with which it has been rendered. After all, you don't say of a ballet dancer, "He jumped in the air, then he twirled around, etc. . . ." You are just *carried away* by his dancing. The nicest readers are—and I know by the letters I receive—youngish people who are still eager and uncontaminated, who approach a book without hostility. But when I read Anita Brookner's novel *Look at Me,* I feel I am in the grip of a most wonderful, imaginative writer. The same is true of Margaret Atwood. Also, great literature is dying because young people, although they don't talk about it much, feel and fear a holocaust.

· · ·

As you know, the future itself is perilous. But as regards books, there is first the financial aspect of publishing. Already books are very expensive, so that a first novel of quality will have less of a chance of being picked up. Say a new Djuna Barnes, or indeed Nathalie Sarraute, might not get published. If Woolf's *The Waves* were to be published today it would have pitiful sales. Of course, "how-to" books, spy stories, thrillers, and science-fiction all sell by the millions. What would be wonderful—what we *need* just now—is some astonishing fairy tale. I read somewhere the other day that the cavemen did not paint what they saw, but what they *wished* they had seen. We need that, in these lonely, lunatic times.

INDEX

A NOTE ON THE TYPE

The principal text of this Modern Library edition
was set in a digitized version of Janson,
a typeface that dates from about 1690 and was cut by Nicholas Kis,
a Hungarian working in Amsterdam. The original matrices have
survived and are held by the Stempel foundry in Germany.
Hermann Zapf redesigned some of the weights and sizes for Stempel,
basing his revisions on the original design.

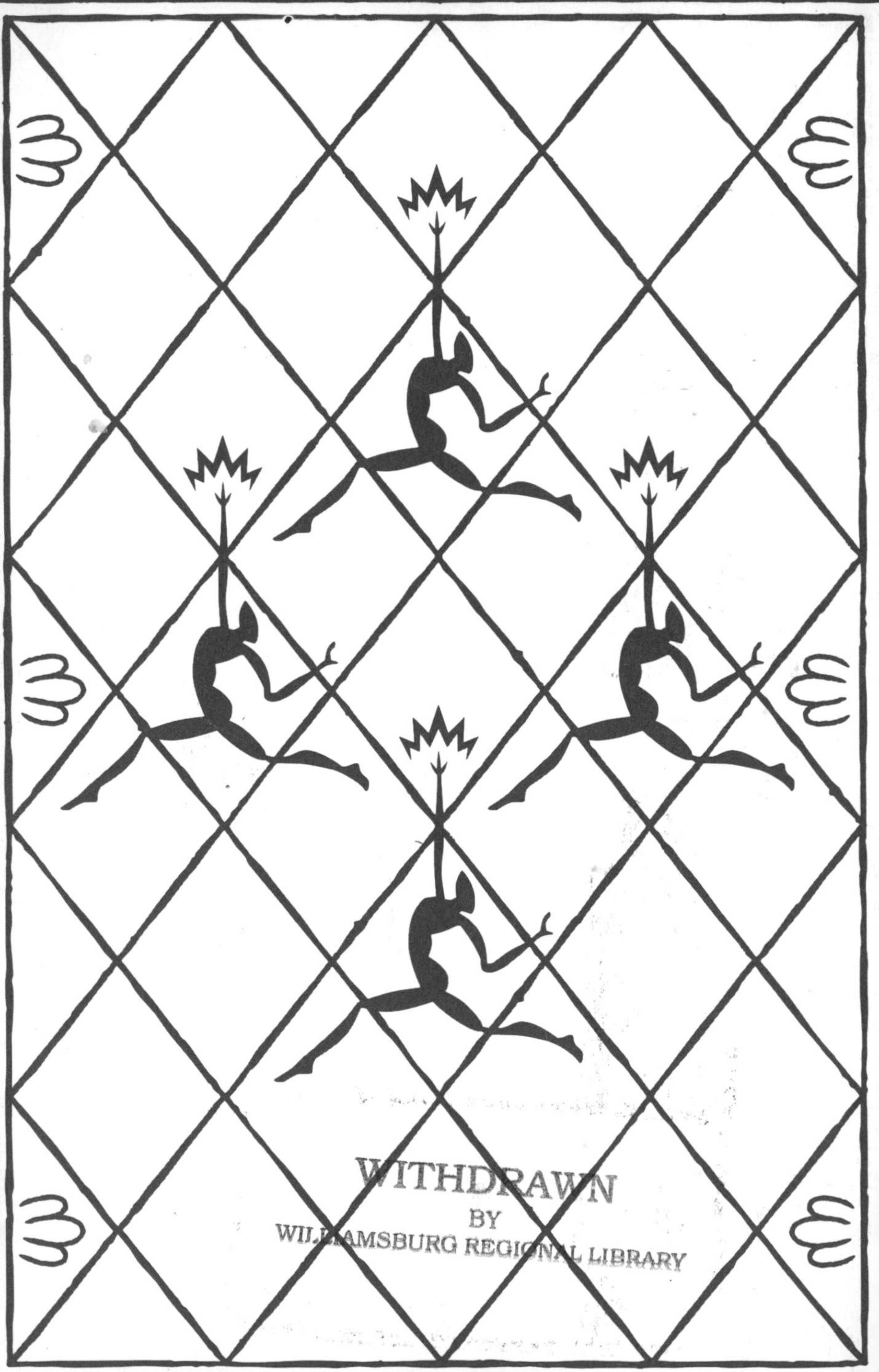